LEGITIMACY PROCESSES
IN ORGANIZATIONS

RESEARCH IN THE SOCIOLOGY OF ORGANIZATIONS

Series Editor: Michael Lounsbury

RESEARCH IN THE SOCIOLOGY OF ORGANIZATIONS
VOLUME 22

LEGITIMACY PROCESSES IN ORGANIZATIONS

EDITED BY

CATHRYN JOHNSON

Emory University, Atlanta, GA, USA

2004

ELSEVIER
JAI

Amsterdam – Boston – Heidelberg – London – New York – Oxford – Paris
San Diego – San Francisco – Singapore – Sydney – Tokyo

ELSEVIER B.V.
Sara Burgerhartstraat 25
P.O. Box 211,
1000 AE Amsterdam
The Netherlands

ELSEVIER Inc.
525 B Street, Suite 1900
San Diego,
CA 92101-4495
USA

ELSEVIER Ltd
The Boulevard, Langford
Lane Kidlington,
Oxford OX5 1GB
UK

ELSEVIER Ltd
84 Theobalds Road
London
WC1X 8RR
UK

First edition 2004

Library of Congress Cataloging in Publication Data
A catalog record is available from the Library of Congress.

British Library Cataloguing in Publication Data
A catalogue record is available from the British Library.

ISBN: 0-7623-1008-1
ISSN: 0733-558X

⊗ The paper used in this publication meets the requirements of ANSI/NISO Z39.48-1992 (Permanence of Paper). Printed in The Netherlands.

CONTENTS

LIST OF CONTRIBUTORS

Matthew E. Archibald	Department of Sociology, Emory University, Atlanta, USA
Timothy J. Dowd	Department of Sociology, Emory University, Atlanta, USA
Mary Ann Glynn	Goizueta Business School, Emory University, Atlanta, USA
Karen A. Hegtvedt	Department of Sociology, Emory University, Atlanta, USA
Anna C. Johansson	Beth Israel Deaconess Medical Center, Boston, USA
Cathryn Johnson	Department of Sociology, Emory University, Atlanta, USA
Christopher Marquis	University of Michigan Business School, Ann Arbor, USA
Anna Rubtsova	Department of Sociology, Emory University, Atlanta, USA
Jane Sell	Department of Sociology, Texas A&M University, USA
Lisa Troyer	Department of Sociology, University of Iowa, USA
Henry A. Walker	Department of Sociology, University of Arizona, USA
Jody-Clay Warner	Department of Sociology, University of Georgia, Athens, USA
Morris Zelditch, Jr.	Department of Sociology, Stanford University USA

INTRODUCTION: LEGTIMACY PROCESSES IN ORGANIZATIONS

Cathryn Johnson

This volume offers a collection of papers, by scholars in both social psychology and in organizations, that focuses on legitimacy processes in organizations. Over the last two decades social psychologists in sociology have developed legitimacy theories that strive to understand how legitimacy processes merge into structures. And, in organizational research, issues of legitimacy processes have been, and continue to be, of central concern for predicting organizational growth and survival. Therefore, I thought it worthwhile to produce a volume of *Research in the Sociology of Organizations* that addresses specifically how legitimacy processes operate within and external to organizations.

This volume accomplishes two goals. First, it provides a space dedicated solely to addressing questions of how legitimacy processes internal and external to organizations operate. This is no easy task. Legitimacy has long been recognized as a key and fundamental process in social life, and in organizations in particular (Weber, 1924/1978; Zelditch, 2001). Despite wide recognition that legitimacy is fundamental to understanding the internal structure and viability of an organization, articulating the general processes that underlie legitimacy has remained a difficult and persistent problem. The authors in this volume grapple with these processes, enhancing our knowledge of how legitimacy operates. Second, it is my hope that this volume stimulates more discussion and beneficial ties between social psychologists and organizational researchers on issues of legitimacy.

In this introduction, I provide a context for this collection of papers for the RSO readers. First, I discuss three key issues that are raised consistently in any

Legitimacy Processes in Organizations
Research in the Sociology of Organizations, Volume 22, 1–24
Copyright © 2004 by Elsevier Ltd.
All rights of reproduction in any form reserved
ISSN: 0733-558X/doi:10.1016/S0733-558X(04)22010-9

analysis of legitimacy. There are many more than three, so I picked what I thought would be the most relevant here. The first issue focuses on the core elements in the definitions of legitimacy offered by the theories used by the contributors in this volume. The second issue pertains to the range of objects of legitimation and delegitimation examined by the theories and the contributors. And the third issue concerns how behavioral patterns become legitimated, instantiated, or made real. While solutions to these issues may remain elusive, drawing attention to them demonstrates some links between legitimacy theories in social psychology and organizations. In the second part of this introduction, I outline the content of each paper, and provide a brief conclusion.

LEGITIMACY PROCESSES IN ORGANIZATIONS: THREE ISSUES

Before addressing these three issues, I provide some background on the key theoretical approaches to legitimacy employed in this volume: two legitimacy theories in social psychology and institutional theory in organizational analysis. Virtually every contributor draws upon at least one of these theories; several authors draw upon two of these theories, offering a way to bridge them and/or apply them to a substantive concern.

Background on the Theories

Legitimacy and the Stability of Authority

Zelditch and Walker (1984, 2003; Walker & Zelditch, 1993) emphasize the sources of legitimacy that maintain the stability of an organization's authority structure inside the boundaries of the organization. The theory stems from a number of concepts first developed by Max Weber, and then extended by Dornbusch and Scott (1975). Weber argued that an order is legitimate, ". . . only if action is approximately or on the average oriented to certain determinate 'maxims' or rules" (1924/1978, p. 31). He notes that, even though individuals may not believe in the same norms, values, and beliefs, their behavior becomes oriented to the valid social order. Individuals perceive that others support the legitimated system and thus act in accord with that system, even if they privately disagree. Thus, Weber captures the collective nature of legitimation processes (Zelditch, 2001).

Dornbusch and Scott (1975) extended Weber's ideas on legitimacy in their theory of evaluation and the exercise of authority. They define propriety as an actor's belief that the rules and norms of conduct are desirable, proper, and appropriate patterns of action. Validity, in contrast, refers to an individual's belief that he or she is obliged to obey these norms even in the absence of personal approval of them. Norms, values, beliefs, practices and procedures are valid if they observably govern the behavior of actors in an organization. The views of others in the social context enhance the validity of rules. An authority exists and is binding when participants see that other participants act in accord with it and support it. If an individual believes, and believes that others believe, that the authority structure is valid, he or she expects others to act in accord with it and support it. He or she will also expect that others expect him or her to act in accord with and support it. Validity, then, acts through the expectations as well as the behavior it creates. Order, then, is greatly facilitated when there is a collective belief in the legitimacy of an authority structure. When an order is valid, people do not question the authority; rather, they comply.

Sources of support include authorization, which occurs when support for the norms comes from individuals who occupy higher positions within the organization, and endorsement, which occurs when there is support for the norms from people of equal or lower positions. Both authorization and endorsement are external sources of collective support for the rules (or an authority). Propriety, on the other hand, refers to individual level support by an actor.

Zelditch and Walker (1984; Walker & Zelditch, 1993), building upon Weber and Dornbusch and Scott, provide a theory that examines sources of legitimacy that maintain the stability of an organization's authority structure even when there is impropriety. Key to this theory is that legitimacy of authority is fundamentally a collective process rather than a question of private individual consent. The authority of any person, act, position, or structure of positions rests on the cooperation from others. When a source is strongly authorized and endorsed, individuals are more likely to comply even if propriety is weak because they expect formal sanctions from superiors or informal sanctions from peers. Insofar as authorization and endorsement operate independently of propriety, the likelihood of responding on the basis of propriety may decrease. A consequence of these legitimating forces is the suppression of reactions by individuals who feel themselves improperly treated. In effect, this argument provides another untested explanation of the failure of inequitably treated individuals to attempt to restore justice (see Hegtvedt & Clay-Warner, this volume).

Zelditch and Walker's theory allows for predictions that account for the countervailing effects of validity. First, validity has a direct effect on compliance and control of actors by others partly because it induces a sense of obligation and partly because actors often accept "the way things are." A number of studies provide support for specific predictions of the theory about the effects of validity on collective mobilization by group members as a form of non-compliance. Results of these studies show that validity, independent of propriety, reduces attempts to mobilize collective action (e.g. Thomas, Walker & Zelditch, 1986).

Second, the theory also predicts that validity will have indirect effects through its effects on authorization, endorsement, and propriety. Validity affects actors' sense of propriety which in turn affects actors' collective actions. Endorsement also decreases attempts to mobilize change in the structure and creates more favorable private perceptions of the structure over time, even when private acceptance of the inequitable structure is initially low (Walker, Rogers & Zelditch, 1988; Walker et al., 1986). And, similar to the effects of validity, endorsement increases propriety of the structure over time.

Other research by Sell and Martin (1983; Martin & Sell, 1986) supports the idea that both authorization and endorsement are sources of legitimation, and these two sources are conceptually and empirically independent. They find that, under certain conditions, authorization can be overcome. Finally, research using vignette methodology shows that authorization and endorsement of a manager who denies a worker a pay raise increases acceptance of the pay denial and decreases the likelihood of forming a coalition or going over the superior's head with a pay request (Johnson & Ford, 1996). Also, endorsement of a superior reduces subordinates' feelings of resentment and excitement resulting from conflict with that superior (Johnson, Ford & Kaufman, 2000).

Zelditch and Walker's theory, then, argues that although an authority structure may be improper – that is, there may be considerable tension, dissatisfaction, and pressure to change it – there are also countervailing factors due to other sources of its legitimacy that dampen the likelihood of any attempts to change the structure, or of actual changes in the structure. When an authority structure is improper but valid, validity will decrease the effect of impropriety. (See papers by Zelditch, Walker, Hegtvedt and Clay-Warner, and Johansson and Sell in this volume for discussions and applications of this theory.)

Legitimacy Theory in the Expectations States Approach
A second prominent legitimacy theory in sociological social psychology is Ridgeway and Berger's (1986; Berger et al., 1998) legitimacy theory. This theory builds on status characteristics theory in the expectation states approach to describe the process by which status structures of groups within organizations are legitimated or delegitimated. Status characteristics theory focuses on how status hierarchies develop and stabilize in decision-making groups (Berger et al., 1977, 1980). It examines how diffuse and specific status characteristics organize interaction in task groups where members are collectively oriented. Diffuse status characteristics, such as gender, race, age, and physical attractiveness are

characterized by at least two states that are differentially valued in the larger society and are associated with general and specific performance expectations. These expectations are estimates about how well a member will perform on a task compared to other members. Information on status characteristics becomes salient when group members differentiate on that characteristic or when the task is directly relevant to the characteristic (e.g. a sex-typed task). Members who possess a high state of a status characteristic, such as whites in a mixed-racial group, are expected to do better than members who possess the low state within the group, e.g. blacks. This is so even when the status characteristic is not directly relevant to the task. Specific status characteristics, such as legal expertise, consist of two or more differentially valued states with expectations for performance related directly to the task, if the task involves these abilities (Berger et al., 1977, 1980).

The theory examines how these status characteristics are related to: (1) the frequency of members' task behavior such as giving opinions or suggestions; (2) the expression of socioemotional behavior (e.g. positive and negative responses to opinions such as complimenting, showing consideration, or withdrawing); and (3) who has more influence in the group (Wagner & Berger, 1997; Webster & Foschi, 1988). High status members are more likely than low status members to offer their opinions, receive positive evaluations, and achieve influence. There is substantial evidence to support this theory (see summaries by Wagner & Berger, 1997, 2002; Webster & Foschi, 1988).

Ridgeway and Berger (1986; Berger et al., 1998), building on status characteristics theory, describe the process by which legitimation and delegitimation operates in decision-making groups. In their theory, legitimacy refers to the process by which members come to believe that a group's status structure is collectively supported by the members. Key to Ridgeway and Berger's (1986; Berger et al., 1985) argument is the activation of various types of referential structures – socially shared systems of beliefs relating states of status characteristics and task outcomes or rewards to expectations for valued status positions. They discuss three elements that characterize actors in a situation and related referential beliefs. The diffuse status characteristics of group members prompt realization of categorical structures that suggest that individuals of one level of a status characteristic have higher positions than others (e.g. men occupy higher status positions). Specific status characteristics of group members trigger ability structures indicating that individuals who do better at the task are in higher status positions. And, reward or outcome characteristics, which often take the form of evaluations, correspond to outcome structures prescribing that actors who have higher evaluations will occupy higher positions in the status order.

Ridgeway and Berger (1986; Berger et al., 1998) suggest that when referential beliefs are activated in a group, they give rise to expectations for valued status positions in that group. That is, group members form expectations regarding who should occupy higher status positions in the group. Just as members draw on referential beliefs to form assumptions about the distribution of status in the group, they also create assumptions regarding the type of status order they expect other members will support. Because group members presumably draw on the same referential beliefs, each actor believes that the other actors share their same expectations. Therefore, they are likely to treat each other in accordance with their shared status expectations. In doing so, they act as if the positions held in the group actually carry the differences in status value implied by their expectations for valued status positions. Group members thus tend to behave in ways that validate the status order. As these behaviors confirm the status order, they create a presumption of collective normative support for the order (Ridgeway & Berger, 1986).

Ridgeway and Berger (1986) suggest that the structural condition that drives the process of legitimation mentioned above is the differentiation of expectations for valued status positions. The greater the differentiation in status expectations, the greater the likelihood that the group's status structure will be perceived as legitimate by group members. Several studies provide support for this claim (Ridgeway, Diekema & Johnson, 1995; Ridgeway, Johnson & Diekema, 1994).

Just as status structures may become legitimated, they also may become delegitimated. Delegitimation occurs when the order of performance expectations becomes incongruent or inversely related to the initially legitimated status hierarchy (Berger et al., 1998). For example, delegitimation occurs when group members work on new tasks that require new skills, making new status distinctions salient, or when there are explicit inconsistent evaluations of the actors' performances on the task. Typically, these evaluations come from an external source who has a right to do this evaluation.

This theory, then, focuses on the processes by which groups' status structures become legitimated or delegitimated. In addition, Ridgeway (1997) shows how these status and legitimacy processes occurring in interaction help to create and maintain inequality within organizations and within labor markets. (See papers by Johansson and Sell, and Rubstova and Dowd in this volume for discussions and applications of this theory.)

Institutional Theory of Organizational Analysis

The new institutionalism of organizational analysis is a theory of organizational legitimacy rather than the legitimacy of the organization's authority structure. This prominent theory in organizations, developed by Meyer, Scott and colleagues (e.g. Meyer & Rowan, 1977; Meyer & Scott, 1983; Powell & DiMaggio, 1991) is rooted in an earlier form of institutional theory (e.g. Selznick, 1949) and the social constructionists accounts of reality (Berger & Luckmann, 1967). (See Jepperson (2002) for a detailed account of this theory.)

The theory shows how organizations change structures to be more isomorphic (i.e. to become similar) with one another. It highlights the importance of the social and cultural environment in its explanation of the importance of legitimacy processes (Scott, 1995). An organization and its environment are located in a larger organizational field (DiMaggio & Powell, 1983; Scott & Meyer, 1983). An organizational field is composed of the organizations that produce the same good or service, supply the resources they require, consume their products, and also of the regulative agencies and various occupational associations that govern them. The survival of an organization depends on the field for resources. The flow of these resources, in turn, depends on the organization's legitimacy. Legitimacy of an organization is based on how well it accords with the institutions of its environment. The institutions of the environment are its consensual norms, values, and beliefs, and also its consensual category beliefs (e.g. beliefs about the nature of its actors). Organizations often try to attain legitimacy by using isomorphic practices that symbolically link them to valued norms. Yet the adoption and conformity to these norms and practices will legitimate the organizations only to extent that these norms and practices are themselves acceptable, appropriate, and valued (Glynn & Abzug, 1998, 2002). The theory argues that organizations incorporate the institutions of the environment into its formal structure because its survival depends on its legitimacy. And, because each organization incorporates the same institutions, the organizations in any particular organizational field become and remain isomorphic (Meyer & Rowan, 1977). Thus, organizations adopt the institutions of their environment into their structure and the structure becomes and remains similar to that of other organizations in the same environment.

Specifically, organizations attempt to pursue legitimacy by creating and maintaining structures, routines and practices that are isomorphic with their socioeconomic, cultural, and political environments. Socioeconomic and political pressures promote homogeneity of organizational structures. Regulatory (coercive), normative and cultural constraints in the environment promote homogeneity among organizations. Isomorphic mechanisms promote homogeneity and legitimacy through coercion (rooted in the political control and in legitimacy-seeking), normative influence (rooted especially in professionalism), and cultural imitation (rooted in the development of standard responses to uncertainty) (DiMaggio & Powell, 1983; Jepperson, 2002). Homogeneity often fosters legitimacy, which in turn, increases survival (Scott, 2001).

Recent elaborations of institutional theory contend that complexes of taken-for-granted cultural accounts, referred to as institutional logics, provide the basis for rationalized myths. Institutional logics refer to widely held beliefs about the legitimacy of structures, routines, and practices found within society (Friedland & Alford, 1991; Stryker, 2000). In so far as these logics are often contradictory, they provide a context for political conflicts within society. For example, Stryker (1994), in her study of the emergence of scientific-technical logics in the legal sector, shows how formal-legal and scientific-technical rationalizations offer alternative sources of legitimacy for actors' behavior within legal systems. Relatedly, recent studies show how shifts in institutional logics bring about attendant changes in the way that organizations and their fields conduct their business (e.g. Dobbin & Dowd, 2000; Schneiberg & Bartley, 2001; Thornton & Ocasio, 1999).

As predicted by institutional theory, organizational survival and success depends on legitimacy. Organizational legitimacy decreases when organizational structures do not adjust and adapt to the changing rules that make up an organizational field. (See Glynn and Marquis, Archibald, Zelditch, Troyer, and Sell and Johannson for discussions and applications of institutional theory.)

Definitions of Legitimacy

Do sociologists in social psychology and organizations define legitimacy in a similar fashion? The definitions of legitimacy in legitimacy theories in social psychology are rooted in the Weberian tradition. Weber's formulation of legitimacy is conceived simultaneously as conformity with a set of rules that actors accept as either: (1) a set of obligations; or as (2) a desirable model of action (see Walker, this volume). Dornbusch and Scott (1975) separated out these ideas by defining validity as the acceptance of norms, values, beliefs, and procedures as matters of objective fact. Propriety, on the other hand, is the individual's acceptance and support of norms, values, beliefs, and procedures as desirable and proper – the way things ought to be. Zelditch (2001, p. 33) provides a broad definition of legitimacy in the Weberian tradition: "... something is legitimate if it is in accord with the norms, values, beliefs, practices, and procedures accepted by a group." Walker et al. (1986) offer a similar definition: legitimacy is "... the belief that a norm or normative system governs or should govern one's actions" (p. 622). This Weberian tradition emphasizes the collective nature of legitimation processes. It also suggests a cognitive dimension and an evaluative dimension of legitimacy.

Contributors to this volume in the social psychology area use definitions consistent with the above. For example, Johannson and Sell note that legitimation is the process through which individuals come to adhere to, defer to or support a socially defined set of rules (written or unwritten) even when there are no obvious incentives to do so. They note that this process is often taken for granted in the establishment and maintenance of social structure. Hegtvedt and Clay-Warner, drawing from Zelditch and Walker (1984), describe legitimacy as the collective sources of support for an authority. More recently, Zelditch and Walker (2003) define a regime as legitimate if its rules, constituent beliefs, and values are normative. "Legitimacy converts power into authority and makes compliance with the directives of dominating actors obligatory" (Walker, this volume).

Similarly, authors of legitimacy theory in the expectation states program refer to legitimacy as the process by which group members come to believe that a group's status structure is collectively supported by the members (Ridgeway & Berger, 1986). They emphasize that the process of legitimation is an inherently collective social process that "... mediates the relationship between power and authority and affects the establishment, persistence and change of social organizational forms" (Berger et al., 1998, p. 379). This process can occur at different levels of interaction such as the group or the organization.

Form the institutional point of view, Meyer and Scott (1983, p. 201) define legitimacy as, "... the degree of cultural support for an organization." Troyer (this volume), borrowing this definition, notes that legitimacy arises from conformity to taken-for-granted expectations regarding appropriate repertoires of action that are aligned with recognizable organizational structures and processes. One of the most cited definitions in the organizations literature is Suchman's (1995, p. 574): legitimacy is "... a generalized perception or assumption that the actions of an entity are desirable, proper or appropriate within some socially constructed system of norms, values, beliefs and definitions." This definition includes both the evaluative and the cognitive dimensions and it also acknowledges the role of the social audience in legitimation processes. Suchman notes that,

> ... when one says that a certain pattern of behavior possesses legitimacy, one asserts that some group of observers, as a whole, accepts or supports what those observers perceive to be the behavioral pattern, as a *whole* – despite reservations that any single observer might have about any single behavior, and despite reservations that any or all observers might have, were they to observe more (1995, p. 574).

Suchman's definition is strikingly similar to the definitions found in the social psychological legitimacy theories. Archibald (this volume) uses Suchman's definition, stating that an organization's legitimacy is based on the collective perception that audiences (both internal and external) support or accept it. Examples of external audiences may include federal and state agencies, as well as social movement entrepreneurs. Examples of internal audiences may include workers and managers. In addition, Suchman (1995) and others refer to types of legitimacy, such as pragmatic legitimacy, moral legitimacy, and cognitive legitimacy. All three types involve a generalized perception that the activities of the organization are appropriate and desirable within a taken-for-granted system of norms, values, beliefs and definitions. They each rest on a different set of behavioral dynamics. Pragmatic legitimacy is based on interest; moral legitimacy is based on evaluations about whether an organizational activity is the right thing to do; and cognitive legitimacy is based on cognition, that is, acceptance based on some taken-for-granted cultural account. (See Suchman (1995) for a detailed discussion of legitimacy; and see Archibald (this volume) for a discussion of the importance of distinguishing between sociopolitical and cultural legitimacy.)

Glynn and Marquis (this volume) tackle the issue of defining illegitimacy. They note that illegitimacy also necessitates some shared understanding or consensus about the inappropriateness of organizational activity (Elsbach & Sutton, 1992). To say that an action is illegitimate involves comparing it against existing norms and values. Consistent with other researchers, these authors view illegitimacy as the devaluation of an organization based upon a perceived misalignment with institutional norms (Davis et al., 1994; Kraatz & Zajac, 1996).

Some definitions above emphasize an evaluative aspect of legitimacy, while others emphasize a cognitive aspect (i.e. acceptance without any evaluative undertones). Some definitions allow for either aspect of legitimacy. Importantly, however, all the definitions from the theoretical traditions in social psychology and organizations have two fundamental similarities. First, in both areas legitimacy is viewed as a process that always has a collective aspect (i.e. a social audience is always present). Often, this audience is perceived to be superordinate to the individuals in the situation. Legitimacy, then, is always dependent on a collective audience. Second, legitimacy involves the appearance of consensus in situations, in that actors perceive that others accept what ever it is that is the object of legitimacy. What is important is the appearance of consensus, not actual consensus. (See Walker (this volume) for a good discussion of the concept of legitimacy in which he describes several problems that confront the definition.)

Objects of Legitimacy

Scholars of legitimation draw our attention to the multiple objects and multiple sources of legitimation (Bell et al., 2000; Dornbusch & Scott, 1975; Walker, Rogers & Zelditch, 2002; Walker & Zelditch, 1993). An object that may or may not become legitimated in organizations and organizational fields may include an act, a rule, a procedure, a routine, a distribution, a position, a group or team, a group's status structure, teamwork, a system of positions, an authority structure, an organization, organizational symbols, an organization's form, practices, services, programs, a regime, a system of power, and a system of inequality (to name a few).

The contributors focus on legitimacy of objects at different levels of analysis. Hegtvedt and Clay-Warner focus on the legitimacy of an act by a person in an organizational position and its effect on perceived justice. Troyer examines the legitimacy of teamwork within a set of competing institutional logics between the organization and teams. Johannson and Sell explain how three sources of legitimation of group structures make groups more or less hierarchical and how these sources make group routines more or less flexible. Rubtovsa and Dowd examine how the subcultural habitus and subcultural capital constructed in organizational departments legitimate hierarchical relations between these departments. Zelditch shows how the internal and external legitimacy processes of an organization combine to determine the legitimacy of an organization's authority structure. Glynn and Marquis examine how organizational symbols (specifically organizational names) that once legitimated organizations can subsequently illegitimate organizations. They note that names dramatize the organization's ceremonial face, proclaiming certainty about its identity and legitimacy in the organizational field (Meyer & Rowan, 1977). Archibald also examines the legitimacy of organizations, distinguishing between the consequences of an organization's sociopolitical and cultural legitimacy on its viability. Finally, Walker examines both legitimacy of the adoption of organizational practices and regimes, and how this adoption can create processes that spread the legitimacy of ideas to arenas external to the organizations that initially proposed them.

This review of the objects of legitimation found in these papers shows that objects can be any shared pattern of behavior that can include both socially related acts and actors. All patterns of behavior examined here acquire legitimacy in a situation when actors perceive that some social audience, as a whole, accepts this socially related act or actor, even if they hold reservations about this pattern of behavior or actor. Recently, Walker et al. (2002) provide an important direction in their work by asking whether the legitimacy of a given object is dependent upon the other objects of legitimacy within the same context. Under what conditions would they be dependent? For example, would the illegitimacy of an act of a person undermine that person in her position within the organization? They explore the possibility that different objects of legitimacy contribute independently toward the probability of compliance of group members.

Legitimacy as a Social Process

Theories and research surrounding legitimacy address the issues of the process, objects, sources, conditions, and consequences of legitimation (and more recently, delegitimation). Some contributors of this volume focus more on the sources and consequences of legitimation; others examine how legitimation (and delegitimation) occurs. It may be fair to say that we have done a better job thus far of studying the former than the latter.

One of the key questions the theories in this volume address is: How do objects gain social support (i.e. legitimacy)? How does legitimacy happen and how does it not happen? Here I provide only a brief discussion of how the theories used in this volume describe or explain the ritualized enactment that occurs for anything to acquire legitimacy, and then provide some examples from the contributors that address legitimacy as a social process.

Legitimacy theories in social psychology view legitimation as a social process that mediates the relationship between social actors and social structures (Berger et al., 1998). Actors create and recreate social reality, and this process is truly collective in nature. Actors must believe that others will also treat objects as valid in order for these objects to be perceived and accepted as legitimate. Inherently, legitimacy is a multilevel process. For example, for Berger et al. (1998), referential belief structures exist at the cultural and societal level and then become relevant in the immediate group situation. They argue that the process of legitimation has its roots in cultural elements, and is created within the group interaction process as members reenact relatively enduring cultural elements. Just as larger structures of power and influence are often formed through interaction is groups, so is the process of legitimation (and delegitimation). From this point of view, structural features drive the process of legitimation; yet at the same time legitimation also requires agreement at the socially constructed local level in order for an object to become legitimate.

How do we study this process? Johannson and Sell (this volume), for example, examine how legitimacy of a social object or person might spread, not only to other objects, but also to the structure and the routines of the group. For example, consider a manager in one activity is granted legitimacy. Under what conditions would this legitimacy be generalized to a completely different set of activities? These authors attempt to identify the process by which legitimation diffuses, or spreads, and to describe the role of the social actor in that process. With their formal theory, they explain how structures created in one interaction shape and constrain future interaction.

More recently, Zelditch and Walker (2003) suggest four conditions that are jointly sufficient to establish and sustain legitimacy. Specifically, they examine how organizations can establish and sustain legitimate regimes. Regimes are defined as, ". . . a set of rules that define a system of positions, position-specific acts and relations between positions" (Walker, this volume). A regime is legitimate if its rules, constituent beliefs and values are normative. These four conditions include: consensus, impartiality, objectification, and consonance. They propose how these conditions affect legitimacy processes within organizations. Walker (this volume), using this extension of Zelditch and Walker's legitimacy theory, shows how regimes get legitimated, and then importantly, how, in turn, this creates processes that spread the legitimacy of ideas and behaviors to arenas outside of the organization that initially proposed them.

Institutional theory focuses on the incorporation of the institutions of the environment into the internal structures of an organization. It argues that legitimacy is gained through structural alignment under isomorphic regimes (see details above). Scott (1995) identifies three "carriers of institutions" which explicate some mechanisms through which legitimation may "diffuse" or spread. These carriers include cultural, social structural and routines. Cultural carriers rely on "... codified patterns of meanings and rule systems" (p. 53). Social structural carriers are based on patterned expectations or "role systems" and create structural isomorphism (p. 53). Routines as carriers rely on structured activities, which can embody institutions (p. 380).

Glynn and Marquis (this volume), drawing from institutional theory, argue that shifts from legitimate to illegitimate states of organizations involve change and periodicity. Examining the boundaries between these states provides one useful way to understand the dynamics of legitimation and delegitimation processes. Different degrees of institutionalization characterize organizational fields. Hence, there are different degrees of demarcation between legitimacy and illegitimacy (Zucker, 1991). (Walker, this volume, also argues that Weber referred to validity as a matter of degree.) Periodicity suggests that each temporal era consists of a discrete set of sanctioned norms, which are different from those in other eras.

Drawing from these ideas, Glynn and Marquis provide the initial stage of a theoretical model of legitimacy as both static and process. They argue that if isomorphism legitimates, then non-isomorphism illegitimates. Illegitimacy seems to result from a misalignment between organizational practices, forms, or symbols and institutional standards of appropriateness. They suggest that this misalignment or incongruence may come from initiatives from inside the organization or situations where the institutional environment changes in ways that are not matched by changes in the organization. Organizational illegitimacy, then, seems to involve a state of misalignment with the environment, which can be predicated upon the processes of institionalization and changing valuations, norms, and beliefs. Institutionalization is not static; norms, values and beliefs change over time. As well, they argue, boundaries demarcating illegitimacy from legitimacy are dynamic. Delegitimation (and legitimation), then, is perceived as both a process and a state.

Also drawing from institutional theory, Troyer (this volume), argues that the way work is structured, rationalized, and accounted for in the organization is based on common cultural beliefs regarding appropriate ways of structuring work. Troyer argues that a discrepancy between the institutional logics that rationalize teamwork within teams and the institutional logics of the organization in which teams are embedded may threaten the legitimacy of these teams. Teamwork, for many teams, represents democratic logics that may contradict bureaucratic logics that often characterize many organizations. When the organization is not characterized by similar expectations or logics as teams within the organization, the external evaluations of these teams suffer (i.e. their legitimacy is questioned). In this case, the discrepancy between the institutional logics that rationalize teamwork and the organization represents one mechanism that can affect a team's legitimacy.

The contributors of this volume study legitimacy as a social process at different levels of analysis. It is our task to discover the underlying features of this process. How do these various objects examined become legitimated, instantiated, made real? To what extent must there be some sort of ritualized enactment for an object to acquire legitimacy? Is this process similar for any object at different levels of analysis?

CONTENTS OF THE VOLUME

The contributors grapple with some or all of the three issues above. In, "Institutional Effects on the Stability of Organizational Authority," Zelditch integrates Dornbusch and Scott's (1975) theory of evaluation and the exercise of authority (EEA), Zelditch and Walker's (1984) theory of legitimacy and the stability of authority (LSA), and Meyer and Rowan's (1977) theory of institutionalized organizations (IO) into a single consistent theory that is able to interrelate the internal and external legitimacy processes of an organization. EEA and LSA see legitimacy processes mostly from inside the organization's boundaries. They have much to gain from opening the organization to its environment. Drawing from IO, the institutions of the environment link the external legitimacy of organizations to their internal legitimacy processes of the organization. On the other hand, IO under-theorizes the internal legitimacy processes of organizations; therefore, it has much to gain from theories of the internal processes of organizations. Zelditch shows how internal and external legitimacy combine to determine the legitimacy of an organization's authority structure. Specifically, this theory integration allows the author to predict the institutional effects on the stability of organizational authority and use them to explain the conditions under which sanctions, evaluations, and performance come to be decoupled. Using three variables – the type of environment on which the organization depends, the extent to which it depends on it, and its organization – Zelditch predicts the strength and direction of an environment's pressures towards evaluation and control. This paper shows the promise of how these theories may complement and benefit each other to enhance understanding of legitimacy processes and organizational outcomes.

In "Democracy in a Bureaucracy: The Legitimacy Paradox of Teamwork in Organizations," Troyer examines a key "legitimacy paradox" that face teams in organizations. Troyer's framework conceptualizes teams as open systems (e.g. Scott, 1998), which are embedded in the social structure of an organization. In addition, teams are collectives with scripts that are based on institutional logics. The institutional logics that rationalize teamwork are the basis for peripheral knowledge structures – i.e. individual-level cognitive representations of expectations for work behavior and the institutional logics that validate those expectations. The legitimacy paradox, then, ". . . reflects the fact that the processes reflected in teams may not conform to those that more commonly characterize work within the organization, leading to a withdrawal of support for the team in the form of adverse evaluations" (Troyer, this volume). The approaches to work that may facilitate teamwork may, at the same time, undermine perceptions by external evaluators of the team's effectiveness. Specifically, Troyer argues that teamwork represents democratic logics that may contradict bureaucratic logics that often characterize many organizations. Drawing from new institutional theory (Meyer & Rowan, 1977; Meyer & Scott, 1983; Powell & DiMaggio, 1991), she argues that such a contradiction threatens a team's legitimacy.

To test her propositions, Troyer analyzed data from surveys of 62 teams in four organizations, spanning three industries: aerospace, computer, and heavy equipment manufacturing. She finds that, although teams whose members consistently draw upon expectations of egalitarianism are less likely to experience internal problems such as miscommunication, the external evaluations of the team suffer when the organization is not characterized by similar expectations and logics. Importantly, this finding holds even though team members do perceive the differences between the team's expectations and the generally held expectations held in the organization.

In "Sources of Legitimation and Their Effects on Group Routines: A Theoretical Analysis," Johansson and Sell also examine a paradox that groups face in organizations. They argue that one goal of organizations is to develop group routines that are efficient, but at the same time also flexible. The paradox here, however, is that routines that are efficient at one point in time may become increasingly inefficient for the group and the organization, yet still remain. As the authors note, "Routine can numb analysis." For example, the authors quote Vaughan (1996) in regard to the *Challenger* disaster: "... its origins were in routine and taken-for-granted aspects of organizational life that created a way of seeing that was simultaneously a way of not seeing" (1996, p. 394). In this paper, the authors develop a formal theory that articulates the processes by which legitimation of particular group structures affect the development and use of group routines. Based on Scott (1995) and Knottnerus (1997), they define group routines as, "... sequential decision structures which two or more actors in a group use to engage in patterned and repeated behaviors which are cued by both external stimuli, as well as one another, in order to solve a problem." Their theory draws upon status/legitimacy theories in the expectation states tradition (Berger et al., 1980, 1998; Ridgeway & Berger, 1986; Walker & Zelditch, 1993; Zelditch & Walker, 1984), and institutional theory (DiMaggio & Powell, 1983; Meyer & Rowan, 1977; Scott, 1995). The multilevel formulation articulates three sources of legitimation: a referential belief structure (i.e. a set of cultural beliefs) about expertise and leadership, authorization (i.e. superordinate support) of a leader, and endorsement (i.e. support by the group) of a leader. Specifically, Johannson and Sell describe how these three sources of legitimation make groups more or less hierarchical and how these sources make group routines more or less flexible. In doing so, they identify the process by which legitimation may spread and the role of the social actor in that process. Their analysis helps to solve the paradox between development of group routines and the creation of flexibility.

In "Cultural Capital as a Multi-Level Concept: The Case of an Advertising Agency," Rubtsova and Dowd address the question, what is the role of culture in the reproduction and legitimation of inequality? They argue that, although Bourdieu's theory of cultural capital provides the processes by which cultural capital facilitates this reproduction and legitimation of inequality at the societal level, there is little detail regarding such processes at the organizational and individual levels (e.g. Lahire, 2003). To address this gap, the authors draw upon three seemingly unrelated theories – Bourdieu's (1977, 1990) theory of cultural capital, social representations theory, and expectations states theory in social psychology – to develop a multi-level concept of cultural capital. All three theories emphasize how culture contributes to the reproduction of inequality, but at different levels of analysis. From Bourdieu's theory they define cultural capital as knowledge, practices and goods that are seen as rare, "high" and desirable. This macro-level concept refers to legitimate culture produced by institutions at the societal level. From social representations theory (Moscovici, 1981, 1988), they define "subcultural capital" (a meso-level concept) as a legitimate culture that operates one level removed from the broader societal culture. This theory suggests that macro-produced categories may be modified in group interaction to form distinctive cognitive schemas that serve in the reproduction of groups at the meso-level (e.g. departments within the organization). From expectation states theory, they define "multicultural capital" as the "... aggregation of cultural and subcultural forms of capital that are salient in a particular interactional context." Rubstova and Dowd illustrate the utility of their multi-level concept through their study of an Eastern European advertising agency. They show how subcultural habitus and subcultural capital of two departments in the organization are constructed as a result of organizational change (i.e. founding, leadership change) and how both, in turn, contribute to the legitimation of hierarchical relations between the two departments. They conclude with a telling discussion of what this multi-level concept holds for research on legitimacy processes within organizational settings.

In "When Good Names Go Bad: Symbolic Illegitimacy in Organizations," Glynn and Marquis examine how organizational symbols, in this case names, that once legitimated organizations can subsequently undermine such legitimacy. They note that institutional processes of imitation, diffusion, and normative precedent often lead organizations to adopt strategies and structures quickly (Fligstein, 1990). Once in place, however, such institutional practices tend to be resistant to change. When it comes to the "dot-com" rush, however, the authors ask, how can we account for such a swift delegitimation of the "dot-com" names? They use the Internet as a window on legitimacy processes to uncover what it can illuminate about institutionalism and symbolic isomorphism (Glynn & Abzug, 2002). Specifically, they study illegitimacy in the context of changes in the valuation of the Internet, from boom to bust, by viewing "dot-com" names as markers for these changes. They begin their analysis by analyzing the case of software retailer Egghead, the first firm to append "dot-com" to its name. Drawing from this case, they develop hypotheses that relate legitimacy to symbolism, and then test these hypotheses in a second study using survey and archival methods. This second study examines how the changing legitimacy of the Internet affected the legitimacy of dot-com names adopted by firms. Their results illustrate how swift and definitive the process of deinstutitionalization can be; good organizational names can go bad rather quickly, both for financial and public audiences.

Building on these findings, Glynn and Marquis develop a theoretical framework that models how symbols initially adopted by organizations in their quest for legitimacy can ultimately illegitimate. They theorize that illegitimacy is institutional misalignment, and that boundaries partitioning illegitimacy from legitimacy are dynamic. Therefore, illegitimating processes in organizations involve both *state* and *process* considerations. They conclude by suggesting how their framework could be applied and tested in other contexts in which deinstitutionalization occurred swiftly, such as corporate governance, compensation structures, and executive pay in the post-Enron world. Notably, the authors tackle the under-researched, yet extremely important, question of how delegimation processes may work.

In "Between Isomorphism and Marketing Partitioning: How Organizational Competencies and Resources Foster Cultural and Sociopolitical Legitimacy, and Promote Organizational Survival," Archibald draws upon the institutional and resource-based perspectives to examine how isomorphism and marketing partitioning foster legitimacy and promote organizational viability. He argues that institutional frameworks suggest that organizations that become isomorphic with their institutional environments gain social fitness that, in turn, promotes viability (Scott, 2001). Resource-based perspectives argue that competitive fitness, gained through the process of differentiation, promotes viability (Carroll, 1985; Oliver, 1997). Archibald distinguishes between cultural and sociopolitical legitimacy, both theoretically and empirically, arguing that this distinction is important because the processes generating organizational viability based on isomorphic pressures may be markedly different from those associated with mechanisms of market partitioning. Specifically, he formulates hypotheses on the extent to which between-organizational homogeneity in competencies (organizational programs and services) and resources (human capital) foster these two types of legitimacy, and promote organizational viability. He analyzes data from an original database of life histories of all active national self-help/mutual aid organizations in the U.S. between 1955 and 2000. Results show that cultural legitimacy and sociopolitical legitimacy have unique relationships with competencies and resources. This study extends the institutional framework by linking institutionalism with resource-based explanations of organizational viability.

In "Linking Legitimacy and Procedural Justice: Expanding on Justice Processes In Organizations," Hegtvedt and Clay-Warner argue that both legitimacy and justice processes affect worker and organizational outcomes, such as compliance, job satisfaction, and commitment. The effects of legitimacy and justice processes may not be independent, given that a single event in organizations can elicit concerns about both legitimacy and justice. Drawing upon Zelditch and Walker's (1984, 2003; Walker & Zelditch, 1993) legitimacy theory in sociology and Tyler's (1990) work on procedural justice in psychology, the authors present two models that explicate how legitimacy (collective sources of support for an authority) and procedural justice (use of fair procedures) affect individuals' interpretations and responses to situations involving unfair outcomes such as underpayment. Both theoretical approaches fundamentally agree that perceived obligation to obey and, in turn, compliance, characterize the success of a legitimate structure. In addition, they both emphasize the importance of group-level contextual factors.

Hegtvedt and Clay-Warner's first model focuses on the independent effects of legitimacy and use of fair procedures on employees' perceptions of fairness about outcomes they receive. They predict that the presence or absence of authorization/endorsement and the use of fair or unfair procedures by a manager affect whether an employee attempts to redress the manager's unfair pay decision or simply acquiesces. Building on the first model, in the second model the authors explicate a dynamic reciprocal relationship between *perceptions* of legitimacy and of fair procedures that affect how workers perceive and react to unfair outcomes. This model shows how the procedurally fair treatment of workers may give rise to the perception that workers, in general, support the authority – i.e. that endorsement exists. In addition, the model proposes how perceptions of collective support may enhance perceptions of procedural justice. Their work represents a notable advancement in our knowledge of how legitimacy and justice processes work together in organizations.

In "Beyond Power and Domination: Legitimacy and Formal Organizations," Walker revisits and extends the multiple-source, multi-object theory of legitimacy in organizations (Dornbusch & Scott, 1975; Walker & Zelditch, 1993; Zelditch & Walker, 1984, 2003) beyond its usual focus on power and domination. Key to this extension is the idea of legitimated *regimes*. The theory describes the mechanisms that establish the legitimacy of new or contested regimes, and facilitates the "spread of legitimacy" to structures and processes that exist outside organizational boundaries. The analysis examines how organizations use legitimized elements of the regimes that lead to the transfer or spread of legitimacy to new, and sometimes controversial, ideas and behaviors. Using current debates about affirmative action policies and practices, Walker illustrates how organizations try to redefine what is legitimate. From this legitimacy theory, adoption of practices like targeted discrimination creates processes that spread the legitimacy of ideas with potentially negative social consequences to arenas external to the organizations that initially proposed them. Although Zelditch and Walker's framework set out initially to understand much of the routine day-to-day activity that characterizes life in a typical organization, Walker shows, importantly, how this framework can also set the stage for understanding how legitimacy processes within organizations extend beyond organizational boundaries.

CONCLUSION

This volume merely scratches the surface of understanding how legitimacy processes work in organizations. A future direction suggested by these papers for enhancing this understanding is to investigate how the theories highlighted in this volume may complement each other. As Zelditch (this volume) notes, legitimacy theories that examine legitimacy processes within organizational boundaries have much to gain from opening the organization to its environment.

As well, institutional theory would benefit from theories of the internal legitimacy processes of organizations.

Zelditch (this volume) provides the most explicit step in this direction. He provides an initial attempt at integrating these theories by showing how concepts in legitimacy theories of the organization's authority can be extended to concepts in institutional theory. He states that institutional theory's:

> ... concept of legitimacy is equivalent to validity; its concept of the effects of "regulatory agencies" is equivalent to authorization; its concepts of functions of occupational associates is equivalent to endorsement. And where they differ, organizational legitimacy can be both directly and indirectly linked to the legitimacy of authority.

In addition, using his integrated theory, he predicts that:

> It is reasonable to suppose that the similarity of the organization to the other organizations in its environment increases its validity, dissimilarity from them undermines it. . . . The more isomorphic the authority structure of an organization is with the structure of authority of the organizations in the environment, the more valid it is in the eyes of the participants in the organization.

This integration allows for specific predictions of the likelihood of decoupling. The next step, of course, is to test these predictions.

Troyer, Sell and Johannson, and Walker (this volume) also provide examples of how these theories may be used together to further enhance our understanding of legitimacy processes. And Rubstova and Dowd draw upon several theories in culture and social psychology to investigate how hierarchical relations between organizational departments are legitimated. Finally, a recent, although not the only, example of bringing together legitimacy theory in social psychology and institutional theory is found in Lucas's (2003) work on the legitimation of female leadership in organizations. Using institutional theory and status characteristics theory within the expectation states program, Lucas (2003) shows the importance of institutionalizing female leadership in addition to female leaders. He found that women who attain leadership based on ability in institutionalized structures (i.e. structures where group members feel that it is proper and right for women to hold leadership positions) are more influential than women who attain leadership based only on ability. These women also have as much influence over members as do male leaders with comparable ability when female leadership is not institutionalized.

My hope for this volume was to provide a stage where sociologists from both social psychology and organizations could address a common issue of enhancing understanding of legitimacy processes in organizations. Legitimacy theories in social psychology and institutional theory in organizations have something to offer each other. Over the last 25–30 years, both areas have built solid theoretical and empirical foundations for our understanding of legitimacy processes. This volume provides a foundation for a constructive dialogue between these two areas of sociology. The contributors of this volume have accomplished this goal, setting the stage for this dialogue, and for that, I thank them.

I also wish to thank Sam Bacharach – the former editor of *Research in the Sociology of Organizations* – for giving me the opportunity to edit this volume. I initially approached him about editing a volume of *RSO* that would address legitimacy, power, and status processes in organizations. He told me quite directly that this approach was too broad and unfocused. Instead, he encouraged me to focus "simply" on legitimacy processes in organizations. Fortunately, legitimacy is at the heart of my own interests. His advice was clearly sound. I am also indebted to Edward Lawler and Morris Zelditch. They both encouraged me to pursue the project. Ed Lawler connected me to Sam Bacharach, for which I am grateful. Morris Zelditch contributed a key piece to this volume, and provided me with ongoing support. Finally, I thank the current editor of *RSO*, Michael Lounsbury, who has been very helpful and supportive during the course of this volume.

ACKNOWLEDGMENTS

I am indebted to my colleagues, Karen Hegtvedt and Timothy Dowd, for their insightful comments and guidance on a previous draft of this introduction.

REFERENCES

Bell, R., Walker, A., & Willer, D. (2000). Power, influence, and legitimacy in organizations: Implications of three theoretical research programs. *Research in the Sociology of Organizations, 17*, 131–177.

Berger, J., Fisek, M. H., Norman, R. Z., & Zelditch, M., Jr. (1977). *Status characteristics and social interaction: An expectation states approach.* New York: Elsevier Scientific.

Berger, J., Ridgeway, C., Fisek, M. H., & Norman, R. Z. (1998). The legitimation and delegitimation of power and prestige orders. *American Sociological Review, 63*, 379–405.

Berger, J., Rosenholtz, S., & Zelditch, M., Jr. (1980). Status organizing processes. *Annual Review of Sociology, 6*, 479–508.

Berger, J., Wagner, D. G., & Zelditch, M., Jr. (1985). Expectation states theory: Review and assessment. In: J. Berger & M. Zelditch, Jr. (Eds), *Status, Rewards, and Influence: How Expectations Organize Behavior* (pp. 1–72). San Francisco: Jossey-Bass.

Berger, P. L., & Luckmann, T. (1967). *The social construction of reality.* New York: Doubleday.

Bourdieu, P. (1977). *Outline of a theory of practice.* Cambridge: Cambridge University Press.

Bourdieu, P. (1990). *The logic of practice.* Stanford, CA: Stanford University Press.

Carroll, G. (1985). Concentration and specialization: Dynamics of niche width in populations of organizations. *American Sociological Review, 100*, 720–749.

Davis, G. F., Diekmann, K. A., & Tinsley, C. H. (1994). The decline and fall of the conglomerate firm in the 1980s: The de-institutionalization of an organizational form. *American Sociological Review, 59*, 547–570.

DiMaggio, P. J., & Powell, W. W. (1983). The iron cage revisited: Institutional isomorphism and collective rationality in organizational fields. *American Sociological Review, 48*, 147–160.

Dobbin, F., & Dowd, T. J. (2000). The market that antitrust built: Public policy, private coercion, and railroad acquisitions, 1825–1922. *American Sociological Review, 65*, 631–657.

Dornbusch, S. M., & Scott, W. R. (1975). *Evaluation and the exercise of authority.* San Francisco: Jossey-Bass.

Elsbach, K. D., & Sutton, R. (1992). Acquiring organizational legitimacy through illegitimate actions: A marriage of institutional and impression management theories. *Academy of Management Journal, 35*, 699–738.

Fligstein, N. (1990). *The transformation of corporate control.* Cambridge, MA: Harvard University Press.

Friedland, R., & Alford, R. R. (1991). Bringing society back in: Symbols, practices, and institutional contradictions. In: W. W. Powell & P. J. DiMaggio (Eds), *The New Institutionalism in Organizational Analysis* (pp. 232–263). Chicago: University of Chicago Press.

Glynn, M. A., & Abzug, R. A. (1998). Isomorphism and competitive differentiation in the organizational name game. In: J. A. C. Baum (Ed.), *Advances in Strategic Management* (Vol. 15, pp. 105–128). Greenwich, CT: JAI Press.

Glynn, M. A., & Abzug, R. (2002). Institutionalizing identity: Symbolic isomorphism and organizational names. *Academy of Management Journal, 45*, 267–280.

Jepperson, R. L. (2002). The development and application of sociological neoinstitutionalism. In: J. Berger & M. Zelditch (Eds), *New Directions in Contemporary Sociological Theory* (pp. 229–266). Lanham, MD: Rowman & Littlefield.

Johnson, C., & Ford, R. (1996). Dependence power, legitimacy, and tactical choice. *Social Psychology Quarterly, 59*, 126–139.

Johnson, C., Ford, R., & Kaufman, J. M. (2000). Emotional reactions to conflict: Do dependence and legitimacy matter? *Social Forces, 79*, 107–137.

Lahire, B. (2003). From the Habitus to an individual heritage of dispositions: Towards a sociology at the level of the individual. *Poetics, 31*, 329–355.

Lucas, J. W. (2003). Status processes and the institutionalization of women as leaders. *American Sociological Review, 68*, 464–480.

Knottnerus, J. D. (1997). The theory of structural ritualization. *Advances in Group Processes, 14*, 257–279.

Kraatz, M. S., & Zajac, E. J. (1996). Exploring the limits of the new institutionalism: The causes and consequences of illegitimate organizational change. *American Sociological Review, 61*, 812–836.

Martin, M. W., & Sell, J. (1986). Rejection of authority: The importance of type of distribution rule and extent of benefit. *Social Science Quarterly, 67*(4), 855–868.

Meyer, J. W., & Rowan, B. (1977). Institutionalized organizations: Formal structure as myth and ceremony. *American Journal of Sociology, 83*, 340–363.

Meyer, J. W., & Scott, W. R. (1983). *Organizational environments: Ritual and rationality.* Beverly Hills, CA: Sage.

Moscovici, S. (1981). On social representations. In: J. P. Forgas (Ed.), *Social Cognition: Perspectives on Everyday Understanding* (pp. 181–203). London: Academic Press.

Moscovici, S. (1988). Notes towards a description of social representations. *European Journal of Social Psychology, 18*, 211–250.

Oliver, C. (1997). Sustainable competitive advantage: Combining institutional and resource-based views. *Strategic Management Journal, 18*, 697–713.

Powell, W. W., & DiMaggio, P. J. (1991). *The new institutionalism in organizational analysis.* Chicago: University of Chicago Press.

Ridgeway, C. L. (1997). Interaction and the conservation of gender inequality: Considering employment. *American Sociological Review, 62*, 218–235.

Ridgeway, C. L., & Berger, J. (1986). Expectations, legitimation, and dominance behavior in task groups. *American Sociological Review, 51*, 603–617.

Ridgeway, C. L., Diekema, D., & Johnson, C. (1995). Legitimacy, compliance, and gender in peer groups. *Social Psychology Quarterly, 58*, 298–311.

Ridgeway, C. L., Johnson, C., & Diekema, D. (1994). External status, legitimacy, and compliance in male and female groups. *Social Forces, 72*(4), 1051–1077.

Schneiberg, M., & Bartley, T. (2001). Regulating American industries: Markets, politics, and the institutional determinants of fire insurance regulations. *American Journal of Sociology, 107*, 101–146.

Scott, W. R. (1995). *Institutions and organizations.* Thousand Oaks, CA: Sage.

Scott, W. R. (1998). *Organizations: Rational, natural, and open systems* (4th ed.). Upper Saddle River, NJ: Prentice-Hall.

Scott, W. R. (2001). *Institutions and organizations* (2nd ed.). Thousand Oaks, CA: Sage.

Scott, W. R., & Meyer, J. W. (1983). The organization of societal sectors. In: J. W. Meyer & W. R. Scott (Eds), *Organizational Environments: Ritual and Rationality* (pp. 129–153). Beverly Hills, CA: Sage.

Sell, J., & Martin, M. W. (1983). The effects of group benefits and type of distribution rule on noncompliance to legitimate authority. *Social Forces, 61*(4), 1168–1185.

Selznick, P. (1949). *TVA and the grass roots.* Berkeley, CA: University of California Press.

Stryker, R. (1994). Rules, resources and legitimacy processes: Some implications for social conflict, order and change. *American Journal of Sociology, 99*, 847–910.

Stryker, R. (2000). Legitimacy processes as institutional politics: Implications for theory and research in the sociology of organizations. In: S. B. Bacharach & E. J. Lawler (Eds), *Research in the Sociology of Organizations: Organizational Politics* (Vol. 17, pp. 179–223). Greenwich, CT: JAI Press.

Suchman, M. (1995). Managing legitimacy: Strategic and institutional approaches. *Academy of Management Review, 20*, 571–610.

Thomas, G. M., Walker, H. A., & Zelditch, M., Jr. (1986). Legitimacy and collective action. *Social Forces, 65*, 378–404.

Thornton, P., & Ocasio, W. (1999). Institutional logics and the historical contingency of power in organizations: Executive succession in the higher education publishing industry, 1958–1990. *American Journal of Sociology, 105*, 801–843.

Tyler, T. R. (1990). *Why people obey the law.* New Haven, CT: Yale University Press.

Vaughan, D. (1996). *The challenger launch decision: Risky technology, culture, and deviance at NASA.* Chicago: Chicago Press.

Wagner, D. G., & Berger, J. (1997). Gender and interpersonal task behaviors: Status expectation accounts. *Sociological Perspectives, 40*, 1–32.

Wagner, D. G., & Berger, J. (2002). Expectation states theory: An evolving research program. In: J. Berger & M. Zelditch, Jr. (Eds), *New Directions in Contemporary Sociological Theory* (pp. 41–76). Lanham, MD: Rowman & Littlefield.

Walker, H. A., Rogers, L., & Zelditch, M., Jr. (1988). Legitimacy and collective action: A research note. *Social Forces, 67*, 216–228.

Walker, H. A., Rogers, L., & Zelditch, M. (2002). Acts, persons, positions, and institutions: Legitimating multiple objects and compliance with authority. In: S. C. Chew & J. D. Knottnerus (Eds), *Structure, Culture, and History: Recent Issues in Social Theory* (pp. 323–339). Lanham, MD: Rowman & Littlefield.

Walker, H. A., Thomas, G. M., & Zelditch, M., Jr. (1986). Legitimation, endorsement and stability. *Social Forces, 64*(3), 620–643.

Walker, H. A., & Zelditch, M., Jr. (1993). Power, legitimation, and the stability of authority: A theoretical research program. In: J. Berger & M. Zelditch, Jr. (Eds), *Theoretical Research Programs: Studies in the Growth of Theory* (pp. 364–381). Stanford, CA: Stanford University Press.

Weber, M. ([1924]1978). *Economy and society* (Vols I and II). G. Roth & C. Wittich (Eds). Berkeley, CA: University of California Press.

Webster, M., Jr., & Foschi, M. (1988). *Status generalization: New theory and research*. M. Webster & M. Foschi (Eds). Stanford, CA: Stanford University Press.

Zelditch, M., Jr. (2001). Theories of legitimacy. In: J. Jost & B. Major (Eds), *The Psychology of Legitimacy: Emerging Perspectives on Ideology, Justice, and Intergroup Relations* (pp. 33–53). Cambridge: Cambridge University Press.

Zelditch, M., & Walker, H. A. (1984). Legitimacy and the stability of authority. *Advances in Group Processes, 1*, 1–25.

Zelditch, M., & Walker, H. A. (2003). The legitimacy of regimes. In: S. R. Thye & E. Lawler (Eds), *Advances in Group Processes* (Vol. 20, pp. 217–249). Greenwich, CT: JAI Press.

Zucker, L. G. (1991). The role of institutionalization in cultural persistence. In: W. W. Powell & P. J. DiMaggio (Eds), *The New Institutionalism in Organizational Analysis* (pp. 83–107). Chicago: University of Chicago Press.

INSTITUTIONAL EFFECTS ON THE STABILITY OF ORGANIZATIONAL AUTHORITY

Morris Zelditch, Jr.

ABSTRACT

Three theories of legitimacy – Dornbusch and Scott's "Evaluation and the Exercise of authority" (EEA), Walker and Zelditch's "Legitimacy and the Stability of Authority" (LSA), and Meyer and Rowan's "Institutonalized Organizations" (IO) – are integrated into a single consistent theory interrelating the internal and external legitimacy processes of organizations. One consequence of IO, the decoupling of sanctions, evaluations, and performance, contradicts EEA and LSA. The contradiction is addressed by aligning the scope of the three theories, which proves to be the source of the contradiction, accommodating their principles to the change in their scope. Translating their terms into a single, consistent language, auxiliary principles are formulated that interrelate their legitimacy processes and conditionalize pressures for evaluation and control and therefore the decoupling of sanctions, evaluations, and performance – the conditions depending on type of environment, extent of dependence on it, and its organization. Integration does not alter the basic principles of EEA or IO but does correct LSA's over-estimation of the stability of authority and provides IO with a mechanism by which and refines the conditions under which sanctions, evaluations, and performance come to be decoupled.

Legitimacy Processes in Organizations
Research in the Sociology of Organizations, Volume 22, 25–48
ISSN: 0733-558X/doi:10.1016/S0733-558X(04)22001-8

1. INTRODUCTION

1.1. Problem

Evaluation and control are fundamental elements of the classical theory of organizations (Fayol, 1916[1949]; Gulick & Gurwick, 1937; Mooney & Reiley, 1939). Unity of action towards a common purpose depends on the capacity of a hierarchy to transmit control. The capacity of a hierarchy to transmit control depends on basing sanctions on evaluations and evaluations on performance. Hence, the coupling of sanctions, evaluations, and performance is one of the theory's fundamental principles.

The classical theory of organizations presupposed a closed system. The coupling of sanctions, evaluations, and performance has also been presupposed in organizations open to their technical environments (Thompson, 1967). But in organizations open to their institutional environments, things are quite otherwise. "Institutionalized" organizations depend for their survival on the resources of an institutional environment – an environment of norms, values, and beliefs, especially beliefs that define and classify organizational actors and their participants and theorize their functions. The supply of the resources of this environment depends on the legitimacy of the organization. The legitimacy of the organization depends on the extent to which the form of its structure accords with the institutions of its environment. Hence, organizations incorporate the institutions of their environment into their structure and the structure becomes and remains like that of other organizations in the same environment. But to the extent that the participants in the technical core of institutionalized organizations are nevertheless oriented to efficient, effective performance of its tasks, the structure of institutionalized organizations becomes decoupled from its technical activities, and its technical activities become decoupled from their effects. This is accomplished by decoupling sanctions from evaluations and/or evaluations from performance (Meyer & Rowan, 1977).[1]

This is a profoundly unsatisfying conclusion if one happens to be interested in legitimacy processes in organizations. The theoretical strategy of many theories of legitimacy processes in organizations sees them mostly from inside the organization's boundaries. They obviously have much to gain from opening the organization to its environment and therefore from the theory of institutionalized organizations. On the other hand, the open-systems strategy of the theory of institutionalized organizations under-theorizes the internal legitimacy processes of organizations. Because it under-theorizes them, the theory of institutionalized organizations also has something to gain from theories of the internal legitimacy processes of organizations. But not if the closed-system theories presuppose evaluation and control while the theory of institutionalized organizations contradicts it. If they contradict each other, all one can achieve by their integration is a logically inconsistent theory.

For example, Dornbusch and Scott's theory of evaluation and the exercise of authority (EEA) (Dornbusch & Scott, 1975) and Walker and Zelditch's theory of legitimacy and the stability of authority (LSA) (Zelditch & Walker, 1984), although neither is entirely sealed off,[2] both focus largely on variables inside the boundaries of the organization. EEA is a theory of the compatibility of the rights that make up an organization's authority structure. Although not quite how Dornbusch and Scott put it, the rights of an authority structure are "incompatible" if they require participants to do something but at the same time prevent them from doing it. Incompatibility undermines individual beliefs in the legitimacy, and therefore the stability, of an organization's authority structure (Dornbusch & Scott, 1975). LSA is a theory of other sources of legitimacy that nevertheless maintain the stability of an organization's authority structure even if it is incompatible (Zelditch & Walker, 1984).

Both theories have much to gain from Meyer and Rowan's theory of institutionalized organizations (IO). The external legitimacy processes of IO play a central role in the incorporation of the institutions of the environment into the internal structure of an organization (Meyer & Rowan, 1977). These institutions link the external legitimacy of organizations to their internal legitimacy processes. But like the classical theory of organization, also both presuppose that organizational effectiveness depends on tightly coupling sanctions, evaluations, and performance (e.g. cf. Dornbusch & Scott, 1975, p. 336). Because IO problematizes evaluation and control, allowing it to deduce that under some conditions sanctions, evaluations, and performance in an organization open to its institutional environment come to be decoupled, it contradicts both EEA and LSA.

Were it not for the fact that IO also has something to gain from EEA and LSA, the simplest solution would be to displace EEA and LSA in favor of IO. But IO is vague about the process by which decoupling actually occurs. It makes ad hoc assumptions, grounded neither in IO nor any other theory, about both the internal legitimation processes of an organization (e.g. Meyer & Rowan, 1977, Proposition 4) and the good faith of participants in the technical core of an organization, without which decoupling does not occur. Therefore, the objective of the present paper is to address the contradiction between EEA, LSA and IO with a view to unifying them in a single, consistent theory. But there are considerable obstacles in the way of unifying them. IO draws from a very different theoretical strategy and a somewhat different family of basic concepts and propositions than EEA and LSA. There is considerable overlap in how the three theories conceptualize legitimacy. But in most other respects there are more differences between them than similarities.

But most of these differences turn out to make no difference to the contradiction that must be addressed by the present paper. For example, differences over the agency of the actor appear at first sight to be irreconcilable. Institutionalism denies the agency, autonomy, and boundedness of either individuals or organizations: Actorness is socially constructed, not given in nature (cf. Jepperson, 2002 and the critique by DiMaggio, 1988). On the other hand, both EEA and LSA presuppose the agency of both individual and collective actors. But by institutionalism's own account, an ontology of agency and norms of rationality are institutions in the environment of any organization in the modern world system (Meyer et al., 1987). However socially-constructed, both organizations in the modern world-system and the participants in them behave as if they are actors, as reviews of the evolving literature on institutional organizations repeatedly discover (Scott, 1991, 2001, pp. 74–77; Scott & Christensen, 1995, pp. 302–308; Scott et al., 2000, pp. 36, 172). Hence, to organizations in the modern world-system, the difference over agency is a difference that makes no difference. Most of the many other differences among the three theories are equally reconcilable because most are complementary rather than contradictory. For example, at first sight a difference over objects of legitimation also looks irreconcilable. IO is a theory of the legitimacy of organizations; EEA and LSA are theories of the legitimacy of an organization's authority structure, not the organization. While all three theories have an overlapping concern with evaluation and control, what IO has to say about the legitimacy of an organization looks at first sight irrelevant to what EEA and LSA have to say about the legitimacy of authority. But the two objects complement each other, as we will find in Section 2.3. In fact, there is just one difference between IO and EEA/LSA that yields a contradiction – that IO problematizes the coupling of sanctions, evaluations, and performance while EEA and LSA take it as given.

1.2. Objectives

Thus, the purpose of the present paper is to integrate EEA, LSA, and IO into a single consistent theory that interrelates the internal and external legitimacy processes of an organization. To accomplish the purpose, Sections 2.1 and 2.2 open EEA and LSA to the environment, align their scope with that of IO – relaxing the presupposition that evaluation and control are given – and accommodate their concepts and assumptions to the change in their scope. Section 2.3 translates the terms of the three theories into a common language and uses it to formulate a small number of auxiliary principles needed to interrelate the internal and external legitimacy processes of organizations. Section 3.1 addresses the contradiction between

IO, on the one hand, and EEA and LSA on the other, conditionalizing the divergent processes by which they describe evaluation and control in organizations. Finally, Section 3.2 uses the theory that results from all this to refine IO's explanation of the coupling and decoupling of evaluation and control in organizations.

There are two important ways in which the scope of the present paper is limited. First, it is concerned only with the governance of organizations. It makes no attempt to extend anything that either EEA or LSA has to say about the governance of organizations to the governance of environments. Second, it is concerned only with the evaluation and control process of organizations. It has nothing to say about the coupling or decoupling of the goals or units of an organization – both of which are also within the domain of IO – hence nothing to say about the size or complexity either of organizations or their administrations.

1.3. Preliminaries

But first, "decoupling" itself is a problem. Meyer and Rowan, following March and Olsen (1976) and Weick (1976), take decoupling to mean that "structure is disconnected from technical (work) activity and activity is disconnected from its effects" (Meyer & Rowan, 1978, p. 79). But the term is also used with reference to many other elements of organizations and describes many kinds of disconnection: Goals are disconnected from goals, from activities, from outcomes, units from units, structure from activities, activities from effects. There are gaps, buffers, evasions, goals not implemented, rules not used, not followed, not enforced, inspection avoided. The term has become stretched to the point that it is too ambiguous for present purposes. Particularly difficult are a few hard cases that are difficult to classify either as coupled or decoupled, such as formal and informal structure, professional authority, and the institutional elements of organizations.

The often observed gap between formal and informal structure is taken by institutionalism to be one of the problems it solves by its capacity to explain decoupling (Jepperson, 2002, p. 235; Scott, 1981, pp. 254–256). But "activity," hence informal structure, can be tightly as well as loosely coupled, whether or not it conforms with formal rules. A tightly coupled operant structure of authority that departs from the rules of formal structure is in fact one of the possible outcomes of an incompatible authority structure in Dornbusch and Scott (1975). An informal structure can therefore be both tightly and loosely coupled at the same time.

Professional authority is equally a problem and for the same reason. Is it loosely coupled, as it is in Meyer and Rowan (1978), because final-decision-making rights are delegated, peers rather than superiors review outcomes, and technical activities are disconnected from administrative activities, giving rise to dual, disconnected, hierarchies? Or is it tightly coupled, Dornbusch and Scott (1975), because, where the outcomes of a task are unpredictable, hence the task requires more independent judgment, more skill, and more knowledge, knowledge is coupled with both decision-making and evaluation, while differentiating them from other tasks?

Finally, institutional activities can be said to be tightly coupled, on the one hand, because organizations invest much time and effort in evaluation and control of conformity to them (Meyer & Rowan, 1978), but can also be said to be loosely coupled, on the other, because evaluation of conformity is purely "ceremonial," evaluation *only* of conformity rather than the quality of performance or its outcomes (Scott & Meyer, 1983).

Despite the ambiguity of the term, it clearly has to do with the extent to which organizations control the outcomes of performance by means of sanctions that depend on their evaluation. Thus, for present purposes, we can say that: With respect to a given a task, the more that sanctions depend on their evaluations and the more that evaluations depend on outcomes, the more tightly sanctions are coupled with outcomes. But, following Scott and Meyer (1983, pp. 148–149), the extent of coupling is a matter of degree: It is tightest if sanctions depend on evaluations that depend on the quality of performance or its outcomes, loosest if sanctions do not depend on evaluations at all. Sanctions that depend on evaluation of "process," i.e. of the amount of effort expended or of conformity to formal rules or explicit directives, such as the number of patients seen, students enrolled, or rules followed, is less tightly coupled than evaluation of the quality of performance or its outcomes but more tightly coupled than evaluations of "structure." Sanctions that depend on evaluations of "structure," i.e. of characteristics of participants such as their credentials, are less tightly coupled than evaluations of the quality of performance or its outcomes, but more tightly coupled than sanctions that do not depend on evaluation at all.

This definition can be extended to multiple tasks if they are interdependent. If they are independent, the issue of coupling does not arise. Coupling has to do with coordination and control. Independent tasks demand no coordination, hence no coupling. This holds even for pooled interdependence, i.e. tasks that jointly but independently contribute to some aggregate outcome (Thompson, 1967). On the other hand, if two sub-tasks are sequentially or reciprocally interdependent, they are coupled to the extent that each is subjected to the same evaluation/control structure and oriented to the same final outcome.

Note that, like EEA, this definition of coupling is task-specific. In addition, it refers only to behavior, not to the rules. By this definition, informal structure may be either tightly or loosely coupled. There is no harm in saying that formal structure is tightly or loosely coupled by design, but what matters is actual behavior. That informal structure departs from formal structure says nothing about coupling, but operant structure itself may be either tightly or loosely coupled.

On the other hand, in accord with Dornbusch and Scott's intuitions about professional authority, by this definition it is tightly rather than loosely coupled: Delegation of final decision-making rights to a person competent to solve a problem tightly couples quality of performance to quality of outcomes, peer review tightly couples competence to evaluate performance to sanctions for performance. The differentiation of the (directive) administrative and (delegated) technical hierarchies characteristic of professional organizations only loosely couples the two hierarchies but is consistent with tight coupling within each of them because the interdependence of the two different kinds of task is pooled rather than sequential or reciprocal.

But, in accord with Meyer and Rowan's intuitions about the institutional elements of organizations, the "ceremonial" coupling of institutional activities can be said to be tightly coupled to the extent that sanctions depend on evaluations of the conformity of structure or process to rules but nevertheless be said to be decoupled from task activities because sanctions do not depend on evaluation of either the quality of performance or the effectiveness and efficiency of outcomes.

2. INTERRELATING INTERNAL AND EXTERNAL PROCESSES OF LEGITIMATION

2.1. Extending EEA

In EEA the labor in authority is divided into rights to make final decisions, make rules, and direct performance, and to sample, set criteria for, evaluate, and sanction performance. From the point of view of an actor p, a particular distribution of these rights is *compatible* only if the evaluation of the performance of p justly attributes causality for its outcome to p. A distribution of rights in authority is *incompatible*[3] if it requires of p that p do X at the same time that it prevents p from doing it – the directives given to p or the criteria by which p is evaluated are contradictory, or the facilities provided by the organization to do X are inadequate to satisfactorily accomplish it.

EEA assumes that if an authority structure is compatible it is stable. If it is incompatible, it is unstable. The basic social psychology of the theory is that no one wants to be faulted for something that isn't their fault. Incompatibility therefore creates pressure for change of the structure of authority. But instability is a matter of degree, ranging from: (a) unexpressed tension; to (b) expression of the tension, i.e. communication of dissatisfaction to others; to (c) attempts to change the structure of authority; to (d) actual change in work arrangements. If there is change it is in the direction of compatibility. The compatibility principles in themselves say nothing about the particular path taken towards compatibility. But the scope conditions of the theory, the conditions that define and limit the kinds of organizations to which it applies, presuppose the evaluation/control principle – that sanctions depend on evaluations, evaluations on performance (Dornbusch & Scott, 1975, p. 336). Therefore, if there is change towards compatibility the path it takes is through tighter rather than looser coupling of evaluation and control.

To align the scope conditions of EEA with those of IO, we assume that EEA applies to a functionally specific, purposive, complex, hierarchical organization that depends in whole or in part on one or more external environments for the resources on which its survival depends. The environment is governed by an ontology of agency and norms of rationality. Its resources can be given or withheld as sanctions at the level of the organization and deployed by the organization as sanctions motivating the performance of its participants providing that its participants care about them. But, where the conditions that originally limited the scope of application of EEA conflated the conditions of evaluation and control with the conditions of responses to incompatibility, the realigned scope of EEA depends only on the fact that participants care about the organization's sanctions. The extent to which sanctions are coupled to evaluations or evaluations to performance is free to vary.[4]

What are the implications of an open system for the internal legitimacy processes described by EEA? While opening the organization to its environment fundamentally alters what EEA has to say about the formal structure of the organization – which now incorporates elements of the environment into it – it turns out to have surprisingly modest implications for the compatibility principles of the theory. What does have an effect is relaxing the evaluation/control conditions presupposed by the scope conditions of the theory. If the coupling of sanctions to evaluations and evaluations to performance is free to vary, the compatibility principles themselves are untouched by relaxing the scope conditions of the theory but the outcome of the process is indeterminate. The theory predicts change in the direction of compatibility but either tighter or looser coupling are possible paths to compatibility.

To see this requires introducing a concept, *vacuous compatibility*, not found in EEA. But EEA's "compatibility" is an example of a larger family of "balance" concepts (Heider, 1946). Explicating the concept of "balance," Cartwright and Harary (1956) give the following meaning to "vacuous" balance: A relation between any pair of the elements of a structure either does or does not exist. If it exists, the structure can be balanced or imbalanced. Imbalance creates pressure towards change in the structure. But if the relation does not exist there is no imbalance. The unrelated elements can be said to be "vacuously balanced." If they are vacuously balanced, they create no pressures towards change in the structure of the elements. In the same way, a decoupled evaluation/control structure is "vacuously compatible." The importance of vacuous compatibility is that it creates no pressures towards change of an authority structure.

Restoring determinacy to the compatibility principle will have to wait on conditions to be derived from IO in Section 3 below. But there is another side to EEA, its conceptualization of legitimacy, that also plays an important role in opening the theory out. In EEA, the instability of an incompatible authority structure is mediated by its legitimacy: The incompatibility of an authority structure undermines its legitimacy in the eyes of the participants in the organization. Its illegitimacy makes it unstable.

But EEA makes a distinction between the legitimacy of authority in the eyes of a particular participant p and p's recognition that it is legitimate in the eyes of others. It presupposes pre-given norms that are binding on the organization's participants. A participant p is capable of recognizing that a norm exists whether or not p willingly approves of it. That the norm is understood by p to be binding induces an obligation to obey. But even if not, recognizing that a norm exists implies support of it by others, hence it is expedient to comply. EEA's concept of *validity* refers to whether or not p acknowledges the existence of a normative order; its concept of *propriety* refers to whether or not p personally believes in and approves of it (Dornbusch & Scott, 1975, pp. 38–40). Because a system of authority is a hierarchy, EEA also distinguishes between two levels of support for authority: Support of the authority of a superior of p by the superior's peers and superiors is *authorization*, support of it by peers of is *endorsement* (Dornbusch & Scott, 1975, pp. 40–42).

Dornbusch and Scott found strong support for the hypothesis that incompatibility gives rise to impropriety and impropriety to much dissatisfaction and much expression of it. But they also found more impropriety than actual attempts to change the structure of authority and more attempts to change the structure of authority than actual change in work arrangements (Dornbusch & Scott, 1975, Chap. 10). While EEA provided the concepts to explain this finding – the countervailing effects of validity, authorization, and endorsement – it did not actually theorize them. This task was undertaken by a proliferant of EEA, LSA.

2.2. Extending LSA

In LSA an organization's authority structure has other sources of legitimacy, reflected in its validity, that are independent of any particular participant's belief that it is improper. A basic assumption of the theory is that the probability of an attempt to change the structure of authority and any actual change in it are inversely proportional to its validity. Hence, an incompatible authority structure may be improper, there may be considerable tension, dissatisfaction, and pressure to change it, but countervailing factors due to other sources of its legitimacy dampen the likelihood of attempts to change the structure and of actual change in it.

There are some differences between the basic concepts of EEA and LSA that will matter both to extending LSA and integrating it with IO. While LSA's concept of propriety is much the same as EEA's, its concept of validity is more elaborate. Not only are norms pre-given, but also values, beliefs, purposes, practices, and procedures. They are valid if they observably govern the behavior of participants in an organization. That is, that an authority structure exists and is binding means that participants see that other participants act in accord with it and support it. If a participant p believes, and believes that others believe, that the authority structure is valid, p expects others to act in accord with it and support it and expects that others expect p to act in accord with and support it. Hence, validity acts through the expectations as well as the behavior it induces. It is assumed by LSA to have an effect on the stability of authority independent of any effect of propriety. But, while it's concept of validity is more elaborate, LSA's concept of stability is less elaborate than EEA's. In LSA, stability refers only to attempts to change a structure of authority or to actual change in it. There may be considerable tension, dissatisfaction, and expression of it without any attempt to change the structure of authority, but LSA's operationalization of stability neglects potential in favor of actual pressure to change the structure of authority.

When an authority structure is improper but valid, validity is assumed to dampen the effect of impropriety. In LSA, four mechanisms account for the countervailing effects of validity.

First, it has a direct effect on compliance by p and control of p by others due in part to the sense of obligation it creates and in part due to unthinking mimesis of things as they are. But it also has indirect effects through its effects on propriety, authorization, and endorsement.

A second mechanism of its effect is through its effect on propriety. While the effect may be small, there is some chance that, because p believes that others act in accord with a valid structure of authority and support it, p comes to personally believe that the structure of authority is in fact right.

But even without propriety, a third mechanism through which validity induces compliance and control is that it both causes authorization of authority by p's superiors and induces in p expectations that authority will in fact be authorized. The latter aborts attempts to change the structure of authority before the fact; the former counters attempts to change the structure of authority after the fact.

A fourth mechanism through which validity induces compliance and control is a similar effect through endorsement. Validity both causes endorsement of authority by peers of p and induces in p expectations that it will in fact be endorsed. The latter aborts attempts to change the structure because they will be futile, the former counters them after the fact if in fact they occur.

What are the effects on these processes of opening the theory to the environment? Unlike the extension of EEA, the extension of LSA requires some revision of a basic assumption of the theory. Opening the organization to the environment, as in the case of EEA, will mean the incorporation of institutional elements in the environment into the formal structure of the organization.[5] Furthermore, as shown in Section 2.3 below, the incorporated institutions will be valid. But as in the case of EEA, opening LSA to the environment also relaxes the presupposition, that LSA simply took over from EEA, that sanctions depend on evaluation and evaluation on performance. If realigning the scope of LSA with that of IO does not presuppose tight coupling of sanctions, evaluations, and performance, one possible response to an incompatible authority structure is to loosen the coupling of evaluation and control – because decoupling is vacuously compatible, it is a change that redresses incompatibility. But it is also a change that does not threaten the validity of an authority structure if it is at least "ceremonially" coupled (see Section 1.3). Ceremonial coupling tightly couples sanctions to evaluations of conformity but decouples them from evaluations of the quality of performance or its outcomes.

Thus, the initial formulation of LSA overdetermined the stability of authority of an organization if it is open to its environment. To open the theory to its environment, its validity assumption must be weakened: In an open system, the probability of an attempt to change a structure of authority and of actual change in it is inversely proportional not to its validity but to the likelihood that a change in the structure of authority threatens its validity.

·

2.3. Interrelating Internal and External Processes of Legitimation

Sections 2.1 and 2.2 align the scope of EEA and LSA with that of IO. They open them to the environment and relax the assumption that tight coupling is a given. That coupling is free to vary removes the source of the contradiction between IO, on the one hand, EEA and LSA on the other – although the divergent processes by which the three theories describe the evaluation/control process must still be conditionalized – making possible a single consistent theory of the interrelation of the internal and external legitimacy processes of organizations. In this theory, internal and external legitimacy complement each other. But how do they combine to determine the legitimacy of an organization's authority structure?

In order to answer this question, the terms of the legitimacy processes described by the three theories must be translated into a common language. A common language makes possible three auxiliary hypotheses that describe the interrelation of the external processes of legitimation to the internal processes of legitimation of the organization's structure of authority. But before accomplishing either purpose, more needs to be said about how IO understands external processes of legitimation.

IO is a theory of organizations in larger systems of organizations that form their environment. An organization and its environment constitute an organizational field (DiMaggio & Powell, 1983; Scott & Meyer, 1983). An organizational field is made up of organizations that produce the same good or service, supply the inputs they require, consume their outputs, and also of the regulative agencies and various occupational associations that govern them. Each of the organizations that produces a good or service depends on the field for the resources on which its survival depends. The supply of these resources, in turn, depends on the organization's legitimacy. The legitimacy of an organization is a matter of the extent to which it accords with the institutions of its environment. The institutions of the environment are its consensual norms, values, and beliefs, especially its consensual category beliefs (e.g. beliefs about the nature of its actors) and consensual theories of its functions, such as classic theories of organization taught by the business schools, schools of management, schools of education, or other professional schools from which an organization draws its participants and carried by the occupational associations of which the organization's participants are members. Because its survival depends on its legitimacy, an organization incorporates the institutions of the environment into its formal structure. Because each organization incorporates the same institutions, the organizations in any particular organizational field become and remain isomorphic (Meyer & Rowan, 1977).

IO's theory of legitimacy differs from both EEA's and LSA's in that it is a theory of organizational legitimacy rather than the legitimacy of an organization's authority and it has no concept of propriety. But in other respects, there are substantial similarities among the three theories. They all make use, in one way or another, of the same concepts of power-dependence (cf. DiMaggio & Powell, 1983; Dornbusch & Scott, 1975, pp. 32–33, 91–99; Zelditch & Walker, 2000, pp. 173–174). While power-dependence is not a basic principle of EEA or LSA, it has an important auxiliary function in them and all three theories make the same assumptions about it. For the most part, the legitimacy concepts of EEA and LSA are also readily extended to IO: IO's concept of legitimacy is equivalent to validity; its concept of the effects of "regulatory agencies" is equivalent to authorization; its concept of the functions of occupational associations is equivalent to endorsement. And where they differ, organizational legitimacy can be both directly and indirectly linked to the legitimacy of authority (see the last paragraph of this section). Propriety is more of a problem and for understanding the part played by internal legitimacy processes in decoupling it's needed. To allow it, one has to allow EEA's distinction between recognizing that a norm, value, or belief exists and personally believing in it. Furthermore, with respect to the latter, one has to relax the presupposition of consensus,[6] allowing individual differences in personal beliefs in legitimacy. But propriety is not determined by external legitimacy processes except indirectly, through their effect on validity. Hence, for the present, validity, authorization, and endorsement are all that is needed.

Using them, three auxiliary hypotheses are sufficient to describe the interrelation of the external legitimacy process of IO to the internal legitimacy processes of EEA and LSA. Because all three theories make the same assumptions about power-dependence, organizations incorporate the institutions of their environment into their structure and are therefore isomorphic with other organizations in their environment. It is reasonable to suppose that the similarity of an organization to the other organizations in its environment increases its validity, dissimilarity from them undermines it. Hence,

Hypothesis 1. The internal validity of the structure and processes of an organization is directly proportional to its external validity.[7]

Thus, validity doubly constrains the pressure to change the structure of an organization. In LSA, it is beyond the reach of any particular participant because it governs a collective process of authorization and endorsement that supports it. Opening LSA to its environment, it is also beyond the reach of any particular participant because it governs external as well as internal processes of support for it. The more isomorphic the authority structure of an organization is with the structure of authority of the organizations in its environment, the more valid it is in the eyes of the participants in the organization. Furthermore,

Hypothesis 2. The external authorization of the internal structure and processes of an organization is directly proportional to its external validity.

Hypothesis 3. The external endorsement of the internal structure and processes of an organization is directly proportional to its external validity.

If internal and external validity are not congruent, the effect will be to undermine the legitimacy of the organization's structure. But to the extent that internal validity is proportional to external validity, external support will be consistent with internal support and add to its effect.

If these three hypotheses are accepted, environmental structures and processes have both direct and indirect effects on the legitimacy of an organization's authority structure, adding much to our understanding of how its stability is maintained and the conditions under which it is stable. The institutions of an organization's environment have a direct effect through their theories of organizational design, such as the classical theory of organization's evaluation/control principle. But the legitimacy of the organization itself has an indirect effect on it because, where there are multiple objects of legitimation (such as acts, persons, positions, and groups), each object of legitimation has an independent, additive effect on the amount of compliance and control of an organization's authority structure (Walker, Rogers & Zelditch, 2002).

3. INTERNAL LEGITIMACY, EXTERNAL LEGITIMACY, AND DECOUPLING

3.1. Conditionalizing Pressures Towards Evaluation and Control

Under what conditions are there pressures towards evaluation and control? Extending EEA and LSA has relaxed the conditions that take evaluation and control as given. These conditions are the source of the contradiction between IO and EEA/LSA. Relaxing them removes the source of the contradiction. But to accomplish a single, consistent theory it remains to conditionalize evaluation and control.

The conceptual resources required are already available in an elaboration of IO by Scott and Meyer (1983) that theorizes the organization of societal sectors. In IO there are two types of environments: *Technical environments* are environments in which a product or service is exchanged and in which organizations gain from efficient and effective control of the work process (Scott & Meyer, 1983, p. 140). Dependence on a technical environment, because it creates pressures for efficiency and effectiveness, creates pressures on an organization for evaluation and control. *Institutional environments* are environments in which the supply of resources depends on conformity to values, norms, and beliefs, particularly beliefs that define and classify actors and theories of how they function (Scott & Meyer, 1983, p. 140). Dependence on an institutional environment, because it creates pressures for legitimacy, creates pressures on an organization for conformity to the beliefs in its environment. But organizations vary in the extent to which they depend on different types of environment; the dependence of an organization on one type of environment can vary independently of its dependence on the other; and institutional environments can vary in how coherently they are organized (Scott & Meyer, 1983, p. 145).

With these three variables: (1) the type of environment on which the organization depends; (2) the extent to which it depends on it; and (3) its organization – one can predict the strength and direction of an environment's pressures towards evaluation and control. But the baseline from which an analysis must start is that absent any environmental pressures, the technical core of an organization tends towards closure (Scott & Meyer, 1983, p. 141, from Thompson, 1967). In so far as the technical core of the organization is sealed off from its institutional environment, it is oriented to efficient and effective performance of its task and therefore towards evaluation and control: Its sanctions therefore depend on evaluations; its evaluations depend on performance.[8]

Furthermore, if an organization does not depend on an institutional environment for resources, as dependence on its technical environment increases, the pressure for efficiency and effectiveness also increases, hence also the pressure for evaluation and control.[9]

Hypothesis 4. The strength of the pressures towards evaluation and control of the quality of performance and its outcomes is directly proportional to the extent of an organization's dependence on its technical environment.

But as dependence on an organization's institutional environment increases, pressures for external legitimacy also increase and therefore pressures for conformity to the institutions the organization has incorporated from its environment. Assuming the organization has achieved isomorphism with it institutional environment,

Hypothesis 5. Holding the pressures of the technical environment constant, the strength of the pressures towards evaluation and control of the quality of performance and its outcomes is inversely proportional to the extent of an organization's dependence on its institutional environment.[10]

An institutional environment can vary not only in the strength of its pressures on an organization but also in the number of its environments. If multiple, their institutional logics can vary in their consistency. Inconsistent, or fragmented, institutional environments create repeated legitimacy crises. One way of avoiding repeated legitimacy crises is to decrease the pressure for evaluation and control of the quality of performance and its outcomes.

Hypothesis 6. Holding the pressure of the institutional environment constant, the strength of the pressures towards evaluation and control of the quality of performance and its outcomes is inversely proportional to the fragmentation of the institutional environment.

A by-product of Hypotheses 4–6 is that they make the compatibility principles of EEA, left indeterminate by its extension to an open system, determinate.

3.2. Institutional Effects on the Stability of Organizational Authority

It remains to predict institutional effects on the stability of organizational authority and use them to explain decoupling – i.e. to describe the processes by which and the conditions under which it occurs. The initial conditions of the process are given by the type of environment on which an organization depends, the extent of its dependence on it, and its organization. There are four cases to consider.[11]

3.3. Organizations Highly Dependent on Both Their Technical and Institutional Environments

An organization highly dependent on both its technical and institutional environments, such as a general hospital, is likely to feel strong pressures towards inconsistent goals of conformity, on the one hand, efficiency and effectiveness on the other. Inconsistent goals are likely to give rise to conflicting criteria of evaluation, hence incompatibility of the organization's structure of authority.

If the participants care much about the organization's sanctions, the incompatibility of the structure of authority should undermine its propriety. Hence, there should be a great deal of pressure for change towards compatibility.

But, because the organization is highly dependent on its institutional environment, the external validity of its structure is high. Hence there are strong pressures from external authorization and endorsement to maintain it, enhancing the strength of the internal validity, authorization, and endorsement of the organization's structure of authority. Its impropriety is therefore counter-balanced by an enhanced resistance to change.

If there *is* instability, the most likely outcome is the decoupling of the technical from the institutional activities of the organization. The institutional activities themselves remain tightly coupled. Decoupling technical from institutional activities is made possible by decoupling evaluations from the quality of performance and its outcomes. The tight coupling of institutional activities is made possible by ceremonial coupling – coupling sanctions to evaluations of conformity.

Why this particular direction of change? If there is change, it is unlikely that the organization gives up the goal of conformity, because of the threat to external validity (cf. Meyer & Rowan, 1977, pp. 38–39). But it is also unlikely to give up efficiency and effectiveness, because of the threat of organizational failure (*ibid.*). If it pursues both goals, it is unlikely to change in any way that threatens the validity of the organization's authority structure. But ceremonial coupling, which couples sanctions to evaluations of conformity, is no threat to the validity of the organization's structure of authority. And ceremonial coupling, because it decouples evaluations from the quality of performance or its outcomes, is vacuously compatible, hence a change in the direction of compatibility.

3.4. Organizations Highly Dependent on Their Technical But Not Their Institutional Environments

An organization highly dependent on its technical environment but not on its institutional environment, such as a general manufacturing firm, should feel strong pressure to meet goals of efficiency and effectiveness but little pressure for conformity. Hence, there should be no inconsistency of its goals. Its environments should give rise to no inconsistency of its criteria of evaluation and therefore no incompatibility of its structure of authority.

But an authority structure may be incompatible for a number of other reasons (cf. Dornbusch & Scott, 1975, Chap. 9). For example, authority may be divided, participants may be held responsible for outcomes they do not have the authority to control or the resources to achieve. If there are other sources of incompatibility, and if participants in the organization care about its sanctions, the authority structure of the organization should be improper and there should be pressure to change it in the direction of compatibility.

If there is pressure to change the organization's structure of authority, there is little pressure from the external institutional environment to resist it. The external environment does not enhance internal validity, does not externally authorize or endorse it. If there are other sources of the incompatibility of an organization's structure of authority, it is very likely to be unstable.

If it is unstable, the most likely outcome is tighter coupling of sanctions, evaluations, and performance. There is little pressure from the external institutional environment to ceremonialize coupling, while the pressure of the technical environment towards goals of efficiency and effectiveness is strong external pressure towards tighter coupling of sanctions, evaluations, and performance.

3.5. Organizations Highly Dependent on Their Institutional But Not Their Technical Environments

An organization highly dependent on its institutional environment but not on its technical environment, such as a public elementary school, should feel strong pressure to meet goals of conformity but little pressure for efficiency and effectiveness. Hence, there should be no inconsistency of its goals. The environment should therefore give rise to no inconsistency in its criteria of evaluation and therefore no incompatibility of its structure of authority.

But there may be other sources of incompatibility – again, divided labor, or responsibility without authority or resources. If there are, and if participants in the organization care about its sanctions, the structure of authority should be improper and there should be pressures to change it in the direction of compatibility.

But there should also be strong external pressures to resist change. Because the organization is highly dependent on its institutional environment, the external validity of its structure is high. Hence there are strong pressures from external authorization and endorsement to maintain it, enhancing the strength of internal validity, authorization, and endorsement of the organization's structure of authority and counter-balancing the effects of its impropriety.

Thus, the third case is more likely to be stable than the second. But if there is change, the direction of change is towards decoupling of sanctions from the quality of performance or its outcomes. Because the organization depends little on its technical environment, there is little pressure from it for efficiency and effectiveness. Therefore, even if the technical core of the organization is itself highly task-oriented, there is little external pressure for tightly coupling sanctions, evaluations, and performance. On the other hand, because the organization depends highly on the institutional environment, there is strong external pressure for conformity. The pressure for conformity will induce pressure to tightly couple the institutional activities of the organization, ceremonially coupling sanctions to evaluations and evaluations to conformity. But tight coupling of the institutional activities of the organization is made possible by decoupling them from technical activities, decoupling evaluations from performance.

3.6. Organizations Highly Dependent on Multiple, Fragmented, Institutional Environments

An organization highly dependent on multiple, fragmented, institutional environments, such as a mental health organization, whether or not it is highly dependent on its technical environment, is likely to incorporate external institutions into its structure that are inconsistent (cf. Meyer, 1994). Hence, the validity of its structure is likely to be contested, external authorization and endorsement are likely to be inconsistent. Criteria of evaluation are therefore also likely to be inconsistent and the authority structure of the organization likely to be incompatible.

If the participants in the organization care about its sanctions, the organization's structure of authority should therefore be improper and there should be a great deal of pressure to change it in the direction of compatibility. Furthermore, if the validity of its structure is externally contested, hence external authorization and endorsement inconsistent, internal validity, authorization, and endorsement are weakened, reducing resistance to such change.

But the organization cannot give up conformity to any of the institutions it has incorporated from its external environments without loss of external validity somewhere. Nor, if it is also dependent on its technical environment, can it give up efficiency and effectiveness without threat of failure. If there is change towards compatibility, the path it takes is therefore towards decoupling of technical from institutional activities, hence sanctions from evaluations of the quality of performance or its outcomes, while tightly, ceremonially, coupling evaluations to conformity. But – although units and programs are outside the scope of the present theory – it also can't give up any of its institutional logics. Hence, it is a reasonable conjecture that unless they are sequentially or reciprocally interdependent, there is also pressure to decouple evaluations of conformity to institutions incorporated from different institutional environments.

4. CONCLUSIONS

Once evaluation and control are free to vary there is no contradiction between IO, EEA, and LSA. But reformulating EEA and LSA to accommodate the required changes in their scope had the following results: Extending the scope of EEA makes no difference at all to its compatibility principles except that without presupposing evaluation and control they are indeterminate – if an authority structure changes towards compatibility, the theory no longer predicts the direction of the path it takes to get there. On the other hand, extending the scope of LSA makes a considerable difference to its basic assumption that attempts to change, and actual change, of an authority structure are inversely proportional to the belief by participants in the organization that others in it believe the structure valid, inducing counter-pressures authorizing and endorsing the structure. If evaluation and control are free to vary, not all change threatens the validity of authority. Hence, the likelihood of attempts to change, and actual change, of an authority structure depend not on validity itself but on the extent to which change threatens it. Finally, while extension of EEA and LSA easily dispensed with their evaluation/control conditions, they could not dispense with the condition that the sanctions of the organization matter to its participants. In fact, though left implicit by it, this is also a condition of the application of IO to organizations and of any more comprehensive theory integrating the three theories. It determines the magnitude of pressures towards change, hence the instability of an organization's authority structure, whatever the direction of the change.

But aligning the scope of EEA and LSA with that of IO makes possible a theory of the interrelation of the internal and external legitimacy processes of an organization only if one can translate the terms of the three theories into one common language. "Decoupling" itself made some difficulties because of the many ways in which it has been used. But there was no difficulty at all about the resource-dependence concepts on which IO depends because, though only auxiliary to other processes, they were also presupposed by EEA and LSA. Nor was it difficult to translate their concepts of legitimacy into a common language, except for "propriety" – individual-level legitimacy – which has no counterpart in IO. Translating it required relaxing IO's presupposition of consensus at the individual level. Given translation of the terms of the three theories into one common language, it was possible to interrelate internal and external legitimacy processes by deducing from isomorphism three auxiliary hypotheses linking the validity, authorization, and endorsement processes of an organization to the validity, authorization, and endorsement processes of its environment.

Conditionalizing the divergent evaluation/control processes described by EEA, LSA, and IO assured that in fact there was no contradiction between them. It was the environmental variables of IO that made conditionalizing them possible. The type of environment, the extent of an organization's dependence on it, and its organization each affects, in the first instance, the extent to which the goals of efficiency and effectiveness conflict with the goal of conformity. Hence it affects the consistency or inconsistency of the organization's goals, the compatibility or incompatibility of its authority structure, and therefore the magnitude of the pressures towards the instability of authority. But, second, they also affect the external validity of the authority structure of the organization, hence external support for it. Through the effect of external validity, authorization, and endorsement on the structure's internal validity, authorization, and endorsement they affect the extent of its resistance to change. Finally, because they affect the strength of the pressures for efficiency and effectiveness, they also affect the pressure for evaluation and control, through which, if the authority structure of the organization is incompatible, they determine the path taken towards compatibility and therefore the extent to which sanctions, evaluations, and performance are coupled or decoupled.

Interrelating the external and internal legitimacy processes of an organization and conditionalizing the evaluation/control process made it possible to fill some gaps in the description of the process by which the sanctions, evaluations, and performances of an organization are coupled and the conditions under which coupling them occurs. The internal legitimacy processes of the organization provide the intervening variables that mediate between the environmental conditions of the process and the stability of the authority structure of the organization; and, if it is unstable, the path it takes towards stability. If the pressures of the external environment are inconsistent, inconsistency of the organization's goals, reflected in inconsistent criteria of evaluation, makes its structure of authority incompatible. Because it is incompatible, it is improper, which induces pressures to change it. But the other side of the organization's dependence on its institutional environment is that validity, authorization, and endorsement, hence the resistance of the structure to change, are also strengthened by its openness to the environment. If nevertheless it changes, the boundary conditions given by the external environment condition but compatibility and validity at the same time constrain the direction in which it changes – conditions and constraints that only decoupling satisfies.

All three theories gain from integration. EEA gains from IO the conditions that determine the path of an incompatible authority structure towards compatibility. LSA gains an explanation of the strength of other sources of legitimacy that it took as given, additional factors that back it, and corrects for over-determination of the stability of authority. IO gains a mechanism that refines its explanation of decoupling and a condition – the importance of the organization's sanctions to its participants – that determines the magnitude of change towards either coupling or decoupling, whichever direction the process takes.

A final comment: I had at first assumed that IO's contradiction of EEA and LSA was due to irreconcilable differences over the foundations of sociology – specifically, over the agency of the actor. It turned out that differences over the agency of the actor did not make much difference, because the institutional environments of organizations in the modern world-system imbue both organizations and their participants with agency and rationality. But institutionalism's rhetorical defocalization of the actor (cf. DiMaggio, 1988) did obscure the mechanism of decoupling. In a sense, the present paper, because it unpacks the process that mediates the effects of an organization's environment on its authority structure, is a matter, more or less, of bringing the actor back in. In this sense, it aligns itself with the increasing trend of many papers using neo-institutionalist theories to explain the structure of organizations such as DiMaggio and Powell (1983), Scott (1991, 2001, pp. 74–77), Scott and Christensen (1995), and Scott et al. (2000, pp. 36, 172).

NOTES

1. The theory of institutionalized organizations is a program as well as a theory. It has undergone considerable evolution since Meyer and Rowan (1977). In the course of its evolution, the conflict between the institutional and technical environments has become less necessary, more conditional, hence more variable. See especially Scott and Meyer (1983).

2. Like IO, EEA and LSA are also programs as well as theories. In the case of EEA, some of its evolution occurred even in the course of the book that described the initial

theoretical formulation. This was to some extent true of the openness of the theory to the environment. Its study of professional organizations brought external standards and organizations into the picture (Dornbusch & Scott, 1975, Chap. 4). And, although it did not dwell much on the fact, its hierarchy of authority was always open at the top, the level of directors and trustees, the ultimate source if authorized power, who brought norms from outside the organization into it. More was made of this by Scott in analyzing the theory in Scott (1981, p. 282), even further elaborated in Scott (2003, pp. 315–316).

3. This differs from the definition given by Dornbusch and Scott (1975, pp. 241, 375). "Incompatibility" in EEA is both a structural condition and a psychological response to it. Its psychology matters to both the likelihood and the magnitude of the response to the condition, but I prefer here to focus on the structural condition.

4. The scope of EEA is limited by two other conditions that are not relaxed by this reformulation of it. EEA applies to organizations of evaluators (1) who are themselves evaluated by evaluators who (2) differ from those they themselves evaluate (Dornbusch & Scott, 1975, p. 336). The significance of the first condition is that the theory is concerned with authority, which is normatively regulated, rather than pure power. The significance of the second is that the theory is not reducible to a theory only of endorsement by subordinates.

5. Because organizations often depend on more than one institutional environment, the external sources of validity may be inconsistent, weakening its strength. This has important consequences for the validity of an organization's structure of authority. These consequences are discussed in Section 3.

6. On the presupposition of consensus see Zelditch and Floyd (1998).

7. If multiple institutional environments are inconsistent, their inconsistency weakens external, and therefore internal, validity (see Section 3), but the hypothesis holds whether or not there are multiple environments and whether or not they are consistent.

8. This default assumption differs from the hypothesis most nearly comparable to it in Scott and Meyer (1983), where organizations with weak pressures from both environments are small and their capacity for survival weak (Scott & Meyer, 1983, p. 141, Hypothesis 6). The difference is that Scott and Meyer's analysis of sectoral effects is focused on the organization rather than its authority structure.

9. Hypothesis 4 simply paraphrases the most nearly comparable hypothesis in Scott and Meyer (1983). Although comparability is less straightforward in the case of Hypotheses 5 and 6, all three hypotheses are modeled as closely as possible on their analysis of sectoral controls.

10. For organizations dependent *only* on their institutional environment, such as a church, the hypothesis is moot. But one can say that as the dependence of such ritual organizations on their institutional environment increases, the pressure for conformity increases and with it the coupling of sanctions to evaluations and evaluations to structure and process (cf. Scott & Meyer, 1983, p. 149).

11. Because of the default assumption that absent any environmental pressures – the fifth case to consider – the technical core of an organization tends towards closure, organizations that depend on neither their technical nor institutional environment, such as beauty shops, are likely to be tightly coupled whether or not their authority structures are incompatible. The environment is neither a source of incompatibility nor external support for authority. But if there are other sources of incompatibility, for example divided authority, or responsibility without authority, or responsibility without the resources it requires

(cf. Dornbusch & Scott, 1975, Chap. 9), there will be pressure for change towards compatibility. They will be counter-balanced by any other internal sources of the validity of authority – for example, pre-given cultural beliefs carried by organizational participants – even if not enhanced by external support. But if there *is* change, the default assumption implies that it will maintain or tighten the coupling of sanctions, evaluations, and performance.

ACKNOWLEDGMENTS

I would like to acknowledge the support of NSF grants SOC 7817434 for research on the "Group Determinants of Agenda Setting," SES 8420238 for research on "Legitimacy and the Stability of Authority," and SES 8712097 for research on "Agenda Gate-keeping." In addition, I would like to thank W. Richard Scott for his exceptionally helpful comments on a previous draft of this paper.

REFERENCES

Cartwright, D., & Harary, F. (1956). Structural balance: A generalization of Heider's theory. *Psychological Review, 63*, 277–293.

DiMaggio, P. J. (1988). Interest and agency in institutional theory. In: *Institutional Patterns and Organizations: Culture and Environment* (pp. 3–21). Cambridge, MA: Ballinger Publishing Co.

DiMaggio, P. J., & Powell, W. W. (1983). The iron cage revisited: Institutional isomorphism and collective rationality in organizational fields. *American Sociological Review, 48*, 147–160.

Dornbusch, S. M., & Scott, W. R. (1975). *Evaluation and the exercise of authority*. San Francisco: Jossey-Bass.

Fayol, H. (1916[1949]). *General and industrial management*. C. Stours (Trans.). London: Pitman.

Gulick, L., & Gurwick, L. (1937). *Papers on the science of administration*. NY: Columbia University Press.

Heider, F. (1946). Attitudes and cognitive organization. *Journal of Psychology, 21*, 107–112.

Jepperson, R. L. (2002). The development and application of sociological neoinstitutionalism. In: J. Berger & M. Zelditch (Eds), *New Directions in Contemporary Sociological Theory* (pp. 229–266). Lanham, MD: Rowman & Littlefield.

March, J. G., & Olsen, J. P. (1976). *Ambiguity and choice in organizations*. Bergen: Universitetsforlaget.

Meyer, J. W. (1994). Institutional and organizational rationalization in the mental health system. In: W. R. Scott, J. W. Meyer & Associates (Eds), *Institutional Environments and Organizations: Structural Complexity and Individualism* (pp. 215–227). Thousand Oaks, CA: Sage.

Meyer, J. W., Boli, J., & Thomas, G. M. (1987). Ontology and rationalization in the western cultural account. In: G. M. Thomas, J. W. Meyer, F. O. Ramirez & J. Boli (Eds), *Institutional Structure: Constituting State, Society, and the Individual* (pp. 12–37). Newbury Park, CA: Sage.

Meyer, J. W., & Rowan, B. (1977). Institutionalized organizations: Formal structure as myth and ceremony. *American Journal of Sociology, 83*, 340–363.

Meyer, J. W., & Rowan, B. (1978). The structure of educational organizations. In: M. W. Meyer & Associates (Eds), *Environments and Organizations* (pp. 78–109). San Francisco: Jossey-Bass.

Mooney, J. D., & Reiley, A. C. (1939). *The principles of organization*. NY: Harper.

Scott, W. R. (1981). *Organizations: Rational, natural, and open systems*. Englewood Cliffs, NJ: Prentice-Hall.

Scott, W. R. (1991). Unpacking institutional arguments. In: W. W. Powell & P. J. DiMaggio (Eds), *Institutionalism in Organizational Analysis* (pp. 164–182). Chicago: University of Chicago Press.

Scott, W. R. (2001). *Institutions and organizations* (2nd ed.). Thousand Oaks, CA: Sage.

Scott, W. R. (2003). *Organizations: Rational, natural, and open systems* (5th ed.). Upper Saddle River, NJ: Prentice-Hall.

Scott, W. R., & Christensen, S. (1995). Conclusion: Crafting a wider lens. In: W. R. Scott & S. Christensen (Eds), *Institutional Construction of Organizations: International and Longitudinal Studies* (pp. 302–313). Thousand Oaks, CA: Sage.

Scott, W. R., & Meyer, J. W. (1983). The organization of societal sectors. In: J. W. Meyer & W. R. Scott (Eds), *Organizational Environments: Ritual and Rationality* (pp. 129–153). Beverly Hills, CA: Sage.

Scott, W. R., Ruef, M., Mendel, P. J., & Caronna, C. A. (2000). *Institutional change and healthcare organizations: From professional dominance to managed care*. Chicago: University of Chicago Press.

Thompson, J. D. (1967). *Organizations in action*. NY: McGraw-Hill.

Walker, H. A., Rogers, L., & Zelditch, M. (2002). Acts, persons, positions, and institutions: Legitimating multiple objects and compliance with authority. In: S. C. Chew & J. D. Knottnerus (Eds), *Structure, Culture, and History: Recent Issues in Social Theory* (pp. 323–339). Lanham, MD: Rowman & Littlefield.

Weick, K. E. (1976). Educational organizations as loosely coupled systems. *Administrative Science Quarterly, 21*, 1–19.

Zelditch, M., & Floyd, A. S. (1998). Consensus, dissensus, and justification. In: J. Berger & M. Zelditch (Eds), *Status, Power, and Legitimacy: Strategies and Theories* (pp. 339–368). New Brunswick, NJ: Transaction.

Zelditch, M., & Walker, H. A. (1984). Legitimacy and the stability of authority. *Advances in Group Processes, 1*, 1–25.

DEMOCRACY IN A BUREAUCRACY: THE LEGITIMACY PARADOX OF TEAMWORK IN ORGANIZATIONS

Lisa Troyer

ABSTRACT

Teamwork represents a democratic logic that may contradict the bureaucratic logic characterizing many organizations. I develop arguments based on new institutional theory suggesting that such a contradiction threatens a team's legitimacy. My study of 71 teams lends support for two claims that capture a legitimacy paradox confronting teams: (1) Egalitarian work processes do correspond to more effective interactions within teams, however (2) To the extent that egalitarianism is uncommon in the organization in which a team is embedded, external evaluations of team effectiveness are less favorable. I discuss the implications of these arguments for subsequent research on organizational teamwork.

INTRODUCTION

Over the past three decades, teams have become an integral component of organizational work design (Barker, 1999; Barley & Kunda, 1992; Drucker, 1988; Katzenbach & Smith, 1993; Reddy & Jamison, 1988). The implementation of a team structure in the work place spans projects and work ranging from strategic decision making, to research and development, to manufacturing (e.g. Cohen &

Legitimacy Processes in Organizations
Research in the Sociology of Organizations, Volume 22, 49–87
Copyright © 2004 by Elsevier Ltd.
ISSN: 0733-558X/doi:10.1016/S0733-558X(04)22002-X

Zhou, 1991; Hackman, 1990; Larson & LaFasto, 1989; Vallas, 2003). Although managers and social theorists alike often espouse the benefits of a team approach to work, social science has yet to provide convincing evidence of the superiority of this form of work. For example, Fiorelli (1988) found that the teams he studied were unable to approximate the egalitarian ideals often embodied in the ideology of teamwork. Vallas (2003) found resistance to teamwork on the part of both managers and workers (see also Vallas & Beck, 1996). Silver et al. (2000) documented the rapid re-emergence of a status hierarchy in a work group that had undergone intensive team-building training aimed at reducing status hierarchies in the group, despite the member's espoused commitment to an egalitarian work culture. Also, Kaplan (1986), Janis (1972), and Manz and Sims (1982) have documented significant inefficiencies in teamwork (e.g. poor quality outputs, failure to meet deadlines, faulty communication). In fact, Kaplan (1979) has argued that we lack convincing evidence that teams offer advantages over other forms of work design (see also Woodman & Sherwood, 1980).

These findings raise important questions regarding the conditions under which teams are effective. In this paper, I propose that the gap between conceptual arguments supporting the advantages of teamwork and consistent empirical evidence in support of claims emanating from these arguments can be attributed to the lack of a systemic perspective on teamwork. Thus the framework I am proposing rests on a conceptualization of teams as open systems (e.g. Katz & Kahn, 1966; O'Connor, 1980; Scott, 1998), embedded in the social structure of an organization. In the following sections, I advance this argument, demonstrating that teams are collectives with scripts for work that are based on culturally accepted rationales, or institutional logics (e.g. Friedland & Alford, 1991). The institutional logics that rationalize teamwork are the basis for *peripheral knowledge structures* (e.g. Lyles & Schwenk, 1992), which provide actors with both a script for work and the reasoning behind those scripts. I suggest that the peripheral knowledge structure held and enacted by team members may diverge from other scripts and rationales that characterize work in organizations. Furthermore, because organizational evaluations are often based on process rather than outcome, such divergence can be detrimental to the team. More specifically, I assert that teamwork can undermine a team's legitimacy within an organization.

The insight that divergence between knowledge structures enacted by teams and organizations may undermine team effectiveness is prompted by a prior case study of two teams (Troyer & Silver, 1999). In this study, we found that one team that reflected participatory and egalitarian norms failed to compete successfully for organization resources (e.g. space, personnel, funds), while a more hierarchically structured and bureaucratic team was highly successful. The organization in which the two teams were embedded was a highly bureaucratic division of a municipal government. The administrator to whom the two teams reported was touting teamwork as a strategy of positive organization change within the division and had encouraged leaders and members of both teams to study a number of handbooks on teamwork that stressed participatory management and egalitarian norms. Yet, it seemed that the more egalitarian team was not only less successful at securing needed resources; it was sometimes viewed by the administrator and other high-ranking organizational managers as less effective on the basis of how work was done, irrespective of the outcomes it achieved.[1] In hindsight, evaluations based on process are not surprising, since teams are often evaluated prior to the completion of their work. Also, teams are often engaged in work for which objective measures of performance (e.g. profitability, product quality) may not be immediately available, such as work involving long-range strategic planning or the development of new products. Consequently, in assessing team performance, evaluators may focus on process, rather than outcome.

When evaluation is based on process and when teams enact scripts that diverge from those that more commonly characterize work in an organization, then the team may be trapped in a legitimacy paradox. I adopt Meyer and Scott's definition of legitimacy as, "... the degree of cultural support for an organization" (1983, p. 201). This support (i.e. legitimacy) arises from conformity to taken-for-granted expectations regarding appropriate repertoires of action that correspond to recognizable organizational structures and processes. When the knowledge structures enacted in teams differ from those more commonly recognized within the organization, it may be difficult for non-team members to make sense of the team's work. This runs the risk of rendering the team's actions incomprehensible within the larger organization meaning system, akin to a cultural conflict (e.g. Martin, 2002; Wuthnow et al., 1984). I argue that under such circumstances, non-team evaluators will withdraw support for the team (as manifested in unfavorable performance evaluations). Thus, the "legitimacy paradox" reflects that fact that the processes reflected in teams may not conform to those that more commonly characterize work within the organization, leading to a withdrawal of support for the team in the form of adverse evaluations.[2]

In the sections that follow, I begin by explicating why theoretical assertions on the benefits of teamwork may not always be supported by empirical evidence. This discussion sets the stage for conceptualizing work *teams*, and elaborating the expectations and rationales that make teams a distinct form of organizational work design. I propose that discrepancies between these expectations and rationales (e.g. shared participation in decision making, egalitarian norms, equally distributed authority) and others common to organizations (e.g. reliance on elite sets of decision-makers, status differentiation, hierarchical authority structures) generate a legitimacy paradox for teams that can explain their failure to achieve their theoretical potential. I offer an initial empirical test of these arguments and discuss avenues for further research.

THE RIFT BETWEEN THEORY RELEVANT TO TEAMWORK AND EMPIRICAL FINDINGS

The disjuncture between theoretical arguments and empirical evidence on team effectiveness[3] may stem from three sources. First, researchers and managers have confused ideals of team interaction with actual observations of team processes. For example, social scientists frequently argue that because teams are (ideally) egalitarian units and can be comprised of diverse members, they should be superior at problem-solving and innovation (e.g. Collins & Guetzkow, 1964). In practice, however, teams are not always as democratic, cooperative, and consequently, effective as many would like to believe (e.g. Cohen & Zhou, 1991; Hackman, 1990).

Second, for some types of work, attempts to impose a team design may be unnecessary, if not an impediment to effective work (e.g. Goodman, 1986; Hackman, 1976; Janz & Tjosvold, 1985; McGrath, 1984; Steiner, 1972). The advantages of distributed authority, shared reward systems, and norms of egalitarianism often associated with teamwork may depend on the group's assignment. In general, though, researchers note that teams may be particularly effective in dealing with tasks involving uncertainty, and tasks demanding creativity and/or commitment from a large and diverse constituency (e.g. Collins & Guetzkow, 1964; Dyer, 1987; Hollenbeck, Williams & Klein, 1989; Tjosvold, 1991). Also, researchers claim that highly interdependent tasks benefit from these characteristics (Cohen & Arechavala-Vargas, 1987; Lawrence & Lorsch, 1967; Thompson, 1967; Van de Ven, Delbecq & Koenig, 1976). Whether a team design for work is most effective depends on the extent to which the projects that organizations assign to teams require creativity and commitment, and impose interdependence between members.

Third, social scientists have only recently begun to recognize that teams are embedded in a larger organizational structure. Weick (1979) and Tjosvold (1986, 1991) have argued that we will gain a more comprehensive understanding of organizations by examining the *interrelations* between individuals, groups, and organizations. Along these lines, Ancona (1993; see also Ancona, 1990; Ancona & Caldwell, 1992) has noted that team performance depends in part on how teams manage their external dependencies. Ancona's work offers an insightful approach to theory and research on teams by wedding the classic theorizing on group dynamics of Homans (1950) and Lewin (1951) to the contemporary problem of organizational teamwork. Of particular note in Ancona's conceptualization is her emphasis on effective strategies of linkage between teams and environments as a prerequisite to high performance. She demonstrates that teams whose members engage in activities that actively link the team and its work to the organization are more effective than teams whose members do not implement such activities. For instance she found that when teams actively promote their progress and achievements to others in the organization outside the team, then the teams were more successful in meeting their goals (Ancona, 1990).

Likewise, Sundstrom et al. (1990) claim that it is important to consider organizational context and boundaries to understand team effectiveness. Along these lines, in a case study of two teams in a municipal bureau, Troyer and Silver (1999) found that the team that mirrored the bureau's rigid hierarchy, well-defined division of labor, and close adherence to formalized policy consistently secured more resources for its work than the team characterized by a flat hierarchy, minimal role differentiation, and reliance on informal working relations. In a particularly telling qualitative study of the introduction of team initiatives (i.e. the expansion of worker autonomy, reduced salience of authority lines) in organizations, Vallas (2003) demonstrates how pre-existing managerial practices may doom teamwork. For instance, Vallas found that attempts to encourage worker autonomy in organizations characterized by a high degree of managerial control resulted in more robust hierarchy and greater conflict in those organizations.

Following on these insights, I argue that perceptions of a team's effectiveness are influenced by the team's "fit" with the organization. Often, teams are embedded in organizations embodying social structural characteristics that are inconsistent with those often associated with "teamwork" (i.e. egalitarianism, shared accountability, shared authority). For instance, it is not uncommon for a highly bureaucratic organization with formal lines of authority and explicit hierarchy to organize some of its work within teams. While a group may in isolation appear to function smoothly as a team, the implementation and assessment of its work in the organization, and hence the team's effectiveness, also depend on perceptions of how the team functions within the prevailing organizational social structure outside the team.

In sum, team effectiveness is a complex issue. Some collectivities identified as teams fail to achieve the social structures and processes that many theorists argue are critical advantages of teamwork. Simply calling a group a team does not ensure that members will behave in accordance with the connotation of and expectations associated with that label. Furthermore, whether adopting the structural and interactional characteristics associated with teamwork is optimal depends on the nature of the work in which the group is engaged. Finally, the point which is perhaps most neglected in theory and research on teamwork is that even collectivities with work that may benefit from a team orientation and that achieve that orientation may fail because they are not perceived as functioning in accord with predominate organizational expectations. Underlying the first two of these three points is the questions, "What does it mean to be a team?" and "Under what conditions is it desirable to be a team?" I turn to these two issues first, and then return to the implications of the answers to these questions for an open systems model of organizational teamwork.

CONCEPTUALIZING TEAMS

Social science has had an ongoing interest in the study of organizational work groups since the influential Hawthorne studies (Mayo, 1933). Following the explicit recognition of the effects of group structure and process on work that this investigation generated, researchers have attempted to refine and critique understandings of both the functional and social implications of groups within organizations (e.g. Blake & Mouton, 1964; Likert, 1961; McGregor, 1960; Sayles, 1958; Trist & Bamforth, 1951; Whyte, 1951). This research emphasizes both the effects of groups on organizations and the effects of groups on members. From both of these emphases, it is clear that groups can be either a detriment or an asset to individuals and organizations. Pursuant to this realization, managers and researchers have attempted to engineer groups that optimize the benefits and reduce costs of group processes for both individuals and organizations. By some accounts, the concept of a "team" embodies these explicit attempts to design groups, which maximize the advantages of collective interaction, while minimizing the costs.

While it is clear that researchers and managers are increasingly recognizing the importance of teams in organizations, it is also clear that the term "team" is applied loosely to a broad array of collectivities. Research articulating the distinctive features of organizational work teams has recently appeared in four areas spanning social psychology and organizations: group dynamics research, industrial and organizational psychology, organizational behavior, and organization development. Studies in the first three of these traditions have conceptualized teams by identifying common structural characteristics of teams that distinguish them from other types of work units in organizations (e.g. shared authority rights, interdependent work flows (between members, and between the team and the organization), division of labor). Organization development practitioners have tended to emphasize normative arrangements among members as defining elements of teams.

In a review of conceptualizations of teams in social scientific research (Troyer, 1995), I found that most researchers seemed to agree that a team: (1) is a recognizable organization unit; (2) is engaged in an interdependent relation with the organization; (3) consists of members confronted with shared accountability for performance with respect to a common task; and (4) is engaged in work involving role differentiation and coordination among the members. Yet, as these characteristics reveal, it is not clear exactly how a team might differ from a department or other group within an organization. That is, for instance, members of an administrative department are recognizable, rely on the organization and are relied on by the organization, may be held accountable for outcomes as a group to some extent (at some level of the organization), and are likely to experience some degree of differentiation and coordination in their work. Consequently, these characteristics do not clearly delineate a team from other types of organization collectivities.

Although often neglected in sociological approaches, the perspective of the organization in applying the label "team" to a collectivity may provide insight on the distinctive features of such units. Practitioners in organization development (OD) suggest some of the distinctive features of a team. In this literature, it is clear that the term "team" is not used in a purely structural sense, but also highly normative one (e.g. Beer, 1976; Dyer, 1987; French & Bell, 1984; Rosen, 1989). The design of teams using an OD approach is based on the premise that those closest to the issues comprising a task are most capable of making and carrying out the necessary decisions with respect to the task. Furthermore, researchers and practitioners in the OD tradition argue that teams are especially well suited to assignments involving strategic decision-making and/or innovation particularly where uncertainty is high (e.g. Dyer, 1987; Hollenbeck, Williams & Klein, 1989; Orive, 1988; Rosen, 1989; Tjosvold, 1991). Central to the design of teams for such purposes is the bringing together of diverse points of view, styles of work, and expertise. Also, though, OD approaches recognize longstanding social scientific findings on the difficulties that such heterogeneity can engender in work processes. The very characteristics that establish diversity in team membership are likewise the basis for the rapid evolution of a "power and prestige order" in the group (e.g. Berger et al., 1972). If this hierarchy operates unchecked, it may undermine the benefits of diversity by structuring the interaction so as to restrict the participation of some members. Other problems that plague diverse groups include communication difficulties, coordination problems, and interpersonal conflict (e.g. Forsyth, 1983; Johnson & Johnson, 1989). While it may be impossible to entirely eliminate such effects, some researchers argue that it may be possible to moderate them. Process consultation (e.g. Dyer, 1987; Tannenbaum et al., 1992) represents one approach to remedying dominance, conflict and other problems in group interaction. This "team-building" strategy involves sensitizing members to dominance and conflict, imposing norms for interaction to lessen their effects, and generating commitment among members to a "team approach" to work. As a "team" the group emphasizes shared participation, cooperation, and equally distributed privileges among members.

On the basis of this work, I propose that organizations are not necessarily using the "team" label as a faddish label for any collectivity. Rather, the term "team" in organizational settings seems to also connote norms of participation, cooperation, and equality. I refer to these connotations collectively as "egalitarianism." It appears that managers and researchers alike share in the belief that this connotative component is critical to a team's success. When teams adopt an egalitarian approach to work, it is believed that they will circumvent many of the internal problems (e.g. conflict and miscommunication) that can be generated in the interaction of a diverse group. Nonetheless, the extent to which members of a team actually hold such representations of the team is an empirical question that must be examined in any research investigating teamwork. This conceptualization of teams suggests two propositions that have been investigated in a wide array of research on team performance:

Proposition 1. Socially diverse teams will experience lower levels of internal problems if members hold and enact egalitarian norms than if they do not.

Proposition 2. Socially diverse teams that experience higher levels of internal problems will be less effective than those that experience lower levels of internal problems.

Proposition 1 reflects important insights on teams discussed above. First, teams tend to be comprised of diverse members (although the degree of diversity may vary across teams). Indeed, diversity is often an asset in solving complex problems and in promoting innovation. This diversity, however, is often a source of conflict in the team, leading to misunderstandings and conflict. Practitioners and researchers argue and have demonstrated that promoting egalitarianism can reduce conflict and alleviate misunderstandings. Proposition 2 reflects the more intuitive notion that internal problems (e.g. conflict and misunderstandings) undermine a team's ability to accomplish its work and generate valued outputs for the organization. Together, these two propositions reflect common insights on why teams are viewed as a promising strategy for organizing work. Yet, the notion that particular normative expectations do or should characterize teamwork begs the question, "What is the source of these expectations?" Neo-institutional theory, a sociological perspective on organizations, provides insight on this issue.

INSTITUTIONAL LOGICS AND ORGANIZATIONAL TEAMS

Neo-institutional theory, developed by Meyer, Scott and colleagues (e.g. Meyer & Rowan, 1977; Meyer & Scott, 1983; Powell & DiMaggio, 1991) is an influential contemporary perspective on organizations. Arising from a combination of institutional theory (e.g. Selznick, 1949) and social constructionist accounts of reality (e.g. Berger & Luckmann, 1967), this perspective asserts that organizational structures (e.g. hierarchy, reward systems, divisions of labor) reflect *rationalized myths* corresponding to cultural values and beliefs in the organization's environment (Meyer & Rowan, 1977). In other words, the structures found within organizations that guide work practices are rationalized, or accounted for, in terms of common cultural beliefs regarding appropriate or legitimate ways of structuring work. These accounts represent myths, however, insofar as their existence within the broader structure is itself a social construction. For instance, merit-based incentive systems in organizations correspond to widely held beliefs in society regarding the legitimacy of rewarding actors on the basis of their contributions and achievements. As Berger and Luckmann (1967) note, such cultural beliefs are not objective realities (in part, because legitimacy is itself a social construction), but rather are objectified social constructions. As a result, the appropriateness of such beliefs (and structures corresponding to them) assume a take-for-granted status in society (and organizations) and are rarely questioned.

Recent elaborations of this perspective have explicated the concept of a rationalized myth, arguing that complexes of taken-for-granted cultural accounts, referred to as *institutional logics*, provide the foundation for rationalized myths. According to Friedland and Alford (1991), modern societies are comprised of key institutions (e.g. capitalist economies, bureaucratic states, democratic legal systems). Each institution provides accounts that define the actor's place in the institution (and society), as well as scripts for action. Moreover, these definitions and scripts provide social actors with assumptions about how social life should proceed. For example, as Friedland and Alford note, the logic of capitalism reflects beliefs regarding commodification and accumulation as governing principles of social activity; bureaucratic logics correspond to assumptions regarding rationalization and the regulation of social action through hierarchy; and democratic logics reflect participation and the control of social action by the majority.

Institutional logics, then, reflect widely held beliefs about the legitimacy of routines and structures found within society. Furthermore, as demonstrated by Stryker (1994), these logics are not bound to particular situations, but rather can be imported and mobilized by actors as source of legitimacy. As Friedland and Alford argue (see also Stryker, 2000), these logics are often contradictory, providing fodder for political conflicts within society. An analysis of the evolution of medical organizations by Scott, Mendel and Pollack (forthcoming) demonstrates how organizational structures shift over time to reflect the changing alternative, overlapping, and simultaneously conflictual logics that exist within the wider society in which medical organizations are situated. They argue that each logic provides a legitimating rationale for the appearance of particular organizational structures in the medical sector. Similarly, Stryker (1994) describes the emergence of scientific-technical logics in the legal sector. In this analysis, she shows that formal-legal and scientific-technical rationalizations (i.e. institutional logics) offer alternative sources of legitimacy for actors' behavior within legal systems.

These analyses are instructive in that they point to the multiplicity of and conflict between potential logics on which organizational structures may rest. Just as organizations as a whole may draw on alternative logics, so may units within the organizations. That is, units and actors within organizations may orient themselves to the structure of organizational work by drawing on one or a combination of institutional logics. In particular, I discuss two logics that may compete in orienting actors towards work structures: bureaucratic logics and democratic logics.[4]

Organizations, as a whole, are frequently characterized by a form of work design involving (among other factors) hierarchical authority systems, strict divisions of labor, and formal procedures. These components of work are supported by an institutional logic that permeates society, that of bureaucracy. Scott (1998) notes that bureaucratic logics represent legitimating accounts that provide a foundation for a distinctive strain of administrative structures that coordinate complex activities in society. Scott (drawing on the work of Berger et al., 1973) points out that:

> ... bureaucracy connotes distinctive spheres of competence, the importance of proper procedures, orderliness, predictability ... Conforming to authorized structures and to certified procedures – regardless of their outcomes – provides a rationale and justification to organizational participants. Formal rationality often stands for functional rationality (Scott, 1998, p. 163).

Despite the sterility and coldness often attributed to bureaucratic structures and the actors within them, the adoption of hierarchy, formal rule systems, and strict division of labor signals a concern with goal-directed efficiency and attempts to remove idiosyncratic tendencies from organizational work. In this respect, these structures correspond to a legitimizing institutional logic, which (following Friedland & Alford, 1991) I refer to as a "bureaucratic logic," that is understood and taken-for-granted by actors in the environments of organizations.

Democracy, however, may represent an alternative competing logic. The cultural acceptance of democracy, with its emphasis on broad participation and equality, provides external legitimacy to structures and processes emphasizing the egalitarianism and broad participation that characterize some modern organizations. As such, organizational actors have an alternative pre-existing legitimate framework toward which to orient themselves in the structure of work: democratic logics.

As this discussion has indicated, the design of organizational work may, in part, reflect institutional logics (i.e. cultural rationalizations, which provide a basis for the legitimacy of a particular organizational form) that characterize institutions within the society in which the organization is embedded. Similarly, though, it is important to note that the work groups within organizations are embedded in institutional logics. While a work group may more closely correspond to particular logics, it may be embedded in an environment characterized by other alternative logics. As such, it is important to think of work groups (like organizations) as open systems, subject to influences and evaluations from the broader organizations in which they are embedded. One consequence of an open systems conceptualization of organizational work groups is that it makes salient the fact that work groups may be subjected to multiple institutional logics. Also, as I have alluded to, these logics may represent competing or even conflicting rationales upon which work relations are based. I turn now to a discussion of how institutional logics become embodied in the enactment of work at the individual and group level and the implications of such enactments for evaluations of team effectiveness.

AN OPEN SYSTEMS FRAMEWORK FOR UNDERSTANDING TEAM EFFECTIVENESS

As emphasized throughout this paper, an understanding of team effectiveness demands looking beyond the boundaries of the team itself. Teams do not exist and work in isolation, but rather are situated within organizations. Furthermore, the *de facto* expectations and rationales that members hold for the team may or may not entail the frequently advocated egalitarianism discussed above. Regardless, the expectations and rationales held within a team may diverge from those held by other actors outside of the team in the organization. As a result, members may develop a style of interaction and an approach to work that differs markedly from that of organizational actors outside of the team. The potential for such divergence has important implications that have only recently begun to be recognized in existing research on organizational teams. As I argue in this section, the logics that define how work should be conducted guide the actors' expectations for behaviors. If these expectations and logics diverge from those more commonly held by non-team employees, and if such others are in a position to evaluate the team, then the team may not receive favorable evaluations of its work from these others. This argument requires the explication of two important and linked processes: (1) how institutional logics are represented in expectations at the level of the individual actor; and (2) how evaluations of team performance are generated. I begin with an examination of the former process.

Institutional Logics, Expectations for Work, and Individual Actors

The intersection of social cognition and organization behavior may provide further insight into the nature of team effectiveness. Research in social cognition holds that social conduct is guided by cognitive representations, referred to as schemata (Fiske & Taylor, 1984), scripts (Schank & Abelson, 1977), or knowledge structures (Galambos et al., 1986). Research in the tradition of social cognition shows that these cognitive structures provide actors with a template for behavior, and as such, are an important guiding force behind social action (e.g. Markus & Zajonc, 1985).

Developing this line of work further in the context of organizational learning, Lyles and Schwenk (1992) refer to knowledge structures, which correspond to and guide procedural activities of actors in organizations as "peripheral knowledge structures." A peripheral knowledge structure is a cognitive representation containing information regarding *how* to achieve objectives, as well as the *rationale* behind those procedures. That is, a peripheral knowledge structure represents the link between an expectation for behavior and the general grounds elaborating why the expectation is appropriate. Also, we see that the rationale behind the procedures corresponds to the notion of institutional logics. A peripheral knowledge structure, then, can be conceptualized as an individual-level cognitive representation of expectations for work behavior and the institutional logics that validate those expectations.

An important foundation of social action in a group, then, is not only the expectations group members hold, but also the institutional logics held by the group members that validate the expectations. It is important to note, however, that members may not all appeal to the same logics, and thus the extent to which particular expectations appear legitimate and are enacted may vary among group members. For instance, some members may subscribe more to the logic of bureaucracy (i.e. the role that differentiation, hierarchy, and authority plays in facilitating organizational work), while others may subscribe more to the logic of democracy (i.e. the contribution that cooperation, participation, and equal valuing of individuals plays in facilitating organizational work). Such differences may engender miscommunication and conflict among members. In other words, the greater the variation in the peripheral knowledge structures held by group members, the greater the likelihood of internal problems in the group. Furthermore, to the extent that members of a group all receive the same explicit instructions regarding work expectations and the rationale behind these expectations, we would expect to observe less variation in the peripheral knowledge structures members hold.[5] On the basis of this discussion, I propose:

Proposition 3. There will be less variation in the peripheral knowledge structures that team members hold in teams in which more members have undergone joint, explicit training regarding the expectations for behavior in the team.

Proposition 4. The greater the variation in the peripheral knowledge structures held by members of a team, the higher the level of internal problems in the team.

As this discussion suggests, the explicit training of teams with respect to particular expectations for behaviors and the rationale behind the expectations generates a shared understanding regarding how work will proceed in the team, and why such procedures are valuable. This shared understanding provides members with a means for effectively navigating their responsibilities within the team. Team members may receive such training through externally hired consultants or in-house programs. The key point is that the more members who receive explicit training, the greater the shared understanding of how members will conduct work in the team (i.e. the repertoires of action) and why those repertoires exist (i.e. rationales for repertoires of action). Again, these are the two key features of a peripheral knowledge structure. These ideas foreshadow another question regarding teamwork, "How does the inculcation of a particular set of expectations and rationales affect external evaluations of the team?"

Evaluations of Team Effectiveness

Two factors may work jointly in generating assessments of team effectiveness: (1) the level of ambiguity involved in team performance, which affects the likelihood that procedure-based evaluation criteria will be employed; and (2) the cognitive strategies actors engage in when making evaluative judgments, which lead them to invoke knowledge structures that may not correspond to those held by the object of evaluation.

First it is important to note that performance is often difficult to assess. Dornbusch and Scott (1975) argue that performance (i.e. the actual enactment of work) is rarely completely and directly discernible. Consequently, evaluators often use indirect measures of performance including outcomes, or other indicators of performance. Outcome information (e.g. quality and quantity of outputs), however, is often unavailable. This may be the case when evaluations must be made although the work is incomplete, or when the outcome itself is known to require an "incubation period" before objective assessments may be made. As an example, take the work of product design teams or research and development teams. Usually, the fruits of such a team's work cannot be easily measured. Comparisons to standard criteria, such as usability, marketability, or profitability, may not be available for a long period after the outcome of the team's work reaches a final stage. Nonetheless, evaluations of the team are often made without such information. Moreover, the evaluations reflect the degree of support (i.e. cultural approval) in the organization for the team. That is, evaluations indicate the legitimacy of the team in the organization. These evaluations, in turn, are used to make critical decisions, like whether the team will receive ongoing resource support from the organization (e.g. time, personnel, material, and financial support). Irrespective of the bases for such evaluations, the evaluations themselves have crucial implications for the team's subsequent success (both in terms of performance and outcomes). As such, under certain conditions, evaluations can assume a kind of self-fulfilling prophecy status with respect to performance.

Scott (1977), following on Suchman (1967), asserts that in the absence of full performance or outcome information, organizations commonly rely on two types of indicators to assess performance: process and structural criteria. Process indicators focus on how work is performed, under the assumption that particular procedures are linked to particular outcomes. For example, an evaluator might consider whether members of a team are regularly observed working in their offices or other designated work space. The assumption underlying this considera-tion may be that employees who are visible are more productive (and hence, so are the units with which they are affiliated). Teams, however, may take members away from designated work spaces for collaborative work and meetings, leading to less visibility.

Like process indicators, structural indicators place heavy emphasis not on actual performance, but rather on symbols of performance. Structural criteria stress indicators of capacities for performance. For instance, an evaluator may consider the educational credentials of team members (i.e. types of degrees and levels of educational attainment) and how those credentials correspond to the authority different team members wield. In this case, the assumption is that: (1) particular types of training (e.g. financial, engineering) and levels (e.g. graduate degrees) provide critical competencies that improve the quality of the team's work; and (2) vesting more authority with members holding higher status credentials improves the decision-making in the team. That is, the type and level of team members' credentials and the distribution of authority across the membership represent structural indicators of the team's performance. As noted earlier, however, teams may benefit less from a homogeneous membership characterized by replication of educational level and training. Rather, diversity (both in level and type of training) may facilitate the team's ability to innovative and to address complex problems. And, allocating authority equally across the membership may also enhance interaction within the team. Yet, populating the team with individuals of different status (rather than merely high statuses) and failing to assign formal authority on the basis of status may lead an external evaluator to question the competency of the team.

Note that both process and structural indicators emphasize conformity to organizational rule regimes (e.g. requirements and standards to which employees in different organizational positions are expected to adhere). Organizational actors generally perceive conformity to organizational rule systems as an indirect indicator of performance. As such, I refer to both process and structural indicators as procedural standards. The important point here is that when either direct performance or outcome information is missing, procedural standards may become the main criteria for evaluation as an indirect indicator.[6] When this occurs, evaluations represent evaluator's assessments of the appropriateness of a team's process. Also, as I noted previously, these assessments correspond to the cultural support for the team – the team's legitimacy in the organization.

Second, it is important to note that the cognitive strategies that evaluators rely on when assessing team performance may generate a bias in the evaluation that works against the team. Cognitive social psychologists and social scientists have noted that evaluation is often based on cognitive referents (e.g. Fiske & Taylor, 1984; Niedenthal et al., 1985; Rosch & Lloyd, 1978). When an actor evaluates another, the process of judgment involves calling up a cognitive referent as a standard, and evaluating the extent to which the evaluator's perceptions of the actor being evaluated (i.e. the evaluatee) map onto that standard. High correspondence between the referent and perceptions of the evaluatee generates positive evaluations, while low correspondence generates negative evaluations. Obvious referents, however, may be unavailable for a variety of reasons. For instance, the evaluator may lack adequate experience with the object of evaluation (evaluatee and/or evaluatee's action/outcome), information regarding the state of the object may be unavailable, or standards for evaluation (and hence the appropriate cognitive referent) may be unknown to the evaluator.

Research on cognition suggests that knowledge structures are used not only to generate expectations (and hence, guidelines or scripts for action), but also to interpret stimuli (e.g. Bargh et al., 1988; Sharkey & Mitchell, 1985). When evaluators rely on procedural criteria, it is not surprising that the cognitive referent they would invoke would be their own peripheral knowledge structures representing procedures for meeting organizational expectations. Even if an evaluator is aware that the team has undergone training targeted at changing the structure of interaction within the team (e.g. "team building" training), this awareness does not necessarily provide the evaluator with an interpretative schema (i.e. peripheral knowledge structure) for assessing the procedures enacted within the team. That is: (1) the evaluator may be relying on procedural criteria as the basis for the evaluation; and (2) the observations the evaluator makes of the team may not fit the peripheral knowledge structure held by the evaluator. In other words, when objective criteria are unavailable, yet an evaluation is demanded, evaluators may generate proxies as cognitive referents. These proxies may be based on the peripheral knowledge structures held by evaluators, which may or may not coincide with those held and enacted by the team.

The Legitimacy Paradox of Teamwork

The above discussion alludes to a problem that teams face in their work: Divergent expectations regarding *how* work should be performed. On the one hand, teams may be trained or otherwise come to adopt expectations for work that are distinct from those found more commonly in their organization. In particular, it is not uncommon for the expectations developed within a team to embody an egalitarian ideology, based on the logic of democracy. The conduct that these expectations engender can facilitate work within the team by reducing internal problems like miscommunication and conflict. While there is a dearth of consistent evidence that egalitarian teams are higher performers than non-egalitarian work units, there is evidence that problems involving conflict and communication are reduced by such approaches to work (e.g. Hackman, 1980; Johnson & Johnson, 1989; McGrath, 1984). That is, teamwork (in the sense of realizing egalitarian ideals) does seem to have a positive effect on the internal functioning of teams.

On the other hand, teamwork also involves ascribing to an institutional logic that may be inconsistent with a logic of bureaucracy that is more common in organizations. This is where the legitimacy paradox of teamwork is found. When an organization is generally characterized by more structured forms of interaction (i.e. adherence to formal procedures and formal lines of authority) corresponding to the logic of bureaucracy, then the procedures whereby team members conduct work may seem unfamiliar, even deviant to external observers. At the same time, the nature of the work assigned to teams may make objective evaluations difficult to conduct. Nonetheless, evaluations are likely to occur, and as argued above, in the absence of objective criteria, such evaluations are likely to involve procedural criteria. Moreover, the procedural criteria invoked are likely to correspond to the peripheral knowledge structures guiding how evaluators expect work to be generally conducted in the organization. To the extent that assessments of how the team conducts work do not map onto the peripheral knowledge structures evaluators hold, teams are likely to receive unfavorable evaluations. Thus, I propose:

Proposition 5. The greater the divergence between the peripheral knowledge structures team members hold for conducting work in the team and the peripheral knowledge structures evaluators hold for conducting work in the organization, the less favorable the evaluations of the team.

In summary, the lack of consistent evidence on the effectiveness of teamwork, may in part, be accounted for by considering the fact that teams are situated in a broader organizational structure. An egalitarian approach to work in teams may facilitate team effectiveness by reducing internal problems. Also, formal training of team members may buttress members' acceptance of such norms by rationalizing egalitarianism with a democratic institutional logic. As a result, members are more likely to develop and share the same peripheral knowledge structures dictating how work is to be accomplished. At the same time, the expectations for work processes in the organization outside of the team may conform more or less to those held for work processes in the team. An egalitarian peripheral knowledge structure, in particular, may be held by team members, but not by other individuals in the organization. It is also important to note that under certain conditions (namely lack of objective criteria), the standards for work processes within the organization may be applied to assessments of teams. When this occurs, I argue that teams will receive unfavorable evaluations if the peripheral knowledge structure enacted within the team diverges from that held by others outside the team (especially evaluators). The critical point, and hence paradox, is that the same approaches to work that facilitate team processes may undermine external perceptions of the team's effectiveness.[7] I turn now to an empirical test of the propositions I have offered.

METHOD

To test these assertions, I conducted a survey of 71 teams in five organizations, spanning three industries (aerospace, computer, and heavy equipment manufacturing).

Sample

I constructed a strategic sample of teams (and organizations) to test my assertions. An ideal test would require variation in both the level of egalitarianism in the organization and level of egalitarianism in the teams I studied. The selection of aerospace, heavy equipment manufacturing, and computer as the three industries from which to draw organizations and teams represented a strategy to achieve the kind of variation that would facilitate testing of the claim on divergence.

Organizations in the aerospace industry tend to be: (1) large and complex; (2) heavily reliant on both domestic and international government contracts; and (3) subject to a long history of federal regulation (e.g. McKenna, 1992; O'Lone, 1990). This was the case for the organization included in this study. The heavy equipment manufacturing company, was subject to federal regulations and standards, though its contracts were largely held with private companies. Nonetheless, these private companies were themselves large, complex organizations. Size and complexity increase the likelihood of bureaucracy (Blau, 1963). Also, isomorphic processes (e.g. DiMaggio & Powell, 1983) increase the likelihood that an organization will assume the characteristics of other organizations on which the focal organization is reliant. Finally, the nature of work is likely to affect the degree of bureaucracy in an organization. The products manufactured by both the aerospace and heavy equipment manufacturing companies were large, complex, and required a correspondingly large and diverse labor force. Together then, these factors increase the likelihood that the aerospace and heavy equipment manufacturing organizations would embody a bureaucratic logic in their orientation toward work.

In contrast, federal regulations and standards did not pose such formidable constraints on the work of the teams in the study from the firms representing the computer industry. Furthermore, the products generated by these companies were marketed mostly to individual consumers, as opposed to the contracted production of the companies in the aerospace and heavy equipment manufacturing organizations. Additionally, the computer industry reflects a greater degree of egalitarianism in its tradition and culture, relative to aerospace and heavy equipment manufacturing (e.g. Dennison & Mishra, 1995; Lee et al., 2000; Rogers & Larsen, 1984). Nonetheless, one of the organizations was quite large, with a diverse array of products, while the others computer organization were relatively small, marketing a narrower line of products. As such, the strategic selection of these organizations increased the likelihood of testing my assertions in organizations with more democratic logics in their orientations toward work than in the other two industries. The differences between these organizations, however, suggested that one (the larger one) might ascribe to a more bureaucratic logic than the others.

I worked closely with a liaison from each organization to try to identify ten to fifteen teams in each company for participation in the survey. This would allow me to exercise some control over industry and organization effects, while still testing my assertions on team effectiveness and divergence in peripheral knowledge structures. I asked each organizational liaison to identify teams that varied in terms of the stage of work they were conducting in the organization. I felt this was important, since it is reasonable to expect that teams near the end of their project work may be viewed as more effective than those just starting out or far from completion. Furthermore, research suggests that teams in early stages of work may experience greater internal problems (e.g. Tuckman, 1965). Thus, I sought variation in the team's stage to protect against introducing confounds in testing the theoretical propositions I have offered. In addition, I sought to include teams working on projects that would be difficult to evaluate along objective dimensions (for example, usability of a product, market success of a product, or lack of production errors). More specifically, I suggested that long-term decision-making and/or product design and development teams might represent suitable candidates for the study.

For each team participating in the study I identified a non-team evaluator to provide assessments of the team along different dimensions, as well as information regarding the expectations the evaluator held for how work was generally conducted in the organization. Evaluators also answered questions regarding the criteria they used to assess the teams. I provide details regarding each of these items below in the discussion of dependent, independent, and control variables. It is important to note that the evaluators were individuals who were formally charged with the responsibility of regularly assessing the teams I studied. In other words, whether or not I had conducted this study, the evaluators who participated in it would have supplied the organization with assessments of the teams. In every case, the evaluators were high-level executives to whom team leaders reported.

All members of each team participating in the study also completed a questionnaire. Team members and evaluators completed their surveys within a few days of one another. The questionnaire included items addressing how work was usually conducted within the team and within the organization. Additionally, members answered questions regarding communication and information flows in the team, and like evaluators, members provided assessments of their teams' effectiveness. Also, the questionnaire included items eliciting information on each member's age, occupation, education, and ethnicity to test assertions on diversity. I also asked team members to report on the length of time the team had been working on the project and whether the team had received formal training in team processes (as, for example, from organization/management consultants). Details regarding these items are provided below in the discussion of dependent, independent, and control variables.

Dependent Variables

The primary dependent variables of interest include internal problems (INT-PROB) experienced in the team (P1 and P4, also an independent variable in

P2), effectiveness (EFFECTIVE) (P2 and P5), and variation in the peripheral knowledge structures held within the team (VTPKS) (P3, also an independent variable in P4). I operationalized each of these variables through member and/or evaluator responses to multiple items on the survey questionnaire. I included the items representing each variable as observed variables representing latent structures in confirmatory factor analyses. I employed the resulting measurement model from these analyses in structural equation models to test study hypotheses. Below, I briefly describe the items relevant to each dependent variable.

The questionnaire included two items assessing evaluator perceptions of internal problems (INTPROB) in the teams. The first item asked evaluators to report the extent to which problems arose because members failed to supply one another with information (INFO). The second item asked evaluators to report the extent to which problems arose in the team because members did not hold clear understandings of their work assignments in the team (CLARITY). Responses were made on a seven-point scale (1 = Not at All Problematic, 7 = Highly Problematic). In addition to evaluator perceptions of internal problems, I also obtained team member reports of information difficulties and problems in clarity of assignments (TINFO and TCLARITY, respectively). I constructed team-level indicators for these items by taking the mean response for each item. Although I did not hypothesize on whether members and evaluators would vary in their perceptions of problems, a comparison of team and evaluator perceptions may provide additional insight on the nature of how teams are viewed within an organization.

I operationalized effectiveness through evaluator responses to three items: the extent to which the respondent agreed that the team was productive (PRODV), innovative (INNOV), and generated high quality work (QUALITY). Responses were made on a seven-point Likert-type scale (1 = Strongly Disagree, 7 = Strongly Agree). I used responses to these three items as indicators of a latent variable, effectiveness (EFFECTIVE). Although the propositions generated by my framework explore effectiveness from an external perspective (i.e. that of the evaluator), I also measured team members' assessments of productivity, innovativeness, and quality of work. Thus, although not captured in formal study hypotheses, further insight may be generated by comparing team and evaluator responses to these items. To obtain team-level indicators of effectiveness, I calculated the arithmetic mean of team member responses to these items.

I calculated variation in the peripheral knowledge structures to which members of the same team ascribed (VTPKS) by taking the coefficient of variation (e.g. Blalock, 1979) in the team for each of the four components of the peripheral knowledge structure described below. Each coefficient of variation was treated as a separate indicator contributing to the overall VTPKS.

Independent and Control Variables

As stated in the discussion of P1 and P2, egalitarianism is argued to offer an important benefit to socially diverse teams. Furthermore, the idea that egalitarian practices bridge socially diverse actors often receives emphasis in the training that teams may receive. Although the sampling of teams participating in the survey was targeted to include socially diverse units, I sought to confirm this through items on the survey instrument. Consequently, members were asked to report their age (AGE), number of years employed by the organization (SENIORITY), gender (GENDER), level of education (EDUC), ethnicity (ETHNIC), and occupational background (OCCUP). As a measure of diversity for the continuous variables of AGE and SENIORITY, I calculated the coefficient of variation for each team. For the categorical variables, GENDER, EDUC, ETHNIC, and OCCUP, the measure of diversity was Blau's index of heterogeneity (Blau, 1977).

I initially used two sources to assess whether members had participated in joint, explicit training regarding expectations for work in the team (P3). First, all team members were asked to indicate whether they had participated with other team members in seminars or training sessions to facilitate teamwork. Second, I obtained information regarding the team-related training of team members prior to administering the survey to teams in the sample. This information was obtained through unstructured discussions with non-team representatives (usually the study liaison) of each organization participating in the study in which I requested details (and documentation, where available) regarding the training that team members and/or teams as a whole were given in preparation for their work. For all of the teams in the sample in which some members indicated that they had participated collectively in formal team training, organizational representatives also indicated that the team had been formally trained. At the same time, not all of the members on these teams participated in the training. Consequently, the measure I used as an indicator of the extent of joint team training was the percentage of members on the team who reported receiving joint, formal team training (PTRAIN).

I assess the peripheral knowledge structure guiding work in the team (TPKS) by asking members to indicate the extent to which particular expectations and beliefs guided work-related interactions in the team. Respondents were asked the extent to which most members would agree with four statements: (1) all team members are expected to participate in team discussions (TPART); (2) if team members experience difficulty in their work, they can depend on another member for assistance (THELP); (3) it is important for all members to participate in team decision making (TDECM); and (4) the contributions of all members are taken seriously in the team's work (TSERS). Responses were made on a seven-point scale (1 = Most Members Would Strongly Disagree, 7 = Most Members Would

Strongly Agree). To obtain team-level indicators, I calculated the arithmetic mean of team member responses on each item.

A parallel set of items represented expectations guiding work-related inter-actions in the organization outside of the team (OPKS). Team members and evaluators were asked to consider how work was generally conducted in the organization outside of the team and then both members and evaluators were asked the extent to which most employees would agree with four statements representing expectations that paralleled those asked with respect to the team: (1) everyone present during a discussion about work is expected to participate (OPART); (2) if employees experience difficulty in their work, they can depend on another employee for assistance (OHELP); (3) it is important for every employee to participate in the decision making in his/her unit of the organization (ODECM); and (4) the contributions of all employees are taken seriously in the organization's work (OSERS). Responses were made a seven-point Likert-type scale (1 = Most Employees Would Strongly Disagree, 7 = Most Employees Would Strongly Agree). Evaluator responses represent indicators of evaluator perceptions of organizational peripheral knowledge structures (OPKS$_e$), while the arithmetic mean of team responses on each item represent indicators of team perceptions of organizational peripheral knowledge structures (OPKS$_t$).[8]

To assess divergence between the team and organization with respect to the expectations guiding work (DIVPKS), I calculated the absolute value of the difference between evaluator responses on each item representing organizational expectations and the mean of the team responses to the parallel item representing expectations within the team. Thus, there are four indicators of divergence between the team and the organization in the peripheral knowledge structures (i.e. expectations and rationale) capturing the conduct of work.

Because team members also responded to items regarding organizational peripheral knowledge structures, I can explore whether team perceptions of the organizational peripheral knowledge structures were consistent or inconsistent with those held by evaluators. While I do not hypothesize on the outcomes or effects of such (in)consistencies, this analysis provides additional insight into issues surrounding divergence in peripheral knowledge structures and evaluations of teams.

RESULTS

Questionnaires were distributed to 573 members of 71 teams in five organizations. Five hundred and fifty-nine members returned questionnaires, yielding a response rate of 97.67% among team members. Sixteen teams represented organization A, from the aerospace industry; fifteen teams represented organization B, from the heavy equipment manufacturing industry; fifteen teams represented organizations C and D, both from the computer industry; and ten teams represented organization E, also from the computer industry.

At the time the teams were initially identified for participation, external evaluators for each team were also identified. At the time the survey was administered, however, evaluators for only 65 of the 71 teams were still in a position to evaluate the teams. All of the teams lacking evaluators were from the same organization (E). Although the time between identification and actual survey administration was no greater than eight weeks for any of the teams, this lapse was long enough for evaluators in this organization to either be transferred out of the division relevant to the team's work (and hence no longer be responsible for formal team evaluations), leave the organization, or be obligated to other organizational duties which precluded participating in the survey. Thus, the response rate for evaluators was 91.55%.

I also examined within-team response rates, and found that among four teams in the study, response rates were 50% or lower. For all remaining teams, the response rates were 100%. I excluded the four teams with response rates below 100% from my analyses. These teams were all from the same organization, the same one in which six evaluators were no longer available (E). Later, it was revealed that the company was undergoing a major reorganization at the time of the survey. Only one viable team was left in the sample from this organization and it was clear that this particular team was situated in a highly disrupted organizational environment. I decided to exclude this team (and organization) from subsequent analyses. Thus, the final sample included 61 teams spanning four organizations in three industries.

Description of Teams and Organizations

The types of teams in each organization included research and development teams, product design teams, product development teams, and strategic long-term planning teams. In Table 1, I provide descriptive statistics, broken down by organization, relating to the team size, length of time teams had been working on their projects, and diversity (along the dimensions of age, seniority, gender, education, ethnicity, and occupation of team members). The table also indicates the industry of each of the organizations and the level of egalitarianism in the organizations (as reported by evaluators). As this table shows, organization A

Table 1.   Industry, Level of Organization Egalitarianism, Mean Size and Age of Team, and Diversity Represented in Teams by Organization (Standard Deviations in Parentheses).

Variable	Organization			
	A ($n = 16$)	B ($n = 15$)	C ($n = 15$)	D ($n = 15$)
Industry	Aerospace	Heavy equipment manufacturing	Computer	Computer
Organization egalitarianism	4.23 (1.35)	3.05 (1.05)	5.87 (0.82)	5.53 (0.78)
Size	12.06 (4.07)	6.00 (0.00)	6.80 (1.57)	6.00 (0.00)
Team age (in months)	47.38 (6.35)	6.27 (4.20)	3.93 (1.33)	9.00 (5.73)
Diversity				
Age	0.22 (0.05)	0.23 (0.07)	0.15 (0.05)	0.20 (0.04)
Seniority	0.95 (0.31)	0.68 (0.21)	0.50 (0.19)	0.60 (0.13)
Gender	0.19 (0.15)	0.13 (0.14)	0.24 (0.17)	0.27 (0.16)
Education	0.53 (0.18)	0.59 (0.20)	0.58 (0.13)	0.56 (0.09)
Ethnicity	0.13 (0.12)	0.00 (0.00)	0.06 (0.13)	0.27 (0.16)
Occupation	0.65 (0.12)	0.50 (0.20)	0.48 (0.19)	0.61 (0.16)

Note: Organization Egalitarianism is the mean of evaluator responses to the four questions related to the peripheral knowledge structure characterizing how work is generally conducted in the organization outside the team (i.e. OPART, OHELP, ODECM, OSERS). Size reflects the average number of members in the teams participating in the study from each organization. Team age reflects the average number of months the teams had been in existence in each organization. For Age and Seniority, the measure of diversity is the Coefficient of Variation (e.g. Blalock, 1979); for Gender, Education, Ethnicity, and Occupation, the measure of diversity is Blau's index of heterogeneity (Blau, 1977).

tended to have larger teams than the other organizations. Also, the teams affiliated with organization A had existed longer than teams in other organizations. This variable may be taken as a proxy for the stage of work teams were at when the study was conducted and indicates that the sample is comprised of teams at varied stages of work, as I had hoped to capture with my sampling strategy. Importantly, the table indicates that the organizations vary with respect to level of egalitarianism. Consistent with the logic underlying my sampling strategy, the two organizations representing the computing industry have the highest levels of egalitarianism. The aerospace organization and heavy equipment manufacturing organization had lower levels of egalitarianism. Finally, Table 1 indicates that the teams included in the study represent varying but relatively high degrees of diversity across all of the organizations. This is important for testing the first two propositions, which apply to teams characterized by diversity.

Egalitarianism and the Internal Functioning of Teams

I tested the propositions offered above through three latent structural models using EQS (Bentler, 1995). The correlations between all indicator variables in each model are given in Appendix A. Means and standard deviations for the indicator variables are given in Appendix B.

The first proposition asserts that, for teams characterized by a diverse membership, if team members hold a peripheral knowledge structure promoting egalitarianism then the team will experience lower levels of internal problems. Also, if the team has lower levels of internal problems, then it will be perceived as more effective. As described above, I assessed the peripheral knowledge structure of the team through member reports along four indicators of egalitarianism. The model includes two indicators of internal problems and three measures of effectiveness. I began this analysis by conducting a confirmatory factor analysis (CFA) to assess the measurement model. The results of the CFA indicated that three pairs of error terms should be permitted to covary to achieve a good fit to the model (ε_{THELP} and ε_{TSERS}, ε_{THELP} and ε_{PRODV}, and ε_{TDECM} and ε_{INFO}, respectively). After freeing these terms, a Comparative Fit Index (CFI) (Bentler, 1990) of 0.982 was obtained, indicating that the model fit reasonably well.

Once the measurement model was estimated, I again used EQS to generate structural estimates for the model parameters. The results of this analysis are illustrated in Fig. 1. This figure shows that for these heterogeneous teams, internal problems in the teams were perceived by evaluators to be lower when the team members reported holding peripheral knowledge structures that corresponded more rather than less to democratic logics ($\beta = -0.570, p < 0.01$). This supports Proposition 1. Also, teams with perceived lower levels of internal problems were also perceived by evaluators as more effective ($\beta = -0.672, p < 0.01$), supporting Proposition 2. Thus, we find support for the oft-cited observation that egalitarianism reduces internal problems and enhances team performance.

Team Training and the Internal Functioning of Team

As noted in the third and fourth propositions, I hypothesized that the variation in the peripheral knowledge structures held by team members would be lower for teams that had undergone explicit, joint team training than for those not experiencing such training. Of the 61 teams included in the analyses, 25 had received team training, with varying percentages of the memberships of different teams participating in the training. I began this analysis by examining the measurement model representing the multiple indicator latent variables, variation in team

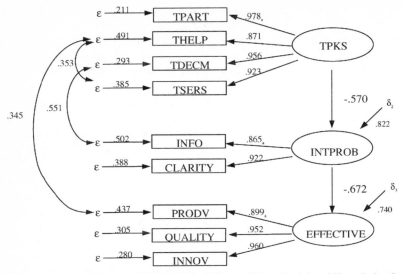

Fig. 1. Standardized Structural Estimates for Effects of Team Peripheral Knowledge Structures (TPKS) on Internal Problems (INTPROB), and Effects of INTPROB on Evaluator Perceptions of Team Effectiveness (EFFECTIVE). *Note:* Subscript (a) indicates fixed parameter. $\chi^2 = 33.57$, df $= 22$; CFI $= 0.971$. All estimates significant at or below $p < 0.01$.

peripheral knowledge structures (VTPKS) and internal problems (INTPROB). This analysis indicated that the error terms for two of the indicators of team peripheral knowledge structures (ε_{VTHELP} and ε_{VTDECM} should be freed to covary in the model in order to generate a good fit. The CFI for the final model was 0.972.

The structural modeling based on this measurement model is illustrated in Fig. 2. This model indicates further support for the third and fourth assertions from my framework. We see that the greater the percentage of team members participating in team training, the lower the variation among members' perceptions of the peripheral knowledge structures guiding the team ($\beta = -0.267, p < 0.01$). Furthermore, variation in peripheral knowledge structures is related to increased levels of internal problems in these teams ($\beta = 0.660, p < 0.01$).

Divergence in Peripheral Knowledge Structures and Team Performance

The key claim of this study is that divergence between the peripheral knowledge structure held within the team and the peripheral knowledge structure more

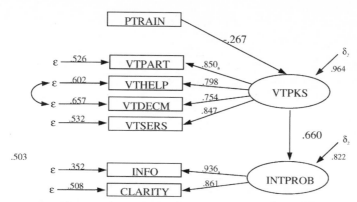

Fig. 2. Standardized Structural Estimates for Effects of Team Training (PTRAIN) on Variation in Members' Peripheral Knowledge Structures (VTPKS), and Effects of VTPKS on Internal Problems (INTPROB). *Note:* Subscript (a) indicates fixed parameter. $\chi^2 = 15.49$, df = 12; CFI = 0.972. All estimates significant at or below $p < 0.01$.

generally characterizing the organization will be linked to lower evaluations of the team on the part of external evaluators. Once again, I began the analysis testing this claim with an assessment of the measurement model. This analysis suggested that a good fitting model would be obtained by allowing two error terms to covary (εDIVHELP and εDIVSERS). With this parameter freed, the CFI for the model was 1.00.

Figure 3 depicts the structural model estimated on the basis of this measurement model. As predicted, divergence between the peripheral knowledge structures characterizing the team and those characterizing the organization has a significant negative effect on external evaluations of the team ($\beta = -0.686, p < 0.01$).

Interestingly, of the 61 teams in the sample, the results indicated that egalitarianism was *lower* for 17 of the teams relative to the organizations in which they were embedded. Of these, eight teams had mean egalitarianism levels that were one-point or more below the organization mean (those with less than a one-point difference could be considered as virtually equivalent to the organization in egalitarianism). Removing these eight from the analyses, all of which were from organization A, did not render any of the path coefficients in Fig. 3 insignificant. For these eight, however, the mean of the indicators for evaluator's perceptions of effectiveness was notably low (2.98), compared to the overall sample mean of 4.44. This suggests that when the team differs in either direction from the organization (i.e. by being more egalitarian or less egalitarian than the organization), then evaluators perceive the team as less effective. Yet, the decrement to perceptions of

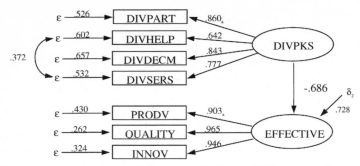

Fig. 3. Standardized Structural Estimates for Effects of Divergence Between Team and Organization Peripheral Knowledge Structures (DIVPKS) on Evaluator Assessments of Team Effectiveness (EFFECTIVE). *Note:* Subscript (a) indicates fixed parameter. $\chi^2 = 9.21$, df $= 12$; CFI $= 1.00$. All estimates significant at or below $p < 0.01$.

team effectiveness may be exacerbated when the team is *less* democratic than the organization in which it is embedded. With such a small sub-sample ($n = 8$), however, we should treat this result cautiously. In summary, the results do show that the greater the divergence between the team and organization with respect to peripheral knowledge structures, the lower the evaluations of the team and for the majority of teams in these analyses, the team was more egalitarian than the organization in which it was embedded.

Comparing Team and Evaluator Perceptions

The above analyses are suggestive of the paradox of teamwork I have described. On the one hand, teamwork (as indicated by approximation of egalitarian knowledge structures) appears to facilitate the internal functioning of teams. On the other hand, the greater the divergence between these knowledge structures and those that more generally characterize the organization, the less favorable view of the team that external evaluators will hold. An important remaining issue is whether team members are cognizant of the differing peripheral knowledge structure of the organization along these dimensions (i.e. participation, cooperativeness, decision making, and individual value). If members are unaware that expected patterns of behavior in the organization outside of the team are different from those in the team, then it may be that team members are behaving in deviant ways in their extra-team interactions. This deviance, in turn, may generate unfavorable assessments of teams on the part of external evaluators. That is, the fact that teams follow different expectations in their within-team interactions may not itself be the source of problematic evaluations. Rather, it may be an ignorance of organization expectations that generates illegitimacy, and hence decrements in evaluations of effectiveness.

To examine this possibility, I calculated matched pairwise Pearson's moment correlations between team perceptions of the organization expectations pertaining to participation, cooperativeness, decision-making, and individual value and those of evaluators. All correlations were moderate to high and significant at $p < 0.01$ (correlations were 0.59, 0.42, 0.55, and 0.75 for participation, cooperativeness, decision making, and individual value, respectively). Thus, it appears that ignorance of the patterns of behavior expected in the organization does not explain the lowered evaluations in the face of divergent peripheral knowledge structures. Nonetheless, I did not measure the enactment of peripheral knowledge structures within the team or organization. Consequently, the possibility remains that extra-team behaviors did not conform to the peripheral knowledge structures characterizing the organization. Clearly, additional research explicitly designed to test the enactment of peripheral knowledge structures would shed further light on these issues.

In a related vein, it may also be the case that evaluators view the internal functioning of teams differently than the team members do. For example, evaluators (perhaps because they do not recognize teamwork) may view the team as experiencing higher levels of internal problems than team members perceive. Since internal problems are related to decrements in external evaluations, it is possible that it is divergence in perceptions of internal problems rather than in peripheral knowledge structures that generates lower evaluations of the team.

I investigated this possibility by examining the matched pairwise Pearson's moment correlations between team and evaluator perceptions of problems related to information flows in the team and clarity in member assignments. Both correlations were significant ($p < 0.01$) and high (0.74 and 0.68 for information problems and problems in clarity of member assignments, respectively). Thus evaluators and team members hold comparable views of the internal functioning of the teams. As such, attributing unfavorable evaluations of the team to divergent perceptions of team functioning is less tenable than the hypothesis that unfavorable evaluations arise from divergence in peripheral knowledge structures.

Finally, it may be the case that team members possess different perspectives on team effectiveness than evaluators. Moreover, the kinds of patterns that guide teamwork may depend, in part, on the team's assessment of its own effectiveness. If the team perceives itself as less effective, then it may adopt norms and institutional logics that are different than those it would adopt given high levels of effectiveness. That is, peripheral knowledge structures may be an outcome of perceived effectiveness. Under this premise, if team assessments run counter to evaluator assessments, then the resulting norms and institutional logics adopted within the team may be contrary to those the evaluator expects (which may or may not be held more broadly throughout the organization). I explored this possibility by examining Pearson moment correlations between team and evaluator assessments of the team along the dimensions of productivity, innovativeness, and quality of work. The correlations were all significant ($p < 0.01$) and high (0.80, 0.64, 0.76 for productivity, innovativeness, and quality, respectively). Thus, members and evaluators appear to hold corresponding views of the team's effectiveness in these dimensions.[9]

DISCUSSION

As these results suggest, the paradox of teamwork is that it is often at odds with alternative expectations and logics that provide a rationale for particular forms of organizational action. Yet, on the one hand, teams whose members consistently subscribe to expectations of egalitarianism are less likely to experience internal problems (like problematic information flows and miscommunication). On the other hand, to the extent that: (1) team members subscribe to such expectations; and (2) the expectations are not consistent with the expectations and logics more generally characterizing the organization (outside the team), the external evaluations of the team are likely to be less favorable. That is, external evaluations of the team may suffer to the extent that the team is successful at inculcating members with egalitarian expectations and logics corresponding to democracy (if the organization is not characterized by similar expectations and logics). What is perhaps most striking about this finding is that that these relations hold despite the fact that team members do perceive the differences between the team's expectations and the expectations more generally held in the organization.

Although this study offers important insights on organizational teamwork and its effectiveness as a mode of work design, there are at least two key limitations worthy of note. First, it is important to recognize the limitations of the survey methodology I employed. In this study, I examined actors' perceptions of work expectations within the team and the organization. As is well recognize actors' reports are not always consonant with realities or behaviors (e.g. Nisbett & Wilson, 1977). Whether and how these perceptions translate to enactment represents the next critical step in exploring the arguments I have offered on the relations between teamwork and effectiveness. Toward these ends, a field study of organizational teams in which both perceptions and enactments are recorded would represent an important complement to the study described here.

A second limitation of the present study is the limited number and diversity of organizations and teams represented in the survey. As I previously indicated, this sample was strategically chosen to represent variation in the knowledge structures that might characterize work in the organization (and allow a test of the claim on divergence). Nonetheless, greater insight will be gained by testing these arguments on a wider array of organizations and work groups.

Even in light of these limitations, though, the study provides striking evidence of the legitimacy paradox of teamwork – that teamwork, even when it is successful at reducing internal problems, may not always lead to positive evaluations of team effectiveness and support for the team. I have demonstrated that this paradox is linked to conflict between expectations for the enactment of work within the team and work within the organization (outside of the team). It is perhaps most interesting to note that evaluations suffer despite evaluator's and team members' perceptions of such differences. That is, evaluators and members appear to perceive the fact that scripts for action in the team differ from the scripts for action that more generally characterize work in the organization. Also, evaluators do perceive their reliance on process (rather than outcome) in the evaluation process. Despite these perceptions, we see a decrement in evaluations.

In many ways, the theory and research discussed here may pose more questions than they answer. For instance, despite the overwhelming strength of these findings, the fact remains that some teams with divergent knowledge are successful. What factors contribute to that success? Ancona (e.g. Ancona, 1990; Ancona & Caldwell, 1992) has demonstrated the importance of a variety of external strategies that link teams to the organizations in which they are situated. In particular, she shows that teams with roles that involve managing "external dependencies" out-perform teams lacking such roles. Combining these results with those of the present study, we might expect that such external bridging strategies would be all the more important for teams who have: (1) come to accept democratic logics as a foundation for structuring work; and (2) exist in an organizational environment that embraces a bureaucratic logic.

Additionally, my argument suggests that the legitimacy paradox of teamwork arises, in part, from the ambiguity that characterizes the evaluation of organizational work. Assessments of team performance have important consequences for teams in terms of the longevity and resourcing of the team's work. Yet, whether decrements in assessments that relate to divergent knowledge structures generate negative consequences is still an empirical question that needs to be addressed.

Another factor, the conflicting institutional logics that may permeate organizations, is also a fundamental source of the legitimacy paradox of teamwork that I have described. This point (on conflicting institutional logics) is particularly worthy of further theoretical and empirical elaboration. In the present study, I did not directly examine institutional logics, but only inferred that peripheral knowledge structures are formed, in part, from institutional logics. An exploration of the linkage between institutional logics and peripheral knowledge structures is an important step, insofar as it would link macro social ideologies with individual expectations, and subsequently actions. Demonstrating and explicating this linkage would not only enhance sociological knowledge regarding organizational work design, but would also link two important theoretical orientations: institutional theory and theories of group dynamics. As such, the arguments and initial study offered here represent only a first step in an ongoing and timely agenda on the study of organizational work design.

NOTES

1. For example, although the team consistently met its deadlines and there was no objective indication that it would not meet its goals, administrators complained about the team's failure to follow formal bureaucratic processes and expressed confusion regarding why the team used some of the processes it did, which negatively affected their evaluations of the team.

2. In anticipation of the empirical research that I will present, the knowledge structures enacted in teams may be more or less egalitarian than those more common to the organization. The point is that it is the degree of consonance between the team knowledge structure and organizational knowledge structure that matters, not whether the team enacts knowledge structure embodying more or less egalitarianism. Nonetheless, as described below, the term "team" is generally used to connote a unit that reflects egalitarian norms.

3. By "effectiveness" I mean the extent to which team members and non-team members view the team as generating outputs that are valuable to the organization.

4. Organizations or the units within them may be characterized by other logics (e.g. the logic of family, religious logics). Also, there may be multiple logics operating in an organization at any moment in time, leading to alternative subcultures (e.g. Martin, 2002). Exploring these other logics is beyond the scope of this paper; however, Friedland and Alford (1991) offer an interesting discussion of the genesis and content of alternative institutional logics.

5. As Lyles and Schwenk (1992) note peripheral knowledge structures may arise from different sources. For instance, employees' prior experiences in an organization (or in different organizations) may be a source of peripheral knowledge structures. Some organizations may hire consultants or use in-house trainers to train teams in team-building strategies that may impart peripheral knowledge structures to the members of the team. Also, team leaders may be more or less influential in conveying their own peripheral knowledge structures to team members. My prior research (Troyer, 2003; Troyer & Silver, 1999) and that of others (e.g. Barnard, 1938; Deal & Kennedy, 1982; O'Reilly & Chatman, 1995) suggests that managers, founders, and leaders play an important role in the culture (and hence knowledge structures) that permeates organizations.

6. It is important to emphasize, however, that organizational actors may not be conscious of their reliance on such indicators (or even that direct criteria are not clearly available).

7. Although I have emphasized the (mis)fit between a democratic team and a bureaucratic organization in this discussion, the theoretical arguments I have presented are generalizable to the opposite case: Bureaucratic teams in democratic organizations. My emphasis in this paper is on developing and testing a theoretical argument that explains the empirical case of teamwork (i.e. why teams have not seemed to live up to their promise as a superior form of organizational work design). The general theory, however, can be extended to addressing a range of situations in which the logics of two units conflict and objective standards for evaluation are absent.

8. I elected to assess the extent to which teams and organizations adhered to democratic logics through these items, rather than explore alternative logics. There are two primary reasons for this decision. First, as noted in the introduction of the paper, I am interested in assessing how egalitarian knowledge structures corresponding to democratic logics relate to team performance (as represented in Proposition 1). Second, I sought to clearly compare the degree of correspondence between the team logics and organization logics. Using a different set of indicators (e.g. to assess a different type of logic) within the organization would have made such comparisons difficult and inconclusive.

9. While these *post hoc* analyses suggest that some obvious alternative explanations may be implausible, I have not ruled out all possibilities. For example, it may be that evaluators have worked with the teams or team members in the past and those working experiences may affect evaluations. Additionally, the teams' prior performance records (especially for teams that were in place for several years, as in organization A) may affect subsequent performance assessments. An evaluator's own prior work experiences in teams may also affect assessments. My data do not permit me to assess these or other alternative explanations, but they are alternatives that are worthy of consideration in future research and I am grateful to the editor, Cathryn Johnson, for suggesting them to me.

ACKNOWLEDGMENTS

This project was supported by grants from the National Science Foundation (SES9300723) and the Stanford Center for Organizations Research. I thank the companies that participated in this project and their employees, who completed the questionnaires. Although they must remain anonymous, I am grateful to these participants who generously contributed their time and advice, making this project possible. Additionally, I thank Bernard P. Cohen, W. Richard Scott, Sanford M. Dornbusch, Joseph Berger, and Jerald Herting, who provided invaluable insight and suggestions related to the theoretical ideas, research design, and analyses. Finally, I thank the editor, Cathryn Johnson, whose careful and constructive critique enhanced the quality and presentation of the ideas and analyses.

REFERENCES

Ancona, D. G. (1990). Outward bound: Strategies for team survival in an organization. *Academy of Management Journal, 33*, 334–365.

Ancona, D. G. (1993). The classics and the contemporary: A new blend of small group theory. In: J. K. Murnighan (Ed.), *Social Psychology in Organizations: Advances in Theory and Research* (pp. 225–243). Englewood Cliffs, NJ: Prentice-Hall.

Ancona, D. G., & Caldwell, D. F. (1992). Bridging the boundary: External activity and performance in organizational teams. *Administrative Science Quarterly, 37,* 634–665.

Bargh, J. A., Lombardi, W. J., & Higgins, E. T. (1988). Automaticity of chronically accessible constructs in person × situation effects on person perception: It's just a matter of time. *Journal of Personality and Social Psychology, 55,* 599–605.

Barker, J. R. (1999). *The discipline of teamwork: Participation and concertive control.* Thousand Oaks, CA: Sage.

Barley, S. R., & Kunda, G. (1992). Design and devotion: Surges of rational and normative ideologies of managerial control. *Administrative Science Quarterly, 37,* 363–399.

Barnard, C. I. (1938). *The functions of the executive.* Cambridge, MA: Harvard University Press.

Beer, M. (1976). The technology of organization development. In: M. D. Dunnette (Ed.), *Handbook of Industrial and Organizational Psychology* (pp. 937–994). Chicago: Rand McNally.

Bentler, P. M. (1990). Comparative fit indexes in structural models. *Psychological Bulletin, 107,* 238–246.

Bentler, P. M. (1995). *EQS structural equations program manual.* Encino, CA: Multivariate Software.

Berger, J. B., Cohen, B. P., & Zelditch, M., Jr. (1972). Status characteristics and social interaction. *American Sociological Review, 37,* 241–255.

Berger, P. L., Berger, B., & Kellner, H. (1973). *The homeless mind: Modernization and consciousness.* New York: Random House.

Berger, P. L., & Luckmann, T. (1967). *The social construction of reality.* New York: Doubleday.

Blake, R., & Mouton, J. S. (1964). *The managerial grid.* Houston, TX: Gulf.

Blalock, H. M. (1979). *Social statistics.* New York, NY: McGraw-Hill.

Blau, P. M. (1963). *The dynamics of bureaucracy.* Chicago: University of Chicago Press.

Blau, P. M. (1977). *Inequality and heterogeneity: A primitive theory of social structure.* New York: Free Press.

Cohen, B. P., & Arechavala-Vargas, R. (1987). Interdependence, interaction and productivity. Working Paper No. 87–3. Center for Sociological Research, Department of Sociology, Stanford University, Stanford, CA.

Cohen, B. P., & Zhou, X. (1991). Status processes in enduring work groups. *American Sociological Review, 56,* 179–188.

Collins, B. E., & Guetzkow, H. (1964). *A social psychology of group processes for decision-making.* New York: Wiley.

Deal, T. E., & Kennedy, A. A. (1982). *Corporate cultures: Rites and rituals of corporate life.* Reading, MA: Addison-Wesley.

Dennison, D. R., & Mishra, A. K. (1995). Toward a theory of organizational culture and effectiveness. *Organization Science, 6,* 204–223.

DiMaggio, P. J., & Powell, W. W. (1983). The iron cage revisited: Institutional isomorphism and collective rationality in organizational fields. *American Sociological Review, 48,* 147–160.

Dornbusch, S. M., & Scott, W. R. (1975). *Evaluation and the exercise of authority.* San Francisco: Jossey-Bass.

Drucker, P. F. (1988). The coming of the new organization. *Harvard Business Review* (January–February), 45–53.

Dyer, W. (1987). *Team building: Issues and alternatives* (2nd ed.). Reading, MA: Addison-Wesley.

Fiorelli, J. S. (1988). Power in work groups: Team member's perspectives. *Human Relations, 41,* 1–12.

Fiske, S. T., & Taylor, S. E. (1984). *Social cognition.* New York: Random House.

Forsyth, D. R. (1983). *An introduction to group dynamics.* Monterey, CA: Brooks/Cole.

French, W. L., & Bell, C. H., Jr. (1984). *Organization development: Behavioral science interventions for organization improvement* (3rd ed.). Englewood Cliffs, NJ: Prentice-Hall.

Friedland, R., & Alford, R. R. (1991). Bringing society back in: Symbols, practices, and institutional contradictions. In: W. W. Powell & P. J. DiMaggio (Eds), *The New Institutionalism in Organizational Analysis* (pp. 232–263). Chicago: University of Chicago Press.

Galambos, J. A., Abelson, R. P., & Black, J. B. (Eds) (1986). *Knowledge structures.* Hillsdale, NJ: Lawrence Erlbaum.

Goodman, P. S. (1986). Impact of task and technology on group performance. In: P. S. Goodman & Associates (Eds), *Designing Effective Work Groups.* San Francisco: Jossey-Bass.

Hackman, J. R. (1976). Group influences on individuals. In: M. D. Dunnette (Ed.), *Handbook of Industrial and Organizational Psychology* (pp. 147–161). Chicago: Rand McNally.

Hackman, J. R. (1980). *Work redesign.* Reading, MA: Addison-Wesley.

Hackman, J. R. (1990). *Groups that work (and those that don't)* (1st ed.). San Francisco: Jossey-Bass.

Hollenbeck, J. R., Williams, C. R., & Klein, H. J. (1989). An empirical examination of the antecedents of commitment to difficult goals. *Journal of Applied Psychology, 74,* 18–23.

Homans, G. C. (1950). *The human group.* New York: Harcourt Brace and World.

Janis, I. (1972). *Victims of groupthink.* Boston: Houghton-Mifflin.

Janz, T., & Tjosvold, D. (1985). Cost effective and ineffective work relationship: A method and a first look. *Canadian Journal of Administrative Sciences, 2,* 43–51.

Johnson, D. W., & Johnson, R. T. (1989). *Cooperation and competition: Theory and research.* Edina, MN: Interaction Book Company.

Kaplan, R. E. (1979). The conspicuous absence of evidence that process consultation enhances task performance. *Journal of Applied Behavioral Science, 15,* 346–360.

Kaplan, R. E. (1986). Is openness passé? *Human Relations, 39,* 229–243.

Katz, D., & Kahn, R. L. (1966). *The social psychology of organizations.* New York: Wiley.

Katzenbach, J. R., & Smith, D. K. (1993). *The wisdom of teams: Creating the high performance organization.* Boston: Harvard Business School Press.

Larson, C. E., & LaFasto, F. M. J. (1989). *Teamwork: What must go right, what can go wrong.* Newbury Park, CA: Sage.

Lawrence, P. R., & Lorsch, J. W. (1967). *Organization and environment: Managing differentiation and integration.* Boston: Graduate School of Business Administration, Harvard University.

Lee, C., Miller, W. F., Hancock, M. G., & Rowen, H. S. (2000). *The Silicon Valley edge: A habitat for innovation and entrepreneurship.* Stanford, CA: Stanford University Press.

Lewin, K. (1951). *Field theory in social science: Selected theoretical papers.* New York: Harper.

Likert, R. (1961). *New patterns of management.* New York: McGraw-Hill.

Lyles, M. A., & Schwenk, C. R. (1992). Top management, strategy and organizational knowledge structures. *Journal of Management Studies, 29,* 155–174.

Manz, C. C., & Sims, H. P., Jr. (1982). The potential for 'groupthink' in autonomous work groups. *Human Relations, 35,* 773–784.

Markus, H., & Zajonc, R. B. (1985). The cognitive perspective in social psychology. In: G. Lindzey & E. Aronson (Eds), *The Handbook of Social Psychology* (Vol. 1, pp. 137–230). New York: Random House.

Martin, J. (2002). *Organizational culture: Mapping the terrain*. Newbury Park, CA: Sage.

Mayo, E. (1933). *The human problems of an industrial civilization*. New York: Macmillan.

McGrath, J. E. (1984). *Groups: Interaction and performance*. Englewood Cliffs, NJ: Prentice-Hall.

McGregor, D. (1960). *The human side of enterprise*. New York: McGraw-Hill.

McKenna, S. D. (1992). A culture instrument: Driving organizational learning. *Leadership and Organization Development Journal, 13*, 24–29.

Meyer, J. W., & Rowan, B. (1977). Institutionalized organizations: Formal structure as myth and ceremony. *American Journal of Sociology, 83*, 340–363.

Meyer, J. W., & Scott, W. R. (1983). *Organizational environments: Ritual and rationality*. Beverly Hills, CA: Sage.

Niedenthal, P. M., Cantor, C., & Kihlstrom, J. F. (1985). Prototype matching: A strategy for social decision making. *Journal of Personality and Social Psychology, 48*, 575–584.

Nisbett, R. E., & Wilson, T. D. (1977). Telling more than we can know: Verbal reports on mental processes. *Psychological Review, 84*, 231–259.

O'Connor, G. G. (1980). Small groups: A general system model. *Small Group Behavior, 11*, 145–174.

O'Lone, R. G. (1990). Aerospace suppliers adopting TQM to remain competitive. *Aviation Week and Space Technology, 133*, 70–71.

O'Reilly, C. A., & Chatman, J. A. (1995). Culture as social control: Corporations, cults, and commitment. In: B. M. Staw & L. L. Cummings (Eds), *Research in Organizational Behavior* (Vol. 18, pp. 157–200). Greenwich, CT: JAI Press.

Orive, R. (1988). Group consensus, action immediacy, and opinion confidence. *Personality and Social Psychology Bulletin, 14*, 573–577.

Powell, W. W., & DiMaggio, P. J. (1991). *The new institutionalism in organizational analysis*. Chicago: University of Chicago Press.

Reddy, W. B., & Jamison, K. L. (1988). *Team building: Blueprints for productivity and satisfaction*. San Diego, CA: University Associates.

Rogers, E. M., & Larsen, J. K. (1984). *Silicon Valley fever*. New York: Basic Books.

Rosch, E., & Lloyd, B. B. (1978). *Cognition and categorization*. Hillsdale, NJ: Lawrence Erlbaum.

Rosen, N. A. (1989). *Teamwork and the bottom line: Groups make a difference*. Hillsdale, NJ: Lawrence Erlbaum.

Sayles, L. R. (1958). *Behavior of industrial work groups*. New York: Wiley.

Schank, R. C., & Abelson, R. P. (1977). *Scripts, plans, goals, and understanding: An inquiry into human knowledge structures*. Hillsdale, NJ: Lawrence Erlbaum.

Scott, W. R. (1977). Effectiveness of organizational effectiveness studies. In: P. S. Goodman & J. M. Pennings (Eds), *New Perspectives on Organizational Effectiveness* (pp. 63–95). San Francisco: Jossey-Bass.

Scott, W. R. (1998). *Organizations: Rational, natural, and open systems* (4th ed.). Upper Saddle River, NJ: Prentice-Hall.

Scott, W. R., Mendel, P., & Pollack, S. (forthcoming). Environments and fields: Studying the evolution of a field of medical care organizations. In: W. W. Powell & D. L. Jones (Eds), *How Institutions Change*. Chicago: University of Chicago Press.

Selznick, P. (1949). *TVA and the grass roots*. Berkeley, CA: University of California Press.

Sharkey, N. E., & Mitchell, D. C. (1985). Word recognition in a functional context: The use of scripts in reading. *Journal of Memory and Language, 24*, 253–270.

Silver, S. D., Troyer, L., & Cohen, B. P. (2000). Effects of member status on the exchange of information in team decision-making: When team building isn't enough. In: M. M. Beyerlein,

D. A. Johnson & S. T. Beyerlein (Eds), *Advances in Interdisciplinary Studies of Work Teams: Team Development* (Vol. 7, pp. 21–51). San Diego: Elsevier.

Steiner, I. (1972). *Group process and productivity.* New York: Academic Press.

Stryker, R. (1994). Rules, resources and legitimacy processes: Some implications for social conflict, order and change. *American Journal of Sociology, 99,* 847–910.

Stryker, R. (2000). Legitimacy processes as institutional politics: Implications for theory and research in the sociology of organizations. In: S. B. Bacharach & E. J. Lawler (Eds), *Research in the Sociology of Organizations: Organizational Politics* (Vol. 17, pp. 179–223). Greenwich, CT: JAI Press.

Suchman, E. A. (1967). *Evaluation research.* New York: Russell Sage.

Sundstrom, E., de Meuse, K. P., & Futrell, D. (1990). Work teams: Applications and effectiveness. *American Psychologist, 45,* 120–133.

Tannenbaum, S. I., Beard, R. L., & Salas, E. (1992). Team building and its influence on team effectiveness: An examination of conceptual and empirical developments. In: K. Kelley (Ed.), *Issues, Theory, and Research in Industrial/Organizational Psychology* (pp. 117–153). Amsterdam: Elsevier.

Thompson, J. D. (1967). *Organizations in action.* New York: McGraw-Hill.

Tjosvold, D. (1986). The dynamics of interdependence in organizations. *Human Relations, 39,* 517–540.

Tjosvold, D. (1991). *Team organization: An enduring competitive advantage.* Chichester, NY: Wiley.

Trist, E. L., & Bamforth, K. L. (1951). Social and psychological consequences of the Longwall method of coal-getting. *Human Relation, 4,* 3–28.

Troyer, L. (1995). *Team embeddedness: The relations between team social structures, organization social structures, and team performance.* Unpublished doctoral dissertation, Stanford University, Stanford, CA.

Troyer, L. (2003). The role of social identity processes in status construction. In: S. R. Thye & J. Skvoretz (Eds), *Advances in Group Processes* (Vol. 20, pp. 149–172). San Diego: Elsevier.

Troyer, L., & Silver, S. D. (1999). Institutional logics and group environments: Toward an open system perspective on group processes. In: S. R. Thye, E. J. Lawler, M. W. Macy & H. A. Walker (Eds), *Advances in Group Processes* (Vol. 16, pp. 219–252). Greenwich, CT: JAI Press.

Tuckman, B. W. (1965). Developmental sequences in small groups. *Psychological Bulletin, 63,* 384–399.

Vallas, S. P. (2003). Why teamwork fails: Obstacles to workplace change in four manufacturing plants. *American Sociological Review, 68,* 223–250.

Vallas, S. P., & Beck, J. (1996). The transformation of work revisited: The limits of flexibility in American manufacturing. *Social Problems, 43,* 339–361.

Van de Ven, A., Delbecq, A. L., & Koenig, R., Jr. (1976). Determinants of coordination modes within organizations. *American Sociological Review, 41,* 322–338.

Weick, K. (1979). *The social psychology of organizing.* Reading, MA: Addison-Wesley.

Whyte, W. F. (1951). Small groups and large organizations. In: J. H. Rohrer & M. Sherif (Eds), *Social Psychology at the Crossroads* (pp. 297–312). New York: Harper.

Woodman, R. W., & Sherwood, J. J. (1980). The role of team development in organizational effectiveness: A critical review. *Psychological Bulletin, 88,* 166–186.

Wuthnow, R., Hunter, J. D., Bergesen, A., & Kurzweil, E. (1984). *Cultural analysis.* Boston: Routledge and Kegan Paul.

APPENDIX A
CORRELATION MATRIX OF INDICATOR VARIABLES
USED IN STRUCTURAL MODELS

Variable	(1)	(2)	(3)	(4)	(5)	(6)	(7)	(8)	(9)
(1) TPART	1.00								
(2) THELP	0.85	1.00							
(3) TDECM	0.94	0.80	1.00						
(4) TSERS	0.90	0.87	0.87	1.00					
(5) INFO	−0.48	−0.53	−0.37	−0.44	1.00				
(6) CLARITY	−0.51	−0.51	−0.46	−0.45	0.81	1.00			
(7) PRODV	0.46	0.32	0.40	0.39	−0.48	−0.53	1.00		
(8) QUALITY	0.39	0.31	0.33	0.31	−0.49	−0.54	0.87	1.00	
(9) INNOV	0.50	0.46	0.44	0.47	−0.62	−0.64	0.85	0.91	1.00
(10) TRAIN	0.45	0.35	0.57	0.36	−0.14	−0.21	0.30	0.35	0.37
(11) VTPART	−0.62	−0.67	−0.49	−0.57	0.56	0.44	−0.20	−0.16	−0.33
(12) VTHELP	−0.41	−0.68	−0.36	−0.40	0.46	0.43	−0.06	−0.18	−0.29
(13) VTDECM	−0.63	−0.60	−0.63	−0.67	0.46	0.43	−0.31	−0.28	−0.41
(14) VTSERS	−0.70	−0.76	−0.64	−0.75	0.55	0.55	−0.33	−0.35	−0.48
(15) DIVPART	−0.40	−0.39	−0.30	−0.37	0.41	0.43	−0.57	−0.54	−0.56
(16) DIVHELP	−0.37	−0.41	−0.26	−0.31	0.44	0.42	−0.35	−0.34	−0.41
(17) DIVDECM	−0.18	−0.32	−0.06	−0.16	0.51	0.45	−0.50	−0.55	−0.56
(18) DIVSERS	−0.56	−0.52	−0.46	−0.51	0.53	0.54	−0.52	−0.55	−0.57

Variable	(10)	(11)	(12)	(13)	(14)	(15)	(16)	(17)	(18)
(10) TRAIN	1.00								
(11) VTPART	−0.13	1.00							
(12) VTHELP	−0.15	0.70	1.00						
(13) VTDECM	−0.40	0.62	0.40	1.00					
(14) VTSERS	−0.18	0.72	0.67	0.64	1.00				
(15) DIVPART	−0.23	0.34	0.25	0.31	0.51	1.00			
(16) DIVHELP	−0.13	0.42	0.41	0.20	0.46	0.59	1.00		
(17) DIVDECM	−0.03	0.41	0.41	0.13	0.46	0.73	0.52	1.00	
(18) DIVSERS	−0.16	0.45	0.34	0.30	0.61	0.65	0.68	0.66	1.00

APPENDIX B
MEANS AND STANDARD DEVIATIONS FOR OBSERVED VARIABLES IN ANALYSES

Variable	Mean	Standard Deviation
TPART	4.53	1.21
$OPART_e$	4.49	1.39
$OPART_t$	4.17	1.02
THELP	5.04	0.99
$OHELP_e$	5.31	0.99
$OHELP_t$	4.97	0.73
TDECM	4.41	1.41
$ODECM_e$	3.95	1.34
$ODECM_t$	4.00	1.12
TSERS	5.05	1.41
$OSERS_e$	5.48	1.42
$OSERS_t$	4.66	1.24
VTPART	0.24	0.11
VTHELP	0.20	0.13
VTDECM	0.22	0.11
VTSERS	0.20	0.14
DIVPART	1.26	1.00
DIVHELP	0.97	0.78
DIVDECM	1.40	1.28
DIVSERS	1.32	1.23
$INFO_e$	2.95	1.33
$INFO_t$	2.72	1.03
$CLARITY_e$	2.57	1.30
$CLARITY_t$	2.42	1.23
$PRODV_e$	4.64	1.33
$PRODV_t$	4.84	0.75
$QUALITY_e$	4.69	1.52
$QUALITY_t$	5.06	0.80
$INNOV_e$	4.57	1.74
$INNOV_t$	5.06	1.02
PTRAIN	45.71	44.96

Note: Variable subscript "t" indicates team member perceptions, "e" indicates evaluator perceptions.

SOURCES OF LEGITIMATION AND THEIR EFFECTS ON GROUP ROUTINES: A THEORETICAL ANALYSIS

Anna C. Johansson and Jane Sell

ABSTRACT

The use of routines in the decision-making process of individuals, groups and organizations is a well accepted yet taken for granted phenomenon. One goal of organizations is to develop group routines that are efficient, but at the same time flexible. However, this presents a paradox because routines that are efficient at one point in time, or for a particular task, may persist, be unquestioned, and become increasingly inefficient for the group and the organization. This chapter develops a formal theory that describes the processes by which the legitimation of particular group structures impacts the development and use of group routines. The theory presented draws from theories of legitimation, expectation states theory, and institutional theory. The theory formally depicts three sources of legitimation: a referential belief structure (set of cultural beliefs) about expertise and leadership, authorization or superordinate support of a leader, and endorsement (support by group) of a leader. Specifically, the theory addresses: (1) how different sources of legitimation make groups more or less hierarchical; and (2) how the different sources of legitimation make group routines more or less flexible.

Legitimacy Processes in Organizations
Research in the Sociology of Organizations, Volume 22, 89–116
Copyright © 2004 by Elsevier Ltd.
All rights of reproduction in any form reserved
ISSN: 0733-558X/doi:10.1016/S0733-558X(04)22003-1

INTRODUCTION

One goal of organizations, both large and small, is the development of group routines that are efficient, but at the same time flexible. In this goal rests an apparent paradox: if routines are efficient by a set of accepted criteria at one point in time, they are not commonly questioned. But, if they are not questioned, they can become inefficient yet still remain. Or they can become efficient for group functioning, but inefficient or even detrimental for group goals. This paradox has been documented in many case studies, from the famous political "groupthink" cases illustrated by Janis (1982, 1989) to the NASA work groups analyzed by Vaughan (1996). Routine can numb analysis. As Morgeson and Hofmann (1999) suggest in their description of the Air Florida Flight 90 crash into the Potomac, "the routine was so powerful that the crew members were not even aware that the current flight required a non-routine response" (p. 253).

To address this organizational goal, we begin with a broad question: How do different sources of legitimation affect the routines of that group? An answer to this question may help solve the paradox between the establishment of routine and the creation of flexibility. As it happens, the very same routine can become more or less stable depending upon the sources of legitimation.

Specifically, we develop a theory to explain how different sources of legitimation make groups more or less hierarchical, and group routines more or less flexible. The formal theory specifies assumptions about sources of legitimation, and how these sources cumulate. Further, the theory allows us to derive an ordering of the relative strengths of the sources being tested. Three sources of legitimation – a referential belief structure about expertise, authorization, and endorsement – are considered.

Legitimation is the process through which a socially defined principle or set of rules is adhered to, deferred to, or supported even in the absence of obvious incentives to do so. These principles may be written or unwritten and they can refer to persons, positions and acts. This process is often taken for granted in the establishment and maintenance of social structure. Berger, Ridgeway, Fisek and Norman (1998) suggest that the process of legitimation is an inherently collective social process which "mediates the relationship between power and authority and affects the establishment, persistence and change of social organizational forms" (p. 379). The process also can occur at different levels of interaction such as group and organization. Many theorists and researchers studying legitimation suggest multiple objects and multiple sources of legitimation (Bell, Walker & Willer, 2000; Dornbusch & Scott, 1975; Walker, Rogers & Zelditch, 2002; Walker, Thomas & Zelditch, 1986; Zelditch & Walker, 1984). Sources of legitimation include propriety, endorsement and authorization. These sources reflect individual, group, and organizational or institutional levels of legitimation and illustrate the nested nature of this process. This also suggests that different sources of legitimation may also have different strengths.

Another important aspect of legitimation is the process by which it generalizes or spreads (Berger et al., 1998). Relating to Walker, Thomas and Zelditch's (1986) suggestions, we will explore how legitimacy of a social object or person might spread, not only to other objects, but also to the structure and the routines of the group. So, for example if a particular leader in one activity is granted legitimacy, we will demonstrate the conditions under which that legitimacy might be generalized to completely different kinds of activities.

Routines are also a taken-for-granted phenomenon in social and organizational life. March and Simon (1958) assert that "most behavior, and particularly most behavior in organizations, is governed by performance programs" (p. 142), that is routines. Several authors address routines in the context of organizations suggesting that routines are reflected in decision strategies (Cyert & March, 1963), decision rules (March, 1994), procedures, or a host of terms related to and used interchangeably with routines (Levitt & March, 1988). Despite the lack of precision with which routines have been defined, all of the definitions suggest, implicitly or explicitly, that routines are collective structures embedded in a broader social/organizational context. In this chapter, we will propose a particular framework to analyze and separate sources of legitimation, to measure or estimate the strength of these sources and finally, to derive how these sources and their combination might affect the routines of the group. We examine three sources of legitimation: endorsement, at the group level; authorization, at the organizational level; and referential belief structures at the societal/cultural level.

In developing formal definitions and conceptualizations that enable derivations, we will address three large literatures: legitimation, status inequality within group (with special emphasis upon the expectation states framework), and routines/rituals. While we focus on sociological developments, specifically in structural social psychology and organizations, we also integrate materials from organizational psychology and management. For each concept, we discuss issues raised within and across disciplines. We end each discussion with the presentation of the formal definitions. We begin with issues related to legitimation and then discuss routines because this follows the logical, causal progression of our formulation.

LEGITIMATION AND STATUS INEQUALITY

Legitimation

Numerous researchers address the concept of *legitimation* – the process by which an object gains social support. The theory and subsequent research surrounding this concept can be organized with respect to the process, objects, sources and conditions for legitimation. Legitimation is addressed in various areas within sociology, and while the legitimated social objects addressed may vary, and process remains somewhat mysterious, there is much agreement regarding sources and conditions. In this section we emphasize how these different conceptualizations of legitimation can be combined in innovative ways to yield new predictions.

Max Weber was particularly interested in authority systems and the bases for legitimate authority. Power, domination, and authority were central concepts for Weber as was legitimacy. Weber's definition of power or *macht* is "the probability that one actor within a social relationship will be in a position to carry out his own will despite resistance, regardless of the basis on which this probability rests" (1924/1978, p. 53). Authority refers to legitimate power in that it is tied to the social structure; authority represents the structure while power is granted to a position or individual. According to Weber, an order is legitimate "only if action is approximately or on the average oriented to certain determinate 'maxims' or rules" (1924/1978, p. 31), that is, the order is considered valid. Validity is a crucial component of legitimacy because it is when there is collective belief in the legitimacy of an authority structure that imposing order is greatly facilitated. Under these conditions people do not question the authority but rather they comply "voluntarily." This provides for a social order that is stable, efficient and cost effective. When people stop believing in the legitimacy of the order, they begin to question it and are more likely to attempt changing the structure. Thus, delegitimation of a social order makes maintaining that order more difficult and more costly, and often results in the use of coercion.

Weber conceptualized three types of authority: charismatic, traditional, and legal rational. The basis of legitimacy of these three types of authority depends on cultural systems and historical conditions (Weber, 1924/1978). Traditional authority is characteristic of traditional bureaucracies and is based on time-honored traditions. Charismatic authority is an authority that was legitimated based on personal qualities of the leader and then typically becomes routinized and then replaced by either traditional or legal rational authority. (For an interesting discussion of the process of charisma, see Finlay, 2002.) Legal rational authority is characteristic of the modern bureaucracy such as the state or corporations with the intent of ensuring universal rules, calculability and efficiency.

Evan and Zelditch (1961) experimentally investigated authorization as a source of legitimation and tried to separate the *legal* and *rational* components of Weber's theory of bureaucratic authority. They found that the source of legitimation was more important than competency of the authority when it came to eliciting compliance.

Dornbusch and Scott (1975) have elaborated a theory of authority, based on Weberian concepts of power, authority and legitimacy. However, they define power in terms of the application of "valued sanctions" rather than the exercise of will. They also define authority as legitimate power where "social norms legitimate action by defining it as correct, or appropriate, or permissible" (p. 38). They focus on the legitimacy of power relations in their theory of authority which requires that there be persons or positions linked by power relations, and norms or rules which govern how to exercise and respond to power. Organizations, both formal and informal, provide an environment in which there are networks of social relations that regulate behaviors of individuals who are pursuing specific goals. However according to Dornbusch and Scott (1975), in formal organizations hierarchies can develop which allow for control and regulation. The hierarchy is a power system as well as a status system and while not inevitable, it is likely to develop in a formal organization, and formal power systems are expected to be more stable because they relate to positions rather than individuals.

There are different dimensions to authority as specified in the theory. One dimension refers to the norms, which underlie the power relationship. Dornbusch and Scott (1975) refer to this dimension as either validity or propriety. Validity is collective support for, agreement with, or acknowledgment of a normative order, whereas propriety is individual belief in the norms as to how proper or appropriate they are. A normative order may still be considered valid even if not considered proper by certain individuals. This suggests the relative strength of the collective over the individual, and that authority must be considered valid to be stable, even if not considered proper. A second dimension refers to the sources of legitimacy, that is *whose* norms legitimate the exercise of power, those in superior positions or one's colleagues. "Power becomes authority when it is authorized, or when it is endorsed, or both" (p. 42). That is, the power *structure* becomes legitimated through authorization, endorsement, or both. The third dimension of authority refers to its formal or informal character. According to Dornbusch and Scott (1975), formal authority is based on position and informal authority is based on personal characteristics of the position's occupant. This dimension is directly related to Weber's ideal type of bureaucracy in which authority is tied to a position, not a person and thus provides for a more stable authority system.

The process of legitimation has roots in cultural elements and a legitimated order is created within the group interaction process as members reenact relatively enduring cultural elements (Berger, Ridgeway, Fisek & Norman, 1998). This suggests that sources of legitimation are structural and therefore structural features drive the process of legitimation (1998, p. 385). However, legitimation also requires agreement on a socially constructed *local* reality in order for the social entity to become "normatively prescriptive." Actors must sense that others will treat the structure as valid or in accordance with rules justified by larger cultural accounts. Zelditch and Walker (1984) (as well as Dornbusch and Scott) suggest that "validity is both necessary and sufficient to produce most of the effects usually attributed to legitimacy" (pp. 3–4) whereas propriety is neither sufficient nor necessary to produce these effects.

Zelditch and Walker (1984) and Bell, Walker and Willer (2000) point out that the introduction of valid rules can change conceptions of propriety before some action occurs. Whether or not a rule is valid affects individual evaluations of propriety and then both propriety and validity affect behavior. Thomas, Walker and Zelditch (1986) found that introducing valid rules regarding a reward structure reduced the likelihood that subjects would try to change the structure even though they might have personally felt that the structure was improper. "Even though maintaining the communication structure perpetuates inequality and even though it works against the material interests of the S[ubject]s, they do not attempt to change the structure nearly as much when the structure is legitimated and change delegitimated" (p. 389). Thus, collective approval can override personal approval.

Walker, Thomas and Zelditch (1986) suggest that the effects of endorsement, or collective peer support as a source of legitimation, are often confounded with effects of other uncontrolled sources of variation. They found that endorsement of a system of positions delays or prevents attempts to change the system, making that system more stable and enduring. They argued further that *who* legitimates the action makes a difference; endorsement (peers as source) can override personal beliefs. They concluded that while it may be difficult to separate the independent effects of propriety and endorsement, they have demonstrated the relative strength of endorsement as a source over propriety.

While Zelditch and Walker (1984), Walker, Thomas and Zelditch (1986) and Bell, Walker and Willer (2000) have suggested the relative strength of collective beliefs and approval over personal beliefs and approval, Sell and Martin (1983) and Martin and Sell (1986) empirically tested authorization and endorsement as sources of legitimation. Authorization as a source of legitimacy has to do with belief in a superior power or position, whereas endorsement comes from peers. These two dimensions are conceptually independent (Dornbusch & Scott, 1975) in that endorsed power may or may not be authorized. They demonstrated that while authority as a source of legitimacy is quite strong, and often stronger than endorsement, it can be overcome under certain conditions. Following such consideration of different sources of legitimacy, Walker, Rogers and Zelditch (2002) examine different *objects* of legitimacy. They ask whether the legitimacy of a given object is dependent upon the other objects of legitimacy within the same context. For example, does the illegitimacy of an act undermine the person who initiates or maintains them? In their experiments they find that legitimacy is not an all or nothing presence. In fact, they find that compliance of group members (as a measure of legitimacy) varies with respect to the different objects. Further, there is some evidence to support the notion that different objects of legitimacy contribute independently toward the probability of compliance of group members.

Peter Read (1974) experimentally tested the strength of sources of legitimation and bases of authority in small task-oriented groups. He considered separate sources of legitimation such as endorsement and authorization as they related to specifying a leader. He did not refer to endorsement and authorization specifically, but rather specified four criteria of agents of authority: election, appointment by expert external authority; appointment by non-expert external authority; and usurpation by self-appointed leader. He referred to this particular ordering of predicted legitimacy (from highest to lowest) as the "unidimensional view." At the end of the decision-making, the leader would do something very different and even startling, thereby amplifying initial perceptions of legitimacy. Thus, Read concludes, "the leader selection process may establish a relationship between group members and the agent of selection which remains unexpressed until the leader places unusual demands upon group members" (1974, p. 202). Subjects chose to retain the elected leader more than the expert appointed leader even though the expert leader had more task influence. This suggests a complex relationship between source of authority and influence, even in small *informal* groups.

The process of legitimation is recognized as a parallel or underlying process to power and influence processes (Bell, Walker & Willer, 2000) and is often taken-for-granted in the formation and persistence of social structures. However, as Walker, Rogers and Zelditch (2002) indicate, power can be analytically distinct from legitimacy; power is present when the one seeking power is present or observable. Legitimacy (or as Walker, Rogers & Zelditch, 2002 state, "naked legitimacy") induces compliance even when compliance is not monitored.

In face-to-face group situations, however, it is most often the case that power, influence and legitimacy are intertwined. (For discussion of these concepts and how they are similar and different, see Sell et al., 2004.) Berger, Ridgeway, Fisek and Norman (1998) consider specifically the emergence and consequences of the legitimation (and delegitimation) of power within small groups. They have mapped the process of legitimation within an expectation states framework using graph theory to describe the process through which status hierarchies become legitimated and delegitimated. We propose to combine the approaches stemming from the Weberian tradition most generally addressing organizations with the traditions concerning small group interactions.

Berger et al. (1998) describe legitimation as a social process, which mediates the relationship between social actors and social structures. Social actors are involved in this mediation process to the extent that they create and recreate social reality (Berger & Luckmann, 1967). However, the construction of social reality is a collective process. Actors must believe that others will also treat social objects as valid in order for those objects to be considered legitimate. This supports previous theory that legitimation is an inherently collective process (Berger et al., 1998; Dornbusch & Scott, 1975; Zelditch & Walker, 1984). Berger et al. (1998) also suggest that legitimation is an inherently multilevel process. Using an expectation states framework, they describe how "referential belief structures," that is "sets of socially validated beliefs held in common by actors" (1998, p. 382), exist at the cultural or societal level and are then activated and become relevant in the immediate task situation. The authors combine status characteristics theory and theory of reward expectations to describe the process by which status structures form, become legitimated and possibly delegitimated. Status characteristics theory describes how status characteristics become salient and task-relevant, and how the ensuing status organizing process results in differences in observable power and prestige (Berger, Cohen & Zelditch, 1966; Berger, Fisek, Norman & Zelditch, 1977; Berger, Zelditch, Anderson & Cohen, 1972). The theory of reward expectations connects to this process by describing the relationship between performance and reward expectations, which are based on the valued status characteristics. Rewards are then allocated to valued status positions. Referential belief structures become important to the formula because they define "what everyone knows to be true" (1998, p. 382) with respect to status characteristics, and therefore how status characteristics and reward levels are associated.

Legitimacy is also a central concept in the organizational literature, specifically in institutional theory. Institutional theory seeks to explain how organizations change structures to become more isomorphic with one another. Legitimacy becomes central to the theory because organizational structures that appear legitimate are more likely to survive (Meyer & Rowan, 1977). Institutional theory highlights the importance of the social and cultural environment that is, "social knowledge" and "cultural rule systems" (Scott, 1995, p. xiv). Organizations that incorporate societally legitimated rationalized elements in their formal structures maximize their legitimacy, increase their resources, and their chances for survival. Myths about rationality and efficiency (among others), which become institutionalized, give organizations legitimacy. Thus, organizational structures are created and elaborated through institutionalized myths and the more an organization incorporates these myths the greater legitimacy it has and the more likely it is to be successful and survive.

Drawing from theories of legitimation and the expectation states framework in structural social psychology, we hope to identify the connections between institutional theorists who theorize at a meso to macro level (e.g. DiMaggio & Powell, 1983; Meyer & Rowan, 1977) and describe the diffusion of structures, and institutional theorists such as Zucker (1991) who focus on the micro-level processes whereby social actors engage in constructing social reality during interaction.

Some researchers have criticized institutional theory, especially neo-institutional theory on two points (Prechel, 2000): (1) neoinstitutionalism fails to acknowledge a social actor (Stinchcombe, 1997). The theory assumes a diffusion process whereby legitimacy spreads, however does not describe this process or the role of social actors in this process. (This criticism is similar to that offered by social psychologists (Berger et al., 1998; Zelditch & Walker, 1984); (2) neoinstitutionalism's apparent lack of attention to structure. Hirsch (1997) suggests that this is a problem with neoinstitutionalism's more recent emphasis on cognitive systems, emphasizing the social constructionist perspective where compliance is not only assumed but also taken for granted (Scott, 1995). Scott (1995) identifies three "carriers of institutions" which describe some mechanisms through which legitimation may "diffuse." These carriers are cultural, social structural and routines. Cultural carriers rely on interpretive structures or "codified patterns of meanings and rule systems" (1995, p. 53). Social structural carriers rely on patterned expectations or "role systems" (1995, p. 53) and create structural isomorphism. Routines as carriers are structured activities, which can embody institutions.

Berger et al. (1998) acknowledge that discussions of legitimation usually focus on large-scale social structures, presumably because larger structures such as organizations are more stable and enduring. However, these larger structures of power and influence are often formed through informal interaction such as small task or goal-oriented groups (1998, p. 380). They describe how micro-level interaction creates status hierarchies, which once legitimated, then generalize across groups and contribute toward general patterns of inequality.

We attempt to identify the process by which legitimation diffuses, or spreads, and to describe the role of the social actor in that process. Specifically we will explain how structures created in one interaction shape and constrain future interaction.

Status Inequality in Groups and Legitimation of Status Hierarchies

Structural social psychologists are also concerned with the process by which group interaction creates and maintains structures of inequality. Expectation states theory (Berger, Cohen & Zelditch, 1966) describes the status organizing process in task-oriented groups whereby group members develop performance expectations based on status characteristics. These expectations lead to differences in observable power and prestige.

Status characteristics have two or more states or values and are differentially evaluated in terms of moral worth, such as honor or esteem. Expectation states theory specifies two types of status characteristics: diffuse and specific. Diffuse status characteristics are generally more observable, physical characteristics such as race, age or gender, but can also extend to title or occupation. A diffuse status characteristic, evaluated as having a high or low value of moral worth, is based on culturally salient stereotypes. A group member who possesses a diffuse status characteristic with a higher overall evaluation is said to have high status in relation to a group member who possesses diffuse status characteristics of lower overall evaluation. Specific status characteristics refer to characteristics that can either be directly relevant to the task, or can even be a "general performance characteristic" (Freese, 1976), such as reading or math ability. In the case of reading or math ability, the characteristic may not be directly related to the task but the ability, a specific status characteristic, functions much like a diffuse status characteristic in creating high and low status. Specific status characteristics, which are directly relevant to the task, are particularly powerful in that they have a strong effect on the formation of performance expectations.

The process by which status characteristics organize interaction, also known as the burden of proof process (Berger, Fisek, Norman & Zelditch, 1977; Berger, Zelditch, Anderson & Cohen, 1972), is well defined under certain scope conditions. These scope conditions specify task-oriented groups of individuals with no prior history of interaction who are working on a collective task that is meaningful to the group members, all other things being equal (ceteris paribus). If a status characteristic differentiates actors, then it is activated, or noticed. Once activated, the status characteristic becomes relevant to the task. Having become relevant to the task, the status characteristic shapes expectations for the group members – for others as well as for themselves. Once expectations are shaped, group members' behavior is shaped so as to be consistent with the states of the status characteristics. The resulting behavior is manifested in observable power and prestige, whereby high status group members enjoy higher actions rates and opportunities, have greater influence such as in settling disagreements, and receive more compliance by other lower status group members. Thus a status hierarchy is created and maintained by these behavioral differences which originated with initial observed differences.

Expectation states theory is also concerned with the process of legitimation of status hierarchies because it is the legitimacy of power and prestige orders

(Berger et al., 1998) that contributes to the persistence of inequality. Berger et al. (1998) use status characteristics theory to describe how status characteristics and the evaluations and beliefs about characteristics become the basis for observable inequalities in face-to-face interaction (1998, pp. 381, 382). They also use theory of reward expectations to describe how expectations for rewards are formed based on status characteristics and how social objects with reward significance become salient and relevant in the situation. Referential belief structures link valued characteristics with reward levels, and ultimately to valued status positions. They delineate three types of referential belief structures:

(1) *categorical structures* which specify different levels of rewards associated with different diffuse status characteristics (assumes activation of status beliefs in immediate situation);

(2) *ability structures* which specify different rewards levels associated with valued ability characteristics directly relevant to the task (assumes activation of status beliefs unless explicitly prohibited);

(3) *outcome structures* which specify different reward levels associated with actual achievement (assumes activation of beliefs when task accomplishments are evaluated according to agreed upon standards).

The authors describe graphically the status ordering process whereby the referential beliefs link status categories, abilities, and outcomes with valued status positions. They also demonstrate the relative strengths of inequality within a structure, and the relative legitimacy of status structures based on either diffuse or specific status characteristics. The authors assert that it is often assumed that structures which generate greater differentiation in performance expectations generate greater inequality in their power and prestige orders and therefore are more likely to become legitimated (1998, p. 392). However, they argue that this is not necessarily the case. To demonstrate their argument they illustrate these structures using graph theoretic formulations which illustrate the status organizing processes and the relative strengths of status characteristics as they emerge during interaction on a task. In these graph formulations, strength refers to the strength of effect on performance expectations and is measured in terms of path lengths and the number of paths. An effect is considered stronger when path lengths from status characteristics to outcomes are shorter and when there are more paths. The following diagrams are adapted from Berger et al. (1998, p. 393).

Figure 1 depicts a status structure in which two actors p (person) and o (other) are working together on a task (T). The central issue is how can each actor make decisions about who should be given the most influence? If both actors knew exactly who was better at the task than the other, such decisions would be relatively

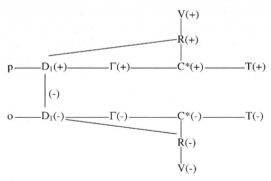

Fig. 1. Diffuse Status Structure.

simple. Such an instance would mean that both actors knew C*, the ability directly associated with task success, T(+). However, actors often do not have such information and instead must make inferences about C* (ability) based on other characteristics. Figure 1 demonstrates the instance where the actors do not have direct information about C*, but they do have information about diffuse status characteristics, D. Figure 1 depicts actor p having a high state of the diffuse status characteristic (for example this actor is a male), and actor o has a low state of the diffuse status characteristic (for example this actor is a female). Associated with these diffuse status characteristics are general expectations that have at least two states and are symbolized as Γ (+ or −). The actors then use *this* information, and from this information make *inferences* about C* (ability). The inferences they make about C* are also associated with a state that is similarly evaluated to the diffuse status characteristic, D. Once the actors have the information about the ability required for task success, they form performance expectations for themselves and for one another. In this instance, actor p (perhaps a male) who has a high state of the diffuse status characteristic (D), is also inferred to have a high state of the ability (C*). The other actor, actor o, has the low state of the diffuse status characteristics and is therefore believed to have a low state of the ability. Both actors now have the information they need to make decisions about who should have the most influence in this task oriented interaction – actor p. Actor p is then also believed to be more deserving of high states of reward levels (R), and high states of valued status positions (P). Thus, a power and prestige order for actors p and o has been formed.

In this status structure, the referential belief structures operate with respect to D, referencing categorical beliefs, and C*, referencing ability beliefs. The referential belief structures specify the rules, norms and beliefs about the different states of D and C* in terms of what actors who possess those characteristics deserve.

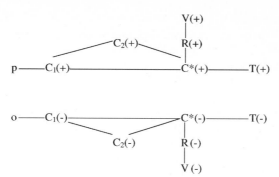

Fig. 2. Specific Status Structure.

However, categorical structures associate reward levels with status characteristics that are based on broad social categories, and while these beliefs are activated in the immediate task situation, they exist outside of the context of the group. Ability structures on the other hand, associate reward levels with status characteristics that are directly relevant to the immediate task situation (Berger et al., 1998). The graph diagram of this structure illustrates how a diffuse status characteristic (D_1), which is *not* initially relevant to the task, is directly linked to reward levels (R) which results in a shorter path to valued status positions (V).

Figure 2 depicts a status structure in which two actors p (person) and o (other) are once again working together on a task (T). In this case, the actors have more information about task ability than did the actors in the previous structure. These actors, p and o, have information about two specific status characteristics which relate to specific abilities, C_1 and C_2. These status characteristics also have either high or low states. The actors use this information to make decisions about which of them have greater ability (C^*) with respect to task success (T). The specific status characteristics in this instance may be directly relevant to the task, such as having previous training on the task, or may be a more general ability such as mathematical ability. Once the actors have the information about the ability required for task success, they form performance expectations for themselves and for one another. In this instance, actor p who has a high state of both of the specific status characteristic (C_1 and C_2), is also inferred to have a high state of the ability (C^*). Actor p has a high state on both specific status characteristics, whereas actor o has low states. Once again, actor p will have the most influence, and actor p is also believed to be more deserving of high states of reward levels (R), and high states of valued status positions (P).

While the actors in this status structure are also making inferences about C^*, it is important to note that they do not have to look beyond the context of the interaction for information to make this decision. In this structure the referential belief structure is activated but only in terms of ability belief structures. Categorical belief structures are not activated in the specific status structure as they are in diffuse status structures.

The path lengths in this structure which connect the specific status characteristics, C_1 and C_2, to task outcomes (T) are shorter than in the diffuse structure making the strength of performance expectations greater. Therefore inequality of power and prestige will be greater in the specific status structure or groups characterized by this kind of structure. While there is greater inequality in the specific status structure, it is not the case that this structure is more likely to become legitimated than the diffuse status structure. There are three reasons for this. First, diffuse status characteristics activate two kinds of referential belief structures: categorical structures and ability structures. Therefore there is a layering effect of referential structures. Second, the direct link (relevance) from the diffuse status characteristic to reward levels results in a shorter path length to valued status positions. Third, the diffuse status structure also has more paths from the status characteristic to valued status positions than does the specific status structure. Shorter paths and more paths have a stronger effect on performance expectations. Therefore, while the specific status structure may result in greater inequality in a specific group, the diffuse status structure is more likely to be legitimated and is therefore more stable over many different groups.

Formal Representation of Legitimation

Based upon the above literature, we now offer some formal definitions related to legitimation as well as a graphic theoretic representation.

Social actors engaged in goal oriented interaction mediate the process of legitimation by creating power and prestige structures at the local level by accessing referential belief structures at the cultural level which specify rules and norms regarding valued status characteristics (Berger et al., 1998). Legitimation is multi-object, multi-level, and multi-source (Bell, Walker & Willer, 2000; Berger et al., 1998; Dornbusch & Scott, 1975; Zelditch & Walker, 1984). Social objects can be persons, positions and acts and can also include systems of positions and hierarchical structures (Berger et al., 1998; Scott, 1995; Walker, Thomas & Zelditch, 1986). Legitimation occurs at multiple levels such as individual, group, organizational, and even societal/cultural levels. Sources of legitimation can be conceptualized as representing the different levels such as propriety (individual), endorsement (group) and authorization (organizational) (Berger et al., 1998; Dornbusch & Scott, 1975; Zelditch & Walker, 1984). This theory considers three sources of legitimation that represent the group level, organizational level and a broader cultural level, that is, referential belief structures (Berger et al., 1998).

Definition 1. *Endorsement* refers to group consensus where consensus is defined as a majority of group members supporting a particular individual or group structure.

This definition derives from Dornbusch and Scott's (1975) discussion of sources of legitimation.

Definition 2. *Authorization* refers to approval or support of a particular individual or group structure from a higher position, a superordinate within an organizational hierarchy.

This definition also derives from Dornbusch and Scott's (1975) discussion of sources of legitimation. Authorization as a source of legitimation is external to the group, initially, but may become endorsed as well if group members support the authority through consensus.

Definition 3. *Referential structures* are "sets of socially validated beliefs" and consist of:

- Valued status characteristics;
- Performance and reward expectations that are consistently evaluated with the status characteristics (from Berger et al., 1998).

Assumption 1. The three sources of legitimation are cumulative; combining sources of legitimation, that is the various levels of legitimation, results in greater legitimation of, or social support for, a social object.

In other words, it is certainly possible for sources of legitimation to conflict. For example, although the organization might support a particular person as a leader, the members of the group might not endorse the person. Assumption 1 simply states that when more sources support a particular person or group structure, that object is viewed as more legitimate than when there are fewer sources of support.

Derivation 1. When these three sources of legitimation are consistent, legitimation is at its greatest strength.

Berger et al. (1998) argue that consistency in status characteristics and performance expectations lead to legitimated power and prestige orders (PPOs). Therefore, when this argument is applied to Assumption 1, sources of legitimation are cumulative, and extrapolated to sources of legitimation, legitimation of the social object in question increases when sources of legitimation are consistent.

Derivation 2. The more extensive the graph connections and the shorter the lengths of the paths, the stronger the legitimation.

From Webster and Hysom (1998) and Berger et al. (1998), we combine the definition of "strength" and status structures more likely to be legitimated based on strength. Structures with shorter paths to valued status positions, or structures with more possible connections to valued status positions or task outcomes are more likely to be legitimated.

Derivation 3. From lesser strength to greater strength, the ordering of the sources of legitimation is: endorsement, authorization, and referential structure (ceteris paribus).

To illustrate how the strength of the sources of legitimation might be depicted graphically, we illustrate endorsed and authorized structures below. To describe the graphs, we need to choose a particular type of characteristic that could be (or could not be) endorsed, authorized or exist within a referential structure. While there are several such characteristics, we choose to demonstrate how *expertise* might function within these contexts. Expertise is particularly important to task groups and it is generally assumed that people who have expertise "should" be those that have leadership roles. Indeed this "should" component is one important aspect of a referential structure.

In this structure shown in Fig. 3, one group member has a specific status characteristic of expertise that is directly relevant to the task. So, for example, perhaps one member has had training on the particular procedure for approaching and solving typology problems and the group is faced with solving such problems. Group members form performance expectations for this person, and for

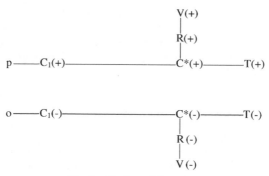

Fig. 3. Endorsed Structure.

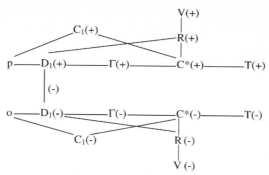

Fig. 4. Authorized Structure.

themselves, which are consistent with the referential belief structure for abilities only. Categorical structures are not activated. Thus, the ability and associated beliefs are only relevant to this specific group. Graphically this is depicted by only one possible path to valued status characteristics. This path connects the specific status characteristic (C_1) to the valued status characteristic but only indirectly through reward expectations (R) via the ability structure (C^*).

In the structure shown in Fig. 4, one group member is given a specific status characteristic of expertise that is related to the group task. In this case, authorization is given for this individual, p, to be the group leader. An example may be that the person trained in topology is appointed as the group leader by the research and development organization. This makes expertise a diffuse status characteristic as well as a specific status characteristic since the referential belief structure, specifically the categorical belief structure, has been activated and brought in from *outside* of the group. Therefore, expertise is no longer only an ability relevant to the group and the task at hand, but has resulted in an esteemed position. The effect is that of superimposing diffuse and specific status structures. Therefore, in addition to the path to the valued status characteristic represented in the endorsed structure above, an additional "shorter" path to the valued status characteristic (V) is now present since the diffuse status characteristic (D) is more directly connected to (V). The result is shorter paths to valued status positions, and *many* more paths than either structure alone would yield. Thus, authorized structures are more likely to be legitimated than endorsed structures.

Referential Belief Structure

The previous two structures are specific to task oriented groups. This structure consists of belief sets linking valued status characteristics and reward levels.

Many such group structures, interacting over time, support and reaffirm referential beliefs which consist of categorical, ability and outcome beliefs. The aggregate effect, that is consistent and comprehensive structures,[1] is a stronger source of legitimation than either of the two individual structures describing endorsement and authorization.

Examples of referential belief structures might include: Men should earn more for the same job than women; leaders should have expertise and should be accorded power and prestige, or a professor should be accorded high prestige but low monetary rewards.

Derivation 4. When the referential structure, authorization and endorsement all enforce a hierarchy, the group structure will be more hierarchical and will be more likely to remain stable (unchanging) over time.

Derivation 4 results from combining Derivation 1, Derivation 2, and the burden of proof process.

ROUTINES

The development and use of routines in the decision-making process of individuals, groups and organizations is a well accepted yet taken for granted phenomenon. Routines range in complexity yet even the most simple of routines allow us to function efficiently. Consider tasks that must be completed by several individuals working in a group where individual actions must be coordinated and where environmental complexity and uncertainty must be managed. Such work groups could be surgical teams, cockpit crews, research and development teams, and committees, such as Institutional Review Boards (IRBs).

Organizations are also decision-making arenas in which routines are developed and used. March and Simon (1958) who are prominent in the area of decision making theory assert that "most behavior, and particularly most behavior in organizations, is governed by performance programs" (1958, p. 142), or routines. According to organizational decision-making theory, human beings are not rational decision makers as classical economic theory assumes. There are cognitive limits to rationality and therefore people can only be at best, "intendedly" rational. Therefore, instead of searching for optimal solutions to problems, people must make decisions according to a pre-defined standard that is considered satisfactory, although less than optimal. Cognitive limits on rationality are not necessarily just a physiological impediment. An organizational environment can also impose limits or boundaries to the decision-making process through what March and Simon call "premise controls" (1958). The assumptions of decision-making theory also suggest that people have imperfect information with respect to their own preferences, alternatives and outcomes. The combination of these limitations creates the requirement for a cognitive and behavioral short cut in decision-making. Thus, the use of routines becomes central to decision making at the individual, group and organizational level because their use is so pervasive, and therefore so are problems related to the inappropriate use of routines.

The definition of routine varies tremendously in a literature that spans many disciplines. Despite the variance in definitions of routines, there are some assumptions that underlie these definitions and they are constant. March and Simon (1958) describe the process of decision-making as a continuum where at one end of the continuum decision-making is completely routinized, and at the other end it is quite effortful. Routinization as an activity is a response to an environmental stimulus "that has been developed and learned at some previous time as an appropriate response for a stimulus of this class . . . a stimulus calls forth a performance program almost instantaneously" (1958, p. 139). At the end of the continuum just described, decision-making is relatively effortless – an activity well suited for a cognitively, rationally limited decision maker, again because the decision maker is searching for a satisfactory solution, not an optimal one (1958, p. 141). The search process for the appropriate routine considering a given environmental stimulus, may itself be a routine. Therefore, just as decision rules in general can be nested (March, 1994), routines can also have a nested structure of routines and subroutines and have great range in complexity (Levitt & March, 1988; Stinchcombe, 1990).

Cyert and March (1963) develop a theory in which their unit of analysis is the firm and they suggest that challenges to rationality also apply to firms. They theorize that firms form "decision strategies" or "rules" (1963, p. 20), and once these rules or decision strategies are developed the firm becomes "an information-processing and decision-making system" (1963, p. 20). According to these authors, decision-making always involves search, which is problem-directed, motivated, simple-minded, and biased by environmental cues, such as premise controls which function to define the situation (March & Simon, 1958). The search process will generally involve looking for a "symptom rule" (Cyert & March, 1963, p. 121), that is a solution which is similar or close to one which has already been used effectively.

Gersick and Hackman (1990) present a theoretical framework for understanding how groups, like individuals, develop and use routines. They explore the functional and dysfunctional consequences of habitual routine use in groups, examine how groups develop and maintain habits over time and changing circumstances, and discuss the circumstances under which groups will change routines. The definition of routines that these authors present is that "a habitual routine exists when a group repeatedly exhibits a functionally similar pattern of behavior in a given stimulus situation without explicitly selecting it over alternative ways of behaving" (1990, p. 69). This definition shares some common features with the definition given by March and Simon (1958). They both refer to a repeated pattern that has been learned and is therefore an outcome of history and experience. Both authors suggest that the selection of a routine does not necessarily involve a conscious search process. Most importantly, both sets of authors refer to an environmental stimulus, a stimulus that calls forth an almost instantaneous solution requiring little cognitive effort. March and Simon (1958) as well as Gersick and Hackman (1990) suggest flexibility in routines ("performance strategies"), whereby individuals and groups can change routines given the right environmental cues.

Cohen and Bacdayan (1994) also emphasize the accepted assumption of the pervasive use of routines in organizations, and stress the importance of routines in organizations in terms of the efficiency they offer. Routines allow organizational skills, experience and knowledge to be stored in such as way that they can be recalled and used in new situations (1994, p. 555). Again, the emphasis on patterns (stored forms of skills and knowledge) and rapid transfer suggests limited cognitive effort. They formally define organizational routines as "interlocking, reciprocally-triggered sequences of skilled actions" (1994, p. 554) and also add that organizational routines are "patterned sequences of learned behavior involving multiple actors who are linked by relations of communication and/or authority" (1994, p. 555). Their definition once again implies dependence on environmental cues for activation of the routine. Individuals within organizations possess *procedural memory*, in which resides skills and habits belonging exclusively to the individual. Organizational members then share parts of this memory, resulting in organizational routines, thus making the routines interlocking and reciprocally triggered where one person's actions is dependent upon that of another. Organizational routines "emerge from the interaction of procedurally remembering individuals" (1994, p. 555) and come to "reside partially in an 'organizational unconscious' " (1994, p. 556). This idea can also be extended to groups within an organization, where one group's actions trigger actions (routines) of another group. The authors test the procedural nature of routines experimentally by creating an organizational context in which there is uncertainty and test *procedural memory* by measuring reliability, speed of formation, repeated action sequences, and occasional suboptimality, and found evidence of all four components.

Levitt and March (1988) use the term routine more loosely and state that "routine" includes a host of concepts, concrete and abstract. Because they discuss routines in the context of organizational learning they focus more on the function of routines, rather than the structure, and employ a more fluid definition of routines. They describe the majority of behavior in organizations as routine and organizational actions as "history dependent." They state that in organizations, "action stems from a logic of appropriateness or legitimacy more than from a logic of consequentiality or intention" and that "routines are based on interpretations of the past more than anticipations of the future" (1988, p. 320). Heimer (1988) focuses less on what a routine is or how it develops, but rather why and when routines are useful. She places heavy emphasis on the implicit efficiency goal of routines and states that routines reward people for "distributing their attention" in certain ways, and punish them for paying attention in undesirable ways (1988, pp. 512–514). Her emphasis on distribution of attention addresses the decision makers' limitations to cognitive rationality, which is similar to March and Simon's (1958) argument. Attention is a scarce resource and therefore focusing on one thing means that attention may be diverted from another. For this reason, there are environments in which routines are inadequate (1988, p. 514) or inappropriate for certain tasks. Heimer gives as an example of such an environment that Perrow (1986) calls a complexly interactive or a tightly coupled system. This means that there are two or more potential and often unplanned interactions that are not linear in nature. This type of a system does not allow for self-correcting responses in the event of a failure (Perrow, 1986, pp. 147–151). A perfect example, according to Perrow's analytic constructs is a space mission, such as those flown at NASA. However, we know from the space shuttle *Challenger* tragedy that even in complexly interactive and tightly coupled environments routines are commonly invoked (Vaughan, 1996). According to Vaughn, with regard to the *Challenger* disaster, ". . . its origins were in routine and taken-for-granted aspects of organizational life that created a way of seeing that was simultaneously a way of not seeing" (Vaughan, 1996, p. 394). We have seen other similar "accidents" due to the failure of routines in complexly interactive environments, such as the Air Florida Flight 90 crash into the Potomac. Thus it seems clear that routines *are* used even in complex environments.

Definitions of routines vary on many dimensions: individual vs. collective focus; structure vs. function (Morgeson & Hofmann, 1999); and cognitive vs. behavioral. Definitions that emphasize individual cognitive processes tend to ignore or at least underestimate environmental influences. Environmental factors such as uncertainty and complexity constrain and enable cognitive processes. Definitions that focus on group or organizational routines consider environmental influences, but also suggest emergent properties such as higher level decision rules (March, 1994), or what Gersick and Hackman (1990) call "meta-norms." In terms of the function of routines, some definitions suggest that routines are cognitive shortcuts which are efficient for individuals as well as organizations. Others, such as Scott (1995) suggest that routines are carriers of institutions, thereby implying that routines are carriers of legitimated social structures.

The concept of ritual is frequently used synonymously with routine. Sell, Knottnerus, Ellison and Mundt (2000) experimentally tested Knottnerus' (1997) theory of structural ritualization using aspects of expectations states theory. According to Knottnerus (1997) the "theory of structural ritualization emphasizes the importance of embedded groups or groups that are nested or located within a more encompassing collectivity" which makes a comparison of rituals to routines appropriate. Sell et al. (2000) investigated newly formed groups since procedures and rituals are missing initially. The researchers combined the theory of structural ritualization and expectation states theory to test whether or not ritualized social practices ("RSPs"), or "schema driven action repertoires" (Knottnerus, 1997), which are present in status hierarchies can be created in new groups. They found that by mere observation of groups by one person randomly designated as the leader could result in the leader and his group reproducing the RSPs and status structure. This observation did not involve explicit punishment or reinforcement of the particular status-linked behaviors; As this is the case, the importance of the four components of the "strength" of RSPs is emphasized: similarity among the RSPs (homologousness), repetition of the RSPs, salience or centrality of the RSPs, and the number and types of resources used to produce the SPS.

If we consider Scott's (1995) assertion that routines are carriers of institutions, then we see that routines and rituals begin to converge in terms of their potential for recreating social structure through social interaction (Giddens, 1984). Scott (1995) defines routines as "carriers [of institutions] that rely on patterned actions that reflect the tacit knowledge of actor – deeply engrained habits and procedures based on inarticulated knowledge and beliefs" (1995, p. 54). As an institutional theorist, Scott tends to overlook the importance of the social actor in recreating social structure. However, this definition combined with Knottnerus' (1997) definition of ritual, and the behavioral aspects of previous conceptualizations allows for the specification of a behavioral definition of routines which will be used in this theory. The crucial components of a definition of routines describe both their structure and function in routine group decision-making. Therefore group routines are sequential decision structures which two or more individuals in a group use to engage in patterned and repeated behaviors which are cued by both external stimuli, as well as one another, in order to solve a problem.

Formal Definition of Routines

The definition of routines consists of elements taken from the previous discussion of routines.

Definition 4. A group routine is a structure characterized by:

- The actions of at least two group members;
- A focus on problem solving;
- Repeated opportunities for interactions;
- Sequential sets of decisions and procedures within groups.

Routines are cued or activated by stimuli external to the routine itself. These cues can be interaction or environmentally based. So, for example, routines might be prompted by group members requesting a particular routine (such as schools promoting a particular procedure for beginning each school day) or by an "asocial" stimulus, such as an environmental event like fire alarm.

RELATING ROUTINES, LEGITIMACY AND TASK STRUCTURE

Using the definitions and derivations already developed, we can now relate routine, legitimacy and task structure.

Derivation 5. Group routines are more likely to form under hierarchical than non-hierarchical structures.

In groups that have assigned a leader (however such an assignment occurs), that leader is immediately given more power than are the other group members. According to expectation states theory, this results in the rapid formation of a PPO, a status hierarchy within the group, which will be reenacted in a self-fulfilling manner. The PPO is reenacted passively because it is not challenged, nor are the activities or procedures of the group. Therefore, the group is likely to develop problem solving routines based on what they already know, or more specifically, what the leader already knows. Furthermore, other members of the group are less likely to challenge established activities. Thus, Derivation 5 results from combining expectation states theory, resultant group structures as determined by PPO, the definition of routines, and Derivation 4.

Derivation 6. Group routines are more stable (less likely to change) over time under hierarchical conditions than under non-hierarchical conditions.

A basic assumption of Berger et al. (1998) is that performance expectations are congruent with valued status positions, and there is greater differentiation on valued status positions. Consequently, there is a greater likelihood of the resulting PPO becoming legitimated (1998, p. 386). The legitimated PPO refers to the hierarchy that is supported at different points in time. Therefore, when combined with Derivation 5,

Derivation 7. Given that a hierarchy is legitimated referentially, through authorization, and through endorsement, groups will form more routines that remain stable.

Derivation 7 results from combining Derivations 4, 5 and 6. Such a setting can occur, for example, when it is generally understood (i.e. the referential structure supports) that expertise provides someone leadership status; further the organization in which the interaction occurs supports the expert as a leader, and; the group members support the expert as the leader of their group.

Under some conditions, the referential structure can be overridden:

Derivation 8. If the authority structure and the endorsement structure are consistent and opposed to the referential structure, the effects of the referential structure will be weakened.

From the graph theoretic formulation of endorsement and authorization, the effects on the PPO are weakened when inconsistent status characteristics are introduced for the same actor. The result is to dilute the strength of the referential structure. Given the illustration of a leader, this derivation suggests even if there is a norm of expertise providing leadership position, the leader does not possess the same amount of power if she or he does not have the support of others in the group and if the organization does not support the expertise criterion.

Derivation 9. If the referential belief structure is weakened, then the hierarchy becomes less stable.

Derivation 9 results from combining the corollary of Derivation 4, and basic assumptions of delegitimation (Berger et al., 1998). This assumption states that when performance expectations become incongruent with the originally legitimated order, the likelihood of delegitimation of the PPO increases (1998, p. 388).

Derivation 10. If the hierarchy becomes less stable, then routines become less stable.

Derivation 10 is a corollary of Derivations 6 and 9.

There are several scope conditions that would be important for further specifying the conditions under which these derivations would apply and could be tested. Many of these conditions are held in common with expectation states theories because our formulations depend on them. For all the sources of legitimation, the groups that are in consideration have no prior interaction, and are engaged in a collective task. The members of this group are task-oriented, caring about the outcomes. Further, there is the expectation that there will be multiple interactions within this group.

SUMMARY AND CONCLUSIONS

This chapter develops a theory to explain how different sources of legitimation make groups more or less hierarchical, and group routines more or less flexible. The formal theory specifies assumptions that sources of legitimation are additive, and derives an ordering of the relative strengths of the sources being tested. Three sources of legitimation – a referential belief structure about expertise, authorization, and endorsement – are discussed.

Berger et al. (1998) describe diffuse and specific status structures and how legitimacy for these structures are created and maintained. Specifically, they argue that specific status structures may demonstrate greater inequality, and are thus more hierarchical, but this does not necessarily mean that these structures are more likely to be legitimated, or have stability. Rather, diffuse status structures are more likely to become legitimated and therefore become more stable. Recall that diffuse status characteristics activate two types of referential structures (categorical and ability), have shorter paths to valued status positions, and have more paths to valued status positions. This theoretical formulation extends the graph theoretical formulations for specific and diffuse status structures to describe endorsed and authorized structures, and even the referential structure. Recall also that endorsed structures resemble specific status structures where one specific status characteristic is present, and authorized structures reflect a layering of specific and diffuse status structures. The referential structure is represented by many authorized and endorsed structures interacting over time. Thus, the referential structure subsumes both authorized and endorsed structures. However, it may be the case that much like specific status structures, endorsed structures are also less stable than authorized structures. This formulation enables separating these concepts and testing their relative effects.

The formal theory presented can address theoretical questions about the relationship between sources of legitimation, group structure, and group routines. The multi-level formulation that incorporates a referential belief structure, and two collective sources of legitimacy, reflects typical organizational settings. The definition of routines used in the theory helps illustrate the degree to which organizational routines can vary and therefore the development of what may seem like innocuous interaction patterns can persist across related "routine" activities.

As it has been suggested, nothing is as practical as a theory. Theories pinpoint the most relevant factors affecting the phenomena under investigation. We believe that this formulation has the potential to serve in application. If the derivations are supported through empirical tests, they will provide guidelines for organizations concerned with the paradox of establishing routines that are efficient for the group's objective but not so inflexible that changing environments cannot be accommodated.

NOTE

1. According to Berger et al. (1998) status characteristics consistent with performance expectations and valued status positions are more likely to result in legitimated PPOs (1998, p. 391), and that adding additional consistent status characteristics ("comprehensiveness") increases the probability of the PPO becoming legitimated (1998, p. 392).

ACKNOWLEDGMENTS

This research was supported, in part, by NSF# SES 0101260. We are indebted to Joseph Berger, Zeng-yin Chen, David Hofmann, Harland Prechel, Charles Samuelson and Morris Zelditch, Jr. for their comments on related papers.

REFERENCES

Bell, R., Walker, A., & Willer, D. (2000). Power, influence, and legitimacy in organizations: Implications of three theoretical research programs. *Research in the Sociology of Organizations, 17*, 131–177.

Berger, J., Cohen, B. P., & Zelditch, M., Jr. (1966). Status characteristics and expectations states. In: J. Berger, M. Zelditch Jr. & B. Anderson (Eds), *Sociological Theories in Progress* (Vol. 1, pp. 22–46). New York: Houghton Mifflin.

Berger, J., Fisek, M. H., Norman, R. Z., & Zelditch, M., Jr. (1977). *Status characteristics and social interaction: An expectation states approach.* New York: Elsevier Scientific.

Berger, J., Ridgeway, C., Fisek, M. H., & Norman, R. Z. (1998). The legitimation and delegitimation of power and prestige orders. *American Sociological Review, 63*, 379–405.

Berger, J., Zelditch, M., Jr., Anderson, B., & Cohen, B. P. (1972). Structural aspects of distributive justice, a status value formulation. In: J. Berger, M. Zelditch Jr. & B. Anderson (Eds), *Sociological Theories in Progress* (Vol. II, pp. 119–146). New York: Houghton Mifflin.

Berger, P. L., & Luckmann, T. (1967). *The social construction of reality.* New York: Doubleday.

Cohen, M. D., & Bacdayan, P. (1994). Organizational routines are stored as procedural memory: Evidence from a laboratory study. *Organizational Science, 5*(4), 554–567.

Cyert, R. M., & March, J. G. (1963). *A behavioral theory of the firm.* Englewood Cliffs, NJ: Prentice-Hall.

DiMaggio, P. J., & Powell, W. W. (1983). The iron cage revisited: Institutional isomorphism and collective rationality in organizational fields. *American Sociological Review, 48*, 147–160.

Dornbusch, S., & Scott, W. R. (1975). *Evaluation and the exercise of authority.* San Francisco, CA: Jossey-Bass.

Evan, W. M., & Zelditch, M., Jr. (1961). A laboratory experiment on bureaucratic authority. *American Sociological Review, 26*(6), 883–893.

Finlay, B. (2002). The origins of charisma as process: A case study of Hildegard of Bingen. *Symbolic Interaction, 25*(4), 537–554.

Freese, L. (1976). The generalization of specific performance expectations. *Sociometry, 39*(3), 194–200.

Gersick, C. J., & Hackman, J. R. (1990). Habitual routines in task-performing groups. *Organizational Behavior and Human Decision Processes, 47*, 65–97.

Giddens, A. (1984). *The constitution of society: Outline of the theory of structuration.* Berkeley, CA: University of California Press.

Heimer, C. A. (1988). Social structure, psychology, and the estimation of risk. *American Sociological Review, 14*, 491–519.

Hirsch, P. M. (1997). Sociology without social structure: Neoinstitutional theory meets brave new world. *American Journal of Sociology, 102*(6), 1702–1723.

Janis, I. L. (1982). *Groupthink: Psychological studies of policy decision and fiascos.* New York: Houghton Mifflin.

Janis, I. L. (1989). *Crucial decisions: Leadership in policy making and crisis management.* New York: Free Press.

Knottnerus, J. D. (1997). The theory of structural ritualization. *Advances in Group Processes, 14*, 257–279.

Levitt, B., & March, J. G. (1988). Organizational learning. *Annual Review of Sociology, 14*, 319–340.

March, J. (1994). *A primer on decision making: How decisions happen.* New York: Free Press.

March, J. G., & Simon, H. A. (1958). *Organizations.* New York: Wiley.

Martin, M. W., & Sell, J. (1986). Rejection of authority: The importance of type of distribution rule and extent of benefit. *Social Science Quarterly, 67*(4), 855–868.

Meyer, J. W., & Rowan, B. (1977). Institutionalized organizations: Formal structure as myth and ceremony. *American Journal of Sociology, 83*, 340–363.

Morgeson, F. P., & Hofmann, D. A. (1999). The structure and function of collective constructs: Implications for mulitlevel research and theory development. *Academy of Management Review, 24*(2), 249–265.

Perrow, C. (1986). *Complex organizations: A critical essay.* New York: Random House.

Prechel, H. (2000). *Big business and the state: Historical transitions and corporate transformation in the United States, 1880–1990s.* New York: State University of New York Press.

Read, P. B. (1974). Sources of authority and the legitimation of leadership in small groups. *Sociometry, 37*(2), 189–204.

Scott, W. R. (1995). *Institutions and organizations.* Thousand Oaks, CA: Sage.

Sell, J., Knottnerus, J. D., Ellison, C., & Mundt, H. (2000). Reproducing social structure in task groups: The role of structural ritualization. *Social Forces, 79*(2), 453–475.

Sell, J., Lovaglia, M. J., Mannix, E. A., Samuelson, C. D., & Wilson, R. K. (2004). Investigating conflict, power and status within and between groups. *Small Group Research, 35*(1), 44–72.

Sell, J., & Martin, M. W. (1983). The effects of group benefits and type of distribution rule on noncompliance to legitimate authority. *Social Forces, 61*(4), 1168–1185.

Stinchcombe, A. (1990). *Information and organizations.* Berkeley, CA: University of California Press.

Stinchcombe, A. (1997). On the virtues of the old institutionalism. *Annual Review of Sociology, 23*, 1–18.

Thomas, G. M., Walker, H. A., & Zelditch, M., Jr. (1986). Legitimacy and collective action. *Social Forces, 65*, 378–404.

Vaughan, D. (1996). *The challenger launch decision: Risky technology, culture, and deviance at NASA*. Chicago: Chicago Press.

Walker, H. A., Thomas, G. M., & Zelditch, M., Jr. (1986). Legitimation, endorsement and stability. *Social Forces, 64*(3), 620–643.

Weber, M. ([1924] 1978). *Economy and society, Vol. I and II*. G. Roth & C. Wittich (Eds). Berkeley, CA: University of California Press.

Webster, M., Jr., & Hysom, S. J. (1998). Creating status characteristics. *American Sociological Review, 63*(3), 351–378.

Zelditch, M. J., & Walker, H. A. (1984). Legitimacy and the stability of authority. *Advances in Group Processes, 1*, 1–25.

Zucker, L. G. (1991). Postscript: Microfoundations of institutional thought. In: W. W. Powell & P. J. DiMaggio (Eds), *The New Institutionalism in Organizational Analysis* (pp. 103–106). Chicago: University of Chicago Press.

CULTURAL CAPITAL AS A MULTI-LEVEL CONCEPT: THE CASE OF AN ADVERTISING AGENCY

Anna Rubtsova and Timothy J. Dowd

ABSTRACT

Bourdieu clearly articulates how cultural capital works at the macro-level and how it leads to the reproduction and legitimation of inequality. He is less clear about other levels of analysis. We address this gap by drawing on social psychological theories and by suggesting that cultural capital is best treated as a multi-level concept – with "cultural capital" produced at the macro-level, "subcultural capital" produced at the meso-level, and "multicultural capital" produced at the micro-level. We illustrate with an exploratory analysis of an advertising agency in Eastern Europe, thereby highlighting legitimacy processes occurring among its departments and personnel.

1. INTRODUCTION

What role does culture play in the reproduction and legitimation of inequality? Two prominent literatures confront this question directly. The cultural capital literature details, among other things, the institutional – and ultimately arbitrary – process by which dispositions of the dominant class are tacitly cast as "natural" and "desirable"; this process, in turn, provides this class with a cultural currency that both facilitates and justifies its success from generation to generation. The

Legitimacy Processes in Organizations
Research in the Sociology of Organizations, Volume 22, 117–146
ISSN: 0733-558X/doi:10.1016/S0733-558X(04)22004-3

expectation states literature documents, in part, how notions regarding desirable – and ultimately arbitrary – attributes both emanate from the broader society and emerge from within particular groups; these notions result in interactions that favor and validate individuals with such attributes. A third literature indirectly addresses this question yet is nevertheless relevant. The social representations literature shows how understandings that are demonstrably arbitrary can emerge within particular groups. Despite their complementary foci, these three literatures are rarely considered together. In this article, it is our modest goal to bring them into dialogue, using both social representations and expectation states to address a gap in the cultural capital literature.

The literature on cultural capital focuses on several domains – including those of education (e.g. Roscigno & Ainsworth-Darnell, 1999) and consumption (e.g. Holt, 1998) – and it contains various definitions of its central concept. In their seminal article, for example, Michèle Lamont and Annette Lareau (1988, p. 153) define cultural capital as "high status cultural signals used in cultural and social selection." Underlying this definition is the idea that groups produce and monopolize distinctive cultural goods (e.g. knowledge, practices, preferences). Indeed, much research shows that signals associated with such distinctive goods not only allow mutual recognition and association among elite group members, they also facilitate the exclusion of outsiders (e.g. Bryson, 1996; Lamont, 1992). In other words, cultural capital can be used as a passkey to elite networks and opportunities, perhaps converting itself into economic capital (e.g. Borocz & Southworth, 1996; Carter, 2003).

Paul DiMaggio (1987, 1991) offers a somewhat different conceptualization of cultural capital. He distinguishes between cultural capital at the societal level – defined as "sets of cultural goods and capacities that are widely recognized as prestigious" (DiMaggio, 1991, p. 135) – and cultural capital at the individual level – defined as "proficiency in the consumption of and discourse about generally prestigious – that is, institutionally screened and validated – cultural goods" (DiMaggio, 1991, p. 134). He focuses, then, on both the creation of sets of goods that are universally valorized in the U.S. and on individuals' familiarity with such goods. Regarding the former, DiMaggio (1982b, c, 1991, 1992) shows the organizational processes by which such goods as visual arts, theatrical plays, and classical music were institutionalized as "high culture" in the U.S. by the mid-1900s. Regarding the latter, he demonstrates that mastery of high culture (e.g. knowledge of and participation in the fine arts) is connected to positive outcomes for individuals. Thus, DiMaggio (1982a) shows that possession of cultural capital by U.S. high school students has a positive effect on their grades, and DiMaggio and Mohr (1985, p. 1231) establish positive connections between an individual's cultural capital and her "educational attainment, college attendance, college completion, graduate attendance and marital selection." In the wake of this work, some further explore the institutionalization of high culture (e.g. DeNora, 1995; Dowd et al., 2002), while others examine how mastery of high culture contributes to educational success (e.g. Aschaffenburg & Maas, 1997; DuMais, 2002).

The work of Pierre Bourdieu (e.g. 1984, 1986; Bourdieu & Passeron, 1990) lies at the center of the cultural capital literature. Given the centrality of his oeuvre – as well as its sprawling coverage and complexity – it is not surprising that a number of reviewers (e.g. Brubaker, 1985; DiMaggio, 1979) and critics (e.g. Gartman, 1991; Lieberson, 1992) address (if not challenge) Bourdieu's theory and empirics, while others debate (if not question) the empirical investigations that his theory has inspired (e.g. Holt, 1997; Kingston, 2001). One criticism, in particular, stands out for us: although Bourdieu clearly articulates the mechanisms by which cultural capital contributes to reproduction at the macro-level (e.g. inter-class differences), he is much less clear about these mechanisms at the meso- (e.g. organizational departments) and micro- (e.g. interacting individuals) levels of analysis (e.g. Erickson, 1996; Lahire, 2003; see DiMaggio, 1997). This relative inattention to the meso- and micro-levels may be an issue in the broader cultural capital literature, as well. Lareau and Horvat (1999, p. 38) – who ethnographically focus on the intersection of class, race, family, cultural capital, and education – offer a telling example when they note, "Although the theoretical potential of offering an intricate and dynamic model is embedded in Bourdieu's original conceptual work, the empirical research has often been disappointing. The translation of the theoretical model into 'variables' has often decontextualized key concepts from the broader theoretical mission."

In this article, we hope to reap – in Lareau and Horvat's words – the theoretical potential of Bourdieu. To do so, we draw on two theories in social psychology. Social representations theory addresses the construction of cultural understandings and dispositions. We use this theory to suggest an organizational (meso-level) analog to the cultural capital that Bourdieu identifies with social class (macro-level) – an analog that we label "subcultural capital." Expectation states theory addresses the extent to which interacting individuals invoke certain evaluations and how these evaluations, in turn, influence their status attainment. We use this theory to suggest that interactional contexts vary in the extent to which they promote or hinder activation of both cultural and subcultural capital by individuals (micro-level) – and we label that aggregation of capitals as "multicultural capital." Simply put, we suggest treating cultural capital as a multi-level concept.

We proceed in three broad sections. First, we turn to Bourdieu's treatment of cultural capital, noting the macro-level at which he casts this concept. Second, we extend the concept of cultural capital to the meso- and micro-levels by drawing on, respectively, social representations and expectation states. We use these two theories to develop the notions of "sub-cultural capital" as a cultural currency serving the reproduction of inequality among meso-level social groups (e.g. organizational departments) and "multicultural capital" as a vehicle of individual status attainment. Finally, we illustrate the utility of the multi-leveled concept of cultural capital with empirical material from an advertising agency located in the Commonwealth of Independent States (i.e. former Soviet republics), focusing on subcultural capital and the legitimation of hierarchical relations between two departments.

2. CULTURAL CAPITAL AT THE MACRO-LEVEL

We consider the theory of cultural capital as originally conceived by Bourdieu, and we argue that cultural capital is primarily a macro-level concept concerned with reproduction of social classes and maintenance of capitalist order. To that end, Bourdieu (1986) describes cultural capital as taking three forms: particular cultural objects that purportedly require special abilities to understand (i.e. objectified form), class-based dispositions for understanding such cultural objects (i.e. embodied form), and credentializing systems that legitimate an arbitrary range of cultural objects and dispositions as esteemed (i.e. institutionalized form).

2.1. Bourdieu and Cultural Capital Theory

The theory of cultural capital – as originally developed by Bourdieu – is intricately connected to his theorizing on fields and social classes. According to Bourdieu (1977, 1990), the reproduction of social inequality through accumulation of various types of capital – economic, social, symbolic, and cultural – is possible only within capitalist societies that are *institutionally differentiated* into autonomous fields. Indeed, such differentiation precedes the particular manifestations that both habitus and cultural capital take in a given context.[1]

The notion of institutional differentiation is crucial to Bourdieu's theorizing (e.g. Bourdieu, 1991a, 1993). In treating cultural capital as socially constructed competencies, he draws on Durkheim's idea of society as providing common cognitive categories, or frameworks of thought, for its members. However, following Max Weber, Bourdieu notes the differentiation of capitalist societies into autonomous spheres (i.e. fields) – with the economic sphere becoming institutionally distinct from the social and cultural spheres, and with the cultural sphere itself becoming differentiated into art, science, politics, religion, and so forth. Bourdieu argues that it is each field – rather than society as a whole – that provides its actors with distinctive cognitive categories – those "schemes of perception," thought, appreciation and action that form the habitus (Bourdieu, 1990,

p. 60). In other words, in pre-capitalist societies with "no self-regulating market...no educational system, no juridical apparatus, and no State" (Bourdieu, 1977, p. 183), social actors share similar frameworks of thought, knowledge and ideologies. However, in the institutionally differentiated societies of capitalism, each autonomous field possesses its own "logic"; each field produces distinctive types of legitimate knowledge, practices and goods; and each field inculcates a distinctive habitus in its actors (Bourdieu, 1991a, 2002; see Verter, 2003).

Bourdieu (1991a) connects the notion of fields to a Marxian theory of class domination and social reproduction. He posits that, due to institutional differentiation, class domination cannot be reproduced only within an economic field through the accumulation of economic capital as theorized by Marx. Instead, because each field has its own logic, similar reproduction processes take place within each particular field. In order to maintain their domination, then, the upper class must have superior ability to accumulate knowledge, competencies and goods valued within such fields as education (educational capital), art (artistic capital), politics (political capital), and religion (religious capital). Consequently, Bourdieu speaks of fields as arenas of struggle and contestation, where actors compete for profits of various types – be they profits of economic or cultural capital (see DiMaggio, 1979; Verter, 2003).

The habitus plays a particular role in the class-based struggles that unfold in various fields. To begin with, the habitus itself – "a lasting, generalized and transposable disposition to act in conformity with a (quasi-) systematic view of the world and human existence" (Bourdieu, 1987, p. 126) – is class-based. Bourdieu (1990) argues that a homogeneity of material conditions leads to a homogeneity of habitus; consequently, the habitus is similar within a class and different across classes. Furthermore, and perhaps more importantly, the habitus of the dominant class is best fit for the appropriation of knowledge and practices valued within different fields, as well as for the accumulation of cultural capital.

Bourdieu (1991a, 1993) locates the superiority of the dominant class' habitus in the historical genesis of autonomous fields. A field of human activity (e.g. religion, art) begins to acquire autonomy with the development of a body of coherent theoretical knowledge pertaining exclusively to its activity. However, rationalization of practice and development of systematized knowledge are only possible with the emergence of a substratum from within the upper class – one that is specifically involved in this intellectual labor. The crucial point is that, at the early stages of field development, ideology specialists do not produce new knowledge *ex nihilo*, but rather they externalize and systematize the implicit schemes of appreciation and action of their habitus (Bourdieu, 1991a). Because intellectual labor is a prerogative of the ruling class, it is the ruling class habitus that forms the basis of the autonomous fields: based on their implicit schemes of appreciation and action, the ideology specialists systematize the *arbitrary* representations and practices existing among the elites and consecrate them as *natural*, desirable and objectively given. This is the basis of class reproduction. From the early stages of autonomous fields' genesis, underprivileged classes become "objectively dispossessed" (Bourdieu, 1991a, p. 9) of the schemes of appreciation and action necessary to appropriate knowledge and practices consecrated by the fields, whereas dominant class members emerge as "exclusive holders of the specific competence" to produce and decode rare cultural symbols (Bourdieu, 1991a, p. 9). This unequal distribution of habitus is perpetuated through family socialization and educational system.

For instance, Bourdieu (1968, 1984) argues that the material conditions of the upper class – which is removed from the struggle for survival and the pressure of "necessity" – leads to the ruling class schemes of appreciation for *form* and *style* of art (e.g. art for art's sake) in contrast to the underprivileged class habitus that stresses appreciation for its *function* (e.g. entertainment). Furthermore, through the historical development of the artistic field, art professionals externalized and systematized this upper class habitus, thus constituting art forms concerned with pure style and aesthetics as "high" in contrast to "low" or popular art forms concerned with entertainment. Such a constitution of artistic field, in turn, supports the existing social structure. The distinctive upper class habitus for decoding art is perpetuated through early socialization and rewarded by the education system. This unequal distribution of artistic habitus leads to the unequal accumulation and distribution of artistic capital: the upper class as a whole is best able to accumulate knowledge, competencies and goods valued within the artistic field (artistic capital) and exchange it for economic capital, social prestige (symbolic capital) and connections (social capital), thus supporting and legitimating its social domination. The same is true for upper class individuals and families: individuals can maintain or improve their social position via "reconversion strategies" (Bourdieu, 1984, p. 137), exchanging their cultural capital for economic capital or *vice versa*.

2.2. Implication for the Meso- and Micro-Levels

Bourdieu's theory of cultural capital is primarily a macro-level theory of social order under conditions of modernity. Thus, he mostly conceptualizes cultural capital as *class* cultural capital.[2] To that end, he speaks of cultural capital as involving knowledge, practices, and goods that are consecrated as rare, "high" and desirable; he also speaks of the institutional production and distribution of cultural capital within autonomous cultural fields and how such processes result in the reproduction of class. Bourdieu does acknowledge that individuals and families employ cultural capital at the micro-level, yet he appears less interested in social interaction *per se*. In fact, he invokes the subjective to the extent that it is "objectively defined" (Bourdieu, 1990, p. 135) and remarks that "interaction itself owes its form to the objective structures which have produced the dispositions of the interacting agents and which allot them their relative positions in interaction and elsewhere" (Bourdieu, 1977, p. 81). Nevertheless, Bourdieu's theory does incorporate what Lamont and Lareau (1988) label a "micro-political framework," as cultural capital and its attendant institutions are maintained through practice. We therefore conclude that Bourdieu's theory is potentially a multi-level one. Our goal for the rest of the paper, then, is to extend the cultural capital concept to the meso- and micro-levels.

3. CULTURAL CAPITAL AT THE MESO-LEVEL: "SUBCULTURAL CAPITAL"

We suggest that Bourdieu's cultural capital theory can be extended to analysis of the reproduction of inequality among groups existing at the meso-level (e.g. organizational departments). Two aspects of his theory make this possible. Consider first his argument regarding the relationship between social class and habitus. Through the processes of historical constitution, different classes acquire different "instruments of perception" and "universes of representations" (Bourdieu, 1968, p. 597), which are instilled in class members through family socialization and education. As a result, each class differently perceives, interprets and evaluates the same stimuli (e.g. art works) and environment. Such differences, in turn, contribute to and legitimate the ongoing reproduction of inequality, whereby working class children become working class adults. Consider next his argument regarding institutional differentiation. The production of cultural knowledge under conditions of modernity is not society-wide and unified but is differentiated into specialized domains (i.e. fields), such as religion and art. Due to the historical constitution of the habitus in such fields, members of particular groups have privileged access to "legitimate" cultural knowledge, which they can accumulate and exchange for economic or social capital (e.g. Bourdieu, 1991a, 1993, 2002).

Both of Bourdieu's arguments are preserved and paralleled at the meso-level, we believe, if meso-level groups (e.g. departments) can similarly inculcate homogenous schemes of appreciation and action in their members and if the following scope conditions are fulfilled: (1) a given entity (e.g. organization) possess at least two distinct groups (e.g. departments); (2) the groups are involved in the production of specialized cultural knowledge and practices; (3) the cultural knowledge and practices produced by each group is differentially valued within the larger entity, thereby producing a hierarchy of distinction; and (4) the cultural knowledge and practices produced by the dominant group leads to advantages and resources (e.g. social and economic capital). Still a question remains: can meso-level groups (e.g. departments) – which have historical life-spans shorter than that of social classes, and which are not inextricably intertwined, as are social classes, with family socialization and education – generate their own respective habitus? Social representations theory suggests that they can.

3.1. Social Representations Theory

Social representations theory (SRT) deals with the origins, structure, and functions of collective cognition (Moscovici, 1981, 1988). SRT speaks to certain issues raised by both Durkheim and Bourdieu. In *Elementary Forms of Religious Life*, Durkheim (1995) makes the case for the social bases of cognition. In doing so, he critiques the approach of empiricism, which ". . . posits that perception is physical sensation and is the caused effect of a determinate object or 'stimulus' upon the visual system" (Crossley, 1996, p. 25). In contrast, Durkheim argues that human beings experience reality not as a direct response to empirical stimuli, but they perceive it through socially constructed categories of understanding (e.g. time, space) – as well as through particular communal beliefs, theories and ideologies. Durkheim uses the term "collective representations" to evoke these categories that both express and construct reality.[3] The "first argument" of Bourdieu described in the previous paragraph resonates with Durkheim's work, as it posits that social classes supply basic cognitive categories (schemes of thought, appreciation and action) through which social reality is conceived and perceived.

Social representations theory moves the societal-level concerns of Durkheim and Bourdieu to the interactional level. French scholar Serge Moscovici and colleagues find that, at the latter level, collective cognition is dynamic; it is "always in the making" (Moscovici, 1988, p. 219). They thus delineate between "social representations" – collective cognition circulating at the meso-level – and "collective representations" – collective cognition circulating at the societal level. More specifically, they define social representations as "a set of concepts, statements and explanations originating in daily life in the course of inter-individual communications," thereby creating realities and common sense (Moscovici, 1981, p. 181). Their concept both evokes and diverges from Durkheim's concept of "collective representations" (Moscovici, 1988). In the Durkheimian treatment, collective representations are historically constituted and may last for several generations, and they become instilled in the society members through the educational system. In contrast, social representations entail a "meso-translation" of sorts. When "categories which structure and express the representation are borrowed from a common culture" (Jodelet, 1984, p. 365; cited in Jovchelovitch, 1995, p. 90), they are modified in interaction to express the interests, history, and identity of a particular group. The concept of social representations likewise evokes and diverges from Bourdieu's concept of the habitus. Social representations can provide a "systematic view of the world and human existence" (Bourdieu, 1987, p. 126) – as does the macro-level habitus. However, rather than being "lasting" (Bourdieu, 1987, p. 126) – as is the macro-level habitus – social representations are potentially malleable.

A series of experiments conducted by Moscovici and colleagues offers a compelling demonstration of SRT.[4] They show that a cognitive element which at first blush appears immutable – color perception – can change as the result of social interaction. The majority of experiments proceed in the following sequence. First, subjects undergo a preliminary color vision test. This ensures that subjects do not suffer from defects in color vision, and it also convinces the subjects themselves that their responses are not due to such defects. Second, subjects confront unambiguous stimuli, namely slides projected on a screen that show blue color of varying intensity. Third, the interaction phase ensues, wherein subjects orally offer color assessments. During this phase, confederates (i.e. those who covertly collaborate with experimenters) exercise their influence by orally describing the blue color as "green." Fourth, a discrimination test establishes whether, as a result of the confederate influence, a change in the color perception of naïve subjects occurs. Finally, a post-experiment questionnaire clarifies the cognitive processes accompanying the conversion behavior. This series of experiments establishes that, under influence of a consistent minority, naïve subjects experience blue color as green. Moreover, the change occurs not only in the subjects' verbal response but also entails a lasting and "genuine modification of color perception" (Moscovici & Personnaz, 1980, p. 272). For instance, Moscovici and Personnaz (1980) evaluate change in color perception by applying a color afterimage test. This test makes use of complementary colors that are perceived on a white screen following the removal of a colored slide; the complementary color of blue is yellow-orange and the complementary color of green is red-purple. Subjects that first perceive particular slides as "blue" but then, under minority influence, perceive them as "green" also perceive red-purple afterimage after seeing blue slides. The results of these experiments demonstrate that interaction can transform even the most basic types of cognition. The demonstration of such dynamism and malleability, furthermore, is "all of a piece with his theory of social representations" (Farr, 1987, p. 349).

Other SRT research demonstrates the import of social representations in "real world" contexts that lie beyond the experimental laboratory. Denise Jodelet's (1991) ethnographic study of a rural community in central France offers a notable example. This community contains a visible contingent of the mentally ill, given local services that provide the latter with family care. Jodelet details how villagers form their representations of insanity by taking the unfamiliar scientific concept of "mentally ill" and anchoring it to familiar notions of "loonies" and "tramps." That is, social representations "conventionalize" unfamiliar concepts borrowed from the wider culture and link them to concepts and images already familiar to community members. Once formed, representations define reality for the community. Social representations of madness, for instance, delineate the villagers from the mentally ill, thus simultaneously expressing and constructing the identity and boundary of each group, as well as the relative worth of each. Moreover, these representations prescribe action. Villagers avoid contact, for example, with water "polluted" by the mentally ill, as they believe that mental illness can be contracted via bodily fluids. Such SRT research shows that meso-level groups do not "invent" new cognitive elements, but rather they change and modify the cognitive elements supplied by the macro-level culture to reflect their particular histories and cultural contexts (e.g. Campbell, 1998; Moscovici, 1976). Put another way, these groups construct a meso-level habitus – albeit one that may not be as enduring and transposable as the macro-level habitus identified by Bourdieu.

3.2. Implication for Cultural Capital Theory

Without contradicting cultural capital theory, SRT emphasizes that meso-level groups engage in the constitution of "instruments of perception" – to borrow Bourdieu's terminology – from which flow boundaries and distinction. This meso-level constitution parallels – but remains distinct from – the constitution that Bourdieu identifies on the macro-level. This emphasis of SRT also resonates with certain work in the cultural capital and organizational literatures. First, extant scholarship acknowledges the "non-dominant" competencies that compete with cultural capital (e.g. Kane, 2003; Thornton, 1996). For example, DiMaggio (1987, 1991) distinguishes between "cultural capital" – competencies that are universally validated – and "cultural resources" – those that are validated within particular contexts. Second, other scholarship notes that competencies particular to certain lines of business may compete with – if not matter more than – competencies that are universally validated (e.g. Erickson, 1996; Hallett, 2003). Finally, scholarship on "hybrid" organizations clearly shows that dispositions (i.e. logics) that emanate from and are validated at the societal level can fitfully co-exist with dispositions that are far less universal in appeal (Glynn, 2000; Liddle, 2004).

Given the emphasis of social representations theory – as well as complementary work mentioned above – we propose the concept of *subcultural habitus* –

schemes of thought, appreciation and action instilled by meso-level groups (e.g. organizational departments) in their members. By logical extension, then, we also propose the concept of *subcultural capital* – knowledge, practices, and goods that are consecrated as rare, "high" and desirable by meso-level groups and that play a role in their social reproduction.[5]

4. CULTURAL CAPITAL AT THE MICRO-LEVEL: "MULTICULTURAL CAPITAL"

We suggest that cultural capital may not only be used for the reproduction of macro-level social categories (e.g. class) and meso-level groups (e.g. departments) but also for individual status attainment. While subcultural capital serves similar functions for the meso-level groups as cultural capital does for macro-level categories, cultural and subcultural capitals can also circulate within the same time and social space, and it is their relationship to each other that is of theoretical interest. An important question arises: how does the activation of these capitals occur on the micro-level (e.g. individuals within organizations)? While some work in the cultural capital literature points to the activation of (sub)cultural capital (e.g. Carter, 2003; Lamont, 1992), the literature generally provides little purchase on the issue. The work of Bourdieu is especially silent on this point (Lahire, 2003). Fortunately, a social psychological theory has long grappled with the activation of status among individuals in group settings. Discussion of this theory should be useful in developing a micro-level concept of cultural capital.

4.1. Expectation States Theory

Expectation States Theory (EST) focuses on how status hierarchies develop and stabilize in task groups (Berger & Conner, 1974; Berger et al., 1980; Wagner & Berger, 2002). The literature produced by the Expectation States Research Program connects, on the one hand, the emergence of status orders in collectively-oriented and task-focused groups with, on the other hand, the formation of performance expectations. According to Berger and Conner (1974, p. 87), a performance expectation is a "generalized belief that an actor holds about the capacity of himself or others to contribute to task completion." In essence, such a belief becomes a self-fulfilling prophecy. Individuals who are expected by group members to perform a task well – when compared to other members – will receive more opportunities to perform, accept performance opportunities more often, exert more influence, and receive more positive reactions on their performances (Berger & Conner, 1974). As a result, highly evaluated group members will make more contributions than others to the tasks that face the group. In turn, given that task accomplishment is valued by the group, prominent contributors to such tasks are accorded high status within the group.

Expectations regarding the potential contribution of group members are based on shared cultural beliefs about the worth of members' attributes, possessions and behaviors (e.g. Ridgeway & Berger, 1986). For example, if a group of strangers is assigned the task of solving a mathematical problem – and if the members of this group share a belief that men are better problem-solvers than women – then the men in this group will receive higher performance expectations than the women. "Status characteristics" refer to the particular attributes of actors that are assessed during interaction and "around which evaluations of and beliefs about them come to be organized" (Berger et al., 1980, p. 479). These characteristics are usually supplied by membership in societal status groups and reflect broader beliefs about the worthiness of either particular social categories – such as class, race, sex (i.e. diffuse status characteristics) – or particular knowledge or skills valued by wider society and/or specific status groups (i.e. specific status characteristics) (Ridgeway & Walker, 1995). Status characteristics can be further characterized as external – where value is defined outside and prior to group interaction – and as internal – where value results from a specific interactional context (Cohen & Zhou, 1991). For instance, the ability to solve a mathematical problem using a particular software program may be valued within a context of a given group (internal), whereas notions about men and their mathematical abilities result from beliefs held by the wider society (external). Finally, as the foregoing examples suggest, status characteristics that arise in interaction are mediated through status cues, "indicators, markers or identifiers of the different social statuses people possess" (Berger et al., 1986, p. 1).

Both expectation states theory and cultural capital theory share a similar focus: the reproduction of social inequality through cultural and cognitive mechanisms. Both theories acknowledge that status hierarchies existing in the wider society are translated into group status orders via the shared beliefs of group members. Simply put, the status of individuals in a particular group is a function of those individuals having attributes, cultural goods, knowledge and competencies that are consecrated as desirable by macro-level social institutions and/or by meso-level groups. The EST propositions considered thus far are quite compatible with the theory of cultural capital. However, a notable difference between the two theories does remain: expectations state theory is much more specific about the interactional mechanisms through which cultural goods become translated into group status. In particular, EST explains how macro-structural and situational elements combine to produce group status orders.

Each social actor participating in the interaction has a unique combination of status characteristics supplied by his/her membership in various status groups. Furthermore, each status characteristic that forms this combination is associated with a particular set of beliefs about its worthiness – beliefs that are shared by society as a whole and/or a particular group. However, the EST literature (Berger et al., 1980) notes a crucial point: not every status characteristic becomes activated and assessed during a specific interactional episode. For instance, if a group's task is to solve a math problem, then upper class membership – as expressed through such status cues as knowledge of classical music – may not be relevant. Instead, performance expectations in this case may be formed based on such diffuse status characteristics as gender. In order for a status characteristic to affect expectations, then, it must become *salient* in a particular situation. It does so when it either highlights categorical differences among the actors or when it differentiates among the actors' knowledge or competencies that are relevant to a group task (Ridgeway & Walker, 1995). Thus, at the beginning of interaction, only certain status characteristics become activated. Interaction participants make assessments for self and others of all these salient status characteristics in their relation to task accomplishment. In doing so, the actors combine all the relevant status information (both positive and negative) into aggregated expectation states for self and for others. On the basis of these aggregated expectation states, relative expectations regarding (dis)advantages are formed for self and other group members. Through the cycle of self-fulfilling prophecy, these expectations of (dis)advantages are, in turn, transformed into group status orders during the process of interaction.

4.2. Implication for Cultural Capital Theory

Without contradicting cultural capital theory, expectation states theory supplies a number of important details pertaining to cultural capital at the micro-level. First, EST shows that, at the micro-level of group interaction, high status characteristics are supplied by multiple groups. Sociologists have long realized that the social identity of individuals is not constituted solely by a membership in one group, but is increasingly influenced by *multiple* group memberships; hence, interacting individuals will not act solely as, say, class members (DiMaggio, 1987). Instead, individuals engaged in group interactions assess multiple status characteristics that are signaled through numerous status cues. Second, EST highlights that high status cues are potentially supplied by groups that range from the macro- (e.g. class) to the meso- (e.g. departments) levels. The perceived desirability of various status characteristics can be defined both outside and prior to a specific interaction (external status characteristics) and within a specific interactional context (internal status characteristics). Finally, EST points to the contingent nature of cultural capital at the micro-level. On the one hand, interacting individuals must share the same cultural beliefs in order for status characteristics to become a basis for distinction; on the other hand, characteristics associated with particular group identities are activated only if salient within a given interaction.

In light of these implications, we suggest that cultural capital – when defined as class cultural capital (i.e. competencies shared by the members of the same class) – may not be a useful concept for examining reproduction at the micro-level, as class identities are not always activated in such interactions. As a result, we propose the concept of *multicultural capital* – which we define as the aggregation of cultural and subcultural capitals that are salient in a particular interactional context.[6] The following formula summarizes:

$$\text{Multicultural Capital} = \sum \text{Cultural Capital} + \sum \text{Subcultural Capital}$$

5. EMPIRICAL ILLUSTRATION

The purpose of this section is to illustrate empirically how concepts of subcultural and multicultural capital may be used in business settings. To achieve this purpose, we draw on materials gathered during fieldwork at an advertisement agency – ABC Advertisement[7] – in one of the Commonwealth of Independent States (CIS) from 2000 to 2001 and gathered in a series of semi-structured interviews with agency members in 2002. The fieldwork resulted in extensive notes – as well as supplementary documents concerning organizational history, structure and procedures. The interviews were carried out with five members of ABC's creative department and five members of its account management department. Each interview lasted for about an hour, on average, and was designed to uncover departmental members' social representations about the skills, knowledge, competencies and goods valued within their respective departments, their agency, and the field of advertisement. In addition, each interview collected information about work routines and communication patterns developed between the creative and account management departments, as well as the history of these inter-department relationships. The format of semi-structured interviews was chosen, as it is commonly used in research on social representations (Flick, 1998).

We proceed by empirically describing the case of ABC Advertisement, focusing on two stages in its history. We then discuss theoretical ramifications offered by this case. Two caveats deserve mention before proceeding. First, given the content of the fieldwork and interviews at our disposal, we focus on the meso-level and, to a much lesser degree at the end of this section, the micro-level.[8] Second, the empirical materials that we draw upon represent a pilot study, the results of which cannot be generalized. Our exploratory analysis should not be seen as the definitive statement regarding the operation of subcultural and multicultural capitals in business settings. The latter concern is a task of future research.

5.1. Meso-Level of Analysis: ABC Advertisement – First Stage

ABC Advertisement was founded as an overseas branch of an international advertising agency. Despite its branch status, however, ABC was initially organized as a unit which was locally run, self-directed and self-financed. To be sure, the branch did inherit several international clients from its parent company – clients who extended their operations to the CIS; the branch also inherited from its parent company creative ideas for certain client brands. Nevertheless, ABC had to construct its day-to-day business operations "from scratch."

This task of setting up a new agency was undertaken by a young local professional, who became both ABC's first employee and its General Manager (GM). Being a skillful administrator and having considerable experience in marketing, this GM was nevertheless new to the world of advertisement. To get ABC operational, then, she had to find a team of reliable managers with extensive experience in advertising industry. Given that the parent company positioned itself primarily as a *creative* agency,[9] one of the first key employees hired was a Creative Director (CD), who came from a well-respected international agency and had an impressive collection of creative works in his portfolio. Because the CD was extremely familiar with the operational intricacies of advertising agencies, his particular vision influenced considerably the initial organization of the agency's day-to-day operations. In particular, he defined the nature and character of creative work and the organization of the creative department – with the latter including work procedures with clients, account managers, and other agency personnel.

5.1.1. Definition of Creative Work
Creative work was initially defined as the purview of the creative department rather than the account management department. From the creative staff's point of view, account managers did not have to be imaginative; instead, the latter simply needed to be good project organizers and productive communicators with clients. Given that the creative department had the means to enforce its definitions of reality throughout the agency, account managers seemed to accept this exclusive location of creativity within the creative department, only rarely employing the

term "creativity" in relation to their own work. Most often this term, and its numerous derivatives (e.g. "creators," "procreators"), emerged in the discourse of account managers concerning the creative department – sometimes seriously, sometimes teasingly, or sometimes angrily.

This initial definition of creative work had two implications. On the one hand, the work performed by creative department was defined as "art" dependent on the unique vision, intuition and experience of its senior staff. For instance, an account manager recalled the following incident in her interactions with the creative department:[10]

> Once the client urgently asked me to add some new text to a leaflet that we were working on. We were including some new prizes in our promotion and the leaflet had to incorporate the description of these prizes. I asked the creative department to write the text. However, they had plenty of immediate work and could do this text only the next day. However, my brand manager needed this text the same day, since she had to approve it with her marketing director. What could I do? It was me who was ultimately responsible for the project, and not the creative department. So, I set down and wrote that text myself. It was really simple. In fact, I happen to have exactly the same linguistic education as our copywriter. So, it was easy for me. And the client liked the text and approved it. However, when the creative department learned that I wrote the text, I was in big trouble. They complained to the general manager. They were talking to me about how inappropriately I behaved. Apparently, only they could do the creative work. Only they had the skills.

This definition of creative work as art also found its expression in activity patterns within the creative department. The senior management of the department, for example, secured the right for a flexible schedule, explaining that artistic work was based on inspiration that required settings other than the office. As a result, departmental brainstorming sessions were often held in cafés and restaurants. The downside of such a definition of "art," from the perspective of many account managers, was that creative work was sometimes turned into an end in itself, with creative staff forgetting that the main goal of advertisement is to sell clients' products.

On the other hand, the agency's creative work became defined as a professional activity performed according to objective science (e.g. laws of perspective and composition) and rationally explained as such in interactions with clients and agency personnel. Thus, the presentation of new works by creative department staff usually stressed the technical character of the texts and layouts, and when explaining the use of particular expressions and colors used in ad copy, references to human psychology and mechanisms of human perception were common. For instance, a designer expressed it this way:

> One explains to the client why exactly this color and why it cannot be different. Most often it is due to the fact that the client does not know the technological requirements of this or other production.

This definition of creative work as objective science was also connected to social representations that neither clients nor account managers should meddle in the creative process. One designer expressed it this way:

> Neither accounts, nor brand managers should intrude into these [creative] questions. Of course, this is an unattainable ideal. As everywhere, there is a human factor that is an element of subjectivity. As a result, [a] brand manager says that he does not like this or that color based on some subjective factors, starting with eyesight, or because he did not have enough sleep this morning. And the same can be said about the accounts in the agency.

5.1.2. Work Procedures

The initial definition of creative work was also reflected in the organization of the creative department and in its interaction with the account management department, as well with clients. Because the creative process was defined as the exclusive domain of the creative department, interactions between it and other agency departments were structured to minimize possible intrusions of non-artistic staff into the design and production of advertisement products. An account manager, for instance, recalled the following about the creative department:

> Before, it [the creative department] was as closed as Japan; it just issued a complete product and was ready to take on responsibility for its every single detail . . .

On a practical note, this meant that work-related communication between the creative department and other departments, as well as communication with clients, was carried out almost exclusively through the CD and senior copywriter.

Indeed, ABC was marked by a formalization of procedures. In most advertising agencies, account managers have to write creative and design briefs,[11] so as to request creative jobs (e.g. designing a poster, writing ad copy, developing the concept for a new advertisement campaign). To be sure, agencies differ in the formalization that accompanies such briefs. For instance, formal briefs may be required to order a key job, whereas a request for small changes might be made orally (i.e. informally). However, formalization reigned at ABC. A number of account managers complained that they had to write a separate brief for each and every small job required; they also had to answer all the questions on a given brief, even though some were not pertinent to particular job. Finally, they complained of having to resubmit the same brief repeatedly, as the CD refused to accept a brief completed in an unsatisfactory fashion. This formalized communication process meant that account managers were not allowed to interact directly with the designers working on their projects. Account managers simply submitted their requests for creative jobs (in the forms of briefs) to the Creative Director, and then they received the completed products from the account director. Should creative personnel working directly on the product have any questions for account managers, or *vice versa*, those questions were conveyed exclusively through the CD or senior copywriter. Such communication procedure had yet another consequence. Because the flow of creative jobs to be completed was directed and scheduled by the Creative Director, who defined these jobs as an artistic process, he was generally in a position to negotiate lengthy terms of completion.

5.2. Meso-Level of Analysis: ABC Advertisement – Second Stage

The situation at ABC changed dramatically when the first General Manager left the agency, which was followed by the departure of senior management in the creative department and several designers. The newly-hired GM at ABC had experience working as a Creative Director. Not surprisingly, he also became the head of ABC's creative department. The new GM/CD hired designers and copywriters to replace those who departed, and he created a new position – namely that of a traffic manager – responsible for handling briefs from account managers and for scheduling creative jobs. Amidst these changes, the agency experienced a perceptible shift in power. The account management department was now composed of "old-timers" who had been with the agency from its beginning and had accumulated prestige and reputation within the agency and with clients, while the creative department was staffed by new people who had yet to develop ways of working with each other and with the members of other departments. Moreover, as the CD was simultaneously acting as ABC's GM, he was concerned with both artistic and business aspects of advertising. This shift in power allowed the senior staff of the account management department to assume a dominant position within the agency. In turn, they were able to redefine the nature of creative work, account management work, and working procedures between the departments.

5.2.1. Redefinition of Creative Work

According to account managers interviewed, advertising products *may* be creative, innovative and approximate works of art, but they do not have to be. The main goal of the advertising is to sell clients' products. Thus, ads that are creatively dull, but nevertheless sell products, are fully acceptable. An account manager expressed it this way:

> Of course, creativity is good, but creativity is only good if it sells the product. The purpose of advertising, the purpose of the advertising business is, first of all, to sell the product, and not to show how creative we are, and which cool stuff we can produce. The experience of such companies as Procter & Gamble shows that the less creative is advertising, the more effective it is.

Another account manager noted:

> My favorite advertising, for instance, is the advertising by Procter & Gamble, which is absolutely rational and pragmatic. According to my criteria, advertising must sell. Creative advertising I just like to look at, as I like to look at the [illustrated] journals. That is, I would not like to work for a client, who is interested in the production of super-creative advertising, which will not go further than an advertising festival. That is, for me the main goals are the sales and the pragmatism. I like advertising, which makes big money.

Under old management, creativity was located exclusively in the creative department, while under new management, account managers appropriated the term "creativity" in relation to their own work. Consider this description offered by an account director:

> In advertising, a person should be able to learn quickly. His breadth of knowledge is very important. That is, due to the nature of his work, a person must be in control of many simultaneous things, even in very different spheres, such as project management, finances, creative work, really lots of things . . . In addition, there are many technical things, which a person should be able to do: to write well, to be able to operate with numbers . . . to have a taste for creativity.

Remarkably, such extension of creativity to the account management department was also supported by the new General Manager/Creative Director:

> The account service people certainly should think creatively as well. They should be able to judge creative [work] and make suggestions. If they do not, I don't think they are in the right business.

Some account managers even claimed that they are better able to do certain creative jobs (e.g. copywriting) than the creative staff because have a better grasp of markets and brands:

> Although I am an account manager, but sometimes I write texts, write articles as a copywriter. Why? Because I can do it better than a copywriter. Not only because I have more information, say about the brand, etc., but sometimes also because I feel that I can write better even stylistically. So that the client even asks me: "I want you to write the copy, do write!"

5.2.2. Redefinition of Procedures

Redefinition of the nature of the creative process was accompanied by several changes in the communication patterns and work routines between the creative and account management departments. First, the creative department became more open than it once was, so that account managers could, in certain cases, communicate directly with those creative personnel working on their projects. One account manager reported:

> Our relationships with the creative department have very much changed with the change of the Creative Director. And changed dramatically. That is, if before the creative department was closed as Japan was closed from Europe, then now they are absolutely open.

Another account manager remarked:

> Our General Manager has introduced this. When we have to solve some problem – for instance, regarding some POS [point of sales] materials – and the client has some small comments in this regards, we can directly approach a designer who is working on these POS and negotiate with him his schedule and how quickly he is able to introduce these small changes.

Second, because the jobs performed by the creative department became defined from a more pragmatic and less artistic perspective, it led to a general reduction in the amount of time required to complete a standard creative job. According to an account manager:

> Now the procedure became easier and more appropriate. Because the agency has very much work now. One cannot require a week to create a poster, now that would not work. 2–3 days for the development of all POS materials.

Another account manager expressed a similar thought:

> They [the creative staff] simply do not have time to indulge in some excessive creativity, since the volume of the work required and the deadlines do not allow them to be too distracted by purely artistic reasons.

Finally, in cases of necessity, account managers sometimes have the opportunity to perform some of the creative jobs (e.g. copywriting) themselves. According to one account director:

> Taking into account that the most important [thing] is the result, one has sometimes to sacrifice some bureaucratic procedures. Because it is the account [manager] who is responsible for the end product. Because the client does not see a copywriter, even does not know a copywriter. Therefore [account manager's name] writes now many texts . . . In other words, this is due mainly to our responsibility [for the project].

5.3. Theoretical Ramifications

5.3.1. Subcultural Capital

The case of ABC Advertisement illustrates how subcultural capital can develop and then serve in the reproduction of meso-level groups. When discussing social classes on the macro-level, Bourdieu (1984) argues that different conditions of material existence produce a divergence of habitus among the classes. Drawing on social representations theory (e.g. Jodelet, 1991), we argue that different conditions also led to a divergence of habitus among two departments at ABC Advertisement (i.e. meso-level). Because creative staff and account management staff were involved in very different activities and routines, they developed dissimilar schemes of thought, appreciation, and action. The habitus of those in the creative department – due to previous training and work requirements – emphasized an appreciation for and performance of artistic works – a scheme dealing with shapes, colors, graphics, words, and abstract ideas. In contrast, the habitus of those in the account service department – due to their training and the nature of their work – emphasized an appreciation for and performance of operations with numbers, concrete problems, human relations, and psychology.

As Bourdieu (1991a) notes with regard to the macro-level habitus, we also note at the meso-level: powerful actors can (and do) uphold one subcultural habitus over others. In the first stage of ABC's history, the GM and CD both enforced the view that ABC was, above all, a creative agency that could not afford to issue advertising products that were substandard or uninteresting in the artistic sense. In essence, these powerful actors endorsed the habitus of the creative department. Consequently, the subcultural capital valorized by the agency in this first stage entailed knowledge, practices and goods that were consistent with the logic by which the creative department operated and were at odds with the operational logic found in the account management department. Regarding valorized knowledge, senior management officials in the creative department were constituted as the "high priests" of specialized knowledge accessible only to an elect few, whereas account management staff became the "laity" having but a basic grasp of this esoteric knowledge. In fact, creative staff considered the knowledge produced by the account management department as more simple-minded and commonsensical than the knowledge they employed within their department.

Regarding valorized practices, the creative department stressed quality over quickness, especially given the blessings of their "high priests." This resulted in delays and deadline extensions for delivery of advertising content. While favoring the logic of the creative department, such delays and extensions went against the logic of the account management department, whose staff preferred sales effectiveness rather than aesthetic quality. When account managers argued that rapid execution of projects was more important to clients than was production of innovative and imaginative content, senior creative staff affirmed that neither account managers nor clients knew what constituted good and effective advertising. Furthermore, creative staff argued that account managers should educate clients about the amount of time necessary for the production of quality advertising rather than succumb to client pressures. Finally, regarding valorized goods, senior management in the creative department were mostly responsible for presenting such goods (e.g. creative ideas, advertising products) to clients. In contrast, account managers were supposed to have some knowledge of the esteemed goods that emanated from the creative department, but they were not allowed to present (nor interpret) these products to clients. According to social representations shared by the members of the creative department, account managers "just" had to be effective communicators who could defend to clients the artistic works that flowed from the creative department.

In the first stage of the agency's history, then, account managers were initially dispossessed of the schemes of appreciation and action (i.e. subcultural habitus) necessary to produce and decipher the competencies that were valorized as high and desirable within the agency (i.e. subcultural capital). As a result, members of the account management department were less able than their counterparts in creative department to promote their particular logic of operation within the agency. While notable in its impact, this subcultural habitus was not immune to change, as social representations theory would suggest (e.g. Moscovici, 1988). In the second stage of the ABC's history, changes in the agency's top management ushered in powerful actors who viewed the agency in a different light – as an organization involved in both creative and business endeavors. Consequently, the subcultural habitus now upheld by the agency was that of the account management department, thereby allowing them to promote their particular operational logic. According to this logic, good advertisement had to sell, and the knowledge and skills required for the creation of good advertisement were not necessarily artistic talent but expertise regarding markets and brands. In other words, the newly valorized subcultural capital consisted of knowledge, practices, and goods largely found within the account management department, and it reproduced a new hierarchy of relations between the two departments.[12]

This case of ABC Advertisement thus shows how subcultural capital can serve to reproduce the hierarchical ordering that exists among meso-level groups. At each stage of the agency's history, powerful actors initially established the legitimate subculture of ABC. This illustrates the constructionist notion regarding the arbitrariness of cultural knowledge, which Bourdieu also shares. That is, the definition of reality that ultimately wins out often does not depend on the plausibility or functional potency of its particular interpretation but on the power of individuals and groups which hold that interpretation (Dobbin & Dowd, 2000). "He who has the bigger stick has the better chance of imposing his definitions of reality" (Berger & Luckman, 1967, p. 127). Once in place however, the agency's legitimate culture became taken-for-granted and served to reproduce the domination of, in the first stage, the creative department and, in the second stage, the account management department.

5.3.2. Multicultural Capital

The case of ABC Advertisement is well suited for the illustration of group-level (i.e. department) processes that legitimate social reproduction. However, given the complete lack of research regarding the valorization of "advertising capital" (i.e. cultural currency circulating at the macro-level) in the CIS region (see

Note 8), we are unable to delve into the aggregated nature of multicultural at the micro-level. Nevertheless, both interviews and fieldwork hint at the importance of the subcultural component for individual status attainment.

Our exploratory analysis shows that definitions of creative work, as well as work procedures, had implications for individual careers. In the first historical stage, when the legitimate subculture of ABC valorized artistic competencies, members of the creative department were well situated to turn mastery of this legitimate culture into social and economic gains. Because they were able to negotiate (if not impose) extended schedules for completion of creative jobs, they were also able to produce content that they deemed innovative and imaginative. As a result, creative staff had the opportunity to accumulate strong portfolios, which, in turn, could enhance their marketability, prestige and bargaining power. In contrast, members of the account management department suffered from the dissatisfaction of clients frustrated by slow completion of projects, thereby limiting their options for social and economic gain. During the second historical stage, when the legitimate subculture of ABC valorized competencies regarding markets and brands, creative personnel could allot far less time to the production of advertising content. In fact, when compared to the previous stage, creative staff now confronted an increased workload, which provided fewer opportunities to render artistically innovative content. This potentially limited their abilities to compile a strong portfolio, thus hampering opportunities for social and economic gain. Meanwhile, when compared to the first stage, account managers now enjoyed an improved condition. Now that they could both press particular designers working on their projects and do some of the creative work themselves, account managers could finish projects in a timely fashion and create efficient ads that sold the clients' products. This contributed to the marketability and prestige of ABC account managers.

Existing research shows that individual status attainment is influenced by the amount of cultural capital that an individual possesses (e.g. Aschaffenburg & Maas, 1997; Borocz & Southworth, 1996). This is most likely true for individuals at ABC Advertisement, although as noted, we do not have data on particular forms of cultural capital employed by individuals in the agency. Still, we can hypothesize that different levels of "advertising capital" (see Note 8) possessed by agency personnel (e.g. competencies valorized at the macro-level) could explain variation in status outcomes within the departments. Yet would we be able to explain different status outcomes of the same account manager under different legitimate cultures by heeding only advertising capital? Conceptualizing multicultural capital as an aggregate of cultural and *subcultural* forms of capital, in our opinion, would allow for a better explanation of individual status dynamics within such a meso-level setting.

6. CONCLUSION

The theory of cultural capital, as originally developed by Pierre Bourdieu, occupies a central position in sociology. It has inspired, for instance, much theorizing and research in the realms of consumption and tastes (e.g. Bryson, 1996) and education (e.g. Aschaffenburg & Maas, 1997). The resulting scholarship, as well as the original theory that inspired it, sheds light on the role that culture (e.g. symbolic competencies) plays in the reproduction and legitimation of inequality. Given its centrality, his theory of cultural capital (as well as his attendant empirics) has also inspired modification (e.g. Verter, 2003) and criticism (e.g. Halle, 1993), as scholars address gaps that they find amidst Bourdieu's expansive work. One criticism is particularly salient for us: Bourdieu details the processes by which cultural capital facilitates the reproduction and legitimation of inequality at the societal level, but he does not provide similar detail regarding such processes at the organizational and individual levels (e.g. Erickson, 1996; Lahire, 2003). Despite this lack of detail, his theory sometimes evokes the meso- and micro-levels. For example, it contains a strong cognitive component, pointing to perceptual schemes by which individuals construct their world, and it acknowledges that individuals can employ cultural capital for status attainment (e.g. Bourdieu, 1968, 1984, 1990; see Lamont & Lareau, 1988).

In this paper, we suggest that two theories in social psychology – social representations and expectation states – permit some specification of these meso- and micro-level processes and allow a treatment of cultural capital as a multi-level concept. Hence, we distinguish between "cultural capital" at the macro-level, "sub-cultural capital" at the meso-level, and "multicultural capital" at the micro-level. Directly drawing on Bourdieu's theory, we define *cultural capital* as knowledge, practices, and goods consecrated as rare, "high" and desirable; we also emphasize that this form of capital is institutionally produced and distributed within autonomous cultural fields and is used for the social reproduction of such macro-level categories as class, gender, and ethnicity (see also Hall, 1992). In other words, cultural capital refers to legitimate culture produced by institutions at the societal level.

While our usage of cultural capital is consistent with that of Bourdieu's theory, our usage of the next two forms addresses a gap in his theory. Regarding the meso-level, social representations theory indicates that groups can also be sites for the production of legitimate culture – in particular, a legitimate subculture that operates one level removed from the broader societal culture. Such subcultures are not completely emergent in group settings, though. According to social representations theory, groups borrow cognitive categories from the common culture; however, these macro-produced categories are modified in group interaction to form distinctive cognitive schemas, or subcultural habitus, that serve in the reproduction of meso-level groups. Therefore, we define *subcultural capital* as knowledge, practices, and goods consecrated as rare, "high" and desirable by some meso-level group and used for its social reproduction. Regarding the micro-level, expectation states theory notes that individuals are members of both macro-social categories (e.g. classes) and meso-level groups. When engaged in group interaction, individuals assess multiple status characteristics; however, status characteristics associated with macro-level categories and meso-level groups are only activated when salient for a given interaction. As a result, we define *multicultural capital* as the aggregation of cultural and subcultural forms of capital that are salient in a particular interactional context. This definition highlights how individuals can pursue status attainment via the mastery of legitimate culture produced at both the macro- and meso-levels.

Our primary goal in this paper was to develop a multi-level concept of cultural capital by bringing three theories, which are rarely considered together, into dialogue. However, we also illustrated the utility of this multi-level concept by considering the case of an advertising agency located in Eastern Europe. Though the case presented here was of an exploratory nature, it is quite suggestive. First, it highlights how both subcultural habitus and subcultural capital are constructed in the wake of organizational change (i.e. founding, leadership change) and how both, in turn, legitimate hierarchical relations between two organizational departments. Second, it offers an example regarding how subcultural capital can be empirically approached. To asses what constitutes this form of capital within an organization, we analyzed the social representations offered by its personnel regarding the knowledge, practices and goods that are valorized as legitimate within their agency. Finally, the case suggests that the multi-level conceptualization of cultural capital could benefit the study of reproduction processes within social organizations, as it casts into bold relief cultural processes by which "firms link the 'macro' and 'micro' dimensions of work organization and inequality" (Baron & Bielby, 1980, p. 738).

NOTES

1. Bourdieu uses "cultural capital" as a general term for various types of capital valued within autonomous fields, into which differentiates modern culture (e.g. political capital in the field of politics, religious capital in the field of religion, scientific capital in the field of science, artistic capital in the field of art). He distinguishes all these various forms of cultural capital, on the one hand, from material economic capital, and on the other hand, from non-material symbolic capital (i.e. prestige) and social capital or social connections (e.g. Bourdieu, 1991b).

2. In contrast to Marx, Bourdieu defined class not only in relation to economic conditions but through the homogeneity of conditions of existence and habitus: "a class or class fraction is defined not only by its position in the relations of production, as identified through indices such as occupation, income or even education level, but also by a certain sex-ratio, a certain distribution in geographical space (which is never socially neutral) and by a whole set of subsidiary characteristics which may function, in the form of tacit requirements, as real principles of selection or exclusion without ever being formally stated (this is the case with ethnic origin and sex)" (Bourdieu, 1984, p. 102). According to the logic of his theorizing, the concept of cultural capital can be used not only in relation to the reproduction of economic classes but also for such macro-level categories as race, ethnicity, sex, or age (see Hall, 1992).

3. Subsequent research in social cognition offers some support for Durkheim: human perception is indeed guided by prior knowledge organized in complex knots of basic categories (see DiMaggio, 1997).

4. See the following works: Moscovici et al. (1969), Moscovici and Neve (1973), Moscovici and Lage (1976, 1978), and Moscovici and Personnaz (1980).

5. Sarah Thornton (1996) uses "subcultural capital" when referring to the competencies (i.e. "hipness") that are valorized in youth-oriented club cultures and that are construed as distinct and in opposition to mainstream popular culture. Hence, her usage emphasizes "subculture." Our usage, however, emphasizes the "sub" of subcultural – that is, the meso-level culture that operates under the macro-level culture. Moreover, we see Thornton's usage of subcultural capital as a particular example of the general usage we employ.

6. Bethany Bryson (1996) uses "multicultural capital" when referring to prestige accorded to those with musical tastes that are both broad (i.e. liking numerous genres) and exclusive (i.e. disliking low-status genres). Thus, she uses "multi" to "specify a content of cultural capital, not to modify its meaning" (Bryson, 1996, p. 888). Our usage, then, departs considerably from hers.

7. The names of the agency and the country where it is located are not named due to issues of confidentiality.

8. Bourdieu (1977, 1984) argues that an autonomous field valorizes certain goods, practices, and knowledge as legitimate. These valorized elements function as cultural capital. We expect that the autonomous field of advertising valorizes certain kinds of special knowledge and goods that, in turn, function as "advertising capital." Unfortunately, we know of no research addressing such valorization in the advertising field(s) of the CIS region. Such field-level analysis – and identification of advertising capital – awaits further study.

9. Advertising agencies differ by how much emphasis they put on either creative work or account management. The agencies specializing in account management may have small creative departments or may not have any at all. In the latter case, account managers subcontract creative work elsewhere. In creative agencies, by contrast, most of the creative work is performed in-house.

10. This incident is recorded in field notes rather than on tape and, therefore, the record conveys the general content of the manager's speech rather than her exact expressions.

11. "Design" briefs are used to request technical jobs (e.g. to prepare a poster for print) from the creative department. A brief is a form that lists questions about possible types of standard jobs, product and deadlines. Whenever a conceptual job is required (e.g. to develop an idea for a new advertisement campaign, to design new packaging for a product), "creative" briefs are used. A standard creative brief form contains a number of questions about advertising and marketing objectives, target audience characteristics, brand charac-teristics, and budget constraints. The creative brief is filled out by an account manager based

on the information received from the client, and it is passed onto the creative department for execution.

12. Both interviews and fieldwork suggest that the legitimate subcultures found in each historical stage were not produced exclusively within the advertising agency. Some agency personnel stressed that their definitions of good and effective advertising were not unique but widespread throughout the advertising industry; one account manager, for example, remarked that the tendency to consider advertising as art was a "common evil" promoted by numerous advertising festivals. This is consistent with SRT research (e.g. Jodelet, 1991) which shows that some cognitive categories found in social representations (meso-level) are borrowed from the wider culture (macro-level).

ACKNOWLEDGMENTS

We thank members of the Emory Sociology Friday-Seminar for their comments on a related paper. We especially thank Cathy Johnson for her editorial guidance and support.

REFERENCES

Aschaffenburg, K., & Maas, I. (1997). Cultural and educational careers: The dynamics of social reproduction. *American Sociological Review, 62*, 573–587.

Baron, J. N., & Bielby, W. T. (1980). Bringing the firm back in: Stratification, segmentation, and the organization of work. *American Sociological Review, 45*, 737–765.

Berger, J., & Conner, T. L. (1974). Performance expectations and behavior in small groups: A revisited formulation. In: J. Berger, T. L. Connor & M. H. Fisek (Eds), *Expectation States Theory: A Theoretical Program* (pp. 85–109). Cambridge, MA: Winthrop.

Berger, J., Rosenholz, S., & Zelditch, M., Jr. (1980). Status organizing processes. *Annual Review of Sociology, 6*, 479–508.

Berger, J., Webster, M., Ridgeway, C., & Rosenholz, S. (1986). Status cues, expectations and behavior. *Advances in Group Processes, 3*, 1–22.

Berger, P. L., & Luckman, T. (1967). *The social construction of reality: A treatise in the sociology of knowledge*. Garden City, NY: Anchor.

Borocz, J., & Southworth, C. (1996). Decomposing the intellectuals' class power: Conversion of cultural capital to income, Hungary, 1986. *Social Forces, 74*, 797–821.

Bourdieu, P. (1968). Outline of a sociological theory of art perception. *International Social Science Journal, XX*(4), 589–612.

Bourdieu, P. (1977). *Outline of a theory of practice*. Cambridge: Cambridge University Press.

Bourdieu, P. (1984). *Distinction: A sociological critique of the judgement of taste*. Cambridge, MA: Harvard University Press.

Bourdieu, P. (1986). The forms of capital. In: J. G. Richards (Ed.), *Handbook of Theory and Research for the Sociology of Education* (pp. 241–258). New York: Greenwood.

Bourdieu, P. (1987). Legitimation and structured interests in Weber's sociology of religion. In: S. Whimster & S. Lash (Eds), *Max Weber: Rationality and Modernity* (pp. 119–136). London: Allen & Unwin.

Bourdieu, P. (1990). *The logic of practice*. Stanford, CA: Stanford University Press.
Bourdieu, P. (1991a). Genesis and structure of the religious field. *Comparative Social Research, 13,* 1–43.
Bourdieu, P. (1991b). *Language and symbolic power*. Cambridge, MA: Harvard University Press.
Bourdieu, P. (1993). *The field of cultural production: Essays on art and literature*. New York: Columbia University Press.
Bourdieu, P. (2002). Поле Науки. *SOCIO/ΛΟΓΟΣ 2002*. Альманах Российско-французского центра социологии и философии Института социологии Российской Академии наук. Москва: Институт экспериментальной социологии.
Bourdieu, P., & Passeron, J.-C. (1990). *Reproduction in education, society, and culture*. London: Sage.
Brubaker, R. (1985). Rethinking classical theory: The sociological vision of Pierre Bourdieu. *Theory and Society, 14,* 745–775.
Bryson, B. (1996). "Anything but heavy metal": Symbolic exclusion and musical dislikes. *American Sociological Review, 61,* 884–899.
Campbell, C. (1998). Representations of gender, respectability and commercial sex in the shadow of AIDS: A South African case study. *Social Science Information, 37,* 687–709.
Carter, P. L. (2003). "Black" cultural capital, status positioning and schooling conflicts for low-income African American youth. *Social Problems, 50,* 136–155.
Cohen, B. P., & Zhou, X. (1991). Status processes in enduring work groups. *American Sociological Review, 56,* 179–188.
Crossley, N. (1996). *Intersubjectivity: The fabric of social becoming*. Thousand Oaks, CA: Sage.
DeNora, T. (1995). *Beethoven and the construction of genius: Musical politics in Vienna, 1792–1803*. Berkeley, CA: University of California Press.
DiMaggio, P. (1979). Review essay: On Pierre Bourdieu. *American Journal of Sociology, 84,* 1460–1474.
DiMaggio, P. (1982a). Cultural capital and school success: The impact of status culture participation on the grades of U.S. high school students. *American Sociological Review, 47,* 189–201.
DiMaggio, P. (1982b). Cultural entrepreneurship in nineteenth-century Boston, Part I: The creation of an organizational base for high culture in America. *Media Culture and Society, 4,* 33–55.
DiMaggio, P. (1982c). Cultural entrepreneurship in nineteenth-century Boston, Part II: The classification and framing of American art. *Media Culture and Society, 4,* 303–322.
DiMaggio, P. (1987). Classification in art. *American Sociological Review, 52,* 440–455.
DiMaggio, P. (1991). Social structure, institutions, and cultural goods: The case of the United States. In: P. Bourdieu & J. S. Coleman (Eds), *Social Theory for a Changing Society* (pp. 133–155). Boulder, CO: Westview Press.
DiMaggio, P. (1992). Cultural boundaries and structural change: The extension of the high culture model to theater, opera, and the dance, 1900–1940. In: M. Lamont & M. Fournier (Eds), *Cultivating Differences: Symbolic Boundaries and the Making of Inequality* (pp. 21–57). Chicago: University of Chicago Press.
DiMaggio, P. (1997). Culture and cognition. *Annual Review of Sociology, 23,* 263–287.
DiMaggio, P., & Mohr, J. (1985). Cultural capital, educational attainment and marital selection. *American Journal of Sociology, 90,* 1231–1261.
Dobbin, F., & Dowd, T. J. (2000). The market that antitrust built: Public policy, private coercion, and railroad acquisitions, 1825 to 1922. *American Sociological Review, 65,* 631–657.
Dowd, T. J., Liddle, K., Lupo, K., & Borden, A. (2002). Organizing the musical canon: The repertoires of major U.S. symphony orchestras, 1842 to 1969. *Poetics, 30,* 35–61.
DuMais, S. A. (2002). Cultural capital, gender, and school success: The role of habitus. *Sociology of Education, 75,* 44–68.

Durkheim, E. (1995). *The elementary forms of religious life*. New York: Free Press.

Erickson, B. H. (1996). Culture, class, and connections. *American Journal of Sociology, 102*, 217–251.

Farr, R. M. (1987). Social representations: A French tradition of research. *Journal for the Theory of Social Behaviour, 17*(4), 343–370.

Flick, U. (1998). *An introduction to qualitative research*. London: Sage.

Gartman, D. (1991). Culture as class symbolization or mass reification? A critique of Bourdieu's distinction. *American Journal of Sociology, 97*, 421–447.

Glynn, M. A. (2000). When cymbals become symbols: Conflict over organizational identity within a symphony orchestra. *Organization Science, 11*, 285–298.

Hall, J. R. (1992). The capital(s) of cultures: A nonholistic approach to status situations, class, gender, and ethnicity. In: M. Lamont & M. Fournier (Eds), *Cultivating Differences: Symbolic Boundaries and the Making of Inequality* (pp. 257–285). Chicago: University of Chicago Press.

Halle, D. (1993). *Inside culture: Art and class in the American home*. Chicago: University of Chicago Press.

Hallett, T. (2003). Symbolic power and organizational culture. *Sociological Theory, 21*, 128–149.

Holt, D. (1997). Distinction in America? Recovering Bourdieu's theory of tastes from its critics. *Poetics, 25*, 93–120.

Holt, D. B. (1998). Does cultural capital structure American consumption? *Journal of Consumer Research, 25*, 1–25.

Jodelet, D. (1984). Les représentations socials: Phénomènes, concept et théorie. In: S. Moscovici (Ed.), *Psychologie Sociale* (pp. 357–378). Paris: Presses Universitaires de France.

Jodelet, D. (1991). *Madness and social representations*. New York: Harvester Wheatsheaf.

Jovchelovitch, S. (1995). Social representations in and of the public sphere: Towards a theoretical articulation. *Journal for the Theory of Social Behavior, 25*, 81–102.

Kane, D. (2003). Distinction worldwide? Bourdieu's theory of taste in international context. *Poetics, 31*, 403–421.

Kingston, P. W. (2001). The unfulfilled promise of cultural capital theory. *Sociology of Education Extra Issue*, 88–99.

Lahire, B. (2003). From the habitus to an individual heritage of dispositions: Towards a sociology at the level of the individual. *Poetics, 31*, 329–355.

Lamont, M. (1992). *Money, morals, and manners: The culture of the French and American upper-middle class*. Chicago: University of Chicago Press.

Lamont, M., & Lareau, A. (1988). Cultural capital: Allusions, gaps and glissandos in recent theoretical developments. *Sociological Theory, 6*, 153–168.

Lareau, A., & Horvat, E. M. (1999). Moments of social inclusion and exclusion: Race, class, and cultural capital in family-school relationships. *Sociology of Education, 72*, 37–53.

Liddle, K. (2004). *Managing contradiction: The competing logics of feminist bookstores*. Unpublished manuscript, Department of Sociology, Emory University.

Lieberson, S. (1992). Einstein, Renoir, and Greeley: Some thoughts about evidence in sociology. *American Sociological Review, 57*, 1–15.

Moscovici, S. (1976). *La Psychoanalyse, Son Image et Son Public* (2nd ed.). Paris: P.U.F.

Moscovici, S. (1981). On social representations. In: J. P. Forgas (Ed.), *Social Cognition: Perspectives on Everyday Understanding* (pp. 181–203). London: Academic Press.

Moscovici, S. (1988). Notes towards a description of social representations. *European Journal of Social Psychology, 18*, 211–250.

Moscovici, S., & Lage, E. (1976). Studies in social influence: III. Majority vs. minority influence in a group. *European Journal of Social Psychology, 6*, 149–174.

Moscovici, S., & Lage, E. (1978). Studies in social influence: IV. Minority influence in a context of
    original judgements. *European Journal of Social Psychology, 8*, 349–365.
Moscovici, S., Lage, E., & Naffrechoux, M. (1969). Influence of a consistent minority on the responses
    of a majority in a color perception task. *Sociometry, 32*, 365–379.
Moscovici, S., & Neve, P. (1973). Studies in social influence: II. Instrumental and symbolic behavior.
    European Journal of Experimental Social Psychology, 3, 461–474.
Moscovici, S., & Personnaz, B. (1980). Studies in social influence: V. Minority influence and conversion
    behavior in a perceptual task. *Journal of Experimental Social Psychology, 16*, 270–282.
Ridgeway, C., & Berger, J. (1986). Expectations, legitimation, and dominance behavior in task groups.
    American Sociological Review, 51, 603–617.
Ridgeway, C., & Walker, H. (1995). Status structures. In: K. Cook, G. Fine & J. House (Eds),
    Sociological Perspectives in Social Psychology (pp. 281–310). Boston: Allyn & Bacon.
Roscigno, V. J., & Ainsworth-Darnell, J. W. (1999). Race, cultural capital, and educational resources:
    Persistent inequalities and achievement returns. *Sociology of Education, 72*, 158–178.
Thornton, S. (1996). *Club cultures: Music, media, and subcultural capital.* Hanover, NH: Wesleyan
    University Press.
Verter, B. (2003). Spiritual capital: Theorizing religion with Bourdieu against Bourdieu. *Sociological
    Theory, 21*, 150–174.
Wagner, D. G., & Berger, J. (2002). Expectation states theory: An evolving research program. In:
    J. Berger & M. Zelditch, Jr. (Eds), *New Directions in Contemporary Sociological Theory*
    (pp. 41–76). Lanham, MD: Rowman & Littlefield.

WHEN GOOD NAMES GO BAD: SYMBOLIC ILLEGITIMACY IN ORGANIZATIONS

Mary Ann Glynn and Christopher Marquis

ABSTRACT

We empirically examine the institutional dynamics attending the process whereby legitimate organizational symbols become illegitimate. We conducted two studies, one historical and one comparative, of those firms that appended "dot-com" to their names during the period of "Internet euphoria," 1998–1999. The first study analyzes the legitimacy over time for one case, that of Egghead software, the first organization to affix "dot-com" to its name. The second study compares the legitimacy of firms named "dot-com" in the wake of the "dot-com" crash, using both public perceptions and financial valuations. Results from the two studies indicate that good organization names can go bad rather quickly and illustrate how swift and definitive the process of deinstitutionalization can be.

INTRODUCTION

In October 1999, there was a corporate rush to embrace the Internet and symbolize this in the organizational name, with a "dot-com" appendix:

Dot-com has become the Internet's indispensable suffix, a terse but unmistakable signal of existence on the Web. The number of registered dot-com addresses has reached a staggering

Legitimacy Processes in Organizations
Research in the Sociology of Organizations, Volume 22, 147–170
© 2004 Published by Elsevier Ltd.
ISSN: 0733-558X/doi:10.1016/S0733-558X(04)22005-5

4.5 million, and businesses routinely pay $10,000 or more to secure prime dot-com names (Weber, 1999, p. B1).

Less than one year later, however, a different corporate rush was on. By the fall of 2000, the "dot-com balloon . . . [which] seemed to float effortless to new heights" (Weber, 2000, p. B1) had deflated:

> What a cruel, cruel illusion it all turned out to be. Stoked by the false promise of office foosball and a lot of irrational exhibitionism, the dot-com phenomenon proved to be shot through with phoniness – an apparition within a hologram wrapped inside two specters of a mirage, with some tulip mania to boot. As for why anyone thought doing business on the Web was a good idea, search us. Amazon.com? More like Amazon.bomb! (Useem, 2000, p. 82).

Many of the same companies, which had expediently appended "dot-com" to their names, just as quickly divorced themselves in name from an Internet gone bust. This symbolic detachment occurred even in those companies whose core business was the Internet. When Phone.com, a provider of Internet software, merged with Software.com, both "dot-com" names were abandoned in favor of a new corporate moniker, Openwave Systems. The CEO explained the rationale: "We wanted to send a message to say we're here . . . We also wanted to distance ourselves from the legacy of dot-coms – *there's just too much of a dot-com stigma*" (italics added; *Wall Street Journal*, 2000, p. B13).

Swiftly, and perhaps unexpectedly, "good" dot-com names had gone horribly "bad." An organizational name that signaled Internet affiliation cast a shadow on the firm, threatening the legitimacy which had been purchased symbolically with the Internet moniker. That organizations quickly conformed to a new institutional order by adopting a meaningful marker was not a surprise; that decoupling occurred so rapidly and so unambiguously was, arguably, not as easily predicted by institutional theories. Institutional processes of imitation, diffusion, and normative precedent often give a corporate rush to adopt strategies and structures (e.g. Fligstein, 1990); once in place, however, such institutionalized practices tend to be resistant to change. As Davis, Dickmann and Tinsley (1994, p. 55) put it, "institutions don't budge" and deinstitutionalization tends to be slow-moving and fairly infrequent. In their study of the "deconglomeration" of the corporate firm, Davis et al. (1994, p. 564) characterize a decade-long period of deinstitutionalization as "relatively brief." How, then, can we account for such a swift delegitimation of the "dot-com" names? In part, perhaps, it may be due to the phenomenon itself: The institutionalization and deinstitutionalization of symbols seem to have been accomplished in "Internet speed." However, this is just a supposition because the Internet is, as yet, relatively understudied: ". . . few sociologists have examined the Internet's institutional structure . . . Some sociologists *are* doing important work; but unless their numbers grow, a magnificent opportunity to build and test theories of social and technical change may go unexploited" (DiMaggio, Hargittai, Neuman & Robinson, 2001, p. 329).

We address this gap in the literature. We use the Internet as a window on legitimacy processes to uncover what it can reveal about institutionalization and symbolic isomorphism (Glynn & Abzug, 2002). We build on previous research that demonstrated positive effects for firms' adoption of the "dot-com" suffix and address what we see as two substantial limitations in earlier studies; one being temporal and the other, theoretical. In terms of the first, prior work on the adoption of "dot-com" names has been conducted only during the era of Internet hype and, even then, limited to a very narrow band of time, e.g. a three-day (Lee, 2001) or five-day window (Cooper, Dimitrov & Rau, 2001) surrounding the announcement date of the name change. Studies from corporate strategy (Lee, 2001) and finance (Cooper et al., 2001) attest to the positive effects of these name changes on stock market valuation, arguing that these name changes were used as symbols to legitimate organizations to investors and provide evidence that these companies had adapted to the new investment environment (Lee, 2001). The "dot-com" crash, which occurred subsequent to these studies, raises questions as to the continuing legitimacy of the "dot-com" names (Glynn & Abzug, 2002) and organization's perceived "social fitness" (Deephouse, 1996).

As well, these prior studies are somewhat undertheorized, particularly in terms of their treatment of legitimacy, as they consider firm valuation exclusively in financial measures, such as stock prices and trading activity (Cooper et al., 2001; Lee, 2001). Certainly, investors' valuations are one source of legitimacy, the "pragmatic legitimacy" described by Suchman (1995, p. 578), i.e. "the self-interested calculations of an organization's most immediate audiences." Overlooked are sources of normative and cognitive legitimacy, both of which are based on a broader set of perceptions about organizational appropriateness and comprehensibility, respectively. As Meyer and Rowan (1977) would have us think about it, names dramatize or narrate the organization's ceremonial face, asserting certainty about its identity and legitimate membership within the field. In their words, "Affixing the right labels to activities can change them into valuable services and mobilize the commitments of internal participants and external constituencies" (Meyer & Rowan, 1977, p. 350).

Our approach is inductive in building a theoretical framework on how symbols that once legitimated can subsequently illegitimate. To start, we analyze the case of software retailer Egghead, the first firm to append "dot-com" to its name. We use this case to develop hypotheses relating legitimacy to symbolism, which we subsequently test in a second study using both survey and archival methods. In this second study, we examine how the changing legitimacy of the Internet affected the legitimacy of "dot-com" names for both public and financial audiences, comparing perceptions in the "dot-com" explosion (1998–1999) to those of the "dot-com" implosion (2000). Based on these findings, we theorize how good organization names can go bad and offer a framework on how legitimating symbols can subsequently illegitimate organizations.

ORGANIZATIONAL LEGITIMACY AND ILLEGITIMACY

Illegitimacy is often defined as the antonym of legitimacy. Extrapolating from the definition of legitimacy as "a generalized perception or assumption that the actions of an entity are desirable, proper, or appropriate within some socially constructed system of norms, values, beliefs and definitions" (Suchman, 1995, p. 574), illegitimacy, then, would be the generalized perception that an entity's actions are undesirable, improper or inappropriate within a socially constructed system of norms, beliefs, and definitions. Indeed, a number of organizational researchers have taken this perspective.

Elsbach and Sutton (1992) describe illegitimate activity as an organizational statement of "not us." They point out that illegitimacy, like its counterpart, necessitates some shared understanding or consensus about its inappropriateness. Zuckerman (1999), who examined product alignment with analysts' judgments, described illegitimacy as a "mis-match between the firm's self-concept and the categories to which others think it belongs." Kraatz and Zajac (1996), in a study of the adoption of professional and vocational programs by liberal arts colleges, found that determining whether an action is illegitimate involves matching it against existing norms and values. They identified the conditions of illegitimacy as: inconsistency, threat, and denouncements by significant actors. They describe how for liberal arts colleges, professional and vocational programs were highly inconsistent with institutionalized norms of liberal education. Thus, these vocational and professional programs were construed threats to the perpetuation of the institutional norms; as a result, institutional actors denounced them and illegitimacy ensued for the college.

The implication from this stream of research turns institutionalization on its head: if isomorphism legitimates, then non-isomorphism illegitimates. Institutionalization is so tied to legitimacy that it is difficult not to see illegitimacy simply as deinstitutionalization or lack of institutionalization. Consequently, a conceptual fuzziness results; the construct of illegitimacy is defined not by what it is, but by what it is not (i.e. legitimacy). Correspondingly, the effects of illegitimacy are also somewhat fuzzy. The literature reports mixed findings: Some researchers testify to the negative consequences of illegitimacy, while others demonstrate that illegitimacy can have positive effects.

The negative consequences of illegitimate organizational forms, symbols, and practices have been well-noted by institutionalists. A core tenet of neo-institutional theory is that isomorphism legitimates (Deephouse, 1996) and that resources flow to more legitimate forms, thus insuring organizational survival and effective performance. By inference, then, illegitimacy is problematic. Several studies attest to this point. Deephouse (1996), in his research on the regulatory environment in the banking industry, observed strong isomorphic pressures for organizational conformity in order to secure legitimacy from critical audiences such as regulators and the media. Davis et al. (1994), examining de-institutionalization in corporate forms, demonstrated how environmental shifts change the definition of legitimacy; they showed how conglomerate forms became less legitimate over time and eventually undervalued, both in the stock market and in denouncements in the business press. Similarly, Zuckerman (1999) demonstrated that firms without a clear "role performance" confronted a legitimacy discount and failed to get reviews from critics who specialize in that products' targeted category because of a perceived mismatch between a firm and its organizational membership.

Conversely, however, illegitimacy has also been found to have positive consequences for organizations. Illegitimate firms often attract more notice and more media attention. Such press – either favorable or unfavorable – is often beneficial to organizations (Fombrun & Shanley, 1990), seemingly validating the old saying that "there is no such thing as bad publicity." The title of a 1990 Wall Street Journal article, expressing skepticism about organizational re-namings, asked "Have the Klingons taken over the banks?" (Christie, 1990). Such suspicions attest to how the organizational name serves as a touchstone upon which organizational legitimacy can be conferred or withheld (Glynn & Abzug, 1998, 2002). Moreover, illegitimacy can enable legitimacy. Elsbach and Sutton (1992) show how illegitimate actions, such as shutting down the film Midnight Caller by the AIDS Coalition to Unleash Power (ACT UP), can ultimately lead to legitimacy through media portrayals and organizational impression management. Consistent with this perspective, Kraatz and Zajac (1996) demonstrate how legitimacy can be a source of inertia; lack of adaptation can lead organizations to engage in illegitimate acts. However, work by Davis and colleagues (1994) suggesting that, as institutional environments change, the definition and meaning of legitimacy should also change, affords a different interpretation of the Kraatz and Zajac (1996) results: When the colleges in the Kraatz and Zajac (1996) sample made changes, they may actually have been maintaining their alignment (or isomorphism) with the environment. Thus, the illegitimate activities may have been organizational attempts at securing legitimacy.

In spite of the divergence of findings on the consequences of illegitimacy, there does seem to be convergence as to its antecedents. Generally speaking, illegitimacy seems to result from a mis-alignment or incongruence in organizational practices, forms, or symbols with institutional standards of appropriateness or with valued standards; in other words, illegitimate organizations lack isomorphism. Sometimes, this results from organizational initiatives; other times, the institutional environment changes in significant ways that are not matched by commensurate organizational changes. Davis and colleagues (1994) map such "deinstitutionalization" processes for the conglomerate form, finding that the definition of what is legitimate changed with environmental changes. Thus, legitimacy declines when organizational structures are inert relative to the changing rules that constitute the organizational field.

We view illegitimacy as the devaluation of an organization based upon a perceived mis-alignment with institutionalized norms, consistent with other researchers (e.g. Davis et al., 1994; Kraatz & Zajac, 1996). Our work is similar to preceding studies in that we focus on organizational alignment with the institutional environment as a source of legitimacy; likewise, we argue that illegitimacy, in turn, can result from mis-alignment, when changes in norms over time also involve changes in the standards of what constitutes appropriateness and inappropriateness and organizations no longer conform.

Our work departs from preceding research in two important ways. First, while others have focused on organizational form and structure (e.g. Davis et al., 1994; Kraatz & Zajac, 1996), we focus on symbol. Glynn and Abzug (2002) have demonstrated how institutional processes of symbolic isomorphism legitimate; we investigate how such processes can delegitimate. Second, we have chosen a novel but important site – the Internet – which, because of its swift rate of change, affords a view of institutionalization processes through a more compact window. Moreover, through the marker of organizational names, the Internet serves as a boundary, partitioning an organizational field, i.e. "a set of organizations as meaningfully bounded social actors" (Davis et al., 1994, p. 549), that wall off Internet-identified firms ("dot-coms") from those not so identified. For all these reasons, it is a site in need of study, as DiMaggio and colleagues (2001) have pointed out.

Our contributions, then, are to examine deinstitutionalization and illegitimacy in the context of changes in the valuation of the Internet, from boom to bust, by focusing on "dot-com" names as markers for these changes. By mapping such changes over time in institutions and organizational symbols, we uncover some of the institutional processes that reveal the boundaries between legitimacy and illegitimacy in naming practices. Understanding patterns and changes in organizational names over time can make transparent the processes of "ceremonial conformity" that Meyer and Rowan (1977) argued was essential to legitimacy. We begin by detailing the case of one company undergoing serial name changes: Egghead.com.

THE CASE OF SERIAL NAME-CHANGER EGGHEAD.COM

Egghead Software was the very first company to adopt the "dot-com" name. The company was founded in 1984 as the first software-only retailer and successfully grew through the early 1990s. However, as mass-market retailers such as CompUSA and Walmart started carrying software products, Egghead's fortunes reversed. By early 1998, the company had suffered five years of decline and dropped from 250 nationwide stores to just 83. It was at this point that Egghead Inc. shifted in strategy and symbolized this in its name, becoming Egghead.com in January, 1998.

In changing its name, Egghead attempted to leverage the Internet fever that had been growing since 1996. In the four years from 1996 to 2000, the technology heavy NASDAQ exchange index grew from a value of 1000 to over 5000 (in early 2003, it traded around 1500). Now known as a period of "irrational exuberance" and seemingly comparable to other famous market bubbles like the Dutch tulip collapse of the 1630s, the "dot-com" euphoria of the late 1990s bestowed virtually any business associated with the Internet or electronic commerce with stratospheric stock market valuations.

As an indication that this name change was an attempt to capture some of the budding legitimacy associated with the Internet, Egghead coupled the name change to a disappointing earnings announcement, perhaps in an attempt to distract investors for a lackluster quarter. At least initially, however, investors were not fooled. The day after the announcements, the stock price lost 18% of its value, closing at $6.375. It soon became clear, however, that Egghead was on to something in its strategic repositioning as a "dot-com." Investors soon forgot the previous five years of disappointing earnings. *Fortune Magazine* describes the shift in the audience reactions:

> Six months ago, Egghead's CEO, George Orban . . . moved the entire business onto the Web, and added "dot-com" to the end of its name. Wall Street, with its untrammeled lust for anything with that beautiful dot-com suffix, gave Orban and his stock a big, wet kiss. Since Orban's bold move, Egghead stock has more than tripled, recently hitting $22 a share (Lee, 1998, p. 194).

By November of 1998, Egghead.com was valued at $108/share, up almost 1400% from the pre-name change period. This seemed to reflect investors' "untrammeled lust for anything with a dot-com suffix." The old rules of business were thrown out and profitability no longer a requirement for exuberant stock market ratings:

> The concept of Internet time also spawned a highly abnormal approach to company-building. Since time immemorial, most businesses had grown organically, using operating profits from early customers ... to fund expansion and ad campaigns. But the Internet craze – invariably described either as a "land grab" or a "gold rush" – turned the process on its head. First build a "brand," the thinking went. Then get eyeballs. Then turn them into paying customers. Then figure out how to make a business of it (Useem, 2000, p. 83).

In this period, corporate names and symbols were key to the investing community and having a "dot-com" name provided short-term alignment with financiers and the stock market (Lee, 2001).

> "A lot of people assumed everything was – this is a bad word, but – Internetable," says (one) financier ... They said, 'Has anyone come up with ItalianCheese.com? Okay, then let's do it.' ... At the trend's apogee, venture capitalists bought up hundreds of domain names in the hopes of assembling a business around each, and eagerly funded such paradigm-shatterers as JustBalls.com (Useem, 2000, p. 82).

Things changed, however. As DiMaggio and colleagues describe it (2001, p. 319), perceptions of the Internet progressed from "unjustifiable euphoria" to "abrupt and equally unjustified skepticism." Egghead.com continued to disappoint investors with poor earnings performance, the company's stock gradually declined, eventually falling under $1.00 (Fig. 1). Reflecting the fickleness of investors and how

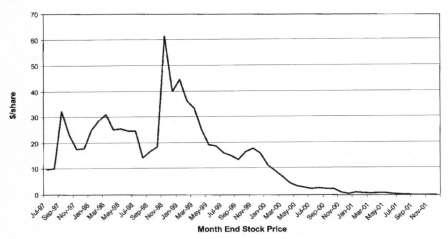

Fig. 1.   The Rise and Fall of Egghead.com.

quickly the investment environment can change, in January of 2001, the president of Egghead.com described in the *Wall Street Journal* (Maio, 2001): "The entire Internet sector is in the doghouse. Just as we were extraordinarily valued at $108 in November 1998, we are undervalued now." However, Egghead.com was not just in the doghouse, but its strategy and name were no longer in alignment with what investors considered legitimate. By August of that year, Egghead.com would declare bankruptcy and eventually liquidate its assets. Like other investment bubbles that preceded it, it was only a matter of time before the tide would turn and bring Internet stock prices back to reality. As described in *Businessweek* in August of 2001, one and a half years after the NASDAQ reached its peak, "everything went suddenly, spectacularly wrong. With a swiftness that caught business leaders and economists off guard, the extraordinary New Economy boom flared like a supernova and went dark. The aftermath has been ugly" (Walczak, 2001).

The Egghead case illustrates two important lessons on legitimacy dynamics in organizational fields. Paralleling Davis et al.'s (1994) finding about organizational structures, the case of Egghead illustrates that symbolic alignment with the environment is also essential for legitimacy; environmental changes can result in illegitimating what was previously legitimate. However, unlike the findings reported by Davis and co-authors (1994), the processes unfolded with breathtaking speed. As the Egghead case reveals, an asset viewed as legitimate – a name with a "dot-com" suffix – became a liability when environmental norms changed. Different, however, from the gradual shift in conceptions of the corporation as a sovereign body (Davis et al., 1994), deinstitutionalization was swift, widespread, and initiated just by the configuration of a name.

The swiftness of the change from legitimate to illegitimate points to what we see as the second important lesson in the Egghead case: the role of elites or key legitimating actors, such as Wall Street investors, media commentators, and the general public, in authorizing symbols and standards of appropriateness. This observation is not unique; others (e.g. Davis et al., 1994; Zuckerman, 1999), have found that the investing community is important in defining what is legitimate. What is different in our research, and revealed in case of Egghead.com, is the rapidity of the change and its extensiveness, occurring not only in the community of investment experts (Davis et al., 1994), but more broadly in public discourse. In our study, the rapidity and extensiveness of the "dot-com" change extended to the public arena. Unlike Zuckerman (1999), where illegitimacy effects are focused on a small and limited population of analysts, illegitimating "dot-com" organizations seems to have been predicated on a fundamental and pervasive shift in the perceptions of several constituencies. We use these lessons to formulate hypotheses which we test in the study that follows.

REVISITING THE LEGITIMACY
OF "DOT-COM" NAMES

To examine the generalizability of legitimacy dynamics we observed at Egghead, we assessed "dot-com" perceptions of public and financial audiences subsequent to the bursting of the Internet bubble. Using the sample studied by Lee (2001), we investigated how the 58 companies that suffixed "dot-com" to their names in 1998–1999 fared in more recent times; we excluded Egghead from this analysis.

Arguing that these name changes were used as symbols to legitimate organizations to investors and evidence organizational adaptation, Lee (2001) found a positive effect for "dot-com" name changes. However, we expected the reverse in the wake of the "dot-com" implosion. We reasoned that the "dot-com" implosion shifted the standards of appropriateness and changed the favorability of norms that initially drove the adoption of "dot-com" names, for both public audiences and the Wall Street community.

More specifically, we hypothesize that firms that suffixed "dot-com" to their name in 1998 or 1999 would be perceived as less legitimate after the dot-com crash. We also hypothesize that firms that suffixed "dot-com" to their name in 1998 or 1999 would have suffered severe stock market devaluation after the "dot-com" crash.

To test these hypotheses, we sampled all publicly traded companies that made name change announcements in 1998 and 1999 to include "dot-com" as part of the name. These firms are listed in Table 1 and are the same firms studied by Lee (2001, p. 797). Because our hypotheses involved different dependent variables, we tested the hypotheses using two different methodologies. For our first hypothesis, positing more negative public reactions to "dot-com" firms, we surveyed the general public to assess their perceptions of organizations' credibility based only on their name, similar to Glynn and Abzug (2002). For our second hypothesis, positing more negative stock market valuations for "dot-com" firms, we followed the logic of Lee (2001) and Cooper et al. (2001), and assessed market values as indicators of legitimacy.

Public Perceptions of Name Legitimacy (H1)

Using a questionnaire we developed, we surveyed 55 twenty-year old undergraduates in the Fall of 2002. We chose this group as a "litmus test" because, for them, the Internet is familiar and comprehensible. The survey was very brief, just one page and took approximately 10 minutes to complete. Using the firm names in Table 1, participants were presented a randomized list of pairs of the old

Table 1. Name Changes and Announcement Date.

Old Name	New Name	Date
Egghead Inc.	Egghead.com	1/28/1998
Alpha Microsystems	AlphaServ.com	1/20/1999
Asset Retrieval	Creditgroup.com	2/1/1999
Boraxx Technologies	QuadXSports.com	3/12/1999
Bridgeport Communications	WealthHound.com	5/28/1999
Cardiovascular Laboratories Inc.	CLIXhealth.com	3/25/1999
Cellular Vision, USA	SpeedUs.com	12/21/1998
Charter Investor Relations of North America	Millionaire.com	12/16/1998
Computer Literacy Inc.	Fatbrain.com	3/29/1999
Conagen Corp.	Planet411.com	2/10/1999
Connect Inc.	ConnectInc.com	12/15/1998
Didax Inc.	Crosswalk.com	5/5/1999
e-Casino Gaming Corp.	e-Vegas.com	6/4/1999
Eduverse Accelerated Learning Systems	Eduverse.com	6/7/1999
First Virtual Corp.	FVC.com	7/30/1998
Formquest International	MegaChain.com	4/19/1999
Freepages Group	Scoot.com	2/22/1999
FSGI Corp.	TMANGlobal.com	12/22/1998
Genisys Reservations Systems	Netcruisetravel.com	2/11/1999
GoodNoise Corp.	Emusic.com	6/2/1999
Group V Corp.	TotalAxcess.com	5/17/1999
HHHP Inc.	Wcollect.com	2/12/1999
Home Care America	BizRocket.com	6/7/1999
Interactive Processing Inc.	Worldtradeshow.com	3/17/1999
International Barter Corp.	Ubarter.com	4/27/1999
IPVoice Communications Inc.	IPVoice.com	4/19/1999
JetFax, Inc.	EFax.com	2/3/1999
Medirisk Inc.	Caredata.com	6/3/1999
MIS International	Cosmoz.com	1/15/1999
Modacad Inc.	Styleclick.com	6/1/1999
Motorcycle Centers of America	eUniverse.com	4/15/1999
New York Bagel Exchange Inc.	Webboat.com	2/1/1999
Okane International	Superwire.com	4/28/1999
OneStopCar of Florida	OneStop.com	4/14/1999
Ozone Technology	Enwisen.com	5/13/1999
PetMed Express Inc.	PetMedExpress.com	4/8/1999
Phon-Net Corp.	Phon-Net.com	6/14/1999
Pivot Rules Inc.	Bluefly.com	10/29/1998
Prosoft I-Net Solutions	ProsoftTraining.com	9/18/1998
RDI Marketing	HouseholdDirect.com	3/17/1999
RLD Enterprises	Go-Rachels.com	1/28/1999
RNL Realty, Inc.	Netmaximizer.com	3/11/1999
Score Medical Corp.	IMatters.com	3/22/1999
Shop TV	Site2shop.com	2/11/1999

Table 1. (*Continued*)

Old Name	New Name	Date
Sloan Electronics	SalientCyber.com	4/20/1999
Software.net Corp.	Beyond.com	8/25/1998
Spectrum Information Technologies	Siti-Sites.com	12/17/1998
Staruni Corp.	Ubid4it.com	4/6/1999
SUNCOM Telecommunication	VirtualSellers.com	5/4/1999
SyCo Distribution Inc.	SyCoNet.com	2/3/1999
Tao Partners	we-NetVisionz.com	5/12/1999
Technology Horizons Corp.	CKDNET.com	12/1/1998
TeleServices International Group, Inc.	TSIG.com	3/2/1999
Tel-Save Holdings	Tel-Save.com	11/16/1998
The Henley Group	CIS.com	3/31/1999
USA BancShares	USABanc.com	5/12/1999
Virtual Brand Inc.	Ubrandit.com	3/3/1999
Westergaard Online Systems, Inc.	Westergaard.com	1/13/1999
ZapPower Systems	ZapWorld.com	5/18/1999

(non "dot-com") name and new ("dot-com") name; we sometimes listed the old name first and sometimes the "dot-com" name first. We used this strategy to decrease the risk of response bias. We asked respondents to make two judgments: (1) How similar are the two names? Respondents made their determinations using a 5-point scale, anchored by 1 (not similar) and 5 (very similar); and (2) Which of the two names (e.g. the "dot-com" name or the other "non-dot-com" name) is more credible? Here, respondents were asked to choose the more credible of the two names.

Survey Results. Responses to the first survey question, assessing name similarity, averaged 2.65 across all subjects and all names, indicating that the old and new ("dot-com") names were generally perceived to be dissimilar. For 32 of the 58 name changes (55%) the modal response was "1" (not similar), suggesting that these name changes may have been opportunistic grabs at the legitimacy the Internet symbol offered, rather than a signaling of more substantive and particularistic organizational change. Moreover, the perceptual gap suggests that firms were not leveraging existing social capital but rather seeking the emerging social capital of the Internet. More generally, this first finding indicates a lack of resemblance of the old name to the new "dot-com" name, suggesting that, as in the case of Egghead, these "dot-com" firms may be attempting to seize a ready-made legitimating symbol.

The second survey question assessed name credibility. We found that 56 of the 58 "dot-com" names (96.5%) were perceived as less credible than their non "dot-com" counterparts. This implies that, in the face of changed norms about the favorableness of Internet business, "dot-com" names lost the luster of legitimacy, even to a young, friendly, Internet savvy public.

Taken together, the results of the two survey questions offer strong support for our first hypothesis: Nearly all organizations suffixing "dot-com" to their name in 1998–1999 were perceived as less legitimate following the Internet crash. Thus, it seemed that, in the wake of changed norms about the Internet, organizational symbols connoting Internet businesses lost credibility.

Stock Market Valuations of Name Legitimacy (H2)

We investigated the stock market valuation of our sample of firms (see Table 1), using a five-day period from November 25 to November 29, 2002 (a time when the Internet bubble had clearly burst) and employing numerous sources, including CRSP and COMPUSTAT databases, SEC filings and Internet sources such as Google, Yahoo Finance, company websites, and two over-the counter exchange websites: www.picksheets.com and www.otcbb.com.

The results of this investigation are quite striking (see Fig. 2). Of the 58 "dot-com" name changes identified by Lee (2001), we were able to find information on 57.[1] Of the 57 remaining, 10 had been acquired and 47 are still traded on the stock exchanges. Of these 47 companies still traded, only 7 (14.8%) are valued at over $1.00, a critical threshold for assessing legitimacy because this is the price at which a firm's listing on the NASDAQ market comes into question. Of the other 40 firms still traded, 32 trade for under ten cents ($.10), and 21 trade for less than a penny ($.01); effectively, such stocks are not traded as they are not listed on any significant exchange, but simply trade infrequently on Internet bulletin boards. It is important to note however, that even a $1.00 cut off price to assess legitimacy is liberal, because as the *Wall Street Journal* indicates, even NASDAQ traded firms below $5.00 per share have a difficult time attracting investors:

> NASDAQ-listed companies with stocks trading for less than $1 for 30 consecutive trading days are in danger of delisting. Companies in this strait generally have 90 days to get their stock back above $1 and keep their listings, which is widely seen as critical in attracting institutional investors. At Merrill Lynch & Co., brokers are prohibited from recommending shares that aren't rated by the firm's research analysts, a spokesman said. And the spokesman said the analysts generally don't rate penny stocks – defined by many investors as any stock trading below $5 a share (Elstein, 2001, p. C17).

Beyond financial collapse, further evidence that the "dot-com" name had become illegitimate is that of the 47 firms still trading, 19 had changed their names back to a "non-dot-com" name (Table 2). For instance, PetMed Express Inc. announced

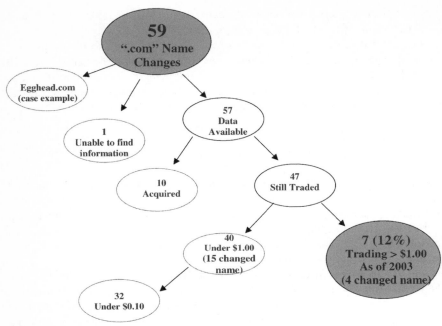

Fig. 2. What Happened to the 59 "dot-com" Name Changes that Occurred in 1998 and 1999? (As of November 2002.)

on April 8, 1999, that it was changing its name to PetMedExpress.com. Less than a year later, however, it changed its name back to Petmed Express Inc, and then, in May 2001, it began doing business as 1800PetMeds (ironically, perhaps, naming itself for a pre-Internet technology, the telephone!) As of late November 2002, 1800PetMeds was trading for just under $2.00 per share.

The findings on stock market valuations overall lend robust support for hypothesis two: The majority of the 58 companies that suffixed "dot-com" to their name in 1998 or 1999 had negative stock market valuation following the "dot-com" crash.

Taken together, the results from the questionnaire survey and stock market assessments indicate that companies that renamed themselves in 1998 or 1999 with a "dot-com" suffix found that they were no longer legitimate. Perceptions of appropriateness concerning Internet affiliations had shifted so dramatically and so swiftly that "dot-com" firms were seen as less credible by public audiences and perceived as less investment-worthy. Building on these findings, as well as insights from the Egghead case, we develop a theoretical framework that

Table 2. Firms from Lee's Sample of 59 "dot-com" Name Changes in 1998 and 1999 that Changed Their Name.

Original Name	"dot-com" Name Change	"dot-com" Change Date	Next "non-dot-com" Name Change[a]	Next Change Date
Prosoft I-Net Solutions	ProsoftTraining.com	9/18/1998	ProsoftTraining	1/17/2002
Tel-Save Holdings	Tel-Save.com	11/16/1998	Talk America	5/01/2001
MIS International	Cosmoz.com	1/15/1999	Financial Content, Inc.	10/13/2001
RLD Enterprises	Go-Rachels.com	1/28/1999	Rachel's Gourmet Snacks Inc	11/13/2001
New York Bagel Exchange Inc.	Webboat.com	2/1/1999	Federal Security Protection Services Inc	3/25/2002
Shop TV	Site2shop.com	2/11/1999	Intermedia Marketing Solutions Inc	05/16/2001
Score Medical Corp.	Imatters.com	3/22/1999	National Health Scan, Inc.	05/09/2002
Cardiovascular Laboratories Inc.	CLIXhealth.com	3/25/1999	Clix group inc	10/05/2000
The Henley Group	CIS.com	3/31/1999	InterAmerican Resources, Inc	9/17/2001
PetMed Express Inc.	PetMedExpress.com	4/8/1999	Petmed Express Inc	03/09/2000
IPVoice Communications Inc.	IPVoice.com	4/19/1999	IPVoice Communications, Inc	1/31/2001
Sloan Electronics	SalientCyber.com	4/20/1999	BrandAid Marketing Corp	12/14/2001
Okane International	Superwire.com	4/28/1999	Superwire Inc.	4/12/2002
SUNCOM Telecommunication	VirtualSellers.com	5/4/1999	Healthtrac, Inc	3/22/2002
ZapPower Systems	ZapWorld.com	5/18/1999	Zap	5/14/2001
e-Casino Gaming Corp.	e-Vegas.com	6/4/1999	Oasis Information Systems, Inc	10/15/2001
Eduverse Accelerated Learning Systems	Eduverse.com	6/7/1999	GeneMax Corp.	5/13/2002
Phon-Net Corp.	Phon-Net.com	6/14/1999	Environmental Strategies & Technologies International, Inc.	5/02/2002
Boraxx Technologies	QuadXSports.com	3/12/99	Bethel Holdings	9/18/2001

[a] In some instances, firms undertook multiple name changes. This change represents the name following a "dot-com" name.

models how symbols initially adopted in a quest for legitimacy can ultimately illegitimate.

TOWARDS A THEORY OF ORGANIZATIONAL ILLEGITIMACY

In the two studies reported in this chapter, we examined organizational names as a touchstone for illegitimacy and sought to understand how changed perceptions about the institutional environment of the Internet affected the process of deinstitutionalization. We observed how the symbol of the organizational "dot-com" name, initially legitimated a firm and, subsequently, illegitimated a firm. How was it, then, that symbols that could so quickly legitimate an organization illegitimate it just as quickly?

In investigating this question, a few basic assumptions guided our inquiry. Our first assumption concerns our view of organizational names. We conceptualize organizational names not simply as passive identity markers but as managerial claims to organizational membership in a targeted institutional field, such as the set of firms doing business on the Internet. Organizations seek legitimacy through isomorphic practices that symbolically link them to valued norms (Glynn & Abzug, 1998, 2002). Thus, we see organizational name changes as a symbolic and opportunistic grab at legitimacy, purchased through alignment with institutionalized practices and legitimacy as a critical driver in firm's adoption of the "dot-com" suffix.

Our second assumption is that "dot-com" names emerged as a marker of an emerging organizational field that sought legitimacy through association with the Internet. Thus, we focus on legitimacy at the level of the organizational field, i.e. the collective set of firms adopting this symbolic practice. We construe the emerging set of firms with "dot-com" names as a loosely focused organizational field that is identifiable through its shared symbolism. In the late 1990s, adding "dot-com" can be seen as a managerial attempt to align the firm with investor values and thus secure legitimacy for the firm. The name served as a boundary marker, cleanly dividing web-based businesses from those that were not, thereby creating a new and distinct category of organizations. As such, we treat this set of firms, at least symbolically, as an organizational field making membership claims as Internet businesses. We believe that such organizational fields, identifiable through a shared symbolic veneer, are not limited to "dot-com" named firms.

Ansell (1997, p. 360) observed that symbolic networks mobilize around potent "condensation symbols" that "create a shared interpretative framework that facilitates coordination, exchange, and ultimately commitment." In many ways, the name "dot-com" served this function, organizing the field of Internet-identified companies through the powerful symbol of a common name, thus representing meanings that helped to integrate groups around a shared sense of ideology, as Ansell (1997) observed.

Other organizational fields that are loosely-coupled but cohering around a common symbol are also evident. For instance, organizations that sponsor the Olympic Games and bear the powerful symbol of the five rings constitute a loosely-connected field of "Olympic Sponsors" although they may not share horizontal or vertical interdependencies. Even firms that constitute a more widely acknowledged organizational field such as the Fortune 500 (or Service 500) can in fact be seen as essentially a symbolic clustering. For example, in the 2002 list, the top seven in this ranking consist of two automakers (General Motors and Ford), a retailer (WalMart) an oil company (Exxon-Mobil), a natural gas and trading company (Enron), a conglomerate in many different industries (General Electric), and a financial firm (Citigroup). How these diverse firms are related in any way besides being large and bearing the label "Fortune 500" is not obvious. However, several institutional studies (e.g. Davis et al., 1994) treat the Fortune 500 as an organizational field. Such fields, organized or defined through symbolism, carry implicit principles of structuration, status, and authority; firms accrue social capital not only because of an actor's position within a social structure, but also because of claimed membership in that social structure. Thus, symbols can structure and even define organizational fields.

Our third and final assumption about organizational names is that, since legitimacy hinges on isomorphism, organizational conformity to norms and practices will legitimate only to the extent that those norms and practices are themselves legitimate, credible, and valued. Thus, although prevailing investor norms in the late 1990s valued – and even hyped – the Internet, this changed by early 2000. When the Internet bubble burst, norms changed accordingly and exposed the institutional dynamics underlying the relationship between legitimacy and illegitimacy. Our findings on these embedded processes of illegitimacy and deinstitutionalization in some ways parallel those hinted at in earlier studies, particularly those found by Davis and colleagues (1994) regarding the deconglomeratization in Fortune 500 firms as well as those of Kraatz and Zajac (1996) regarding professional and vocational programs in liberal arts colleges. However, our research departs from theirs in two significant ways: first, in terms of the antecedents of institutionalization, and second, in terms of the basis for perceptions of credibility.

Rather than being driven by strategic shifts (Davis et al., 1994) or ideological warfare (Kraatz & Zajac, 1996), deinstitutionalization for "dot-com" firms seemed to be predicated on something more fleeting and ephemeral. Just as Wall Street and public audiences seemed taken with all things Internet, bestowing upon them "a big wet kiss" (in the late 1990s), the ardor just as quickly cooled and dissipated. It was as if the illusion were stripped away and the media, rather than simply tracking deinstitutionalization (Davis et al., 1994), actively promoted it, alternatively hyping and hating the promise of the Internet. Given this swift and almost-faddish change in valuations of the Internet, the basis of credibility was similarly thin. By examining nothing more than a firm's name, we were able to note the evolution of legitimacy. It was not performance problems or threats to the institutional order that posed challenges to legitimacy, as in the Davis et al. (1994) and Kraatz and Zajac (1996) studies, but it was seismic shifts in the normative bedrock that created mis-alignments. Thus, the valorization of the Internet, and its subsequent taint, found a parallel in the credibility attached to the "dot-com" names. It was the withdrawal of legitimacy – and not a competing set of legitimating symbols and norms that threatened the established order – and illegitimated the organizational names. The challenge, then, is to account for such shifts that render legitimate symbols illegitimate. Following Zucker (1991) and Deephouse (1996), we postulate that illegitimating processes in organizations involve both *state* and *process* considerations. We develop these foundational ideas to work towards a theory of organizational illegitimacy.

A state perspective on illegitimacy focuses on a static assessment of the mis-alignment between an organization and the norms, beliefs, and values in the institutional environment. If isomorphism legitimates, evident in the positive valuations of "dot-com" named firms in 1998–1999, then a lack of isomorphism, predicated upon a changed environment, illegitimates these same firms and their symbols. However, to explain the latter necessitates a more dynamic model. Of particular note in this study was how swift and strong were the processes of institutionalization (and de-institutionalization) regarding the Internet and, correspondingly, the legitimacy and illegitimacy of "dot-com" names. Our conceptual framework postulating how state and process factors affect illegitimacy is illustrated in Fig. 3.

Figure 3 depicts how legitimacy accrues from a state of organizational-environmental alignment when organizational names conform to institutionalized values, norms, or beliefs, within a particular time period (Time 1 in Fig. 3). This "state" perspective on legitimacy is consistent with Jepperson's (1991, p. 149) argument that "institutionalization is best represented as a particular state, or property, of a social pattern." Implicitly, then, legitimacy (like institutionalization) is the property of the organization. Several definitions cited in Suchman (1995) serve to illustrate. Legitimacy is the state of "Congruence between the social values associated with or implied by (organizational) activities and the norms of acceptable behavior in the larger social system" (Dowling & Pfeffer, 1975, p. 122)

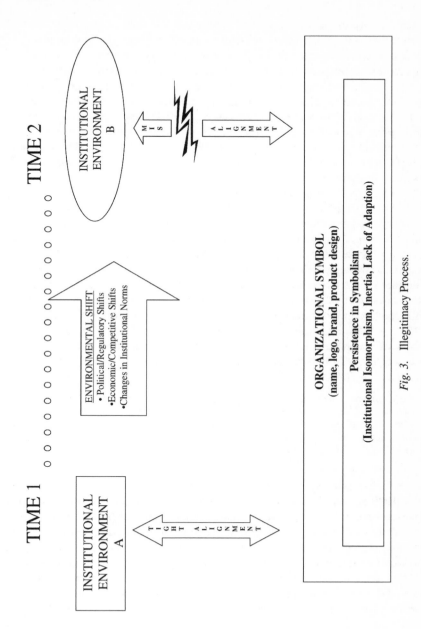

Fig. 3. Illegitimacy Process.

or simply, "Congruence between the organization and cultural environment" (Meyer & Scott, 1983). The "dot-com" names secured positive stock market valuations when Internet business was normatively sanctioned, reflecting an alignment between organizational symbols and institutionalized beliefs.

However, the dynamics of legitimacy, and by implication illegitimacy, involve more than assessing alignment (or mis-alignment) with institutionalized norms. A dynamic view that relates legitimacy and illegitimacy requires a process perspective. What drives delegitimation, or shifts from legitimate to illegitimate states, centers on change and periodicity. We suggest that studying the boundaries between legitimate and illegitimate states is a useful way to understand the dynamics of these processes.

There are two important ways in which such boundaries operate: one is concerned with the clarity with which we can discern the illegitimate from the legitimate; and the other is concerned with the flow from one to the other. The first path shifts the institutional view from one of isomorphism to polymorphism, whereby a less codified (less institutionalized) and variegated set of rules govern the organizational field. As Zucker (1991, p. 104) reminds us, "institutionalization is a continuous rather than a binary variable." Organizational fields are characterized by different degrees of institutionalization and, corresponding, by different latitudes with which legitimacy may be demarcated from illegitimacy. Meyer and Rowan (1977, p. 354) similarly argue that "Institutionalized myths differ in the complete-ness with which they describe cause and effect relationships, and in the clarity with which they describe standards that should be used to evaluate outputs." And that,

> [o]rganizational control efforts, especially in highly institutionalized contexts, are devoted to ritual conformity, both internally and externally .... the idea here is that the more highly institutionalized the environment, the more time and energy organizational elites devote to managing their organization's public image and status and the less they devote to coordi-nation and to managing particular boundary-spanning relationships (Meyer & Rowan, 1977, p. 361).

As 59 organizations re-named themselves with a "dot-com" suffix in the 1998–1999 period, they began to emerge as a collective, albeit loosely coupled, organizational field, that seemed to share not more than a symbolic veneer. Firms seemed to yield to a general normative imperative to align themselves with the Internet and do so rapidly with only an announcement of a name change. The web-based name seemed to represent an opportunistic grab at some newly evolving reputational capital associated with the Internet; startlingly, however, it seemed to be decoupled from other capital bases and traditional business practices. However, this social capital proved to be rather thin. It seemed that low degrees of institutionalization, that characterized the initial emergence of these Internet-identified firms, may breed more cloudy and incomplete legitimating accounts. This may be particularly true in the case of new, entrepreneurial entrants, which carry more uncertainty about their identity (Lounsbury & Glynn, 2001).

The second important way in which boundaries function in the construal of legitimacy and illegitimacy is by demarcating transition points where one process flows to the other. In many ways, legitimacy is a buffer against illegitimacy. Zucker's (1991) view of institutionalization focuses on processes of institutionalization, mapping variation and persistence, and that this may be reflected in the degree of institutionalization that characterizes fields. More generally, the underlying processes that transition between legitimate and illegitimate states hinge on institutitonalists' notion of periodicity, with each temporal era being characterized by a discrete set of sanctioned norms, which are different from those in other eras. In their work on symbolic isomorphism, Glynn and Abzug (2002) described how norms about appropriate naming practices varied from one decade to the next. For instance, in the 1800s, corporate names had long and richly descriptive monikers (The Peninsular and Oriental Steam Navigation Company), but this changed, by the mid-1900s, to reflect more market and brand concerns, typically in a 3-word configuration (United States Steel Corporation). The mid- and late 1900s abbreviated the corporate name further, generating such ambiguous corporate tags as USX and Unisys, but this was reversed towards the end of the century, which saw a shift back to familiar and clear names (Domino Sugar). It was in the late 1990s that corporate names returned to the 3-part configuration, but this time to reflect their internet location (www.amazon.com). How such norms about the appropriateness of Internet symbols in organizational names changed at the turn of the new millennium is our focus in this chapter.

To summarize our perspective, we theorize that organizational illegitimacy involves a state of mis-alignment with the environment, which can be predicated upon the processes of institutionalization and changing valuations, norms, and beliefs. Organizations align themselves with the institutional order by conforming to sanctioned norms in order to secure legitimacy; indeed, this seemed to drive organizations to append "dot-com" to their names in the 1998–1999 period. However, institutionalization is not static and norms, beliefs and values change over time. Organizations that are symbolically inert can become mis-aligned when environments change through processes of deinstitutionalization; this seemed to drive the perceived illegitimacy of "dot-com" names in the wake of the Internet crash. Moreover, this process occurred with great speed and abruptness on the Internet.

We derived our theoretical framework through our studies of "dot-com" names at different points in time, with reference to a critical and quick transformation, i.e. the bursting of the Internet bubble. Future research might test this framework on illegitimacy in sites that afford a different view of institutionalization and deinstitutionalization processes as well as with different types of organizational symbols and structures that signify alignment (or mis-alignment) to the institutional order. And, although the "dot-com" phenomena was somewhat novel in terms of the speed and clarity with which institutionalization and deinstitutionalization occurred, as we have noted, its lessons may extend to other organizational frontiers facing similar rates of change. For instance, another context in which deinstitutionalization occurred swiftly was that of corporate governance, compensation structures, and executive pay in the post-Enron world. Some of these fundamentally changed how boards are composed and how executives are paid. For example, Richard Grasso of the New York Stock Exchange (NYSE) was recently ousted because of perceptions that his pay was excessive and illegitimate; however, his pay was not more than other executives in immediately prior periods, notably the late 1990s, early 2000s. Thus, norms about executive pay seemed to have changed quickly and with significant consequence. As well, former and vocal proponents of stock options (as a form of employee pay) have abandoned them; Microsoft is a well known example. And, finally, there have been fast and furious changes in corporate boards such that companies have tried to do a better job of staffing the committees of the board so they are not so dominated by the CEO and other employees of companies, a practice that was previously well-established and well-accepted. All of these changes, in corporate governance, executive pay, and compensation preferences, have come about at great speed, much like the changes evidenced in the valuation of the Internet. And all offer opportunistic sites for observing institutionalization and illegitimacy, as DiMaggio and colleagues (2001) suggested.

To conclude, we focus on the contributions that this research offers. In theorizing illegitimacy as institutional mis-alignment, we explicitly recognize that the boundaries partitioning illegitimacy from legitimacy are dynamic. Hence, there is a need to conceptualize illegitimacy – as well as legitimacy – as both a process and a state. And, in highlighting the concept of illegitimacy, our objective is to spur research in this theoretically underdeveloped area. Ironically, over 60 years ago, Kingsley Davis (1939, p. 215) lamented that illegitimacy was over-studied and legitimacy under-studied; he noted that, *"The Encyclopedia of the Social Sciences* . . . contains two lengthy articles on illegitimacy but nothing on legitimacy." Our hope is that this chapter may similarly reverse research trends and redirect scholars to investigate illegitimacy dynamics in organizations more expansively.

NOTE

1. The single name change that we were unable to locate is that from Staruni Corp to Ubid4it.com. SEC filings indicated that Staruni had been acquired by Elephant Talk Communications on February 2, 2002. Because Lee's study is based on announced changes, it is possible that this name change was announced but never completed.

REFERENCES

Ansell, C. K. (1997). Symbolic networks: The realignment of the French working class, 1887–1894. *American Journal of Sociology, 2*, 359–390.

Christie, J. (1990, January 31). Have the Klingons taken over banks? It sounds like it. *The Wall Street Journal*, A1, A6.

Cooper, M. J., Dimitrov, O., & Rau, P. R. (2001). A rose by any other name. *Journal of Finance, 56*, 2371–2388.

Davis, G. F., Diekmann, K. A., & Tinsley, C. H. (1994). The decline and fall of the conglomerate firm in the 1980s: The de-institutionalization of an organizational form. *American Sociological Review, 59*, 547–570.

Davis, K. (1939). Illegitimacy and the social structure. *American Journal of Sociology, 45*(2), 215–233.

Deephouse, D. L. (1996). Does isomorphism legitimate? *Academy of Management Journal, 39*(4), 1024–1039.

DiMaggio, P., Hargittai, E., Neuman, W. R., & Robinson, J. R. (2001). Social implications of the Internet. *Annual Review of Sociology, 27*, 307–336.

Dowling, J., & Pfeffer, J. (1975). Organizational legitimacy: Social values and organizational behavior. *Pacific Sociological Review, 18*, 122–136.

Elsbach, K. D., & Sutton, R. (1992). Acquiring organizational legitimacy through illegitimate actions: A marriage of institutional and impression management theories. *Academy of Management Journal, 35*, 699–738.

Elstein, A. (2001, June 21). Deals & deal makers: Battered companies do the reverse split – while tactic boosts share prices, it seldom reverses fortune. *The Wall Street Journal*, C17.

Fligstein, N. (1990) *The transformation of corporate control*. Cambridge, MA: Harvard University Press.

Fombrun, C., & Shanley, M. (1990). What's in a corporate name? Reputation building and corporate strategy. *Academy of Management Journal, 33*, 233–258.

Glynn, M. A., & Abzug, R. A. (1998). Isomorphism and competitive differentiation in the organizational name game. In: J. A. C. Baum (Ed.), *Advances in Strategic Management* (Vol. 15, pp. 105–128). Greenwich, CT: JAI Press.

Glynn, M. A., & Abzug, R. (2002). Institutionalizing identity: Symbolic isomorphism and organizational names. *Academy of Management Journal, 45*, 267–280.

Jepperson, R. L. (1991). Institutions, institutional effects, and institutionalism. In: W. W. Powell & P. J. DiMaggio (Eds), *The New Institutionalism in Organizational Analysis* (pp. 143–163). Chicago: University of Chicago Press.

Kraatz, M. S., & Zajac, E. J. (1996). Exploring the limits of the new institutionalism: The causes and consequences of illegitimate organizational change. *American Sociological Review, 61*, 812–836.

Lee, J. (1998, August 17). Egghead averts annihilation: The computer products retailer still has problems, but a bold move to Web-only distribution could save it. *Fortune Magazine*, 194.

Lee, P. M. (2001). What's in a name.com? The effects of '.com' name changes on stock prices and trading activity. *Strategic Management Journal*, 22, 793–804.

Lounsbury, M., & Glynn, M. A. (2001). Cultural entrepreneurship: Stories, legitimacy and the acquisition of resources. *Strategic Management Journal*, 22, 545–564.

Maio, P. (2001, January 8). Egghead.com reels from slump faced after hacker case. *The Wall Street Journal*, B11A.

Meyer, J. W., & Rowan, B. (1977). Institutionalized organizations: Formal structure as myth and ceremony. *American Journal of Sociology*, 83, 440–463.

Meyer, J. W., & Scott, W. R. (1983). Centralization and the legitimacy problem of local governments. In: J. W. Meyer & W. R. Scott (Eds), *Organizational Environments: Ritual and Rationality* (pp. 199–215). Beverly Hills, CA: Sage.

Suchman, M. (1995). Managing legitimacy: Strategic and institutional approaches. *Academy of Management Review*, 20, 571–610.

Useem, J. (2000, October 20). Dot-coms: What have we learned? Dot-coms soared. Dot-coms crashed. Somewhere in between we uncovered 12 truths about how the Net really changes business. *Fortune*, 82.

Wall Street Journal (2000, November 20). Merged Phone.com sheds dot-com name, B13.

Walczak, L. (2001, August 27). The mood now: The dot-com flameout and ensuing slump have not shaken America's faith in technology and renewed prosperity. *Businessweek*.

Weber, T. E. (1999, October 11). This start-up proposes to dump dot-com, but is it too late? *Wall Street Journal* (Eastern ed.), B1.

Weber, T. E. (2000, July 18). Reality Check: Life after the dot-com crash – What were we THINKING? – Arrogance, greed and optimism plus fear of being left out blinded people to the risks. *The Wall Street Journal*, B1.

Zucker, L. G. (1991). The role of institutionalization in cultural persistence. In: W. W. Powell & P. J. DiMaggio (Eds), *The New Institutionalism in Organizational Analysis* (pp. 83–107). Chicago: University of Chicago Press.

Zuckerman, E. (1999). The categorical imperative: Securities analysts and the illegitimacy discount. *American Journal of Sociology*, 104, 1398–1438.

BETWEEN ISOMORPHISM AND MARKET PARTITIONING: HOW ORGANIZATIONAL COMPETENCIES AND RESOURCES FOSTER CULTURAL AND SOCIOPOLITICAL LEGITIMACY, AND PROMOTE ORGANIZATIONAL SURVIVAL

Matthew E. Archibald

ABSTRACT

This paper analyzes a multidimensional model of organizational legitimacy, competencies, and resources in order to develop the linkage between institutional and resource-based perspectives by systematically detailing relationships among these factors and organizational viability. The underlying mechanisms of isomorphism and market partitioning serve as a point of departure by which the effects on organizational persistence of two sociocultural processes, cultural (constitutive) legitimation and sociopolitical (regulative) legitimation, are distinguished. Using data on 589 national self-help/mutual-aid organizations, this chapter explores how isomorphism and market partitioning foster legitimacy and promote

Legitimacy Processes in Organizations
Research in the Sociology of Organizations, Volume 22, 171–211
Copyright © 2004 by Elsevier Ltd.
All rights of reproduction in any form reserved
ISSN: 0733-558X/doi:10.1016/S0733-558X(04)22006-7

organizational viability. Results show that the more differentiated an organization's core competencies and resources, the greater the sociopolitical legitimacy; the more isomorphic an organization's competencies and resources, the greater the cultural legitimacy. The latter isomorphic processes, however, do not promote greater organizational viability. In fact, while isomorphism legitimates with respect to cultural recognition, it is heterogeneity, not homogeneity, that promotes organizational survival.

INTRODUCTION

Institutional theories in organizational sociology, including recent versions of organizational ecology, are based on the central premise that organizational outcomes are related to the ability to acquire legitimacy, social support, and acceptance from actors in the institutional environment (Carroll & Hannan, 2001; DiMaggio & Powell, 1983; Meyer & Rowan, 1977). In an institutional framework, organizational viability depends largely, although not exclusively, on social, rather than competitive fitness. Rationalized sociocultural and political environments induce homogeneity (i.e. isomorphism) among the formal aspects of different organizations, which enhances organizational viability. Describing the relationship between environmental influences and organizational outcomes is straightforward under this isomorphic regime: regulatory (coercive), normative and cultural (mimetic) mechanisms in the extended institutional environment induce homogeneity among organizations (with regard to their structures, routines and practices) which promotes viability because, it is argued, structural homogeneity signals legitimacy (Scott, 2001).

Resource-based frameworks also detail the relationship between the formal aspects of organizations and organizational viability. In these models, organizations attempt to manage crowding in markets by targeting unique resource segments in an effort to reduce competition when different organizations converge on a single resource or production space (Carroll & Hannan, 2000). By differentiating themselves from potential competitors, along a number of formal dimensions, organizations that do not enjoy scale advantages (e.g. usually newer or smaller organizations) can exploit variations in available resource space even when a market has attained a high degree of concentration. Consequently, environmental constraints induce organizational heterogeneity, rather than homogeneity, which promotes organizational viability. This is so, it is argued, because market differentiation reduces competition through development of structures, routines, and practices that allow organizations to cultivate specialty niches.

Given that organizations confront both institutional and competitive pressures, how are researchers to understand the underlying (cross-cutting) mechanisms generating organizational legitimacy and viability, and, what can organizations do to foster legitimacy, promote viability, and assure persistence? One answer is that distinguishing the organizational consequences of two broad types of legitimation processes (i.e. cultural and sociopolitical legitimacy), and modeling these along with resource-based factors, uncovers the differential effects of isomorphic and resource-partitioning mechanisms, that in turn are expected to influence organizational viability. It is important to distinguish cultural and sociopolitical legitimacy because although organizations are constrained by both social and competitive demands, the processes generating organizational viability based on isomorphic pressures are markedly different from those associated with the underlying mechanisms of market partitioning. I argue in this paper that the differences between the effects of isomorphic and market partitioning processes will emerge when legitimacy is differentiated along cultural and sociopolitical dimensions. The primary reason underlying this claim is that it seems unlikely that regulative, normative and cognitive-cultural legitimation processes have uniform effects on organizational structures, routines and practices. Whether cultural legitimacy, involving constitutive or normative rules, is more likely to entail organizational homogeneity, than sociopolitical legitimacy, involving regulatory regimes based on self-interest, and expedience, is an empirical question that is important to understand.

In addition, it is necessary to distinguish cultural and sociopolitical legitimacy from organizational competencies and resources because institutional theory is unique in emphasizing social fitness, while resource-based theories highlight advantages accruing to material endowments (Tolbert & Zucker, 1996). It is important to distinguish legitimacy from resources (and other non-symbolic capabilities) in order to facilitate greater complementarity between the different strengths of institutional and resource-based frameworks. Use of organizational ecology as a bridge is an obvious choice of analytic strategies. Its succinct operationalization of variables and specification of models detailing the expected relationships between factors derived from the two different theoretical perspectives helps solve the problem of conceptual ambiguity.

In this paper, I draw on institutional and resource-based perspectives to analyze a multidimensional model of legitimacy (Ruef & Scott, 1998). Doing so extends the institutional framework providing greater linkage between institutionalist and resource-based explanations of organizational viability (Jones, 2001; Oliver, 1997). The objective of these analyses is to understand and reconcile divergent elements of institutional and resource-based approaches by: (1) re-conceptualizing the cultural and sociopolitical dimensions of legitimacy, and generating direct measures of the concepts; (2) developing the empirical implications of the relationship between legitimacy, organizational competencies, and resources, based on the two theoretical models and; (3) analyzing contrasting expectations of the relationships between different types of legitimacy (cultural and sociopolitical), organizational competencies, resources, and organizational persistence, using comprehensive data on national self-help/mutual-aid organizations.

This paper draws on two main strands in organizational theory and research. Institutional frameworks suggest that social fitness, gained as organizations become isomorphic with their institutional environment, promotes viability (Scott, 2001). Resource-based theories emphasize that competitive fitness, gained through the process of differentiation, promotes viability (Carroll, 1985; Oliver, 1997). Theoretically, a number of studies have attempted to extend the insights of each in order to create greater complementarity (e.g. Jones, 2001; Oliver, 1997; Scott et al., 2000). Empirically, recent studies have begun to make progress modeling legitimation processes through direct measurement of organizational legitimacy (Barron, 1998; Deephouse, 1996; Edwards & Marullo, 1995; Hybels & Ryan, 1996; Hybels, Ryan & Barley, 1994; Ruef & Scott, 1998; Scott et al., 2000). Research examining legitimation processes and isomorphism suggest that organizational homogeneity in strategies and goals (Deephouse, 1996; Ruef & Scott, 1998), and identities (Glynn & Abzug, 1998, 2001) fosters legitimacy, which promotes viability (e.g. Ruef, 1997; Scott et al., 2000). In contrast, research examining the market partitioning strategies organizations use to out-maneuver other organizations shows that differentiation between organizations promotes viability because as niches become more crowded and resources uncertain, specializing or generalizing strategies permit organizational access to uncontrolled resources (see e.g. Boone et al., 2002; Carroll & Swaminathan, 2000). Although studies with a resource-partitioning focus do not typically model legitimation processes (however see Carroll & Swaminathan, 2000), Scott and Ruef (1997) have shown how divergence in market niches influences legitimacy, as well as survival. I extend the work of these studies by distinguishing, operationalizing, and modeling cultural and sociopolitical legitimacy, core competencies, and resources in order to decipher the variable effects of isomorphism and market partitioning on organizational viability.

To understand how the processes of isomorphism and market partitioning affect organizational legitimacy, and viability, I analyze data from an original database of life histories of all active national self-help/mutual-aid organizations in the U.S. between 1955 and 2000. The central research question is: To what extent does between-organizational homogeneity in core competencies (organizational programs and services), and resources (human capital), foster cultural and sociopolitical legitimacy, and promote self-help/mutual-aid viability? Characterizing both dimensions of legitimacy as recognition by relevant sector authorities, I explore what kind of legitimacy is sought after by organizations that display varying degrees of programmatic, service, and resource homogeneity. In addition, I extend the work of organizational ecologists and others who have used non-profit organizations to analyze legitimation processes such as Singh et al.'s (1991) work on social service agencies, and Baum and Oliver (1991) on day care, as well as studies focusing on non-profits' use of resource partitioning (e.g. Boone et al., 2002; Poplieraz & McPherson, 1995).

This chapter answers the central research question by organizing the analysis in the following manner. I first outline the main arguments linking isomorphism, market partitioning, legitimacy, and organizational viability, and develop several hypotheses. I then discuss the data and methods brought to bear on the hypotheses, followed by analyses and results. The chapter concludes with a discussion of some shortcomings of the model, future directions, and the relevance of models like this one for other organizational contexts.

HOW DO ORGANIZATIONAL COMPETENCIES AND RESOURCES FOSTER CULTURAL AND SOCIOPOLITICAL LEGITIMACY, AND PROMOTE ORGANIZATIONAL VIABILITY?

Distinguishing Cultural and Sociopolitical Legitimacy

Legitimacy is: "a generalized perception or assumption that the actions of an entity are desirable, proper or appropriate within some socially constructed system of norms, values, beliefs and definitions" (Suchman, 1995, p. 574). Organizations are legitimate to the extent that they are able to justify to relevant others their right to exist (Maurer, 1971). They do so by providing appropriate and understandable explanations of their structures, routines, and practices for internal and external audiences. Initially, the concept of legitimacy was applied to organizational goals (Parsons, 1956). Later, the focus shifted to structural and procedural aspects such as "offices, specialized functions, rules, records, routines" (Scott, 2001, p. 152). By emphasizing that actions and patterns of behavior are legitimated (or not) all manner of organizational relationships, purposes, goals, values, routines, and systems of governance become subject to evaluation. To argue that some institution or organization is legitimate based on collective perception is to assert that an audience supports or accepts it. External actors, ranging from federal and state agencies to social movement entrepreneurs, as well as internal actors, ranging from professionals to group members, are culturally and politically empowered to act as authorities. Contemporary institutionalists view legitimacy as a social condition that indicates cultural alignment and normative support consistent with relevant norms and rules governing the form that organizational activities take.

Organizational environments induce actors to adopt structures, routines, and practices that are institutionally based (i.e. created by social convention). New institutionalism in organizational theory problematizes organizational structures, routines, and practices (i.e. what they are, and where they come from) by developing the concept of institutional isomorphism and linking it with legitimation processes. Isomorphism concerns regulatory, normative, and cognitive elements of socioeconomic and political institutions that foster structural, procedural, and strategic homogeneity throughout organizational fields. Through coercion, normative influence, and cultural imitation, isomorphic mechanisms promote formal homogeneity and legitimacy. While legitimation processes operate at a number of different analytic levels, legitimacy gained through structural alignment under isomorphic regimes is more strongly delimited at the level of organizational fields rather than at diffuse societal levels (Scott, 2001). This suggests that analysis of differences between organizations comprising a particular form along the dimensions of legitimating structures, practices, and routines will be fruitful.

Broadly construed, the first "institutional pillar" of neo institutionalist theory emphasizes the instrumental character of legitimacy by way of regulative rules (see e.g. Pfeffer & Salancik, 1978). Regulatory processes structure organizations, organizational sectors, and populations of organizations by fostering expedient, self-interested behavior among sector actors (Meyer & Rowan, 1977). The regulative aspect of institutional processes depends on monitoring, rule-setting, and sanctioning. Rules may be informal or formal and expedience is a central motivation associated with the regulative aspect of an institutional practice. Conformity arises out of actors' best interests, rationally conceived. Organizations might engage in competition in a political market by struggling to alter policies, influence regulations/laws, and garner capital/funding or resources. By way of introducing a subtle contrast, one stream of organization theory emphasizing the more purposive aspect of legitimation processes suggests that it "is an operational *resource* that organizations extract – often competitively – from their cultural environments and that they employ in pursuit of their goals" (italics added, Suchman, 1995, p. 576). For example, Carroll and Hannan (2001) argue that in addition to financial and human capital, organizational resources might consist of endorsements by state officials, status, and legitimacy. The equivalence of legitimacy and resources is confusing since enterprises may have resources but not much legitimacy (e.g. despotic governments), or legitimacy but few resources (e.g. community-based ministries).

The remaining institutional pillars of neo institutionalist theory emphasize the normative and cognitive character of legitimacy by way of constitutive rules. Normative systems define goals and the appropriate way to achieve them. Normative elements may impose constraints on behavior but they also enable (constitute) action. Normative practices enable action in that normative rules confer rights and responsibilities, and privileges.

The cognitive aspect of legitimation processes creates the lens by which social reality is constructed. Cognitive practices shape categories of actors, and expectations about social roles, positions, people, and structures. Cognitive systems create scenes, actors, and scripts for interpersonal interaction. Institutions and organizations become taken-for-granted so that actors accept as given the thing that ordinarily would require the rendering of accounts to justify. The taken-for-granted aspect of legitimacy removes the social constructedness of the behavior so that actors disappear, and the order of things seems always to have existed as it is observed.

For purposes of these analyses, legitimacy is conceptualized as both non-instrumental (cultural) and instrumental (sociopolitical). Cultural legitimacy entails constitutive norms and beliefs that enhance comprehensibility because they create the impression of meaningfulness, predictability and trust. Access to resources, although important, is largely secondary. Sociopolitical legitimacy entails expedience, and it is conferred by authorities whose self-interest is at the forefront of their consideration of organizational designs and purposes. Actors pursuing the practical consequences of organizational designs and activities evince a strong political interest in organizational legitimacy. In this sense, legitimacy becomes a strategy around which sociopolitical interests emerge.

The analytic claim is that legitimacy should be characterized by two major dimensions – cultural legitimacy (constitutive) and sociopolitical legitimacy (regulative). In this paper, tapping the multidimensional characteristics of legitimacy is important because it begs the question whether the same kinds of mechanisms generate cultural and sociopolitical legitimacy, which in turn are expected to enhance organizational persistence.

Cultural and Sociopolitical Legitimacy, Core Competencies, and Resources

An organization's capabilities and resources include all those aspects "that enable it to conceive of and implement strategies" (Barney & Hesterly, 1996, p. 133). Core competencies are stocks of organizational routines, knowledge and skills covering a range of functional activities (e.g. production, research, distribution). Routines might involve core technologies in hospital production and service lines (Ruef, 1997), brewing techniques (Carroll & Swaminathan, 2000) or even social movement service provision (Minkoff, 1999). While an organization's resources are financial (e.g. capital, equity, debt), physical (e.g. machines), human (e.g. training, experience, judgment) and organizational (e.g. teamwork, trust, friendship) (Barney, 1991), some frameworks treat legitimacy as a manageable resource or organizational capability (Hybels, 1995). Yet, conflating legitimacy, core competencies, and resources risks creating an equivalence between acquisition of legitimacy and that of resources. As noted earlier, organizations may be sustained by considerable resource endowments and still fail to be regarded as legitimate (e.g. despotic governments, illegal cartels, Posse Comitatus), while others having acquired legitimacy, remain relatively resource-poor (e.g. substance abuse treatment facilities, neighborhood associations, inner city community ministries).

The analytic challenge is to determine how cultural and sociopolitical legitimacy, core competencies, and resources are distinct. My second analytic claim, although also not a formal hypothesis, is: Cultural and sociopolitical legitimacy are not functionally equivalent to organizational core competencies and resources. That is, competencies and resources may be characterized as legitimate or not, given some environmental imperative, but this does not imply that legitimacy is an organizational competency or a resource.

Having set out these two preliminary expectations regarding the factors in the analysis, I discuss their main relationships and develop formal hypotheses in the following sections.

The Effects of Isomorphism and Market Partitioning on Legitimacy and Organizational Viability

Legitimating processes are essential to organizational persistence for a number of reasons related to organizational growth and survival, such as attracting a broader constituency, and gaining better access to economic and political resources (Baum, 1996). In an early formulation, DiMaggio and Powell (1991) argued that organizations strive for social as well as economic fitness. Organizations compete not just for resources, but also for political power, and status. Legitimacy promotes organizational status, and deflects any criticism of organizational competencies and rights, thereby enhancing survival. Therefore:

Hypothesis 1. Cultural and sociopolitical legitimacy will increase the likelihood of organizational viability.

One way organizations pursue legitimacy (and therefore enhance persistence) is by developing structures, routines, and practices isomorphic with their socioeconomic, cultural, and political environments. "By designing a formal structure that adheres to the prescriptions" of the rationalizing myths in the institutional environment, organizations demonstrate their legitimacy (Meyer & Rowan, 1977 [1991], p. 50). Scott et al. (2000), use several measures of legitimacy, such as accreditation based on professional standards and activities, to show how isomorphic processes foster legitimacy and promote survival among medical organizations. Jones (2001) links organizational capabilities and legitimacy in a dynamic model of film industry careers.

Taking a slightly different approach, market theories also attempt to explain organizational viability based on the formal elements of organizations. Resource-based frameworks hold that:

> rare, specialized and inimitable resources and resource market imperfections cause firm heterogeneity, [. . .] successful firms are those that acquire and maintain valuable idiosyncratic resources for sustainable competitive advantage (Oliver, 1997, p. 700).

In short, capabilities and resources vary significantly across firms, and may be stable instead of converging on one particular form (Barney & Hesterly, 1996). Resource-based frameworks suggest that organizations can manage their environments by outmaneuvering other organizations for access to resources (Aldrich, 1999). In these models, similarity in resource requirements affects competition between organizations: The more similar the resource requirements, the greater the potential for competition (Hannan & Freeman, 1977, 1989). Indeed, competition follows from greater overlap in resource requirements, which increases the chances of organizational failure.

Several explanations contribute to this outlook. Resource partitioning or market differentiation refers to the extent to which organizations attempt to manage crowding in markets. Organizations do so by targeting services and products to various market segments (Carroll & Hannan, 2001). Some target to homogeneous segments and others to narrow segments. The former organizations are referred to as generalists, and the latter, specialists. Specialist organizations concentrate resources while generalists expand resources. So-called r-strategists (who may be specialists or generalists) are first movers in under-exploited niches and k-strategists are efficient, albeit, late movers in niches that have reached their carrying capacity. These types of strategies are not mutually exclusive, such that both specialists and generalists may partition a niche and share its resources. Carroll and Swaminathan (2000) show how specialist organizations (in the brewing industry) take advantage of concentrated markets to fashion a niche that protects them from competition with dominant others. Similarly, Haider-Markel (1997) demonstrate that interest groups avoid direct competition by adapting to different issue niches (i.e. specializing), and, Ruef, Mendel and Scott (1998) detail the ameliorative effects of resource partitioning on competition in the healthcare sector. Although the theory is typically used to explain the emergence of specialist organizations in industries characterized by a high degree of concentration, a number of studies have examined resource partitioning and organizational viability (mortality) (e.g. Carroll, 1985; see Carroll & Hannan, 2001 for a review).

A related explanatory schema is niche overlap (Baum, 1995; Baum & Oliver, 1996; Baum & Singh, 1994a, b). This theory derives from Hannan and Freeman's research examining density-dependence in founding and mortality rates. Baum's models test the proposition that competition and survival are related to the overlap of organizations' resource bases, indirectly measured by different density functions. Like market partitioning, its propositions suggest that greater resource overlap fosters competition between organizations. Subsequent shifts in population rates of organizational formation and survival are based on the extent to which resources are acquired by some, but not all, competitors.

Some resource-based frameworks may also include legitimacy as a predictor of fitness. Here, legitimacy helps organizations secure political, economic, and social capital. Scott et al.'s (2000) study of institutional change in U.S. healthcare shows that the distribution of material resources, as well as legitimacy, fundamentally affect organizational persistence. In another recent study, Edwards and Marullo (1995) examine resource use by peace movement organizations (such as paid staff, membership, and volunteer hours) and legitimacy (based on public support, media relations, co-sponsorship of events, and member's sense of empowerment). Both resources and legitimacy predict social movement viability but their mutual, and, direct and indirect, effects were not specified.

The emphasis in market partitioning differs from that of institutional theory in that in the latter perspective, organizational legitimacy is at the forefront of the relationship between competencies, resources, and viability. In a resource-based perspective it becomes secondary because resource-based views focus on the direct relationship between the degree of organizational differentiation and organizational outcomes rather than the causal mechanism of legitimacy. Note that while resource-based theories may or may not imply an intervening mechanism channeling the effects of heterogeneity, the perspective has yet to suggest that legitimacy serves as that mechanism. It is possible that increased differentiation promotes a unique organizational identity that translates into legitimacy, further enhancing survivability (Carroll & Swaminathan, 2000). Ruef and Scott (1998) found that market partitioning (specialty niche) was salient, and differentially influenced two different types of legitimacy. By emphasizing different aspects of the model, it is possible to develop hypotheses relevant to each perspective.

The second hypothesis highlights expectations consistent with an institutional approach. If regulatory, normative and cognitive pressures originating in organizations, among professionals, within state bureaucracies, the cultural-at-large, and other domains, come to bear on a set of organizations in such a way as to promote large-scale structural uniformity between organizations which in turn foster legitimacy (DiMaggio & Powell, 1991; Scott, 1987; Scott & Meyer, 1991), then:

Hypothesis 2. Isomorphism (homogeneity) rather than market partitioning (heterogeneity) among core competencies and resources will promote cultural and sociopolitical legitimacy.

Institutionalists argue that isomorphism fosters organizational viability because it generates legitimacy. In effect, this involves testing a directional hypothesis based on the signs of the coefficients. That is, homogeneity (rather than differentiation) should promote organizational legitimacy and promote organizational viability.

The central premise in resource-based views is that organizations target resource segments and competition ensues. Overall, economies of scale help generalists (organizations targeting large resource segments) while specialists exploit the narrowness of their segment. Consequently, it is expected that the extent to which organizations differentiate themselves by developing unique structures that (at least hypothetically) facilitate resource acquisition, and endowments, organizational persistence will be enhanced. In the end, the image leads to the prediction that differentiation of core competencies and resources will yield survival while overlap will lead to organizational disbanding. This stands in contrast to expectations generated by an institutional framework. Resource-based theories lead to expectations that contradict institutional expectations that isomorphism functions to promote organizational viability because of its relationship with legitimacy. Hence,

Hypothesis 3. Resource partitioning (heterogeneity) rather than isomorphism (homogeneity) among core competencies and resources will increase the likelihood of organizational viability.

The final hypothesis details a fully specified model of organizational viability based on arguments originating in the institutional framework:

Hypothesis 4. Isomorphism (homogeneity) rather than market partitioning (heterogeneity) among core competencies and resources will promote cultural and sociopolitical legitimacy and will foster organizational viability.

Figure 1 depicts the relationships described by the preceding verbal accounts. It is important to note that the direction of effects from core competencies and resources towards legitimacy is consistent with the hypothesized direction of the latent (unmeasured) influence of isomorphism-differentiation.

In the next section, I detail the data and measures used to unpack and analyze these relationships to better understand how legitimacy, organizational

[A] Cultural Legitimacy, Core Competencies, Resources and Outcomes

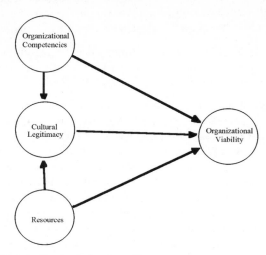

[B] Sociopolitical Legitimacy, Core Competencies, Resources and Outcomes

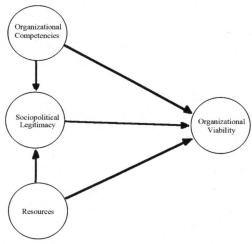

Fig. 1.   Cultural and Sociopolitical Legitimacy, Core Competencies, Resources, and Self-Help/Mutual-Aid Viability.

competencies, and resources influence one another and self-help/mutual-aid persistence.

DATA AND METHODS

Data

I analyze cultural and sociopolitical legitimacy, organizational competencies, and resources underlying organizational persistence using an original database of life histories of all active national self-help/mutual-aid organizations in the U.S. between 1955 and 2000. Self-help/mutual-aid refers to organizations designed to address personal stigmatizing conditions or problems, ranging from medical disability to behavioral dysfunction, in a public but intimate face-to-face group setting. Personal stigmatizing conditions or problems might entail amputation (National Amputee Foundation), cancer (Reach to Recovery), alcoholism (Alcoholics Anonymous), an autistic child (Autism Network), or a relative with Alzheimer's disease (Alzheimer's Disease and Related Disorders Association). Like other formal organizations, self-help/mutual-aid is strongly goal oriented, and supported by a systematic program that is sustained by a differentiated, complex organizational structure comprised of groups, meetings, chapters, boards, volunteers, staff, and affiliated networks (Powell, 1990).

In these analyses, I treat the data cross-sectionally because, in part, the central theoretical questions of interest rely on multiple indicator models of key concepts. Moreover, since hypotheses detail relationships between endogenous latent factors and outcomes, use of simultaneous equations capitalizes on the strengths of this method.[1] The database was constructed from a variety of sources (see Archibald, 2002), including *The Encyclopedia of Associations* (Gale Research Company, 1955–2000), which serves as a chief source of data for this paper. The *Encyclopedia* contains historical information on all self-declared national membership organizations, including voluntary associations devoted to providing health and human services. Each edition and organizational entry of the *Encyclopedia of Associations* consists of a detailed year-by-year record that includes, but is not limited to, organizational founding date, organizational status (e.g. disbanding and changes in name), organizational competencies in the areas of services and programs, and organizational resources, for all national self-help/mutual-aid organizations. In creating the original longitudinal database of the information in the *Encyclopedia*, yearly entries were coded and combined with data drawn from *Index Medicus-Medline, Congressional Information Service, Sociological and Psychological Abstracts*, the *New York Times Index, U.S. Department of Commerce – Bureau of Economic Analysis, U.S. Department of Labor-Office of Education, National Center for Education Statistics.*

Many of the strengths of the *Encyclopedia of Association* are discussed in Minkoff (1995). Despite its comprehensive coverage, some national self-help/mutual-aid organizations may not appear in the *Encyclopedia of Associations* because they are too short-lived (i.e. those failing within a year). This criterion limits variation in organizational life spans to at least a year. It is a reflection of the nature of building a national organization rather than a specific bias on the part of the *Encyclopedia*.

Measures

Table 1 provides summary statistics for variables and factors used in the following analyses. Variables analyzed in this study are arranged by their order in the models depicted in Fig. 1. Each of the latent constructs is represented by observed variables described in the following sections. I begin with a discussion of the endogenous variables and work backwards to the control variables.

Endogenous Variables

There are several endogenous variables in the model: legitimacy, transition, and disbanding. Because core competencies and resources are predicted to affect legitimacy, and the two outcomes, transition and disbanding, they are exogenous. I begin by discussing self-help/mutual-aid organizational transition and disbanding.

Organizational Transition and Disbanding. Organizational theorists distinguish a number of transitional events that affect individual organizations and organizational populations ranging from re-organization, to acquisitions, mergers and disbanding (Carroll & Hannan, 2000). In order to analyze self-help/mutual-aid transition and disbanding, I created two variables. The first variable measures organizational viability by ordering changes in an organization's life history. It has three dimensions: survival, transition (indicated by changes in organizational name), and disbanding (cases without any prior organizational changes). Typically, organizational transition or change is viewed as a vital event that bodes poorly for the survival of the organization. Change in core features such as goals and forms of authority leads to the dissolution of established routines or competencies (Hannan & Freeman, 1989). Name changes are likely to be less drastic, although they may indicate any number of events that have contributed to organizational transition including leadership changes (Glynn & Slepian, 1993) and sociopolitical conflicts such as strikes (Glynn, 2000). In addition, while the decision to alter the public

Table 1. Descriptive Statistics.

Variable	Mean	SD	Min	Max	Definition
Organizational transition (0 = Continue, 1 = Change, 2 = Exit)	0.808	0.882	0	2	50.5, 18.7, and 31.1%
Organizational disbanding (0, 1 = Continue, Change; 1 = Exit)	0.311	0.436	0	1	68.9 and 31.1%
Cultural legitimacy					
Medical	0.501	2.329	0	36	Recognition in medical literature
Academic	0.767	3.302	0	46	Recognition in scholarly literature
Popular	0.788	2.820	0	43	Recognition by press
Sociopolitical legitimacy					
Political	0.795	2.454	0	20	Congressional recognition
Competencies – programs					
Differentiation	0.838	0.097	0.556	1	Program differentiation
Number	2.659	1.372	1	6	Number types of programs
Competencies – services					
Differentiation	0.870	0.045	0.718	0.957	Service differentiation
Number	4.374	2.186	1	12	Number types of services
Resources – human capital					
Differentiation	0.719	0.169	0.143	1	Membership differentiation
Number	2.002	1.196	1	6	Number types of members
Professional affiliation (1 = yes)	0.294	0.456	0	1	Professionals as members
Organizational controls					
Age	15.385	10.416	1	46	Organizational age
Size	7.771	2.172	0.69	14.3	Estimate number members
Founding date	1979	11.176	1919	1998	Organizational founding
Twelve-step program (1 = yes)	0.129	0.336	0	1	Anonymous 12-step program

Table 1. (*Continued*)

Variable	Mean	SD	Min	Max	Definition
Organizational niche[a]					
Medical (1 = medical)	0.472	0.500	0	1	Medical self-help/mutual-aid
Behavioral (1 = behavioral)	0.151	0.358	0	1	Behavioral self-help/mutual-aid
Psychological (1 = psychological)	0.170	0.376	0	1	Psych self-help/mutual-aid

Note: National self-help/mutual-aid organizations (*N* = 589).
[a] General-lifestyle self-help/mutual-aid is the omitted category.

identity of an established organization may improve survival (Ingram, 1996), it is as likely to result in failure, as one organization merges or creates an alliance with, or, is taken over by, a more powerful competitor (Scott, 2003). I analyze changes in organizational identity as a distinct category of self-help/mutual-aid outcome because it represents an intermediate stage between survival and disbanding, and as such, is likely to capture more fully the variations in the effects of legitimacy, organizational competencies, and resources. Moreover, few ecological studies have examined organizational change (Baum, 1996), because one underlying assumption of the framework relies on the notion that organizational structures suffer from inertia and therefore undergo little modification.

Organizational disbanding or mortality is the other central outcome of interest in this study. It occurs when an organization is no longer viable as an entity. Self-help/mutual-aid organizations are defined as either extant or defunct. That is, they survived through the end of the observation period, or they disbanded. This second outcome variable, disbanding, simply treats organizations that changed names as survivors. Group comparison is therefore between organizations whose first transition was disbanding, and those who survived (or tried to adapt through a name change). Self-help/mutual-aid organizations experiencing organizational transition comprised 18.7% (Table 1) whose first transition was a name change, and 31.1% whose first transition was disbanding. Collapsing the transition variable so that outright disbanding constituted the outcome of interest, 31.1% disbanded without any earlier efforts at organizational adaptation. Having two outcome measures allows us to assess whether the independent variables are influencing organizational transition or disbanding alone.[2]

Cultural and Sociopolitical Legitimacy. Voluntary organizations, such as self-help/mutual-aid, are "limited in their ability to demonstrate their effectiveness in terms of conventional output, efficiency or process criteria" (Singh et al., 1991, p. 392). Instead, their effectiveness is judged in terms of "social criteria like the satisfaction and approval of external constituencies" (ibid). Examination of the organizational histories of self-help/mutual-aid reveals that all of them attempt to gain recognition by highlighting political appearances, academic seminars, popular talks and speeches, and other special events that link the organization to important external authorities.

For self-help/mutual-aid organizations, access to agencies, grant monies, and favorable legislation signals to constituents and other audiences that public and political authorities recognize self-help/mutual-aid as a burgeoning social institution. Doing so is likely to enhance longevity (Katz, 1993). Self-help/mutual-aid depends on external authorities who render judgment, and confer legitimacy, based on their beliefs about the organization's appropriateness when it concerns organizational consequences (outputs), procedures, and structure.

I conceptualize legitimacy as recognition of organizational designs and purposes by salient authorities (Scott, 2001), and distinguish cultural legitimacy from sociopolitical legitimacy on the basis of professional and cultural contexts (versus political contexts). The concept of sociopolitical or regulatory legitimacy, with its implied coercive authority, differs markedly from taken-for-grantedness. Sociopolitical (i.e. regulatory) legitimacy can be sought after (or avoided or finessed) by organizations seeking to acquire a particular reputation (Fombrun, 1996) in political spheres (with attendant access to resources that lie in those spheres). Cultural (i.e. normative and cognitive) legitimacy is more difficult (but not impossible) to deploy as a strategy. Rather, it accrues to organizations and to an organizational form over time. I create constructs of organizational legitimacy for each individual self-help/mutual-aid organization using criteria distinguishing cultural (i.e. normative and cognitive) processes from sociopolitical (i.e. regulatory) processes associated with recognition of self-help/mutual-aid organizations by actors in these contexts.

Representatives of self-help/mutual-aid organizations appear before congress and other legislative bodies to give expert testimony on medical and social welfare policy debates. Political authorities (in this case, members of congressional committees) generate sociopolitical legitimacy, based on legal or regulatory regimes. Self-interest and expedience are the mechanisms by which regulative institutions endorse organizational objectives. As Carroll and Hannan (2001, p. 203) note:

> sociopolitical legitimation of an organizational form is usually represented by dummy variables associated with endorsements received by particular organizations or the timing of governmental actions implying endorsement of particular organizational form (for example a legislative act authorizing the right of certain organizations to exist and operate . . .

I extend these operational procedures by measuring sociopolitical legitimacy as the amount of recognition by the political authorities. I locate and enumerate references to appearances and testimony in congressional hearings of each of the 589 self-help/mutual-aid organizations active at one time or another in the U.S. The search task was facilitated by *the Congressional Universe/Congressional Information Services*. The *CIS* subject index includes all regularly produced publications including hearings, testimony, reports of such political bodies as the House Interior and Insular Affairs Committee, Department of Labor, Department of Health and Human Services, Department of Education, and Related Agencies for Appropriations.

Organizations are also subject to normative and cultural pressures at the local and national levels. Cultural authorities (i.e. medical professionals, academics, and the press) generate cultural or constitutive legitimacy, based on normative and cognitive/cultural schema. Cultural legitimacy based on normative regimes entails professional and academic recognition of self-help/mutual-aid. The discussion of self-help/mutual-aid has been fairly widespread in the medical and academic literature. Sectoral evaluators essential for normative recognition of self-help/mutual-aid include medical professionals, the insurance industry, employee assistance programs, non-profit foundations, workshops and conferences (Powell, 1994). To measure cultural legitimacy as the impact of recognition by medical and academic authorities, I locate and enumerate references to each of the 589 self-help/mutual-aid organizations active at one time or another in the U.S. between 1955 and 2000. I measure recognition generated by medical and academic professionals based on counts of articles specifically mentioning the organization. For medical professionals, these counts were conducted by accessing the National Library of Medicine's *Index Medicus-Medline*; for academics, these counts were obtained by accessing journals registered to *Sociological and Psychological Abstracts*.

Another aspect of cultural legitimacy is its "taken-for-grantedness." Cultural legitimacy implies the conceptual appropriateness of an organization rather than its fit under regulatory or normative regimes (Scott, 2003). Cultural legitimacy entails popular recognition and acceptance of individual organizations and of an organizational form, such as self-help/mutual-aid. Organizations become visible and their reputations rise and fall in the course of public discussion and debate. To the extent that the media reflects popular opinion, and widespread cultural beliefs about social organization (McChesney, 1999), indicators of self-help/mutual-aid's cultural legitimacy may be culled from media outlets. The *New York Times* was selected as an appropriate representative of major media for several reasons.[3] To the extent that a newspaper such as the *New York Times* provides major stories and reports about self-help/mutual-aid, familiarity, acceptance and taken-for-grantedness of it and its sources as a national institution becomes widespread. Again, counts of self-help/mutual-aid organizations were used to measure recognition.[4]

Exogenous Variables

Core Competencies and Resources. Organizational competencies are functional capabilities and skills of the organization that create value and provide leverage for gaining competitive advantage. Firms have many competencies covering a range of functional activities (e.g. production, research, distribution). Core competencies for self-help/mutual-aid organizations include programs for goal attainment (social production) and service. In a resource-based framework, competitive advantage derives from competencies that are different from competitors (Oliver, 1997).

Resources can be conceptualized similarly. The resource niche for an organization is comprised of all the resources that sustain the population of organizations in it, including constraints that limit it (Hannan & Freeman, 1989). Organizational ecologists tend to analyze organizational niches based on the properties of organizations, and their environments because their central research question, competition between organizations, is difficult to observe directly. Competition between organizations depends on the extent to which market niches overlap and resources are partitioned. Voluntary associations, like other organizations, occupy and differentiate organizational niches, which are "a set of organizational capabilities and a location in resource space" (McPherson, 1983, p. 520). Market overlap increases competition along these dimensions, while market partitioning decreases competition (Carroll & Swaminathan, 2000). Specialist organizations (such as self-help/mutual-aid) tend to exploit the conditions of market partitioning to avoid direct competition (Carroll, 1985). For example, Haider-Markel (1997) found that interest groups avoided direct competition by adapting to different issue niches.[5]

One way to conceive of competition and market differentiation for self-help/mutual-aid organizations is in terms of program and service capabilities and resources. I measure core competencies and resources in two ways. First, I examine the number of several types of competencies and resources (i.e. members). These quantities are counts of types of competencies and resources. Second, I create an indicator measuring the extent to which a focal organization differs from all other similar organizations on the basis of its core competencies and resources. For self-help/mutual-aid organizations, core competencies are programs and services. Resources are human capital in the form of organizational membership.

Programs are self-help/mutual-aid technologies that serve as organizational strategies for accomplishing self-help/mutual-aid goals. Self-help/mutual-aid goals range from behavior modification and cognitive restructuring to legal advocacy. Programs aimed at actualizing these goals include but are not limited to meetings and support groups, recreational events, and creation of support networks. The social technology of mutual aid is also the most salient characteristic of self-help/mutual-aid. It consists of a small-group setting where members share stories and information concerning their personal experiences dealing with stigmatizing conditions or problems. This technology of self- and mutual-support is a unique characteristic of the self-help/mutual-aid organizational form. Self-help/mutual-aid organizations share a philosophy that promotes individual self-determination, autonomy, and dignity based in this intimate interaction setting. The result is a mutual understanding of members' focal problems, needs, and concerns.

Services include but are not limited to transportation, nutritional programs, study groups, libraries, educational forums, legal and medical referrals, and donations to charities. *Members* who provide human capital for self-help/mutual-aid organizations include those who are stigmatized (such as the mentally ill or disabled), caretakers, relatives, spouses, families, medical professionals, social workers, attorneys, and clergy. For some self-help/mutual-aid organizations, especially those dealing with medical trauma, genetic dysfunction, cancer and other life-threatening conditions, participation by medical professionals is essential to securing information, access to resources and, advancing knowledge of the treatment of traumatic conditions. Member resources are based on the types of members rather than the absolute number (although I control for membership size in the analyses). In addition, for member resources, I use an indicator determining whether or not an organization is specifically affiliated with professionals such as doctors, social workers, teachers and legal professionals. The purpose is to elaborate the kind of human capital benefiting many self-help/mutual-aid organizations.

Following Ruef (2002, 1997), I construct a differentiation coefficient that reflects the partitioning of social production and resource space between organizations along the three dimensions of programs, services, and membership. That is, there is a coefficient for each dimension. Differentiation is operationalized by separating organizations into niche areas based on specialization of function (e.g. marriage and family, infant mortality, cancer, neurological, addiction), and then quantifying differences along the three main dimensions: programs (e.g. meetings, discussion groups, support networks), services (e.g. libraries, computer access, speaker's bureau, publications), and membership (e.g. persons w/problem or stigma, siblings, family members, partner). To create the coefficient(s), I begin by measuring pair wise bilateral overlap among similar types of organizations, and aggregating these pair wise differences across the niche. The formula for the coefficient of difference "*d*" is really just a heuristic for calculating the ratio of niche overlap to non-overlap:

$$d(i,j) = 1 - \left[\frac{a_{i,j}/(a_{i,j} + b_{i,j} + c_{i,j})}{N_j} \right] \qquad (1)$$

where the proportionate difference (d) between a focal organization (i) and the other organizations sharing its particular niche (j) (e.g. marriage and family, infant mortality), is a function of the overlap ($a_{i,j}$) of competencies in programs and services, and member resources (i.e. number of the same programs, services, and resources), relative to $a_{i,j}$ plus $b_{i,j}$ plus $c_{i,j}$. Where "b" represents the unique programs and services, and membership of the focal organization (i), relative to another organization, and "c" represents the unique programs and services, and membership of another organization relative to the focal organization (i). To calculate the quantities $a_{i,j}$ or $b_{i,j}$ or $c_{i,j}$ is the same. For instance: $a_{i,j} = \sum a_{i+1,j}, a_{i+2,j}, a_{i+3,j} \ldots a_{+ki,j}$. The algorithm then averages over all the organizations in the niche (N_j). To make the direction of the relationship consistent with resource-based hypotheses, I subtract this score from 1, such that for d, a score closer to 0 indicates, on average, a greater degree of resource overlap, and lesser differentiation between organizations, while a score closer to 1 indicates greater differentiation. Ruef notes some problems with the formulation of d based on asymmetries in size of organization and potential for exploitation of alternative markets, and makes appropriate adjustments. I control for these asymmetries differently by: (1) using multiple indicators of competencies and resources, which include total number of programs and services, and member resources, and; (2) creating the differentiation measure for clusters of similarly structured organizations based on the diversification of their specialty areas (e.g. marriage and family, infant mortality).

Controls – Organizational Attributes and Niche
In addition to examining the relationships between self-help/mutual-aid legitimacy, organizational competencies, resources, and organizational transition and disbanding, I include the following control variables: organizational attributes (i.e. age, founding date, size, and whether or not the organization has a twelve-step philosophy), and niche (i.e. broad specialty categories such as medical, behavioral and psychological). The first three variables have a considerable pedigree in organizational theory, while being a twelve-step organization is particular to this population of organizations.

With respect to age, one argument suggests that newer organizations have a greater chance of disbanding than older organizations because they lack the experience of established organizations. Yet, some evidence implies that older rather than new organizations are more likely to fail (Baum, 1996). Ruef (2002) shows a consistent pattern of liability of newness. Finally, there may also be a curvilinear relationship between age and failure (see Barnett, 1997; Hannan, 1998 for discussion), although the evidence is limited (Baum, 1996). Age is measured as the time between self-help/mutual-aid founding date and either organizational disbanding or end of observation window (i.e. 2000).

More importantly, perhaps, is the influence of the socioeconomic and political environment on organizational structures (Sacks, 2002; Uzzi, 1999). Here actual age is less important in explaining failure than the consequences of inertia that make structures obsolete over time. Imprinting reflects assumptions about the structures, processes, routines, and activities organizations develop in particular periods of time which are likely to impact the chances of organizational viability (Stinchcombe, 1965). I control for this event by using organizational founding date which represents the historical influence of social, economic, and political factors on organizations.[6]

I control for size because organizational ecology theory, in general, and market partitioning theory, in particular, suggest that the dynamics of organizational environments that yield generalist and specialist strategies depend on economies of scale which in turn influence viability (Carroll & Swaminathan, 2000). I measure size by the number of members a self-help/mutual-aid organization claimed in its membership statistics during the most current period of observation. Similarly, I use a dichotomous variable measuring twelve-step philosophy as a proxy to control for the dominance in membership size of the largest of the self-help/mutual-aid organizations, which happen to be the twelve-step programs.

The last set of controls measure the characteristics of the self-help/mutual-aid niche. I control for niches unique to the self-help/mutual-aid population because some of these may be organizationally denser, and, therefore absorb more resources than other niches, creating intense competition, and contributing to differential failure rates (Brittain, 1994; Hannan & Freeman, 1992). I have, however, no specific expectations about the relationship between an organization's position in any one niche and the likelihood of transition or disbanding. There are three domains in the self-help/mutual-aid population: medical disability organizations for the sick, injured, physically handicapped or impaired, and their family and friends; behavioral organizations that help members change some problematic behavior; and special-purpose psychological organizations that address a range of problems from grief, loss and abuse to anxiety. The omitted category for the three dichotomous variables consists of residual organizations that address general social-psychological problems, and stigmatized statuses, such as sexual orientation and newly released prisoners.

Methods

Several types of methods were used to evaluate the hypotheses. Since quantitative assessments of legitimacy, organizational competencies, and resources are narrowly delimited in the organizations' literature, exploratory analysis of the measurement structure of the variables remained a crucial first step. Moreover, assessing the individual relationships between observed variables and constructs provides basic preliminary information about the validity of the latter. Therefore, I begin the analysis with discussion of key findings from exploratory factor analysis. I then tested the results of these preliminary findings with a confirmatory factor analysis (Bollen, 1989). The purpose of confirmatory analysis is to assess the validity and reliability of legitimacy, organizational competencies, and resources so that interpretation of hypothesized relationships is not biased.

I analyzed a structural equation model to evaluate relationships between legitimacy, competencies, and resources, and, self-help/mutual-aid transition and disbanding. This type of model is best suited for assessing simultaneous direct and indirect relationships, and allows for the use of multiple indicators of legitimacy, competencies, and resources (Long, 1983).

The basic structural equation model follows the form suggested by Jöreskog and Sörbom (1993):

$$\eta' = \beta\eta' + \gamma\xi + \zeta \tag{2}$$

where η and ξ are latent constructs based on vectors of observed variables (y and x); β is a matrix of coefficients expressing the mutual effects of endogenous variables; γ represents the effects of latent exogenous on endogenous variables, and ζ is a vector of random error. One underlying assumption of the model is that the errors are uncorrelated with latent constructs and uncorrelated among themselves.

For the exploratory factor analysis, I used STATA (Statacorp, 2001). In the confirmatory factor analysis, I used maximum likelihood estimates generated by Mplus (Muthén & Muthén, 1998). For analysis of the structural model depicted in Fig. 1, I again used Mplus.

The two outcomes, organizational transition, and, organizational disbanding required multinomial (probit) and binomial logistic analyses, respectively. To assess the influence of legitimacy, competencies, and resources on each other and on organizational transition and disbanding, I used weighted least squares estimates generated by Mplus. Although maximum likelihood estimates are often robust with respect to violations of multivariate, normality (Jöreskog & Sörbom, 1993), weighted least squares is recommended for estimating model parameters with categorical outcomes and nominal indicators (Browne, 1984; Muthén & Christoffersson, 1981; Muthén & Muthén, 1998; Wothke, 1993).

Models for these equations were based on Hosmer and Lemeshow (1989). To calculate the predicted probability of organizational disbanding: If y is a binary outcome variable, and $x = (x_1, x_2, x_3, \ldots x_{p-1})$ are the explanatory variables, the probability of $y = 1| x$ is $= \pi(x)$. The equation for $\pi(x)$ is then:

$$\pi(x) = \frac{\exp(\alpha + \beta_1 X_1 + \beta_2 X_2 + \cdots + \beta_{p-1} X_{p-1})}{1 + \exp(\alpha + \beta_1 X_1 + \beta_2 X_2 + \cdots + \beta_{p-1} X_{p-1})} \tag{3}$$

The predicted probability of organizational transition with the probit model is the same, except that the probit model is based on the assumption that the cumulative distribution function is a standard normal CDF represented by Φ (Liao, 1994; Muthén & Muthén, 1998).

RESULTS

Factor Analysis

There is little prior knowledge to guide us regarding the empirical content and dimensionality of models of organizational legitimacy (Delacroix & Rao, 1994), competencies, and resources. I therefore used exploratory factor analysis to determine the factor components for the theoretical constructs, identifying complex items (i.e. those with multiple loadings), and estimating relationships between items. Specifically, I used an iterative principal axis factoring with varimax rotation to address these measurement issues (Statacorp, 2001).

Table 2 presents results of exploratory factor analysis. An initial scree plot and analysis of random data eigenvalue estimates (Horn, 1965) suggested the possibility of a four-factor solution (see Table 3). Examination of factor coefficients shows that while sociopolitical recognition had a very poor loading on the factor for legitimacy, the remaining observed variables consistently aligned with their hypothesized factors. A four-factor model is therefore not an optimal solution. Since prior theory strongly suggests that cultural legitimacy and sociopolitical legitimacy are conceptually and empirically distinct, I tested an exploratory analysis (not shown) that iterated through to a five-factor solution. In the five-factor solution, the constructs became more distinct and readily interpretable (although the eigenvalues remained weak). Preacher and MacCallum (2003) argue that interpretability of the factor solution is critical to resolving conceptual ambiguity in factor analyses. Another common method is through confirmatory factor analysis (Long, 1983). Confirmatory factor analysis permits adjudication between hypothesized measurement models.

Table 3 presents results of several confirmatory factor analyses. Overall, these analyses support the validity of the constructs emerging from the exploratory solution based on their consistency with the models implied by prior theory.[7] In

Table 2. Exploratory Factor Solutions for Organizational Legitimacy, Competencies, and Resources.[a]

Variables	Factor I	Factor II	Factor III	Factor IV
Legitimacy				
Medical	−0.014	0.854	0.022	−0.007
Academic	−0.028	0.896	0.050	−0.127
Political	0.169	0.352	−0.130	0.137
Popular	0.016	0.848	0.024	−0.045
Competencies – programs				
Differentiation	0.196	−0.180	−0.132	0.768
Number	0.304	−0.028	−0.179	0.656
Competencies – services				
Differentiation	0.782	−0.078	−0.071	0.192
Number	0.807	0.050	−0.157	0.157
Resources – members				
Differentiation	−0.022	−0.018	−0.633	0.236
Number	0.130	−0.045	−0.889	0.066
Professional affiliation	0.118	−0.044	−0.774	0.097
Eigenvalues	2.85	2.27	1.23	0.600
Cumulative% explained	0.38	0.69	0.84	0.92

Note: National self-help/mutual-aid organizations ($N = 589$).
[a] Iterative principle factor with varimax rotation.

these confirmatory analyses, I formally analyzed four- and five-factor solutions, using maximum likelihood least squares estimates.

Fit between the constructs and components of legitimacy, competencies and resources are shown in Table 3. The first point is that while the fit of Model 1 in Table 3 is fair ($\chi^2 = 161.26$, 38 df; CFI $= 0.952$: RMSEA $= 0.074$), the strikingly small loading of political recognition on legitimacy indicates that there exists another factor in the data. Model 2 corrects for the poor standardized loading. Since the second form of legitimacy has only a single observed variable, and therefore is set to 1.0 in order to identify the model, the coefficient for the pseudo-loading is not very helpful in answering the question of whether it is a unique factor or not. However, the overall fit of Model 2 suggests as much. It is clearly better than Model 1 ($\chi^2 = 121.32$, 35 df; CFI $= 0.966$: RMSEA $= 0.065$). Moreover, a chi-square difference between the log likelihoods indicates that the second model represents the data significantly better than the first model, even with the loss of several degrees of freedom (i.e. $-2LL = 39.94$ w/3 df $= p < 0.001$). The other indices of fit (CFI and RMSEA) support this conclusion.[8]

Table 3. Confirmatory Factor Analyses of Cultural and Sociopolitical
Legitimacy, Core Competencies, and Resources.

Factors[a]	Model 1	Model 2	Model 3[c]
Cultural legitimacy			
Medical	1.0 (0.841)	(0.839)	(0.842)
Academic	0.898	0.900	0.896
Popular	0.836	0.835	0.837
Political	0.312		
Sociopolitical legitimacy	0.000		
Political		(0.408)[b]	(0.408)[b]
Competencies – programs			
Differentiation	1.0 (0.718)	(0.723)	
Number	0.776	0.771	
Competencies – general			
Services – differentiation			(0.803)
Services – number			0.750
Programs – differentiation			0.426
Programs – number			0.565
Competencies – services			
Differentiation	1.0 (0.764)	(0.756)	
Number	0.802	0.810	
Resources – members			
Differentiation	1.0 (0.622)	(0.624)	(0.615)
Number	0.914	0.911	0.921
Professional affiliation	0.761	0.764	0.757
N	589	589	589
Goodness-of-fit χ^2 (df)	161.26 (38)	121.32 (35)	140.22 (33)
Log likelihood	−6355.14	−6335.17	−6344.62
CFI	0.952	0.966	0.958
RMSEA	0.074	0.065	0.074

Note: National self-help/mutual-aid organizations ($N = 589$).
[a] Each of the first variables in the factor is constrained to be 1.0 to identify the model and set the factor scale. The software, however, gives estimates of these scale variables. I indicate these variables with parentheses.
[b] In Model 1 and Model 3, sociopolitical legitimacy is treated as a unique factor. The loading for sociopolitical legitimacy on cultural legitimacy is constrained to equal 0 in the remaining models.
[c] Several error variances were freed post hoc to get the program to converge on a solution.

The two forms of legitimacy can now be treated as empirically distinct. Differences between types of legitimacy based on which actors are invested with authority to confer legitimacy find confirmation in these data. The first type of legitimacy is consistent with the constitutive variant of legitimacy promoted by new institutionalism, while the other, sociopolitical legitimacy, is the type of legitimacy consistent with an instrumental approach.

More importantly, the argument for legitimacy-as-resource (or competency) is not confirmed by these data. Results of factor analysis in Tables 2 and 3 do not support this contention nor do additional confirmatory factor analyses (not shown), which model legitimacy and competencies, and, legitimacy and resources as single factors. Not surprisingly, cultural and sociopolitical legitimacy are neither a kind of resource, nor any type of several organizational competencies.

One last peripheral measurement issue arose. It is possible that program and service core competencies are simply aspects of a single dimension. This possibility was suggested by some preliminary analysis of the data using principle components analysis. Loadings showed that services and programs might be a single general competency available to self-help/mutual-aid organizations. To test the chances of mis-specification of these constructs, I ran Model 3, in Table 3, which tests the hypothesis that the two competencies, programs and services, are actually components of a single factor. Examination of the factor loadings and assessment of the fit of the model to evaluate whether this is so or not ($\chi^2 = 140.22$, 33 df; CFI $= 0.958$: RMSEA $= 0.074$), indicate that while Model 3 fits the data about the same or slightly better than Model 1, it is much worse than Model 2 altogether. Therefore, program competencies and service competencies differ conceptually and empirically from one another.

Bivariate Hypotheses

The first formal hypothesis analyzed is that cultural and sociopolitical legitimacy will increase the likelihood of organizational viability. Examination of results in Table 4 shows that consistent with general theoretical expectations expressed in Hypothesis 1, linking cultural legitimacy and sociopolitical legitimacy to organizational viability, both are moderately associated with organizational transition, and somewhat less so with organizational disbanding (-0.251 and -0.211; -0.179 and -0.123, respectively). In a similar pattern, competencies and organizational resources are closely related to organizational transition (-0.269, -0.136, and -0.150), but much less strongly related to organizational disbanding (-0.129, -0.077, -0.083). These results are also consistent with Hypothesis 3, which stated that market partitioning (differentiation) among core competencies

Table 4. Bivariate Correlations Between Latent Factor Scores, and Between Latent Factor Scores and Organizational Viability.

Independent Factors and Outcomes	I	II	III	IV	V	VI
Cultural legitimacy						
Sociopolitical legitimacy	0.813***					
Competencies – programs	−0.248***	0.391***				
Competencies – services	−0.059	0.588***	0.591***			
Resources – members	−0.093#	0.336**	0.276***	0.437***		
Organizational transition (0, 1, 2)	−0.251***	−0.211#	−0.129*	−0.077	−0.083	
Organizational disbanding (0,1 = 0; 2 = 1)	−0.179*	−0.123	−0.269***	−0.136*	−0.150*	0.908***

Note: National self-help/mutual-aid organizations ($N = 589$).
* <0.05 (two-tailed tests).
** <0.01 (two-tailed tests).
*** <0.001 (two-tailed tests).
# <0.10 (two-tailed tests).

and resources will increase the likelihood of organizational viability. Isomorphism with respect to competencies and resources does not directly translate into organizational viability.

Hypothesis 2 argued that isomorphism (homogeneity) among core competencies and resources should promote cultural and sociopolitical legitimacy. Based on results in Table 4, we see that cultural legitimacy is negatively associated with organizational competencies and resources, while sociopolitical legitimacy is positively associated with organizational competencies and resources. In short, the more differentiated (and numerous) an organization's competencies and resources the greater the *sociopolitical* recognition; but the less differentiated (and less numerous – more particularized) an organization's competencies and resources, the greater the *cultural* recognition. This suggests that the drive towards conformity characterizes the relationship between cultural legitimacy and core competencies/resources, but not the relationship between sociopolitical legitimacy and core competencies/resources. Just the opposite: differentiation characterizes the relationship between sociopolitical legitimacy and core competencies/resources. Not surprisingly, from an institutionalist perspective, cultural legitimacy bears a unique relationship with core competencies and resources that differs dramatically from the relationship between sociopolitical legitimacy and competencies and resources.

In light of these results, it is not clear how the relationships between legitimacy, competencies, and resources will *combine* (in a fully specified model) to explain organizational viability. That is to say, the direction of the relationships suggests that the fuller model is not all of one piece. The final question that remains to be analyzed is: Given the pattern of bivariate relationships between the various legitimacies, organizational competencies, resources and organizational outcomes, is organizational viability contingent on legitimacy, and a set of differentiated organizational competencies, and resources, or, do these factors operate independently of one another?

Multivariate Model

Table 5 presents results of probit and logit regression analyses for covariance structure models of organizational transition and organizational disbanding on the main theoretical factors, as previously depicted in Fig. 1, Models A and B. In the analyses in Table 5, a number of controls, including self-help/mutual-aid age, size and founding date, were introduced to assure that the central relationships were not the result of unobserved heterogeneity. This is especially important with organizational data because organizational attributes such as age and size tend to have a powerful influence on organizational persistence (Carroll & Hannan, 2000).[9] In addition, it is important to note that parameter constraints were placed on the models so that the direction of effects flows from organizational competencies and resources to legitimacy (i.e. competencies → legitimacy; resources → legitimacy). The table mirrors this constraint by modeling organizational competencies and resources as exogenous variables, and legitimacy as endogenous. Naturally, the direction of effects could be reciprocal. However, to avoid confusion, and maintain consistency with institutional analyses (e.g. Deephouse, 1996), the models specify that either isomorphism or differentiation in organizational competencies and resources enhance cultural and sociopolitical legitimacy (rather than the reverse), which in turn should benefit organizational viability (Hypothesis 4).

Models 1 and 3 specify the relationships between cultural and sociopolitical legitimacy, organizational competencies, resources, and self-help/mutual-aid *transition* (including a variety of controls), while Models 2 and 4 examine these relationships with respect to self-help/mutual-aid *disbanding*. Note that Table 5 is based on simultaneous equations so that Models 1 and 3 resemble Model A in Fig. 1, and, Models 2 and 4 resemble Model B in Fig. 1. The two outcomes, transition and disbanding, were regressed on legitimacy, organizational competencies, and resources (and controls), while at the same time, legitimacy was regressed on organizational competencies and resources. Self-help/mutual-aid transition and disbanding were modeled as a direct function of cultural and

Table 5. Regression Analyses for Simultaneous Equations of Organizational Transition and Disbanding on Cultural and Sociopolitical Legitimacy, Organizational Competencies, and Resources, and, Cultural and Sociopolitical Legitimacy on Organizational Competencies and Resources.

	Endogenous Variables – Viability (Y1)			
	Organizational Transition (0, 1, 2)		Organizational Disbanding (0, 1)	
	Model 1	Model 2	Model 3	Model 4
Explanatory variables				
Cultural legitimacy	$-0.090(0.028)^{***}$		$-0.088(0.033)^{**}$	
Sociopolitical legitimacy		$0.099(0.122)$		$0.173(0.136)$
Competencies – programs	$-5.515(0.718)^{***}$	$-5.557(1.774)^{***}$	$-6.85(1.82)^{***}$	$-7.144(1.864)^{***}$
Competencies – services	$3.267(0.640)$	$1.51(3.114)$	$2.749(2.888)$	$0.08(3.473)$
Resources	$-0.981(0.689)$	$-1.178(0.758)$	$-1.245(0.754)$	$-1.648(0.845)^{\#}$
Control variables				
Organizational attributes				
Age	$-0.100(0.006)^{***}$	$-0.1(0.006)^{***}$	$-0.058(0.007)^{***}$	$-0.058(0.007)^{***}$
Size	$-0.055(0.024)^{*}$	$-0.055(0.024)^{**}$	$-0.064(0.026)^{*}$	$-0.064(0.026)^{*}$
Founding date	$-0.078(0.005)^{***}$	$-0.078(0.005)^{***}$	$-0.05(0.006)^{***}$	$-0.05(0.006)^{***}$
Twelve-step program	$-0.014(0.186)$	$-0.014(0.186)$	$0.068(0.202)$	$0.068(0.202)$
Organizational niche[a]				
Medical	$-0.349(0.132)^{**}$	$-0.349(0.132)^{**}$	$-0.406(0.143)^{**}$	$-0.406(0.143)^{**}$
Behavioral	$0.020(0.202)$	$0.02(0.202)$	$0.034(0.218)$	$0.034(0.218)$
Psychological	$-0.311(0.175)$	$-0.311(0.175)$	$-0.316(0.19)$	$-0.316(0.19)^{\#}$
	Endogenous Variables – Legitimacy (Y2)			
Explanatory Variables	Cultural Legitimacy	Sociopolitical Legitimacy	Cultural Legitimacy	Sociopolitical Legitimacy
Competencies – programs	$-3.2681(0.909)$	$2.969(2.339)$	$-3.24(1.925)$	$2.945(2.34)$
Competencies – services	$4.1952(2.667)$	$12.433(3.613)^{***}$	$4.103(2.651)$	$12.47(3.589)^{***}$
Resources	$-0.775(0.840)$	$2.845(1.023)^{***}$	$-0.778(0.843)$	$2.851(1.026)^{**}$
N	589	589	589	589
Goodness-of-fit χ^2 (df)	898.177 (107)	743.192 (77)	966.362 (105)[b]	626.259 (75)
CFI	0.808	0.844	0.838	0.871
RMSEA	0.112	0.121	0.118	0.112

Note: National self-help/mutual-aid organizations ($N = 589$).
[a] General-lifestyle self-help/mutual-aid is the omitted category.
[b] Degrees of freedom differ slightly due to constraints between factors.
* <0.05 (two-tailed tests).
** <0.01 (two-tailed tests).
*** <0.001 (two-tailed tests).
\# <0.10 (two-tailed tests).

sociopolitical legitimacy, competencies, resources, and several organizational characteristics including age, size, founding date, twelve-step program, as well as organizational niche.

Beginning with cultural legitimacy, Models 1 and 3 show that, again consistent with Hypothesis 1, with all factors in the model, including controls for organizational attributes and niche effects, self-help/mutual-aid organizations that enjoyed heightened cultural legitimacy are *less* likely than organizations that did not, to experience a transition, and, therefore more likely to survive. In Model 1, the order of magnitude of the change is 1.462 ($e^{-0.090} = 0.9139 \times 1.6 = 1.462$),[10] which implies that unit increases in cultural legitimacy decrease the likelihood of an organization's chances of transitioning to a name change or disbanding by almost one and a half times (1.46). The same is true for model 3. In addition, age, year of founding, size, and medical niche significantly influence persistence. Older self-help/mutual-aid organizations and those that were founded later in the population's history have a greater likelihood of persistence than younger organizations and those founded when self-help/mutual-aid was just getting started by a factor of 1.46 and 1.48, respectively. Not surprisingly, medical self-help/mutual-aid organizations are 1.13 times more likely to survive than self-help/mutual-aid organizations occupying other specialty niches.

In contrast, the regression of cultural legitimacy on organizational competencies and resources, at the bottom of the columns in Models 1 and 3, shows that cultural legitimacy is not influenced by organizational competencies and resources, and therefore does not serve as an explanatory mechanism by which self-help/mutual-aid competencies and resources influence self-help/mutual-aid transition and disbanding. This disconfirms our prior expectation (Hypotheses 4) that (sociopolitical and) cultural legitimacy arise(s) when either institutional or market (competitive) pressures drive organizations to adopt similar structures, processes and routines (under an institutional regime) or idiosyncratic ones (under a market regime), in turn facilitating chances of survival.

Models 2 and 4 in Table 5 are remarkable by contrast. In these two models, sociopolitical legitimacy has no direct influence on self-help/mutual-aid transition and disbanding, when other factors are controlled. Instead, all variance in transition and disbanding previously accounted for by sociopolitical legitimacy, in the bivariate case, is now channeled by other factors. While the specific explanatory mechanisms remain unexplored, it appears that organizational competencies and resources function to render the main relationship insignificant, although organizational attributes, such as age, size, and founding date, and organizational niche, contribute as well. In addition, unlike the relationship between cultural legitimacy and organizational competencies and resources, which remained non-significant when other factors were controlled, increases in organizational competencies and resources (and greater differentiation) fosters sociopolitical legitimacy. They also directly foster self-help/mutual-aid viability, although, interestingly, their effects do not appear to operate at all through heightened sociopolitical legitimacy. Here again, Hypothesis 4 which suggested that competencies and resources operate via legitimacy to promote self-help/mutual-aid viability is not supported.

Lastly, with regard to organizational niche, only medical and less significantly, psychological, self-help/mutual-aid organizations experience greater fitness. Medical organizations are more likely to survive relative to other specialty groups by a factor of about 1.13 ($e^{-0.349} \times 1.6$). Thus, medical groups, having carved out a niche in the self-help/mutual-aid population, show greater fitness than other groups.

DISCUSSION

The paper advances recent theorizing in institutional theory by distinguishing two main variants of legitimation processes, cultural (constitutive) and sociopolitical (regulative), and subjects them to several empirical tests. By analyzing a multidimensional model of legitimacy (Ruef & Scott, 1998; Scott et al., 2000), organizational competencies, and resources, this paper uncovered several notable relationships among these factors, and between them and organizational viability, that supports recommending the consideration of resource-based assumptions by theories with an institutional focus. It is important to note, however, that multidimensional models of legitimacy not only facilitate but also complicate the task of analyzing mechanisms aligned with different legitimation processes, first, because of conceptual ambiguity, and second, with respect to empirical outcomes detailed in this paper. With respect to the former, while institutional theory alerts us to the potential for unexpected results by calling attention to the importance of different levels at which institutional regimes operate (see e.g. Scott, 2001), it remains unclear how different legitimation processes might unfold within any particular context.

At the organizational level, at least, this study shows that cultural and sociopolitical legitimacy are distinct phenomena, likely to operate under diverse legitimation regimes. Moreover, the contention that legitimacy and organizational competencies and resources are equivalent is not supported by these data. Cultural and sociopolitical legitimacy representing constitutive and regulative regimes, respectively, remain empirically distinct, as do factors for core competencies in programs and services, and, resources (human capital). These results augment the small but growing literature that directly measures and analyzes legitimation processes (e.g. Deephouse, 1996; Hybels et al., 1994; Rao, 1994; Scott et al.,

2000). They also contribute to the task of disentangling complex processes involving institutional and competitive dynamics (cf. Jones, 2001), by focusing on the antecedents and consequences of legitimation processes and their relationship with organizational structures, procedures, and resources.

Once all these factors have been distinguished a number of unexpected relationships emerge. For instance, in bivariate models, *cultural legitimacy* is negatively associated with organizational competencies and resources and *sociopolitical legitimacy* is positively associated with organizational competencies and resources. The more differentiated (and numerous) an organization's competencies and resources the greater the sociopolitical recognition; but the less differentiated (and less numerous – more particularized) an organization's competencies and resources, the greater the cultural recognition. This suggests that organizations have access to either one or the other type of legitimacy depending on their core competencies and resources. To the extent that organizations are isomorphic with their environment by imitating other organizations' core competencies (in programs and services), and resources, they are the recipients of cultural legitimacy. To the extent that they are differentiated along these dimensions, perhaps acting as self-interested, non-conforming, actors, they are recipients of sociopolitical legitimacy. Balancing the two is likely to be problematic given the loose coordination among organizational components typical of voluntary organizations (Knoke & Prensky, 1984).

In another interesting turn, competencies and resources are negatively associated with organizational transition and disbanding in such a way that differentiation increases viability, while, in direct contrast to institutional theory, homogeneity lowers it. The institutional view that isomorphism promotes viability is not supported: a resource-based view of market partitioning is more likely to explain viability. An important caveat (Scott, 2001, p. 161) notes that:

> Although all organizations within a given institutional field or sector are subject to the effects of institutional processes within the context, all do not experience them in the same way or respond in the same manner.

Another ambiguity emerged in the course of analyzing bivariate relationships: If market partitioning in core competencies and resources promotes organizational viability (which it does), but market partitioning in core competencies and resources fosters only sociopolitical legitimacy, how do isomorphic tendencies promote legitimacy? That is, we know that they influence cultural legitimacy in the expected manner, but isomorphic core competencies and resources *did not* explain organizational viability (market partitioning did). In light of these results, it is not clear how the relationships between legitimacy, competencies, and resources will *combine* to explain organizational viability. That is to say, the direction of the relationships suggests that the model is not all of one piece.

A simultaneous multivariate model was analyzed, specifically testing linkages between factors.[11] Results demonstrated that consistent with recent advances in institutional theory, and also consistent with market partitioning frameworks, cultural and sociopolitical legitimacy have unique relationships with core competencies and resources, although some of the relationships raise a number of additional questions. For instance, while the direction of the bivariate relationships held up in multivariate models, the coefficients are not always significant, suggesting that some factors, including controls, play a differential role in determining organizational viability.

Overall, results show that isomorphic processes do not promote greater organizational viability in bivariate and multivariate models: the greater the differentiation between organizations along the dimensions of program and service competencies, and, resources, the greater the chances of persistence. In the different versions of the multivariate models, program differentiation promoted viability (as did controls for organizational attributes such as founding data, age, size, and, medical niche). With regard to the conceptual linkages between variables, the pattern of results illustrated the complexity of the models. For example, in multivariate models, sociopolitical legitimacy is influenced by service competencies and resources (as might be expected given a resource-based model), while cultural legitimacy is not. However, cultural legitimacy is significantly related to viability (even though it is not influenced by competencies and resources), while sociopolitical legitimacy is not related to viability. One response is that a more fully specified model, with temporal lags eliminating the reciprocal influences of variables, would help resolve the issue. Moreover, there may be interactive effects, between age and legitimacy, or founding date and resource differentiation that should be modeled in order to yield a fuller understanding of relationships. Nonetheless, one of the important theoretical implications of these results is that we are now in a better position to understand and specify differences between institutional and resource-based theories. Prior ambiguity concerning outcomes is obviated by empirical support for analysis of the relationships specified in these preliminary models.

Work needs to be undertaken to address the ambiguities in the multivariate models. For example, resources influence sociopolitical legitimacy but do not directly promote viability (all else being equal). Why not? One answer is that the organizational environment contains resources that are essential for the creation of new organizational forms, but that a resource-centric model fails to explain why actors do not always manage to mobilize them. Instead, it is argued, the availability of resources is not a sufficient cause for organizational outcomes; rather, cultural (or political) factors motivating resource use are necessary (Armstrong, 2002;

Fligstein, 1998). This underscores several important points. First, the results of the structural path model are incomplete and provisional: they reveal part of the process, but the reciprocal nature of the underlying relationships must be specified and analyzed. Future studies of these relationships need to carefully model the expected direction of effects in order to more thoroughly answer the question of the mechanisms operating to influence organizational persistence. Because this study focused on cross-sectional data, longitudinal research needs to be undertaken to capture the direction of effects. Both legitimation and market partitioning are dynamic processes that should be addressed with longitudinal data. However, there is as yet no integration of event history models in a simultaneous equation context. Some issues can be finessed by creating scales of the indicators and lagging variables, as is sometimes recommended with latent factor models (Jöreskog & Sörbom, 1993).

More importantly, it is necessary to examine population level processes as well as organizational level ones. The results in this paper are applicable to between-organizations differences but the focus of isomorphism and market partitioning addresses organizational-level and field-level processes. While this paper analyzes the consequences of these processes for individual organizations, by expanding the scope of analyses, we could then test organizational ecology hypotheses; for example, the density dependence form of legitimation (e.g. Hannan & Carroll, 1992).

As for other populations and contexts, self-help/mutual-aid organizations are a special type of voluntary organization that experience greater institutional than technical pressures. Moreover, while these types of social movement organizations differ in some fundamental ways from commercial and bureaucratic organizations (Knoke & Prensky, 1984), legitimacy, structure, procedures, resource management, and sociopolitical interests are likely to affect organizational persistence similarly, largely because the underlying mechanisms of selection regimes have been shown to be comparable in a wide variety of instances (for review see Baum, 1996). By differentiating the components of these frameworks, and providing empirical answers to questions about conditions under which institutional and resource-based theories operate, insights about the influence of material and symbolic culture on organizational dynamics become available to scholars interested in refining understanding of legitimacy in a wide range of organizational contexts.

Organization research is interested in institutional processes, resources, and sociopolitical conflict because of their effects on organizational persistence, population structures, and other outcomes with implications for social systems (Lounsbury & Ventresca, 2002). Modeling political and economic processes provides a richer understanding of institutionalization than offered by explanations devoted to organizational isomorphism. Stryker (1995, 2001) and others propose a view of conflict and actor interests at odds with the theme of isomorphic drift underlying the notion of cultural institutionalism. Yet, this paper shows that structural isomorphism does influence (cultural) legitimacy, and, cultural legitimacy does promote organizational viability, although isomorphism hardly seems to be the mechanism by which the process occurs. It would be immensely beneficial if further models were developed that take into account the variable relationships between different types of legitimacy, competencies and resources while struggling to explain the multiple paths by which these factors influence one another and promote organizational persistence.

NOTES

1. Simultaneous models are intractable when it comes to incorporating longitudinal designs and non-linear outcomes. See Discussion.

2. Because of the cross-sectional nature of the data, right censoring is present. Yamaguchi (1991) and Allison (1994) argue that if duration to event is not theoretically important, analysis of a logistic outcome is "technically adequate," even though it is not an optimal solution since it leads to a loss of information about outcomes.

3. For purposes of original database construction, media coverage of the entire forty-five year period required access to a journal that retained its articles over that time period, while also providing electronic access to search for almost six hundred names (multiplied by forty-five years). The *New York Times* was well-suited to this purpose.

4. The question of whether or not self-help/mutual-aid received a favorable assessment in journal articles, newspaper accounts, and congressional testimony is important. The theoretical issue is discussed at length in Archibald (2002, Chap. 3). Examination of journal articles, newspaper accounts, and congressional reports showed that references tended to be neutral (e.g. reporting the outcome of a study, reporting the founding of a new type of self-help/mutual-aid group) or positive (e.g. praise for an organization's skill in serving a marginalized population such as the mentally ill). In both instances, individual self-help/mutual-aid organizations referred to these opportunities for publicity in their own organizational histories. These histories typically referenced these media as a sign of the efficacy, importance, and legitimation of the organization.

5. Haider-Markel (1997) examines interest groups to determine whether resource sharing or competition is more prevalent. In his study, resource partitioning, or cultivating a specialized niche, takes place among interest groups through the process of developing their focal issues. Interest groups will avoid direct competition by focusing on an issue that distinguishes it from other groups. To circumvent competition, interest groups are likely to focus on narrow issues rather than general ones.

6. Note that in this study, age does not provide a measure of length of survival because cross-sectional data are right-censored.

7. When a construct has validity, it has: (a) item content and a corresponding factor structure that is representative of and consistent with what is currently known regarding the construct; (b) a factor structure that is replicable and generalizable across relevant

populations, and; (c) a clear interpretable . . . and relatively precise scaling of individuals along one or more common dimensions (Reise, Waller & Comrey, 2000, p. 287).

8. Although not uncontroversial, I follow Hull, Tedlie and Lehn (1995, p. 221) in using "ghosted" parameter constraints to create nested models that can be tested with chi-square.

9. For recent reviews of age- and size- dependence in vital rates see Baum (1996), Ruef (2002), Hannan (1998) and Henderson (1999).

10. Multiplying the probit estimate by 1.6 yields the more interpretable logit for the path. Doing so permits us to interpret the parameter as odds of the occurrence of a given outcome (Liao, 1994).

11. This model is provisional in some important sense. A longitudinal model is the more appropriate way to examine the paths between factors in order to rule out reciprocal influence.

ACKNOWLEDGMENTS

I would like to thank Regina Werum, Alex Hicks, Aristide Sechandice, and members of the Emory Friday Five-Seventeen Seminar for their comments on earlier versions of this chapter. Special thanks to Timothy Dowd for his critical reading and thoughtful remarks. I am especially indebted to Cathryn Johnson for her stimulating insights, helpful suggestions, and endless patience. Thanks also to Charity Crabtree and Carrie Coward for editorial assistance. Any remaining errors are my own. Data collection for this paper was supported in part by an NSF dissertation grant (62–5041).

REFERENCES

Aldrich, H. (1999). *Organizations evolving*. Thousand Oaks, CA: Sage.

Allison, P. D. (1994). *Event history analysis: Regression for longitudinal event data*. Thousand Oaks, CA: Sage.

Archibald, M. E. (2002). *The population dynamics of modern self-help/mutual-aid: Institutional and organizational change in the civil sector, 1955–2000*. Ph.D. dissertation, Department of Sociology, University of Washington, Seattle, WA.

Armstrong, E. (2002). Crisis, collective creativity, and the generation of new organizational forms: The transition of lesbian/gay organizations in San Francisco. In: M. Lounsbury & M. Ventresca (Eds), *Research in the Sociology of Organizations* (Vol. 19, pp. 337–359). JAI Press.

Barney, J. B., & Hesterly, W. S. (1996). Organizational economics. In: S. Clegg, C. Hardy & W. Nord (Eds), *Handbook of Organization Studies*. Thousand Oaks, CA: Sage.

Barron, D. N. (1998). Pathways to legitimacy among consumer loan providers in New York City, 1914–1934. *Organization Studies, 19*, 207–233.

Baum, J. (1995). The changing nature of competition in organizational populations: The Manhattan hotel industry, 1898–1990. *Social Forces, 74*, 177–205.

Baum, J. (1996). Organizational ecology. In: S. R. Clegg, C. Hardy & W. R. Nord (Eds), *Handbook of Organizations Studies* (pp. 77–114). Thousand Oaks, CA: Sage.

Bollen, K. A. (1989). *Structural equations with latent variables*. NY: Wiley.

Brittain, J. (1994). Density-independent selection and community evolution. In: J. Baum & J. V. Singh (Eds), *Evolutionary Dynamics of Organizations* (pp. 355–379). New York: Oxford University Press.

Browne, M. W. (1984). Asymptotically distribution-free methods for the analysis of covariance structures. *British Journal of Mathematical and Statistical Psychology, 37*, 62–83.

Carroll, G. (1985). Concentration and specialization: Dynamics of niche width in populations of organizations. *American Sociological Review, 100*, 720–749.

Carroll, G., & Hannan, M. T. (2000). *The demography of corporations and industries*. Princeton, NJ: Princeton University Press.

Carroll, G., & Swaminathan, A. (2000). Why the microbrewery movement? Organizational dynamics of resource partitioning in the American brewing industry after probation. *American Journal of Sociology, 106*, 715–762.

Congressional Universe/Congressional Information Services (1955–2000). (CIS subject index.)

Deephouse, D. L. (1996). Does isomorphism legitimate? *Academy of Management Journal, 39*, 1024–1039.

Delacroix, J., & Rao, H. (1994). Externalities and ecological theory: Unbundling density dependence. In: J. Baum & J. V. Singh (Eds), *Evolutionary Dynamics of Organizations* (pp. 255–269). New York: Oxford University Press.

DiMaggio, P., & Powell, W. (1983). The iron cage revisited: Institutional isomorphism and collective rationality. *American Sociological Review, 48*, 147–160.

DiMaggio, P., & Powell, W. (1991). Introduction. In: W. Powell & P. DiMaggio (Eds), *The New Institutionalism in Organizational Analysis* (pp. 1–38). Chicago: University of Chicago Press.

Edwards, R., & Marullo, S. (1995). Organization mortality in a declining social movement: The demise of peace movement organizations in the end of the Cold War era. *American Sociological Review, 60*, 908–927.

Fombrun, C. J. (1996). *Reputation: Realizing value from the corporate image*. Boston, MA: Harvard Business School Press.

Gale Research Company (1955–2000). *Encyclopedia of associations, National organizations* (Vols 1–36). Detroit, MI: Gale Research.

Glynn, M. A. (2000). When cymbals become symbols: Conflict over organizational identity within a symphony orchestra. *Organization Science, 11*, 285–298.

Glynn, M. A., & Abzug, R. (1998). Isomorphism and competitive differentiation in the organization name game. *Advances in Strategic Management, 15*, 105–128.

Glynn, M. A., & Slepian, J. (1993). Leaders and transition: The role of leadership in corporate name change. In: K. E. Clark, M. Clark & D. Campbell (Eds), *The Impact of Leadership* (pp. 305–312). Greensboro, NC: Center for Creative Leadership.

Haider-Markel, D. P. (1997). Interest group survival: Shared interests vs. competition for resources. *The Journal of Politics, 59*, 903–912.

Hannan, M. T. (1998). Rethinking age dependence in organizational mortality: Logical formalizations? *American Journal of Sociology, 104*, 85–123.

Hannan, M. T., & Carroll, G. (1992). *Dynamics of organizational populations: Density, legitimacy and competition*. New York, NY: Oxford University Press.

Hannan, M. T., & Freeman, J. H. (1989). *Organizational ecology*. Cambridge: Harvard University Press.

Henderson, A. D. (1999). Firm strategy and age dependence: A contingent view of liability of newness, adolescence and obsolescence. *Administrative Science Quarterly, 44*, 281–314.

Horn, J. L. (1965). A rationale and test for the number of factors in factor analysis. *Psychometrika, 30*, 179–185.

Hosmer, D. W., Jr., & Lemeshow, S. (1989). *Applied logistic regression*. New York: Wiley.

Hull, J. G., Tedlie, J. C., & Lehn, D. A. (1995). Modeling the relation of personality variables to symptom complaints: The unique role of negative affectivity. In: R. H. Hoyle (Ed.), *Structural Equation Modeling: Issues and Applications* (pp. 217–236). Newbury Park, CA: Sage.

Hybels, R. C. (1995). On legitimacy, legitimation and organizations: A critical review and integrative theoretical model. *Academy of Management Journal* (Special Volume), 241–256.

Hybels, R. C., Ryan, A., & Barley, S. (1994). Alliances, legitimation and founding rates in the U.S. biotechnology field, 1971–1989. Paper presented at annual meeting of Academy of Management, Dallas.

Index Medicus, National Library of Medicine, 1955–2000.

Ingram, P. (1996). Organizational form as a solution to the problem of credible commitment: The evolution of naming strategies among U.S. hotel chains: 1896–1980. *Strategic Management Journal, 17*, 85–98.

Jones, C. (2001). Co-evolution of entrepreneurial careers, institutional rules and competitive dynamics in American film, 1895–1920. *Organizational Studies, 22*(6), 911–944.

Jöreskog, K. G., & Sörbom, D. (1993). *LISREL 8: Structural equation modeling with the SIMPLIS command language*. Hillsdale, NJ: Scientific Software International.

Katz, A. H. (1993). *Self-help in America: A social movement perspective*. New York: Twayne.

Knoke, D., & Prensky, D. (1984). What relevance do organization theories have for voluntary associations? *Social Science Quarterly, 65*, 3–20.

Liao, T. F. (1994). *Interpreting probability models: Logit, probit and other generalized linear models*. Thousand Oaks, CA: Sage.

Long, J. S. (1983). *Confirmatory factor analysis*. Thousand Oaks, CA: Sage.

Lounsbury, M., & Ventresca, M. (2002). Social structure and organizations revisited. In: M. Lounsbury & M. Ventresca (Eds), *Research in the Sociology of Organizations* (Vol. 19, pp. 3–36). JAI Press.

Maurer, J. G. (1971). *Readings in organizational theory: Open systems approaches*. New York: Random House.

McChesney, R. W. (1999). *Rich media, poor democracy: Communication politics in dubious times*. Urbana: University of Illinois Press.

McPherson, J. M. (1983). An ecology of affiliation. *American Sociological Review, 48*, 519–532.

Meyer, J. W., & Rowan, B. (1991 [1977]). Institutionalized organizations: Formal structure as myth and ceremony. In: W. Powell & P. DiMaggio (Eds), *The New Institutionalism in Organizational Analysis* (pp. 41–62). Chicago: University of Chicago Press.

Minkoff, D. C. (1995). *Organizing for equality: The evolution of women's and racial-ethnic organizations in America, 1955–1985*. New Brunswick, NJ: Rutgers University Press.

Minkoff, D. C. (1999). Bending with the wind: Strategic change and adaptation by women's and racial minority organizations. *American Journal of Sociology, 104*, 1666–1703.

Muthén, B., & Christoffersson, A. (1981). Simultaneous factor analysis of dichotomous variables in several groups. *Psychometrika, 46*, 407–419.

Muthén, B., & Muthén, L. K. (1998). *Mplus user's guide: The comprehensive modeling program for applied researchers*. Copyright Muthén & Muthén.

New York Times Subject Index 1955–2000.

Oliver, C. (1997). Sustainable competitive advantage: Combining institutional and resource-based views. *Strategic Management Journal, 18*, 697–713.

Parsons, T. (1956). Suggestions for a sociological approach to the theory of organizations, Parts I and II. *Administrative Science Quarterly, 1*, 63–85.

Pfeffer, J., & Salancik, G. R. (1978). *The external control of organizations: A resource dependence perspective*. New York: Harper & Row.

Powell, T. J. (1990). *Working with self-help*. Silver Spring, MD: National Association of Social Workers.

Powell, T. J. (1994). Introduction. In: T. J. Powell (Ed.), *Understanding the Self-Help Organization* (pp. 1–20). Thousand Oaks, CA: Sage.

Preacher, K. J., & MacCallum, R. C. (2003). Repairing Tom Swift's electric factor analysis machine. *Understanding Statistics, 1*, 13–32.

Reise, S. P., Waller, N. G., & Comrey, A. L. (2000). Factor analysis and scale revision. *Psychological Assessment, 12*, 287–297.

Ruef, M. (1997). Assessing organizational fitness on a dynamic landscape: An empirical test of the relative inertia thesis. *Strategic Management Journal, 18*, 837–853.

Ruef, M. (2002). Unpacking the liability of aging: Towards a socially embedded account of organizational disbanding. In: M. Lounsbury & M. Ventresca (Eds), *Research in the Sociology of Organizations* (Vol. 19, pp. 195–227). JAI Press.

Ruef, M., Mendel, P., & Scott, W. R. (1998). An organizational field approach to resource environments in healthcare: Comparing hospitals and home health agencies in the San Francisco Bay region. *Health Services Research, 32*, 775–803.

Ruef, M., & Scott, W. R. (1997). A multidimensional model of organizational legitimacy: Hospital survival in changing institutional environments. *Administrative Science Quarterly, 43*, 877–904.

Ruef, M., & Scott, W. R. (1998). A multidimensional model of organizational legitimacy: Hospital survival in changing institutional environments. *Administrative Science Quarterly, 43*(4), 877–904.

Sacks, M. (2002). The social structure of new venture funding: Stratification and the differential liability of newness. In: M. Lounsbury & M. Ventresca (Eds), *Research in the Sociology of Organizations* (Vol. 19, pp. 229–261). JAI Press.

Scott, W. R. (2001). *Institutions and organizations* (2nd ed.). Thousand Oaks, CA: Sage.

Scott, W. R. (2003). *Organizations: Rational, natural, and open systems* (5th ed.). Thousand Oaks, CA: Sage.

Scott, W. R., & Meyer, J. W. (1991). The organization of societal sectors: Propositions and early evidence. In: W. Powell & P. DiMaggio (Eds), *The New Institutionalism in Organizational Analysis* (pp. 108–140). Chicago: University of Chicago Press.

Scott, W. R., Ruef, M., Mendel, P. J., & Caronna, C. A. (2000). *Institutional change and healthcare organizations: From professional dominance to managed care*. Chicago: University of Chicago Press.

Singh, J. V., Tucker, D. J., & Meinhard, A. G. (1991). Institutional change and ecological dynamics. In: W. Powell & P. DiMaggio (Eds), *The New Institutionalism in Organizational Analysis* (pp. 361–390). Chicago: University of Chicago Press.

Sociological and Psychological Abstracts 1955–2000.

StataCorp (2001). *Stata Reference Manuals Release 7*. College Station, TX: Stata Press.

Stinchcombe, A. (1965). Social structure and organizations. In: J. March (Ed.), *Handbook of Organizations* (pp. 142–193). New York: Rand McNally.

Suchman, M. C. (1995). Managing legitimacy: Strategic and institutional approaches. *Academy of Management Review, 20,* 571–610.

Tolbert, P. S., & Zucker, L. G. (1996). The institutionalization of institutional theory. In: S. R. Clegg, C. Hardy & W. R. Nord (Eds), *Handbook of Organization Studies* (pp. 175–190). London: Sage.

Uzzi, B. (1999). Embeddedness in the making of financial capital: How social relations and networks benefit firms seeking finance. *American Sociological Review, 64,* 481–505.

Wothke, W. (1993). Nonpositive definite matrices in structural modeling. In: K. A. Bollen & J. S. Long (Eds), *Testing Structural Equation Models* (pp. 256–293). Newbury Park, CA: Sage.

Yamaguchi, K. (1991). *Event history analysis.* Thousand Oaks, CA: Sage.

LINKING LEGITIMACY AND PROCEDURAL JUSTICE: EXPANDING ON JUSTICE PROCESSES IN ORGANIZATIONS

Karen A. Hegtvedt and Jody Clay-Warner

ABSTRACT

Processes of legitimacy and justice pervade work organizations. Here we focus on how legitimacy (collective sources of support for an authority) and procedural justice (use of fair procedures) affect how individuals interpret and respond to situations involving unfair outcomes such as underpayment. We draw upon the legitimacy perspective of Walker and Zelditch and the procedural justice approach of Tyler to develop two new models, one in which the two factors constitute objective and independent contextual elements and one in which perceptions of legitimacy and procedural justice are reciprocal. Both models have implications for understanding fairness and compliance in organizations.

INTRODUCTION

Processes of legitimacy and justice are endemic to work organizations. Kanter's (1977) classic analysis of female managers reflects the importance of legitimacy, while the study of justice in the workplace has become so expansive that it

Legitimacy Processes in Organizations
Research in the Sociology of Organizations, Volume 22, 213–237
Copyright © 2004 by Elsevier Ltd.
All rights of reproduction in any form reserved
ISSN: 0733-558X/doi:10.1016/S0733-558X(04)22007-9

has emerged as a specialized field of study – "organizational justice" (e.g. Cohen-Charash & Spector, 2001; Cropanzano, 2001; Greenberg, 1990). Only a few explicit attempts, however, have been made to analyze the confluence of the two processes (e.g. Cohen, 1986; Hegtvedt & Johnson, 2000; Jost & Major, 2001; Tyler, 1990). For the most part, organizational researchers have focused on *either* legitimacy *or* justice. As a result, our knowledge of how legitimacy and justice work together is limited. Recognition of the relationship between these workplace processes is necessary in order to augment understanding of fundamental workplace issues such as fairness and compliance.

Consider the following scenario. A university's upper administration (i.e. President and Provost) proposes a re-structuring of its undergraduate college and its graduate school so that both fall under the same administrative rubric with a singular "über-dean." These "authorities" broadcast their proposal, but make no explicit attempts to elicit reactions from faculty, staff, or students. Then, several weeks after they first circulated the proposal, the administration announces the change and the placement of a senior faculty member as the dean overseeing both the college and graduate school. Faculty response is nearly unanimous: they question the benefits of the re-structuring, strongly believe that the idea has not been fully vetted, and condemn the administration for failing to invite comments from employees and students.

This simplified example highlights issues of both legitimacy and justice in organizations. Given the lack of collective support by the faculty for the structural change, the restructuring, itself, may be considered illegitimate. As a result, the legitimacy of the position of "über-dean," as well as the legitimacy of the individual who holds the position is likely to be questioned. This lack of legitimacy may then create dissatisfaction and affect the faculty's willingness to comply with proposals initiated by the new dean. Justice concerns also emerge. For instance, many may call attention to the fairness of the process involved in the restructuring decision, citing that the administration's failure to elicit comments from the university community constitutes a breach of basic procedural fairness by denying faculty, staff, and students a "voice" in the decision-making process. Perceiving themselves to have been treated unfairly, faculty and staff may become less committed to the organization, less productive, and more prone to exit.

As demonstrated in the above example, both legitimacy and justice affect worker and organizational outcomes. This example also suggests that the effects of the two processes may not be independent, given that a single act elicited concerns about both legitimacy and justice. Here we present two theoretical models that explicate the connection between legitimacy and justice. In presenting these models, we draw from both sociological and psychological traditions. In particular, we focus upon intersections between Zelditch and Walker's (1984;

Walker & Zelditch, 1993) treatment of legitimacy and Tyler's (1990; Lind & Tyler, 1988) work on justice, which draws distinctions between unfair procedures and unfair outcomes.

Generally, the models join legitimacy and procedural justice as factors conditioning responses to distributive or outcome injustice. The first model, discussed in more detail elsewhere (Hegtvedt, Clay-Warner & Johnson, 2003), focuses on the independent effects of legitimacy and fair procedures on employees' perceptions of outcome fairness. The second model builds upon the first by suggesting a dynamic relationship between perceptions of legitimacy and perceptions of fair procedures. Taken together, these models suggest that justice and legitimacy cannot be examined in isolation. Instead, justice and legitimacy are processes that work together to influence fairness perceptions and compliance, which have implications for interaction in and the operation of organizations.

Below we discuss the linkages between justice and legitimacy in organizations by first reviewing the sociological approach to legitimacy of Zelditch and Walker (1984; Walker & Zelditch, 1993). We then examine research on "procedural justice," which refers to fairness in the process by which decisions are made (Lind & Tyler, 1988; Tyler, 1990). We explicate the commonalities between these approaches to allow for the development of new theory. We then present our theoretical models and discuss the implications these models have for understanding fairness and compliance processes in organizations.

VIEWS ON LEGITIMACY, LINKS WITH JUSTICE

Legitimacy and Distributive Justice

A rudimentary characterization of the sociological approach to legitimacy and justice emphasizes how *collective* elements of the social context affect individual-level responses to *unfair distributions* in organizational settings.[1] Most sociological approaches to the study of legitimacy stem from the work of Weber (1918/1968). Zelditch (2001b, p. 33) offers a broad definition of legitimacy in the Weberian tradition: "... something is legitimate if it is in accord with the norms, values, beliefs, practices, and procedures accepted by a group." Weber notes that individuals may not believe in the same norms, values, beliefs, etc., but he emphasizes that their behavior becomes oriented to the valid social order. In effect, individuals perceive that others support the legitimated system and thus act in accord with that system, even if their private beliefs vary. In this way, Weber's theory accentuates the *collective* nature of legitimation processes (Zelditch, 2001b).

Both Dornbush and Scott (1975) and Zelditch and Walker (1984; Walker & Zelditch, 1993) build upon Weber by incorporating both individual and group-level processes in their analyses of authority and its implications in organizations. Dornbush and Scott (1975) embed their arguments about legitimacy in a theory of formal authority. As such, they generally circumscribe their theory to apply to an organizational hierarchy of at least three levels. To capture Weber's recognition that individuals may not embrace all the norms or beliefs of a society, they introduce separate concepts to represent individual and collective sources of support. *Propriety* represents individual-level support and reflects one's belief that the rules and norms of conduct are desirable, proper, and appropriate patterns of action. *Validity*, on the other hand, is defined as an individual's belief that he or she is *obliged to obey* group norms even in the absence of personal approval of them. In effect, legitimacy ensures compliance to the norms of a group or system.

Specific collective sources of legitimacy include authorization and endorsement. *Authorization* refers to support by individuals who occupy higher positions within the organization (i.e. authorities), whereas *endorsement* pertains to similar support from people in equal or lower positions. For example a middle manager is authorized when she receives support from her superiors; she is endorsed when she receives support from subordinates. A key consequence of endorsement and authorization is compliance.

Implicit in their work, Zelditch and Walker link legitimacy to issues of distributive justice (Zelditch, 2001b). Hegtvedt and Markovsky (1995, p. 258) state that, "Justice exists when there is congruence between expectations for outcomes based on the normative rule and actual outcomes." In the workplace, distributive justice concerns surround salary decisions, allocation of raises, and employee benefits, among other things. Typically, individuals invoke the equity principle when deciding whether or not a distribution is fair. According to the equity principle, a distribution is fair if the ratio of an individual's outcomes to his or her inputs in equal to those of comparison others (Adams, 1965; see also Homans, 1974). For example, an employee is likely to judge his salary (outcome) as fair if it is comparable to the salaries of others in the organization with similar work hours and skills (inputs). Distributive justice researchers examine the conditions under which individuals perceive outcomes to be just or unjust, as well as how they respond in the case of injustice (see Cook & Hegtvedt, 1983; Hegtvedt & Cook, 2001; Törnblom, 1992).

Classic theories of distributive justice (Adams, 1965; Homans, 1974; Walster, Walster & Berscheid, 1978) typically focus on individual-level processes and reactions without much attention to the validity of the social order in which the assessments are occurring. In contrast, Zelditch and Walker (1984; Walker &

Zelditch, 1993) emphasize such validity in the form of legitimacy and investigate its effects on the propensity of individuals to act collectively to change a structure. Although not originally designed to assess distributive justice processes, Zelditch's (2001a) retrospective description of his theoretical research program explicitly ties legitimacy studies to issues of distributive justice. His experimental situation involves five actors connected in a Bavelas communication wheel in which the central actor controls communication of information from others and thus more readily solves problems, thereby earning greater rewards and creating an inequitable distribution. Results from various experiments show that when the communication structure is said to be valid (Thomas, Walker & Zelditch, 1986) or when peripheral actors endorse the structure (Walker, Thomas & Zelditch, 1986), group members express fewer demands to change the network. Validity (Thomas et al., 1986) and endorsement (Walker, Rogers & Zelditch, 1988) also enhance individuals' beliefs about the propriety of the structure. Similarly, results from a vignette study in which subjects play the role of a subordinate who feels a sense of impropriety over the denial of a pay raise show that endorsement or authorization of their manager stymies attempts to form a coalition or seek recourse from the manager's superior (Johnson & Ford, 1996). Although not stated as such, this pattern of findings suggests that collective sources of legitimacy inhibit responses to perceived injustice over pay and, in effect, ensure compliance with the norms of the existing structure.

Inspired by this previous research, Hegtvedt and Johnson (2000) create explicit bridges between collective sources of legitimacy as key elements of the social context and individual perceptions of and reactions to unfair distributions. Specifically, they detail how collective assessments of an outcome distribution – i.e. its legitimacy – affect workers' perceptions of unfairness and the ways in which workers may react to the perceived unfairness. Hegtvedt and Johnson argue that when conditions are objectively unjust, such as when a worker receives a smaller raise than a colleague with equal rank, experience, and productivity, the worker will perceive the outcome as more fair when the distribution system has been endorsed and authorized than when such collective support is lacking. This occurs because the worker considers the opinions of both her peers and her superiors in assessing the fairness of the raise decision: when others support the distribution, the worker is less likely to judge her own outcomes as unfair. Similarly, the worker will judge the raise to be less unfair if the manager who made the raise decision is authorized and endorsed than if such legitimacy is not present.

In addition, Hegtvedt and Johnson (2000) suggest that these collective sources of legitimacy inhibit negative emotional expressions and decrease the likelihood of a behavioral response because of the likelihood of sanctions (Hegtvedt &

Killian, 1999; Johnson, Ford & Kaufman, 2000). As a result, individuals may not voice their concerns about unfairness because of fears of repercussions. An employee, for example, is less likely to challenge a negative performance review when the performance review system is authorized or endorsed. When the employee's colleagues endorse the system, the worker may fear informal punishment, such as ostracism. The worker may fear retaliation by supervisors when the system is authorized. Supervisors may retaliate by denying the employee promotions, giving less favorable job assignments, as well as filing additional negative performance reviews.

The relative impact of endorsement and authorization, however, may depend upon how much an individual identifies with peers or with authorities, respectively. Hegtvedt and Johnson (2000) contend that endorsement is likely to have a greater effect on responses to injustice when workers identify more strongly with their peers than with supervisors, while authorization will be the more influential factor when workers identify more strongly with their supervisors than with their peers. In crafting this argument, Hegtvedt and Johnson draw from the group-value model of procedural justice (Lind & Tyler, 1988), which highlights the important role that group identification plays in shaping employees' attitudes and behaviors. By incorporating the group-value model, Hegtvedt and Johnson suggest that workers' identities – an issue not considered by Zelditch and Walker – may be key to understanding the impact of legitimacy on justice processes.

Legitimacy and Procedural Justice

The group-value model of procedural justice explicitly focuses upon identity issues to link procedural justice and legitimacy (Lind & Tyler, 1988). By "procedural justice" Lind and Tyler refers to fairness in the way in which decisions are made (see also Hegtvedt & Markovsky, 1995). People generally consider as fair procedures that provide consistency across individuals and time, suppression of bias, representativeness of the opinions of people affected, information accuracy, mechanisms to correct bad decisions, and conformity with moral and ethical standards (Leventhal, Karuza & Frye, 1980). Drawing from Leventhal et al. (1980), Tyler and Lind (1992) propose three "relational" factors that communicate information about the relationship between an individual and representative authorities and thus affect one's evaluation of procedural fairness: standing, neutrality and trust. *Standing* refers to status, which can be communicated through polite behavior, dignified treatment, and respect for one's rights and opinions. *Neutrality* points to equal treatment of all parties and includes honesty and lack of bias. The final factor, *trust*, characterizes the intentions of the decision-maker. Individuals perceive authorities to be trustworthy to the extent that they strive to be fair and ethical. Trustworthiness is especially important because it has implications for how an authority can be expected to behave in the future, as well as for how other similar authorities might behave.

At the root of the argument linking procedural justice to legitimacy is the importance of identification with the group to individuals' self-esteem. In developing the group-value model of procedural justice, Lind and Tyler (1988) draw heavily from social identity theory, which explicates how individuals organize their group identities and respond to in-group and out-group members (Tajfel, 1972, 1978). One basic tenet of social identity theory is that individuals seek membership in highly valued groups because membership in valued groups increases individual self-esteem (Tajfel, 1972, 1978). Tyler and Smith (1999) extend this argument (and build upon the group-value model of procedural justice) by positing that individuals acquire self-esteem from two group-related sources. First, individuals interpret fair procedural treatment as an indication of their own value in the group, which increases their self-esteem; Tyler labels this "respect" in the group. Second, individuals feel "group pride" when they experience procedurally fair treatment from in-group authorities. For example, when a supervisor treats an employee in an honest, trustworthy manner, the employee feels proud to belong to such an organization. As Tyler and Smith (1999) explain, individuals want to be important members of important groups.

Having established why individuals may desire fair procedures, Tyler argues that perceived procedural justice is an important antecedent of legitimacy (1990, 2001; Lind & Tyler, 1988). He argues that when an individual identifies with a group that demonstrates procedural fairness, the individual becomes attached to the social order and is more likely to believe that in-group authorities are legitimate and, as a consequence, ought to be obeyed. In support of this hypothesis, Tyler (1990) shows that citizens' procedural justice judgments significantly affect their perceptions of the legitimacy of police, which, in turn, influence their level of compliance with the law. Other research also consistently finds a relationship between perceived procedural fairness and legitimacy (Lind, 1982; Tyler, 1984; Tyler, Rasinski & Griffin, 1986). In each of these studies procedural justice is significant even when controlling for outcome satisfaction, suggesting that the desire for fair procedures is not driven purely by self-interest (see Thibaut & Walker, 1975 for review of the self-interest model of procedural justice). In fact, procedural justice generally has a stronger effect on legitimacy than does an individual's evaluation of the fairness of the outcome itself (Tyler, 1990).

Differences and Similarities in Theoretical Approaches

Given the centrality of legitimacy processes to understanding social order generally and, more specifically, within organizations, here we examine the intersection between the group-value psychological approach to procedural justice and legitimacy and the sociological approach to the impact of collective sources of legitimacy on perceptions of and reactions to distributive injustice. Below we identify differences between the approaches and then focus upon fundamental convergences that allow for the development of new theoretical models that draw from both approaches.

Although, as discussed further below, there are integral similarities between Tyler's psychological approach to justice and legitimacy and that of sociologists to the same issue, several distinctions are noteworthy. First, Tyler's approach clearly incorporates procedural justice where as the sociological approach focuses implicitly on issues of distributive injustice. Second, the sociologists have explored theoretically and empirically a broad range of what might be legitimated (e.g. a person, a rule, a distribution, power, authority), while Tyler and colleagues have focused upon the legitimacy of authorities, while allowing that more macro-level entities such as regimes or communities may also obtain legitimacy (Tyler, 1990). And, third Tyler's approach to the "group" is quite different from that of Zelditch and Walker. The groups that are of interest in Tyler's model are the groups to which individuals may belong within an organization and, subsequently, from which they derive their identity. And, while there has been some recognition of overlapping group identities (Huo, Smith & Tyler, 1996), there is no discussion of how hierarchical levels of authority influence group processes (see Clay-Warner, 2001). In contrast, Zelditch and his colleagues identify at least three organizational levels (such as employee, supervisor, and company vice-president), which may underlie group identities and allow for comparisons across group allegiances.

Despite the differences noted above, the similarities between the two models are significant. There are three basic ways in which the sociological approach of Zelditch and Walker (1984; Walker & Zelditch, 1993) and the psychological approach of Tyler (1990) converge in examining justice and legitimacy. First, these approaches highlight the importance of group-level phenomenon, especially non-material aspects of the group. The sociological perspective does so by emphasizing collective sources of support and their implications for social influence whereas the psychological approach focuses on issues of group value. By involving these group-level phenomena, the perspectives focus upon characteristics of the social context in order to understand the relationship between justice and legitimacy.

A second commonality is the theoretical emphasis on compliance as a consequence of legitimacy. For Zelditch and Walker, individuals in a legitimated structure are likely to comply with the demands of that structure. For Tyler, individuals who perceive an authority to be legitimate are more likely to carry out his or her dictates. In fact, Tyler (2001, p. 417) argues that legitimacy is so central to securing compliance, that it is more effective and efficient than "command and control" strategies in which managers attempt to gain compliance by appealing to worker self-interest. For both Tyler and Zelditch and Walker, the ultimate consequence of legitimacy in work organizations is that employees are more likely to comply with organizational demands.

Finally, the notion of one's perceived "obligation to obey" is integral to both perspectives. As suggested above, Tyler's conceptualization of legitimacy bears striking similarities to Zelditch and Walker's conceptualization. According to Tyler (1990) there are two components of legitimacy: support for authorities (i.e. trust and confidence in them) and obligation to obey authorities. In more recent work (Tyler, 2001), he focuses largely on the second component, contending

> ...it is feelings of obligation (i.e. of what one ought to do) that are central to legitimacy. Legitimacy exists to the degree that people feel a personal obligation to follow social rules and to obey social authorities, that is, when people feel that authorities 'ought' to be obeyed (Tyler, 2001, p. 419).

Thus, obligation to obey is the key concept in Zelditch and Walker's definition of validity, as well as in Tyler's definition of legitimacy. Zeldtich and Walker argue that endorsement and authorization give rise to validity (perceived obligation to obey, despite personal disapproval), which is an important source of legitimacy (i.e. "the belief that a norm or normative system governs or should govern one's actions" [Walker et al., 1986, p. 622]). Tyler, on the other hand, argues that it is procedural justice that is they key antecedent to legitimacy. In essence, both approaches seek to understand what factors influence people's perceived obligation to obey, above and beyond their own personal beliefs about whether the requested behavior is appropriate.[2]

The commonalities between these sociological and psychological approaches to the study of legitimacy and justice indicate that consolidation is possible and, we argue, beneficial. Below we elaborate upon two theoretical models that undertake this task.

MODELS OF THE LINKS BETWEEN LEGITIMACY AND PROCEDURAL JUSTICE

In our initial attempt at consolidation, we limit our discussion to the legitimation of a person who occupies a position of some control or authority over others, as is typical in organizational settings in which managers have authority over lower-level employees. In addition, our focus is on individual responses to situations in which the distribution of some outcomes are objectively unfair. Two avenues for consolidation exist. The first approach considers procedural justice, which implies relational support, and collective support from authorities or peers as two complementary sources of legitimacy, which may independently affect responses to distributive injustice. The second approach explores the reciprocal effects of perceived procedural justice and perceived endorsement/authorization in predicting reactions to distributive injustice.

Model 1: Legitimacy and Procedural Justice: Conditioning Responses to Distributive Injustice

Epitomizing the first approach, Hegtvedt et al. (2003) provide a theoretical framework pertaining to the legitimacy of a manager in a work group situation who offers a one-time pay distribution to a subordinate that is objectively unfair. The theoretical model identifies collective sources of legitimacy and procedural justice as key contextual factors that shape a person's responses to distributive injustice. They predict that the presence or absence of authorization/endorsement and the use of fair or unfair procedures affect whether, for example, an employee attempts to redress a manager's unfair pay decision or acquiesces. These contextual factors, although addressed independently, clearly situate the manager in relation to others, not in isolation as is typical in many justice studies. In such a context, the actions of the supervisor are of focal interest to the subordinates who are often targets of those actions. When the supervisor does something that comes as a surprise to subordinates, they are likely to wonder why. In other words, their social perceptions about their manager are likely to affect their own subsequent thinking and actions (Fig. 1).

Consider, for example, an employee whose endorsed supervisor refuses to provide pay raises. If everyone supports the manager, then his refusal (especially if this is only one instance) may be unexpected. In wondering why the refusal occurred, workers might think that there is something beyond the manager's own motivations and intentions underlying the refusal. They may reason that, given everyone's support for this supervisor, in the past he has been open to considering the needs of workers. What could be going on to disrupt the previous pattern that had won the supervisor support? Workers may then look to the larger situation to determine why the refusal occurred (e.g. profits for the organization are at an all time low). By presuming that the supervisor's behavior is due to something not under his control, the workers may be less likely to attempt to engage others in

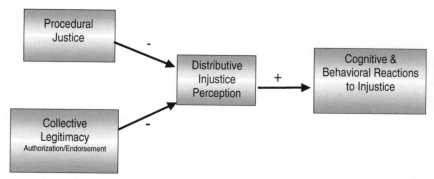

Fig. 1. Illustration of Model 1 of the Effects of Procedural Justice and Collective Legitimacy on Perceptions of Distributive Injustice and Reactions to Injustice.

discussions about a work slow-down or strike. Similarly, if a supervisor generally treats her subordinates in a procedurally fair manner, the subordinates may discount the pay unfairness and continue to comply with the supervisor's requests. These examples capture Model 1 by focusing on the independent operation of collective sources of legitimacy and procedural justice as well as the impact of cognitive interpretations of a supervisor's behavior.

More formally, Hegtvedt et al. (2003) focus on the *independent* effects of *objective* levels of legitimacy and procedural justice on workers' attitudes and behaviors. In their model, explicit information is available with regard to whether peers and/or authorities support the manager and whether or not the manager uses fair procedures, conceptualized as the extent to which he or she demonstrates neutrality and respect toward workers. In Hegtvedt et al.'s model, legitimacy and procedural justice do not overlap but, instead, are orthogonal constructs.

In addition the model includes intervening cognitive processes, specifically attributions. Generally, attributions capture perceived causes of behavior and are more likely to occur when a behavior is unexpected or novel (see Howard, 1995). Two types of attributions are of interest: internal attributions, which suggest that the behavior stems from something about the supervisor's own abilities or intentions; and external attributions, which indicate that the behavior stems from something outside of the supervisor, owing to the situation or other circumstances. Previous work in both distributive and procedural justice (e.g. Hegtvedt, Thompson & Cook, 1993; Utne & Kidd, 1980; van den Bos et al., 1999) notes that perceptions of the causes of a person's behavior (e.g. a manager's refusal to grant a requested transfer) are key to understanding the subjective evaluation of the fairness of that behavior. In addition, research suggests that attributing injustice to another person heightens the severity of felt injustice (Utne & Kidd,

1980), but external attributions reduce the likelihood of an observable response (Hassebrauck, 1987).

Drawing on the works linking justice and attribution processes, Hegtvedt et al. (2003) predict that the legitimacy and procedural fairness of a manager increase the likelihood of external attributions for his or her unjust pay behavior, which in turn reduces the severity of the perception of distributive injustice regarding the pay. The authors also argue that given the circumstances of a one-time payment, procedural justice may be likely to have a stronger impact on perceptions of injustice because use of fair or unfair procedures is a more proximal condition to the subordinates than is general support of the decision-maker. Moreover, the procedures the decision-maker uses directly affect a worker's outcomes.

Regardless of the relative impact of types of support in the situation, Hegtvedt et al. (2003) contend that legitimacy and procedural justice, each in conjunction with perceptions of distributive injustice are likely to affect how a worker responds to his or her pay. When fair procedures have been used and when a supervisor is supported, perceptions of injustice are more likely to spur cognitive reactions (e.g. "My pay level may seem unfair, but it is still more than I would earn at another company. And, besides, here my boss respects me.") than when procedures are unfair and legitimacy is absent. Behavioral responses such as complaints or attempts to change the pay, then, are more likely in the absence of fair procedures or any form of support for a supervisor. Thus both procedural justice and legitimacy indirectly (through attributions and injustice perceptions) and directly (in conjunction with injustice perceptions) limit the range of potential responses to pay unfairness, thereby increasing the likelihood of employee compliance.

The above model assumes: (1) the independent operation of collective sources of legitimacy and procedural justice; and (2) that there is something representing an objective reality about each. In the second model, we focus on how individuals *perceive* collective sources of legitimacy and procedural justice. By doing so we identify potential reciprocal effects of these factors, thus highlighting subjective elements of situations in which workers and their superiors find themselves embedded.

Model 2: Reciprocal Effects of Procedural Justice and Collective Sources of Legitimacy

The second approach to consolidating Zelditch and Walker's and Tyler's perspectives extends the first approach by considering that procedural justice and collective sources of legitimacy may have reciprocal effects on one another. In this approach we acknowledge that it is ultimately individuals' *perceptions* of collective legitimacy and procedural justice that affect how workers perceive and react to unfair outcomes. Moreover, as is recognized in organizations, perceptions of procedural justice and collective sources of legitimacy develop in on-going dynamic processes. We focus first on explaining how social conditions give rise to perceptions of procedural justice, which in turn affect perceptions of endorsement and, second, on how perceptions of both authorization and endorsement may affect perceptions of procedural justice. Although we limit our discussion to these key reciprocal effects, we contend that the resulting perceptions are likely to affect perceptions of and reactions to distributive injustice in much the same way as described for Model 1.

The underpinnings of the model of reciprocal effects between the perceptions of collective sources of legitimacy and of procedural justice include both the conceptual and the empirical strategies of Tyler, on the one hand, and Zelditch and Walker, on the other hand. Conceptually, Tyler's definition of legitimacy and the definition of validity employed by Zelditch and Walker are quite similar, as noted above. Tyler, moreover, contends that when authorities demonstrate lack of bias, respect toward subordinates, and trust in them, such individuals are likely to perceive themselves as valued members of the group and are likely to *perceive* the authorities as legitimate. Empirically, Tyler (1990) measures legitimacy with scales that directly tap respondents' perceived obligation to obey the law. The process and result that Tyler describes seems consistent with Zelditch and Walker's emphasis on endorsement (and authorization) as factors that bolster the acceptance of norms. In other words and as empirical tests reviewed above suggest, compliance with an existing system or structure increases under conditions of endorsement and authorization. What is missing from this early work of Zelditch and Walker, however, is examination of the antecedents to either source of collective legitimacy (see Hegtvedt & Johnson, 2000).[3]

One variant of Model 2 attempts to illustrate how the procedurally fair treatment of subordinates in work organizations may give rise to the perception that subordinates, in general, support the authority – i.e. that endorsement exists. The second variant of Model 2 focuses on how perceptions of collective support enhance perceptions of procedural justice.

Model 2a: How Perceptions of Procedural Justice Affect Perceptions of Endorsement

Sociological approaches to legitimacy in organizations emphasize structural features of the situation. Specifically, such formulations distinguish at least three levels of authority and recognize both upward and downward support (i.e. endorsement and authorization, respectively). The term "middle manager," for example, captures a typical pattern of stratification: the middle manager oversees the work of a number of associates, but she is also supervised by a higher-level manager (e.g. a vice president of the corporation). Endorsement exists to the extent that lower-level workers approve of and support the middle manager. Authorization exists to the extent that the vice president approves of and supports the middle manager. Empirical work reviewed above examines the consequences of the different levels of collective support for the maintenance of a system of distribution and individual beliefs about that system. Omitted from that body of work, however, is consideration of how the dynamics between people within groups shape perceptions and ultimately underlie compliance with organizational norms.

Here we propose that such dynamics are characterized by the relational elements that Tyler identifies as inherent to perceptions of procedural justice and that they may be relevant to the establishment of endorsement. As discussed earlier, Tyler and Smith (1999) argue that feelings of self-worth increase in response to procedurally fair treatment as a result of both *respect* and *group pride* (see also Tyler, Degoey & Smith, 1996). *Respect* refers to an individual's belief that he or she is well regarded in the group as a result of being personally treated in a procedurally fair manner by authorities. *Group pride* refers to the perception that one is a member of a highly valued group, as demonstrated by in-group authorities' strict adherence to standards of procedural justice. The distinction is between one's status within the group (respect) and the status of one's group (pride) (Tyler & Blader, 2002). While a great deal of work in procedural justice has examined the desire for respect as the mechanism explaining individual motivation for procedurally fair treatment, relatively little work explores the role of group pride as a motivating factor or its consequences (see Tyler & Blader, 2002).

We argue that group pride constitutes a theoretical mechanism that may explain the link between perceptions of procedural justice and endorsement. The processes that underlie the development of group pride provide the basis for this link. First, in seeking out procedural justice information as a way to determine whether or not individuals should feel proud of their group membership, these people must examine not only their own treatment but also the treatment others in the group receive. By doing so, individuals observe others and potentially compare themselves to similar others (Goethals & Darley, 1977). For example, in order to determine whether one's group is of high status, and therefore, worthy of pride, a worker must consider how company authorities treat him and others in subordinate positions. The simultaneous examination of one's own treatment and the treatment of others will almost inevitably lead to social comparisons between self and others. It is the comparison information, and not simply the mere observation of others, that is critical to the forging of uniformity in values and perceptions within

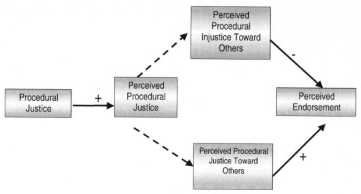

Fig. 2. Illustration of Model 2a of the Effects of Procedural Justice and Perceptions of Endorsement (Dashed Lines Indicate Social Comparison Processes).

the group (Forsyth, 2000). Second, as Tyler (1990) has already shown, when an individual is himself or herself treated in a procedurally fair manner by in-group authorities, the individual's own support for in-group authorities increases. Thus to the extent that observations demonstrate that others are fairly treated and to the extent a person believes that fair treatment by an authority is reciprocated by support for that authority, social comparisons are likely to lead an individual to conclude that others who receive fair treatment also support the relevant authority (Fig. 2).

In effect, an employee bases his or her judgments about procedural justice on his or her experiences and observations of the experiences of those similarly placed in the organization, which provides the basis for group pride – a sense that his group is valued as a result of its consistent display of procedural justice. In addition, to the extent that such fair treatment ensures that the employee supports the relevant authority (perceives the authority to be legitimate), he or she is likely to generalize that other fairly treated people also support the relevant authority. As a consequence, the person is likely *to perceive* the existence of what Zelditch and Walker label endorsement. Conversely, the perception of an authority as procedurally unfair to self and, importantly, to others suggests that subordinates are unlikely to support the authority, leading to the perception on the part of the employee that the authority lacks endorsement.

Critical to this link between perceptions of procedural justice and perceptions of endorsement is the comparisons that individuals make. Ultimately, the degree to which others are treated in a procedurally fair manner determines the extent of endorsement. This is most evident in examining situations in which the treatment of self and others is incongruent. For example, if an individual discovers that only she receives fair treatment while others in the group are unfairly treated, then the employee may surmise that collective support for the authority does not, in fact, exist (e.g. the authority is not endorsed). Conversely, if a person learns that it is only he who is unfairly treated, he is likely to perceive that since others have been treated in a procedurally fair manner that the authority has collective support. In this way, it is the social comparisons evoked by a desire for group pride that allow perceptions of procedural justice to influence perceptions of endorsement.

Model 2a presents procedural justice as an antecedent to the development of perceptions of one form of collective support for an authority. The impact of the perception of others as fairly treated is limited to upward support. What is known and perceived about procedurally fair treatment of peers is independent from authorization as a collective source of legitimacy. Yet, the perception of endorsement and the perception of authorization may color the way in which people perceive the behavior enacted by authorities in the on-going dynamics of workplace settings.

Model 2b: How Perceptions of Collective Sources of Legitimacy Affect Procedural Justice Perceptions

In most psychological work on procedural justice the focal variable is *perceptions* of procedural justice, not some objective indicator (see Tyler et al., 1997 for review). Some studies involve the manipulation of particular elements of procedural justice, such as the relational factors (Tyler & Lind, 1992) or actual procedural rules (Leventhal et al., 1980), and then measure procedural justice perceptions. Other studies, like Tyler's landmark study of Chicago residents' interactions with legal authorities, consider perceptions of procedural justice as the focal independent variable and examine its impact on the perceived legitimacy of legal authorities and subsequent compliance with those authorities. Relatively little work has examined whether contextual factors affect perceptions of procedural justice. Clay-Warner (2001), however, demonstrates that group membership (e.g. attorney vs. judge; male vs. female) and characteristics of the group (e.g. relative status and permeability) affect attorney and judges' perceptions of procedural improprieties in the form of gender discrimination.

Here we assert that an employee's perceptions of the authorization and endorsement of an authority may influence his or her perceptions of the fairness of the procedures used by the authority. Perceptual processes and, again, comparison processes underlie this link. Given the limitations of human information processing, individuals are likely to take short cuts to reduce the amount of potentially available information (see Howard, 1995). People's pre-existing expectations or schema are likely to shape interpretations of new information about particular behaviors. Thus, it is unlikely that individuals fully or separately process information about the actions of an authority from what they generally know about that authority.

To the extent that the employee believes that an authority is authorized or endorsed, the employee then is likely to presume that superiors and subordinates also support the procedures used by the authority. This presumption may be fueled by social comparisons that occur in the absence of self-evaluation among individuals within a social network embedded in an organization. Gartrell (2002) shows that the frequency of interaction, the various types of interaction, and the strength of ties within subgroups of a larger group enhance social comparisons that result in a cluster of support in relationship to the authority. In other words, those to whom an employee is closely tied help him or her to sort through the ways in which an authority has treated him or her as a way to reinforce group pride and to increase self-esteem. Thus, this support augments the perceptual process that transfers the approval of the authority to the perceived approval of the actions of the authority.

Recognition of support for an authority, especially in conjunction with the perceptual transference of legitimacy from the actor to his or her behaviors, may raise the employee's threshold for detecting procedural improprieties. Perceived authorization or endorsement of an authority decreases the probability that the authority's enactment of a procedurally unfair process will be altered and, therefore, there is little motivation on the part of an employee to detect such injustice. For example, among workers who presumably support their supervisors, sharing stories about other supervisors whose unfair behavior was even more egregious than that of their current boss may provide a perspective that decreases the intensity of current unfair procedures. Detecting procedural injustice would reduce self-esteem (through loss of respect and group pride), while offering few alternatives for redress. While workers may be able to form coalitions or in some other way challenge the procedurally unfair act, the probability that these attempts would succeed are likely to be lower when an authority is authorized and endorsed than when collective sources of legitimacy are absent. In addition, the collective sources of legitimacy carry with them the potential for (social) sanctions, resulting in further costs for raising the specter of injustice (see Hegtvedt & Johnson, 2000) (Fig. 3).

The reciprocal effects model acknowledges that it is not simply objective levels of procedural justice and collective sources of legitimacy that ultimately affect compliance behaviors. Much like Younts and Mueller (2001) argue with regard to understanding reactions to distributive injustice, *perceptions* of procedural injustice and legitimacy mediate the relationship between actual procedures/ endorsement/authorization and perceptions of and reactions to distributive injustice. Such a mediation model allows for an examination of the effects of

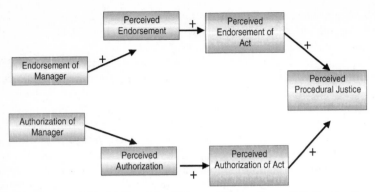

Fig. 3.   Illustration of Model 2b of the Effects of Perceptions of Collective Sources of
Legitimacy on Perceptions of Procedural Justice.

perceived procedural justice on endorsement, as well as the effects of perceived
authorization and endorsement on perceived procedural justice.

JUSTICE AND LEGITIMACY IN ORGANIZATIONS: PATHWAYS TO PERTINENT ISSUES

Justice and legitimacy capture two fundamental processes in organizations. Issues
of justice arise both in terms of how people are treated – both by superiors and by
peers – as well as how they are compensated. The distribution of compensation –
both material and non-material benefits – invites comparisons among individuals.
Both treatment and outcomes are different measures of an individual's worth to
his or her work group. Thus, while it has frequently been only studied at the
individual level, concerns about justice are central to a collectivity. Likewise, issues
of legitimacy are extremely important to the effective functioning of authorities
and feelings of being embedded in a group.

   In this paper we have drawn from Zeldith and Walker's sociological approach
to the study of justice and legitimacy and from the more psychological approach
of Tyler to offer a theoretical analysis of the ways in which justice and legitimacy
processes operate together in work organizations.[4] These theorists fundamentally
agree that perceived obligation to obey and, ultimately, compliance characterize
the success of a legitimate system or structure. Moreover, both perspectives
emphasize the importance of group-level contextual factors. That they feature
different contextual factors allows for greater understanding of how legitimacy
and forms of justice may operate in organizations.

Model 1 brings together collective sources of legitimacy and procedural justice as antecedents to perceptions of and reactions to distributive injustice. To the extent that unfair outcomes disrupt the status quo, they threaten compliance with organizational norms, production efficiency, and commitment. Within an organization, the objective circumstances of the support for a manager by superiors and subordinates and the actual procedures a manager uses may affect the types of attributions a worker who feels unfairly compensated makes, which, in turn, affects his or her sense of perceived distributive injustice and the course of reactions to the unfair situation. In the absence of general support for a manager, especially one who uses unfair procedures, a worker is going to be far angrier over pay inequities and far less likely to demonstrate organizational commitment. The legitimacy of a manager, however, may compensate for the use of unfair procedures or the fairness of procedures may compensate for lack of legitimacy. Such compensation is likely to at least dampen the severity of the perceived injustice, but perhaps not to the point of securing allegiance to the organization. Fair treatment of subordinates and collective support for a manager are key ways to maintain workers' job satisfaction and to prevent turnovers.

But what provides the basis for collective support for a manager? Model 2a offers a possible means by which organizational authorities can foment endorsement for their middle managers. To the extent that they train such managers to treat their subordinates fairly, the observations of and comparisons among the subordinates may lead to the development of group pride, which fosters perceived support for the manager. In addition, as Model 2b illustrates, if workers believe that authorities and their peers support a manager, they are more likely to think that what a manager does constitutes appropriate treatment, especially when their co-workers are available to discuss individual work issues. In effect, the connections among workers themselves can create meanings of the manager's behavior. These reciprocally induced perceptions of procedural justice and of sources of collective legitimacy may ultimately operate in the same way as more objective circumstances to augment or attenuate perceptions of and behavioral reactions to distributive injustice and their concomitant implications for job satisfaction and organizational commitment.

While our general analysis of justice and legitimacy and the specific models we offer have ramifications for understanding justice issues within an organization, they also raise several issues for future basic research. Some of these issues pertain to augmenting the intersection of justice and legitimacy processes while others seem more directly relevant to Zeldtich and Walker's approach or to Tyler's approach.

We note above the importance of group structure – different levels and potential sources of collective support – and group dynamics in understanding justice and legitimacy in organizations. What is largely missing or is only implicit, stemming from the conceptual foundations of Tyler's procedural justice approach, is emphasis on group identity. Individuals are often members of multiple groups with differing interests. Tyler's approach seems to capture the work group as a monolithic whole, without consideration of varying functions or duties as well as lateral positions and departments within an organization. Although Zelditch and Walker do not broach the issue of group identity, Hegtvedt and Johnson (2000) recognize its importance but limit its impact to either identification with peers or authorities (both generally defined, and thus as problematic as Tyler's approach). Thus, one direction for future research is to examine how individuals within an organization conceive of their group identity or identities and the implications of the salience and/or commitment (Burke & Reitzes, 1991) of the identities for the development or impact of collective support on either perceptions of procedural justice or on perceptions of and reactions to distributive injustice. In addition, drawing from current work on the psychology of legitimacy, the understanding of one's workgroup identities may further depend upon whether or not an employee believes that he or she may advance in the organization, thus allowing identification with superiors (Ellemers, 2001; Wright, 1991).

A second avenue for further investigation that pertains to understanding the intersection between justice and legitimacy is a more detailed articulation of the role of social comparisons. As noted by Goethals (1986), social comparison theory is everybody's "second favorite theory" insofar as it often underlies other processes. In a recent volume, Suls and Wheeler (2000) argue that social comparisons pervade evaluations of both individual- and group-level phenomena. Indeed, within any work organization, workers and their supervisors are likely to make comparisons that impact performance assessments and pay decisions at the individual level as well as team evaluations and productivity at the group level. Here, we invoked the process in a general sense in order to understand how comparing one's own treatment to another or developing cohesion among similarly situated individuals may impact perceptions of legitimacy and justice. Omitted from our analysis, however, is a central issue inherent in social comparison research: the direction of the comparison, either upward to authorities, laterally to co-workers, or downward to workers occupying positions of lower prestige. The direction of the comparison may be particularly relevant to understanding whether individuals identify more with their peers or with authorities. For example, an employee who assesses her performance, duties, and responsibilities in comparison with her supervisor may sense greater similarities with upper management than with her own coworkers, which may have implications for the reciprocal relationship between perceived procedural justice and perceptions of collective support for an authority.

That our analysis is limited to the legitimacy of an authority stems from the psychological perspective of Tyler. His work on legitimacy concentrates only on authorities whereas Zelditch and Walker recognize that many things can be legitimated. A third area in which to expand would be to consider how procedural justice may function to legitimate other aspects of organizations – the structure, the distribution of benefit packages, etc. By doing so, it may be possible to extend the models offered here.

Finally, although we examine how perceptions of procedural justice may underlie perceptions of one source of collective legitimacy (endorsement), our analysis did not attempt to examine potential antecedents to authorization. A question that arises is whether the behavior of a middle manager might be a source of authorization. To the extent that such a manager secures the compliance of his or her subordinates, do superior authorities view that manager as more legitimate? In other words, it may be the case that fair treatment of workers has ramifications beyond the creation of endorsement. In addition, authorities who have the potential to legitimate a manager may generalize from what they perceive to be the manager's legitimated actions to the person and they may compare across managers, just like workers examine how their peers are treated. Thus, by delineating mechanisms of perceptual and comparison processes, antecedents of authorization may emerge.

The effects of legitimacy and procedural justice on responses to distributive injustice and the reciprocal effects of perceptions of procedural justice and of legitimacy of authorities is in its initial stages of theoretical development. By building upon Zeldich and Walker and Tyler, a wider understanding may be achieved. Future theoretical work must identify common assumptions and recognize the conditionality of some processes. Future empirical work may address both abstract issues, testable in laboratory situations, as well as concrete issues arising in work settings. Such applied research could draw upon occurrences in organizations, as demonstrated by the opening example in this paper. Ultimately, the applied work may clarify how individuals of various ranks within an organization respond to legitimate, if unfair, outcomes or recognize how the actions of authorities reduce their legitimacy, leaving a potential void in terms of what is fair.

NOTES

1. Because organizations largely involve formal status orders, sociological discussions of the legitimacy of informal status orders (Berger et al., 1998; Ridgeway & Berger, 1986) is largely beyond our purview.

2. Zeldtich and Walker apply the term "propriety" to individual-level sources of legitimacy, while Tyler invokes the notion "personal morality" as an important individual-level antecedent of compliance.

3. More recent work of Zelditch and Walker (Forthcoming) identifies four conditions that are jointly sufficient to establish and sustain legitimacy.

4. See the Jost and Major (2001) volume for other approaches to legitimacy and justice in organizations. The conceptualization of legitimacy is largely different from that offered here, focusing on ideological rationalization for one's own and other people's actions taken on behalf of valued groups.

ACKNOWLEDGMENTS

We would like to thank the editor of this volume for her valuable comments on an earlier draft of this chapter. In addition, support in the writing of this paper came from National Science Foundation grant SES-0136747 to the first author and her colleague, Cathryn Johnson. A previous version of this chapter was presented at the meetings of the Southern Sociological Society, New Orleans, 2003.

REFERENCES

Adams, J. S. (1965). Inequity in social exchange. *Advances in Experimental Social Psychology, 2*, 267–299.

Berger, J. M., Fisek, M. H., Ridgeway, C. L., & Norman, R. Z. (1998). The legitimation and delegitimation of power and prestige orders. *American Sociological Review, 63*, 379–405.

Burke, P. J., & Reitzes, D. C. (1991). The link between identity and role performance. *Social Psychology Quarterly, 44*, 83–92.

Clay-Warner, J. (2001). Perceiving procedural injustice: The effects of group membership and status. *Social Psychology Quarterly, 64*, 224–238.

Cohen, R. L. (1986). Power and justice in intergroup relations. In: R. L. Cohen & J. Greenberg (Eds), *Justice in Social Relations* (pp. 65–84). New York: Plenum.

Cohen-Charash, Y., & Spector, P. E. (2001). The role of justice in organizations: A meta analysis. *Organizational Behavior and Human Decision Processes, 86*, 278–321.

Cook, K. S., & Hegtvedt, K. A. (1983). Distributive justice, equity, and equality. *Annual Review of Sociology, 9*, 217–241.

Cropanzano, R. (Ed.) (2001). *Justice in the workplace: From theory to practice*. Mahwah, NJ: Lawrence Erlbaum.

Dornbush, S. M., & Scott, W. R. (1975). *Evaluation and the exercise of authority*. San Francisco: Jossey-Bass.

Ellemers, N. (2001). Individual upward mobility and the perceived legitimacy of intergroup relations. In: J. T. Jost & B. Major (Eds), *The Psychology of Legitimacy* (pp. 205–222). New York: Cambridge University Press.

Forsyth, D. R. (2000). Social comparison and influence in groups. In: J. Suls & L. Wheeler (Eds), *Handbook of Social Comparison: Theory and Research* (pp. 81–103). New York: Kluwer Academic.

Gartrell, D. (2002). The embeddedness of social comparison. In: I. Walker & H. J. Smith (Eds), *Relative Deprivation: Specification, Development, and Integration* (pp. 164–184). New York: Cambridge University Press.

Goethals, G. R. (1986). Social comparison theory: Psychology from the lost and found. *Personality and Social Psychology Bulletin, 12*, 261–278.

Goethals, G. R., & Darley, J. (1977). Social comparison theory: An attributional approach. In: J. Suls & R. L. Miller (Eds), *Social Comparison Processes: Theoretical and Empirical Perspectives* (pp. 259–278). Washington, DC: Hemisphere.

Greenberg, J. (1990). Organizational justice: Yesterday, today, and tomorrow. *Journal of Management, 16*, 399–432.

Hassebrauck, M. (1987). The influence of misattributions on reactions to inequity: Towards a further understanding of inequity. *European Journal of Social Psychology, 17*, 295–304.

Hegtvedt, K. A., Clay-Warner, J., & Johnson. C. (2003). The social context of responses to injustice: Considering the indirect and direct effects of group-level factors. *Social Justice Research, 16*.

Hegtvedt, K. A., & Cook, K. S. (2001). Distributive justice: Recent theoretical developments and applications. In: J. Sanders & V. L. Hamilton (Eds), *Handbook of Justice Research in Law* (pp. 93–132). New York: Kluwer Academic/Plenum.

Hegtvedt, K. A., & Johnson, C. (2000). Justice beyond the individual: A future with legitimation. *Social Psychology Quarterly, 63*, 298–311.

Hegtvedt, K. A., & Killian, C. (1999). Fairness and emotions: Reactions to the process and outcomes of negotiations. *Social Forces, 78*, 269–302.

Hegtvedt, K. A., & Markovsky, B. (1995). Justice and injustice. In: K. S. Cook, G. A. Fine & J. S. House (Eds), *Sociological Perspectives on Social Psychology* (pp. 257–280). Boston, MA: Allyn & Bacon.

Hegtvedt, K. A., Thompson, E. A., & Cook, K. S. (1993). Power and equity: What counts in explaining exchange outcomes? *Social Psychology Quarterly, 56*, 100–119.

Homans, G. C. (1974). *Social behavior: Its elementary forms*. New York: Harcourt, Brace & World.

Howard, J. (1995). Social cognition. In: K. S. Cook, G. A. Fine & J. S. House (Eds), *Sociological Perspectives on Social Psychology* (pp. 90–117). Boston, MA: Allyn & Bacon.

Huo, Y. J., Smith, H. J., Tyler, T. R., & Lind, E. A. (1996). Superordinate identification, subgroup identification, and justice concerns: Is separatism the problem, is assimilation the answer. *Psychological Science, 8*, 40–45.

Johnson, C., & Ford, R. (1996). Dependence power, legitimacy, and tactical choice. *Social Psychology Quarterly, 59*, 126–139.

Johnson, C., Ford, R., & Kaufman, J. M. (2000). Emotional reactions to conflict: Do dependence and legitimacy matter? *Social Forces, 79*, 107–137.

Jost, J. T., & Major, B. (2001). *The psychology of legitimacy: Emerging perspectives on ideology, justice, and intergroup relations*. Cambridge: Cambridge University Press.

Kanter, R. M. (1977). *Men and women of the corporation*. New York: Basic Books.

Leventhal, G. S., Karuza, J., Jr., & Fry, W. R. (1980). Beyond fairness: A theory of allocation preferences. In: G. Mikula (Ed.), *Justice and Social Interaction* (pp. 167–218). New York: Springer-Verlag.

Lind, E. A. (1982). The psychology of courtroom procedure. In: N. L. Kerr & R. M. Bray (Eds), *The Psychology of the Courtroom*. New York: Academic Press.

Lind, E. A., & Tyler, T. R. (1988). *The social psychology of procedural justice*. New York: Plenum.
Ridgeway, C. L., & Berger, J. (1986). Expectations, legitimation, and dominance behavior in task groups. *American Sociological Review, 51*, 603–617.
Suls, J., & Wheeler, L. (Eds) (2000). *Handbook of social comparison: Theory and research*. New York: Kluwer Academic.
Tajfel, H. (1972). Experiments in a vacuum. In: J. Israel & H. Tajfel (Eds), *The Context of Social Psychology: A Critical Assessment* (pp. 69–119). London: Academic Press.
Tajfel, H. (1978). *Differentiation between social groups: Studies in the social psychology of intergroup relations*. New York: Academic Press.
Thibaut, J., & Walker, L. (1975). *Procedural justice: A psychological analysis*. Hillsdale, NJ: Lawrence Erlbaum.
Thomas, G. M., Walker, H. A., & Zelditch, M., Jr. (1986). Legitimacy and collective action. *Social Forces, 65*, 378–404.
Törnblom, K. Y. (1992). The social psychology of distributive justice. In: K. Scherer (Ed.), *Justice: Interdisciplinary Perspectives* (pp. 177–236). Cambridge: Cambridge University Press.
Tyler, T. R. (1984). The role of perceived injustice in defendant's evaluations of their courtroom experience. *Law and Society Review, 18*, 51–74.
Tyler, T. R. (1990). *Why people obey the law*. New Haven, CN: Yale University Press.
Tyler, T. R. (2001). A psychological perspective on the legitimacy of institutions and authorities. In: J. T. Jost & B. Major (Eds), *The Psychology of Legitimacy* (pp. 416–436, 205–222). New York: Cambridge University Press.
Tyler, T. R., & Blader, S. L. (2002). Autonomous vs. comparative status: Must we be better than others to feel good about ourselves? *Organizational Behavior and Human Decision Process, 89*, 813–838.
Tyler, T. R., Boeckmann, R. J., Smith, H. J., & Huo, Y. J. (1997). *Social justice in a diverse society*. Boulder, CO: Westview Press.
Tyler, T. R., Degoey, P., & Smith, H. J. (1996). Understanding why the justice of group procedures matters. *Journal of Personality and Social Psychology, 70*, 913–930.
Tyler, T. R., & Lind, E. A. (1992). A relational model of authority in groups. *Advances in Experimental Social Psychology, 25*, 115–191.
Tyler, T. R., Rasinski, K., & Griffin, E. (1986). Alternative images of the citizen: Implications for public policy. *American Psychologist, 41*, 970–978.
Tyler, T. R., & Smith, H. J. (1999). Justice, social identity, and group processes. In: T. R. Tyler, R. M. Kramer & O. P. John (Eds), *The Psychology of the Social Self* (pp. 223–264). Mahway, NJ: Erlbaum.
Utne, M. K., & Kidd, R. F. (1980). Equity and attribution. In: G. Mikula (Ed.), *Justice and Social Interaction* (pp. 63–93). New York: Springer-Verlag.
van den Bos, K., Bruins, J., Wilke, H. A. M., & Dronkert, E. (1999). Sometimes unfair procedures have nice aspects: On the psychology of the fair process effect. *Journal of Personality and Social Psychology, 77*, 324–336.
Walker, H. A., Rogers, L., & Zelditch, M., Jr. (1988). Legitimacy and collective action: A research note. *Social Forces, 67*, 216–228.
Walker, H. A., Thomas, G. M., & Zelditch, M., Jr. (1986). Legitimation, endorsement, and stability. *Social Forces, 64*, 620–643.
Walker, H. A., & Zelditch, M., Jr. (1993). Power, legitimacy, and the stability of authority: A theoretical research program. In: J. Berger & M. Zelditch, Jr. (Eds), *Theoretical Research Programs* (pp. 364–381). Stanford, CA: Stanford University Press.

Walster, E., Walster, G. W., & Berscheid, E. (1978). *Equity: Theory and research*. Boston, MA: Allyn & Bacon.

Weber, M. ([1918] 1968). *Economy and society*. G. Roth & C. Wittich (Eds). Berkeley, CA: University of California Press.

Wright, S. C. (1991). Restricted intergroup boundaries: Tokenism, ambiguity, and the tolerance of injustice. In: J. T. Jost & B. Major (Eds), *The Psychology of Legitimacy* (pp. 223–254). New York: Cambridge University Press.

Younts, W., & Mueller, C. W. (2001). Justice processes: Specifying the mediating role of perceptions of distributive justice. *American Sociological Review, 66*, 125–145.

Zelditch, M., Jr. (2001a). Processes of legitimation: Recent developments and new directions. *Social Psychology Quarterly, 64*, 4–17.

Zelditch, M., Jr. (2001b). Theories of legitimacy. In: J. Jost & B. Major (Eds), *The Psychology of Legitimacy: Emerging Perspectives on Ideology, Justice, and Intergroup Relations* (pp. 33–53). Cambridge: Cambridge University Press.

Zelditch, M., Jr., & Walker, H. A. (1984). Legitimacy and the stability of authority. *Advances in Group Processes, 1*, 1–25.

Zelditch, M., Jr., & Walker, H. A. (forthcoming). The legitimacy of regimes. In: S. R. Thye & E. J. Lawer (Eds), *Advances in Group Processes*.

BEYOND POWER AND DOMINATION: LEGITIMACY AND FORMAL ORGANIZATIONS

Henry A. Walker

ABSTRACT

This chapter revisits and extends the multiple-source, multiple-object theory of legitimacy in organizations. It introduces the idea of legitimized regimes and uses it to extend the theory's range beyond the usual focus on power and domination. The theory describes mechanisms that: (1) establish the legitimacy of new or contested regimes; and (2) facilitate the spread of legitimacy to structures and processes that lie outside organizational boundaries. The chapter uses current affirmative action debates to illustrate the mechanisms under study. The work concludes with a summary that includes discussion of prospects for research on extensions of the multiple-source, multiple-object theory.

LEGITIMACY: THE CONDITION OF BEING IN ACCORDANCE WITH LAW OR PRINCIPLE (The Compact Edition of the Oxford English Dictionary, 1971, Oxford University Press)

Legitimacy is a phenomenon that has intrigued students of social behavior since antiquity. The phenomenon is complex, difficult to define and the research literature touches virtually every aspect of social life. Legitimacy is crucial to formal organizations because their survival can depend on their ability to

Legitimacy Processes in Organizations
Research in the Sociology of Organizations, Volume 22, 239–271
Copyright © 2004 by Elsevier Ltd.
ISSN: 0733-558X/doi:10.1016/S0733-558X(04)22008-0

establish and sustain it. Students of formal organizations address a variety of issues including the legitimation of formal structures, practices and procedures (Meyer & Rowan, 1977), legitimacy, isomorphism and institutional "inertia" (Hannan & Freeman, 1989; Meyer & Hannan, 1979), and the role that legitimacy plays in organizational foundings and survival (Hannan & Carroll, 1992; Hannan & Freeman, 1989). Additionally, there is a vibrant and expanding literature on legitimacy processes and organizational politics (Bacharach & Lawler, 1980, 1997; Stryker, 1994, 2000). For a variety of reasons, the general literature on legitimacy and the specialized literature on legitimacy and organizational behavior trace their origins to the study of power and dominance relations.[1]

In this chapter, I extend the study of legitimacy processes beyond a narrow focus on power and domination. The chapter begins by discussing how legitimized power and domination contribute to the creation of social order but it also examines the importance of legitimacy processes to the day-to-day functioning of social and organizational life. The multiple-source, multiple-object theory of legitimacy (Dornbusch & Scott, 1975; Walker & Zelditch, 1993; Weber [1918] 1968, p. 36) informs the discussion. I use it to show how the processes that legitimize orga- nizations, their power and dominance structures and other constitutive elements draw on elements that lie outside organizational boundaries. Next, I show how legitimacy spreads from one organization to others (e.g. to organizations within the same organizational field), and to social structures and processes in the wider, extra-organizational world.

I organize this chapter into four sections. The first section offers a general discussion of the problem of legitimacy as one solution for the general problem of order and for the special case of order in formal organizations. It describes general features of theories of legitimacy and ends with a summary of Weber's classic discussion of the nature and characteristics of the phenomenon. I introduce the multiple-source, multiple-object theory of legitimacy in the second section. Next, I use Zelditch and Walker's (2003) extension of the theory to discuss legitimacy processes as they are played out in organizations and social institutions. The discussion introduces a wider vision of legitimacy processes in organizations *and* extends basic ideas to describe the spread of legitimacy to other institutions and to social life in general. The third section develops a detailed example that illustrates ideas and arguments developed in the preceding sections. The discussion centers on how organizations use legitimized elements of the regimes that define them to effect the transfer or spread of legitimacy to new – sometimes controversial – ideas and behaviors. I use current debates about affirmative action policies and practices to show how organizations try to redefine what is legitimate. The example also illustrates the stabilizing effects of legitimacy that make changing, eliminating or replacing long-standing legitimized practices difficult. The last section summarizes the chapter, draws conclusions and offers suggestions for future theoretical and empirical work.

LEGITIMACY AND THE PROBLEM OF ORDER

Preliminary Remarks: A Problem of Definition

The multiple-source, multiple-object theory of legitimacy (Dornbusch & Scott, 1975; Walker & Zelditch, 1993; Weber [1918] 1968, p. 36) informs the ideas presented in this chapter. However, as I pointed out above (see Note 1), terminological issues abound. The definition that opens this chapter is a narrow door that opens onto a labyrinthine field of investigation. It has the virtue of simplicity but its utility for social science theory and research is limited, in part, because it fails to capture the phenomenon's complexity. I describe several problems that confront the definition.

First, the definition admits phenomena that reasonable observers would describe as not legitimate. Some laws are not legitimate and, as a result, the legitimacy of conditions that are consistent with them is suspect. Legitimacy theories routinely try to explain the variable effects that legitimate and nonlegitimate policies and practices have on social structures and social processes.

A second problem concerns the nature of legitimacy. The Oxford definition is consistent with the inference that legitimacy is an evaluation or attribution made of some object (e.g. a "condition"), with reference to a standard (e.g. a law or principle). The definition describes a state of being and it is accurate as far as it goes. However, it is unclear whether it applies to objective conditions or to both objective and subjective ones. For example, John Ashcroft took office as U.S. Attorney General in January 2001 and fully supported the "Patriot Act" that became law after the events of September 11, 2001. Yet, millions of American citizens consider the law unconstitutional (i.e. illegitimate) when it is compared with a constitutional standard. Whether any person's behavior is classified as illegitimate relative to the law will vary with the evaluator's subjective assessment of the law. Those who claim the law is illegitimate ought to be less likely to attribute illegitimacy to acts that are technical violations of the law. A useful theoretical definition ought to satisfy at least three criteria: (1) It ought to treat legitimacy as an evaluation or assessment of (2) states of being while taking into account (3) the objective character of states of being and the subjective nature of evaluations. I will not offer a general definition of legitimacy here. Rather, I devise a set of *coordinated definitions* that takes into account the purposes for which the definitions are used. In this instance, the definitions must be useful for exploring the multiple-source, multiple-object theory of legitimacy. I begin by introducing the idea of a regime. Next, I devise a working definition of legitimate regimes. The definitions are intended to apply to any group or collectivity that has a minimal degree of social organization.[2]

The multiple-source, multiple-object theory of legitimacy is built on the work of Max Weber ([1918] 1968). Weber analyzed the legitimacy of an *order*, a term that, in English, can mean system (as in social order), or command (or directive). I introduce the term, *regime*, to capture the first meaning. The term comes from political science and political sociology (see Keohane & Nye, 1977) but following Zelditch and Walker (2003) I invest it with slightly different meaning. A command has the status of an element in a regime (as in Definition 2.2 below).

Definition 1 *(Regime)*. A regime, R, is a set of rules that define a system of positions, position-specific acts and relations between positions.

A regime as conceived here is a blueprint that describes a group's design. A fully-specified regime includes descriptions of positions, relations among positions, rules that describe criteria necessary for role occupancy, role enactment, interaction among roles and so on. In the language of formal organizations, a regime is the substructure and the system of rules and procedures that, with the addition of personnel, becomes a living and functioning organization. Hence, hiring criteria, methods of payment, procedures for processing clients and record keeping are all elements of a fully-specified regime. Weber ([1918] 1968) claims that every organizational regime wants to establish its legitimacy which Scott (1981, p. 280) defines as a set of norms "that define situations or behaviors as correct or appropriate." Regimes are sets of rules but legitimacy is not inherent to them; many rules do not possess normative force. On the other hand, legitimized regimes function as normative systems that prescribe what ought to be (i.e. they establish sanctionable standards of behavior). Alternatively, they include proscriptions that describe what should not be (Homans, 1974). Formally,

Definition 2.1 *(Legitimate Regime)*. A regime, R, is legitimate if its rules, constituent beliefs and values are normative.

Definition 2.2 *(Legitimate Element)*. An element, E, is legitimate relative to a regime, R, if E is: (1) consistent with R or constitutive elements of R; and (2) R is legitimate.

With these definitions in hand, I turn to a discussion of legitimacy and the problem of order.

Legitimacy and the Problem of Order

The question, "How is social order possible?," has intrigued protosociologists and sociologists since the dawn of human inquiry. The first students of social life identified the chaotic potential of human existence but they also recognized that power and domination can produce order out chaos (Hobbes [1651] 1998).[3] Powerful actors can use sanctions to establish uniform standards and practices and to compel less powerful actors to comply. Unfortunately, the exercise of power is costly. First, power exercise exhausts resources that could be used more productively (e.g. to produce or secure new benefits). At the macrosociological level, feudal lords invested resources in armies to defend against enemies and to suppress peasant uprisings. Similarly, organizations invest resources in the capacity to deliver negative sanctions as a way of sustaining existing benefits. Power exercise is also costly in a second and potentially more destructive sense. Power exercise creates hostility among its targets and increases the threat of revolt and rebellion. In face-to-face task groups, emergent leaders often sanction uncooperative members at the cost of greater negative affect, increased tension or disharmony and less cohesion (Bales, 1950). The importance of managing such problems leads some groups to create social and emotional specialists who take responsibility for reducing or eliminating them (Slater, 1955). In larger units like organizations or societies, the increased potential for negative behavior makes monitoring more important. As a result, power exercise has the general effect of degrading a group's efficiency and effectiveness.

Power exists as potential and a paradoxical consequence of its potential is the observation that it is most efficient when it is *not* used. The threat of power exercise increases compliance because subordinates *anticipate* power exercise in the event of noncompliance (Nagel, 1975). Legitimacy theorists claim that the efficiency and effectiveness of power and domination increase when their exercise is legitimate (Dornbusch & Scott, 1975; Goldhamer & Shils, 1939; Weber [1918] 1968). Groups that are able to legitimize their constitutive regimes reduce the need for power exercise and ameliorate the negative consequences of power use. Legitimacy converts power to authority and makes compliance with the directives of dominating actors obligatory. Group members who believe that compliance is obligatory are less likely to enact behaviors that are inconsistent with elements of legitimized regimes. Moreover, group members are more accepting of power exercise and their negative reactions to it are less intense when power exercise is legitimate. Legitimized regimes simultaneously minimize the frequency of rule violations, reduce their monitoring costs and enhance their stability.

Modern Organizations, Legitimacy and Order

The social life of early humans was organized almost exclusively by or around family and kin groups. Formal organizations are ubiquitous in contemporary industrial and post-industrial societies and modern humans are involved in and influenced by organizations from conception to death. Prospective parents increasingly turn to fertility clinics to assist conception and pregnant women typically receive prenatal care under the supervision of state-licensed physicians who are members of practices and clinics. In industrialized countries, an overwhelming majority of newborns begin life outside the womb in hospitals or in hospital-affiliated or stand-alone birthing centers.[4] The youngest children continue to receive their early socialization at home. However, public and private day care settings introduce many newborns and toddlers to the skills, values and beliefs that are necessary for them to become well-functioning members of their society. From age five through the end of life, the modern individual lives, learns, works and dies within or under the watchful eyes of a stunning array of formal organizations.

Formal organizations are rule-governed systems (or regimes) and human groups create them to accomplish either specific or general objectives.[5] Organizations must coordinate the actions of members and subunits that often have conflicting needs and interests. Creating and maintaining order within organizations is a special case of the age-old problem of order. If they are to survive, organizations must bring order to systems that have high potential for conflict and chaos. Conflict is disruptive and destabilizing and the application to organizational life of Hobbes' ([1651] 1998) imagery of war of all against all suggests why social order is an important concern for formal organizations.

Theories of Legitimacy and Social Behavior

Theories of legitimacy describe the processes through which legitimacy affects behavior and brings order to social life. Traditionally they have been built on either consensus or conflict frameworks (Zelditch, 2001). Consensus theories argue that legitimacy exists when there is widespread agreement on the desirability or appropriateness of values, norms, beliefs and actions (Parsons, 1951). Homogeneity is an important correlate of consensus. Consensus is "natural" among members of homogeneous groups because their essential similarity assures the convergence of individual interests on a variety of issues. Consensus also occurs when members voluntarily give collective interests higher priority than individual interests. Special circumstances or collective pressures may lead members to recognize the compatibility of collective and individual interests. For example, members may suppress short-term individual interests in deference to collective interests that are compatible with long-term individual interests. In sharp contrast, conflict theories begin by assuming that human association is characterized by basic conflicts of interest that contribute to social disorder if left unchecked. Power and domination can produce order under such circumstances but the unrestrained use of power and domination is destabilizing. Consequently, powerful actors try to legitimize social arrangements as a way of reducing or managing conflict and of establishing a stable social order. (See Zelditch, 2001 for a more detailed discussion of consensus and conflict perspectives on legitimacy.)

Max Weber ([1918] 1968, p. 31) united the two approaches by pointing out that social action is often oriented to an order (i.e. a set of rules or, as in this chapter, a regime). According to Weber, *legitimate regimes* are: (1) those for which members presume that compliance or conformity is obligatory; or (2) regimes that members accept as models of desirable or appropriate action. Weber applied these ideas to his analysis of bureaucratic administration and showed that rational-legal principles are an important foundation of legitimacy for modern organizations. He concluded that legitimacy increases conformity with rules and, ostensibly, the efficiency and effectiveness of administrative procedures.

Weber's conception incorporates assumptions about consensus by claiming that collective consensus is necessary to establish a set of obligations. However, legitimacy does not require complete consensus. Weber used the term, *validity*, to describe the probability that action is oriented to a set of rule-defined obligations. By definition, validity is a matter of degree.[6] The idea implies that regimes can establish obligations and function smoothly without unanimous consent (e.g. some members may fail to orient their actions to obligations established by a regime).[7] Just as important, consider the possibility that all members agree that a regime establishes obligations that govern their behavior. Despite their unanimous recognition of a regime's validity, some members may not agree that the regime establishes desirable models of action. Hence, Weber's formulation also admits the possibility of conflict. Stated simply, a valid regime requires consensus but it can tolerate dissent and the conflict that ensues when some actors fail to accept it as obligatory or as a model of desirable action.

Weber's formulation represented an important conceptual advance but it came at the price of conflating two important ideas. It described legitimacy simultaneously as conformity with a set of rules that group members accept as either: (1) a set of obligations; or as (2) a desirable model of action.[8] Under this conception, the degree to which members, in the aggregate or as individuals, accept either or both elements of a regime varies. Consequently, strict application of Weber's framework leaves the legitimacy status of some regimes indeterminate. Dornbusch and Scott resolved the problem more than fifty years later when they devised the multiple-source, multiple-object theory of legitimacy and organizational effectiveness.

THE MULTIPLE-SOURCE, MULTIPLE-OBJECT THEORY OF LEGITIMACY

The Dornbusch-Scott Theory

Dornbusch and Scott (1975) effected a conceptual separation of the ideas Weber conflated. They also explicated the mechanisms through which legitimized regimes and elements of regimes affect the effectiveness and stability of authority systems. The Dornbusch-Scott theory applies to organizations that have at least three hierarchical levels. Following Weber, the theorists define validity as the condition that exists when group members treat norms, values, beliefs, and procedures as matters of objective fact. They introduce the term, *propriety*, to describe an individual's acceptance and support of norms, values, beliefs, and procedures as desirable models of action – the way things ought to be (Homans, 1974). I revise slightly Dornbusch and Scott's definitions and apply them to the present discussion.[9]

> **Definition 3** *(Validity)*. A regime, R, is valid if group members treat its elements and relations as matters of objective fact. That is, they accept elements of R as binding, normative or obligatory for persons in R's domain.

> **Definition 4** *(Propriety)*. A regime, R, possesses propriety for an individual, *i*, if *i* accepts the elements of R as a desirable configuration or as the way things ought to be.

Finally, Dornbusch and Scott argue that the effects of validity and propriety are buttressed by *authorization* and *endorsement*. A regime is authorized if high status actors support or are perceived to support it. Endorsement refers to the support or perceived support of subordinates or lower participants (Etzioni, 1961).

> **Definition 5** *(Authorization)*. A regime, R, is authorized if high-status actors attribute propriety to it or are otherwise perceived to support its provisions.

> **Definition 6** *(Endorsement)*. A regime, R, is endorsed if lower-status actors attribute propriety to it or are otherwise perceived to support its provisions.

Dornbusch and Scott's formulation is a multiple-source, multiple-object theory. A regime's legitimacy flows from the collectivity (validity) and from individuals (propriety) and is buttressed by the support of high ranking persons (authorization)

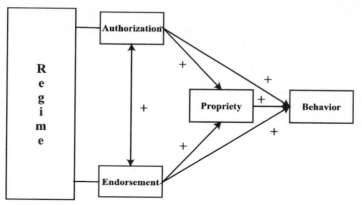

Fig. 1. Schematic Representation of Legitimacy Arguments.

and "the masses" (endorsement). Objects of legitimacy include regimes and their constitutive elements including positions, occupants of positions, and relational ties between positions. The theory shows how superordinates in legitimized positions (authorities) use their legitimacy to secure the compliance and conformity of subordinates. Members comply voluntarily out of a sense of obligation or because they accept as appropriate, behavior that is consistent with institutional rules and organizational directives. For individual members, validity, authorization and endorsement, reinforce their sense of obligation and increase the likelihood that they will assign propriety to the regime. Figure 1 is a schematic representation of the processes the theory describes.

Consider an organization for which R defines a set of authority relations. The Dornbusch-Scott theory claims that subordinates are more likely to comply with directives issued by their superiors if the superordinate-subordinate relation (an element of R) is valid rather than not valid. The effect is reinforced by authorization and endorsement because the two factors imply that members will: (1) support designated agents' access to resources necessary to apply sanctions; and (2) will defend the right of agents to use sanctions. Finally, the theory implies that validity also increases compliance indirectly through its effects on propriety. Group members are more likely to attribute propriety to a regime that is valid, authorized and endorsed.

Legitimacy, Power and Domination in Organizations

The Dornbusch-Scott theory of legitimacy explains well many familiar features of organizational life. The theory implies that propriety has substantial effects on behavior. Members are more likely to comply willingly with superordinates' directives if they attribute propriety to superiors, their directives and to their power exercise (Iannaccone, 1994; Pfeffer, 1981, 1992; Walker et al., 1986). Otherwise, they resist compliance. However, they may suppress their inclination to resist and comply unwillingly if they attribute validity to the regime that defines the system of authority (Walker et al., 1988, 1991).

Valid authority systems secure compliance through their dual effects on behavior and on beliefs and values.[10] Valid regimes affect behavior directly because they establish the boundaries of legitimate or *moral* behavior and because group members treat the regime's governance of their actions as matters of objective fact. Members comply with valid regimes because they recognize that the regime gives superiors the right to direct their behavior and obligates subordinates to comply.

Unlike naked or unconstrained power, legitimized power cuts both ways. Managers or other authorities in valid regimes are obligated to direct the actions of subordinates and, under specifiable conditions, are obligated to levy sanctions against those who fail to comply.[11] Authorization and endorsement buttress validity effects and strengthen conformity pressures (Dornbusch & Scott, 1975; Thomas et al., 1986; Walker et al., 1986).

Valid regimes also affect behavior indirectly through their effects on propriety. Valid systems influence group members to attribute propriety to the norms, beliefs, practices, and procedures that make up a regime. To paraphrase Homans (1974), a valid regime exerts influence on actors to accept that R is desirable and proper – that it describes what ought to be. Experimental research shows that validity affects propriety (Walker et al., 1988, 1991). Furthermore, validity exerts more influence on behavior than propriety in instances of conflict between the two sources of legitimacy (Walker et al., 1988, 1991).

Extending the Multiple-Source, Multiple-Object Theory

Zelditch and Walker (1984, 2003; Walker & Zelditch, 1993) extended the multiple-source, multiple-object theory beyond a focus on organizations with three-levels of hierarchy.[12] In their view, the theory applies to any system of action and legitimacy attaches to acts, persons, and positions, as well as to organizations and institutions. They identify four conditions, claim that they are jointly sufficient to establish and sustain legitimacy and incorporate them in a basic legitimation assumption (Zelditch & Walker, 2003). The integrated arguments show how formal organizations can establish and sustain legitimate regimes.

The Zelditch-Walker framework introduces two new ideas, accepted legitimating elements (ALEs) and regime legitimating formulas (RLFs). Formally,

Definition 7 *(Accepted Legitimating Elements).* Elements of a situation including norms, values, beliefs, practices and procedures are accepted legitimating elements (ALEs), if members of the collectivity believe they are consensually accepted by others in the situation.

A new regime may create beliefs, values, etc. *de novo* and develop a set of logics that justify their acceptance and legitimacy. However, many accepted legitimating elements are drawn from sources outside a given organization's boundaries. State and federal laws establish requirements that every putative corporation must meet before it can be accorded the official designation "corporation." The requirements – or elements – are accepted legitimating elements and company officers may point to them as evidence of their organization's legitimate status as a corporation. Of course, some organizations create many of the formal trappings that legitimize the regimes that describe them without establishing all of the features necessary for full and complete legitimacy. However, once they are identified as, for example, "dummy" corporations, their ill-gotten "legitimacy" quickly dissipates.

Definition 8 *(Regime-Legitimating Formula).* A formula is a regime-legitimating formula (RLF), if for some regime, R, or for some component of R, accepted legitimating elements imply it either logically or empirically and, in turn, the formula logically or empirically implies R's legitimacy.

Regime legitimating formulas function much like translation devices. They consist of statements that lay out the logic of a regime's claims to legitimacy. A regime-legitimating formula devises statements like the following: E (an element of the regime in question) is an instance of an accepted legitimating element therefore E is legitimate. I offer concrete examples below after I introduce a basic legitimation assumption.

The connections between accepted legitimating elements and regime-legitimating formulas and between regime-legitimating formulas and unlegitimated Rs are the mechanisms that permit the legitimation of regimes that lack it and strengthen the legitimacy of regimes whose legitimacy is questioned. Accepted legitimating elements are legitimate by definition but collectivity members must also accept the logic or arguments of a relevant regime-legitimating formula in order for the legitimacy of accepted legitimating elements to spread to a nonlegitimate regime. The conditions under which regime-legitimating formulas and their associated accepted legitimating elements establish the legitimacy of unlegitimized regimes are described in Fig. 2 and are stated formally in the *Basic Legitimation Assumption*:

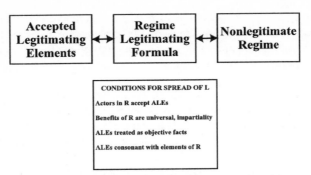

Fig. 2.   Schematic Representation of the Spread of Legitimacy.

Assumption 1 *(Basic Legitimation Assumption).* Given a regime-legitimating formula (RLF) for a regime, R, the undefined or contested elements of R acquire legitimacy if and only if:

Condition 1 *(Consensus).* The elements to which a regime-legitimating formula appeals are consensually accepted within R's domain (i.e. they are ALEs);

Condition 2 *(Impartiality).* Any benefit of R to which a regime-legitimating formula appeals is either in the group's interest or, if the appeal is to self-interest, it can be made universal;[13]

Condition 3 *(Objectification).* Any accepted legitimating element to which a regime legitimating formula appeals is treated as a matter of objective fact; and

Condition 4 *(Consonance).* Any accepted legitimating element to which a regime-legitimating formula appeals is consonant with the nature, conditions, and consequences of R.

Implications of the Revised and Extended Theory

Consensus, impartiality, objectification and consonance are important conditions for legitimizing regimes. I describe how each condition affects behavior within organizations.

Consensus

Consensus is an important condition for organizational legitimacy because it indicates endorsement. The degree to which consensus (or implied consensus) approaches unanimity varies initially with the nature and character of an organization.

Consensus is implied in work organizations – perhaps the most numerous modern organizational form – and voluntary organizations.[14] Members enter such organizations by choice and are presumed to accept either the regime that defines the organization (voluntary organizations) or, in work organizations, the conditions of employment. Both organizational types are expected to have high levels of endorsement or *perceived endorsement*.

Endorsement and perceived endorsement have substantial effects on behavior. Consider Widget Incorporated, a typical work organization with three hierarchical levels (A, B and C) and a nonunion workforce. B, a first-line supervisor tells members of day-shift Unit 2 that Widget is taking unprecedented action. As a consequence of staffing problems, Widget's evening and night shifts are failing to meet production quotas. Level A (management) has directed supervisors to divide workers into five groups and to rearrange work assignments such that members of each group work one evening a week on a rotating basis. That is, members of group 1 are reassigned to work Monday nights, members of group 2 are assigned to Tuesday night and so on. B also tells workers that only those who spend at least 25% of their work hours on evening or night shifts are eligible for night differential pay. A newly-hired day-shift worker, C_{2i}, considers the revised assignment a major change in the terms of her employment and silently questions its legality. How likely is it that C_{2i} publicly expresses her concerns about the new policy? Put simply, the policy's legitimacy status may be unclear to Widget's employees and the central issue is whether workers will identify it as legitimate or contest its claim to legitimacy. In this case, the consensus condition is an important hurdle the policy must clear in its attempt to gain legitimacy.

The multiple-source, multiple-object theory implies that C_{2i} is very unlikely to express her discontent publicly if long-time employees either say nothing during the briefing or simply shrug their shoulders as if to say, "They are the bosses what can we do?" Quiescence in the face of adversity is often treated mistakenly as an indicator of endorsement of the status quo (consensus). In such cases, widespread silence implies tacit support (i.e. consensus or endorsement), of the policy. The silence of group members is functionally equivalent to a majority of employees standing and positively endorsing (i.e. proclaiming support for) company policy during difficult times.[15]

Impartiality

Impartiality is the second condition that Zelditch and Walker discuss. Impartiality is a characteristic of the regime a group uses to allocate the benefits (and costs) it generates. In organizations, impartiality is related directly to elements of the rational-legal principles that govern many modern bureaucratic administrative systems (Weber [1918] 1968). Such systems are organized by rules and employees are presumed to apply them uniformly to other employees and clients. Additionally, bureaucratic regimes require hiring and promotion based on possession of specialized skills or training (Weber [1918] 1968). Demonstrable variation from such principles (i.e. partiality) undermines a regime's legitimacy. Similarly, an organization will experience considerable difficulty sustaining a claim to legitimacy if its actions, whether beneficial or not, appear to advantage some members and not others. Members who identify the offending practice or outcome will label it illegitimate and, subsequently, their evaluation of the regime's propriety will be weakened (Walker et al., 2002).

Consider a situation in which B arbitrarily assigns only some Unit 2 employees to the night shift. B's actions may disrupt personal and family routines, disproportionately target members of specific groups (e.g. older workers, women or those she dislikes), and create general dissatisfaction among the reassigned workers. The failure to offer differential pay is another cost imposed on this select group of employees. Under such circumstances, affected employees are likely to treat the new policy as less legitimate than that described in my earlier scenario. It violates the condition of impartiality. The condition is often written into collective bargaining agreements and its satisfaction is crucial to a regime's claim to legitimacy.[16] An organization can avoid the destabilizing effects of partiality if it masks the disproportionate flow of benefits to specific interest groups. I use a recent example to illustrate the importance of masking.

The airline industry was especially hard hit during the recession that began in 2000 and the industry's economic decline accelerated after the events of September 11, 2001. In a well-publicized case, American Airlines negotiated substantial economic concessions from its employee unions as it tried to avert strikes. Airline executives "sold" pay reductions and other concessions to employee groups as investments in the airline's long-term health. Many airline unions bought the bill of goods but disaster loomed when media reports showed that high ranking executives had received or were promised large pay increases and bonuses. Put simply, company officers masked the fact that their employees' acceptance of contract restructuring including pay cuts would permit management to more easily take actions that served the interests of high-ranking executives. The disclosures placed the new regime (i.e. policies and procedures) in jeopardy. Donald J. Carty, the CEO, and several top executives resigned as the company attempted to block further erosion of its legitimacy (CBSNews.com, 2003).

Objectification
Objectification is a third condition identified by Zelditch and Walker. Elements that a regime legitimating formula links to a nonlegitimate regime (see Fig. 2 above) must be accepted as matters of objective fact if the regime's claim to

legitimacy is to be sustained. Recall that the first scenario I described above used "production problems" to justify the transfer of employees to the night shift. The transfer policy can achieve legitimacy if employees treat the existence of specific problems as matters of fact *and* an element of the regime-legitimating formula asserts that production problems justify policy changes. I make clear that the issue is not whether statements are true or false. Rather, the key concern is whether members accept particular statements (e.g. those a regime-legitimating formula uses to justify a new or contested regime), as matters of fact. In the example, if management can convince employees that a specific problem exists and that it contributes to lower productivity, the idea is objectified. Once it is accorded objective status it can be used as an accepted legitimating element and linked to a policy change by a regime-legitimating formula.

Consonance

Zelditch and Walker argue that the nature, conditions, and consequences of R must be consonant with the accepted legitimating elements to which a regime-legitimating formula appeals in order for the regime-legitimating formula to successfully legitimize R. This condition can be satisfied honestly or through the strategy of masking that I described earlier. On one hand, Widget's policies can achieve legitimacy if the company demonstrates that night-shift production suffers as a consequence of insufficient staffing levels and if it presents the policy change as a temporary measure. Under that scenario, the effects of Widget's policy (e.g. stable production) are consonant with the accepted legitimating elements the regime-legitimating formula claims as justification for a policy change. The more-workers-mean-higher-productivity claim is consistent with common sense.

On the other hand, Widget's policy may fail the consonance test if the benefits it achieves are not consonant with the benefits implied by application of accepted legitimating elements and the regime-legitimating formula. Consider a scenario in which Widget's chief financial officer notifies management that utilities deregulation has reduced power costs substantially during the evening and nighttime hours. Clearly, management can reduce operating costs and increase profitability if it can successfully transfer workers from day to evening and night shifts. Widget's claims about insufficient staffing and productivity are part of a scheme to increase profitability at the workers' expense under this scenario. The plan will not affect overall productivity and, as American Airlines learned, the regime is unlikely to gain legitimacy. Widget's policy violates the consonance condition and members will label it illegitimate if they learn that profitability, not productivity, is the company's motive for change.

The foregoing suggests how the four conditions affect legitimacy processes within organizations. Propriety and validity have direct effects on the behaviors of lower and higher participants in organizations. Validity also affects behavior indirectly through its capacity to enhance the likelihood that individuals attribute propriety to the governing regime. Legitimacy processes are strongest in situations in which: (1) members offer consensual support of a regime; (2) benefits and costs associated with a regime are either distributed universally or their partiality is masked; (3) elements that justify or sustain a regime's claim to legitimacy are accepted and treated as matters of objective fact; and (4) elements that support a regime's claims to legitimacy (ALEs) are consonant with the nature and consequences of the regime.

Beyond Power and Domination

The examples I offered above illustrate the legitimacy effects that are studied most often. Authorities issue directives, subordinates accept the legitimacy of their power and position of dominance and comply with regime policy. I turn now to issues that do not involve power and domination directly.

Regimes also have important effects on matters related to entering and leaving organizations and on the mundane activities that characterize organizational life. Organizational policies establish entrance criteria, the conditions under which members are required to leave, the actions that agents must take when a member voluntarily severs membership and so on. The extent to which organizations and their members adhere to such policies varies directly with the regime's legitimacy. A recent event shows how legitimacy affects such processes.

A professor who was highly-regarded as a writer and poet retired from his post at the University of California's San Diego campus during the 2002–2003 academic year (Wilson, 2003). Retirements are common occurrences in large work organizations and, with few exceptions, proceed without much fanfare. In the case I describe, the professor's resignation sent shock waves through the university. The professor in question retired under the threat of suspension and possible firing. He had not earned the college degree he claimed on his curriculum vitae. Modern universities require their teaching personnel to hold college degrees and in most fields they must have advanced degrees. The requirement seems reasonable and it satisfies all the criteria necessary for legitimacy. In turn, the policy's legitimacy sets in motion a variety of processes and outcomes.

Legitimized requirements for role occupancy (e.g. specification of credentials necessary for professorial employment), shape the pool of potential candidates. Normally, those who fail to satisfy the requirements do not apply for positions unless, like the professor described above, they create false credentials. Similarly, those who are offered and accept positions conform with the legitimized actions expected and required of role occupants. Professors meet their classes at standardized times whereas construction workers wear hard hats, maintain their equipment, and so on. Workers conform with legitimized expectations and deviation from formal rules is minimized or hidden from superordinates. As a consequence, the frequency of overt power exercise is reduced and its rare exercise leads some observers to infer that power is diffuse rather than concentrated in modern organizations (Bell, Walker & Willer, 2000).[17] As a result, organizations generally run like the well-oiled machines they so often house.[18]

The Spread of Legitimacy

Zelditch and Walker's extension of the multiple-source, multiple-object theory implies that accepted legitimized elements can have implications that extend beyond a particular organization's boundaries. It suggests that organizations can use existing accepted legitimating elements to legitimize their nonlegitimate regimes. For example, newly-formed organizations or those whose legitimacy is contested can devise regime-legitimating formulas that link existing accepted legitimating elements with the regimes they hope to legitimize. Accepted legitimating elements associated with successful organizations (e.g. those proved profitable or efficient), are the best candidates for this process. The model implies that regime-legitimating formulas will be more successful if they use existing accepted legitimating elements to effect the spread (or transfer) of legitimacy from an "old" organization to new or contested regimes. The model offers one explanation for the spread of a particular organizational form to new organizations within an organizational field and, in some, instances to organizations in different fields. The legitimizing process encourages mimicry, institutional isomorphism and structural inertia (Hannan & Freeman, 1977, 1989; Meyer & Hannan, 1979; Meyer & Rowan, 1977). Figure 2 describes processes involved in the spread of legitimacy.

The extended multiple-source multiple-object theory does not limit the spread of legitimacy from one organization or class of organizations to other organizations. Modern organizations penetrate every aspect of social life and the generality of legitimacy processes ensures that many extra-organizational regimes will build their claims to legitimacy on accepted legitimating elements that are components of formal organizations to which they are not directly connected. The process is consistent with but its outcomes are different than those associated with the spread of legitimacy from old to new organizations or the prevalence of institutional isomorphism. I offer an extended example to describe the spread of legitimacy and its effects on structures and processes that lie outside an organization's boundaries or its organizational field.

FROM EQUAL OPPORTUNITY TO
DIVERSITY: AN ARCHETYPAL CASE

Affirmative action is a "hot button" issue in American higher education and the split decisions in recent court cases have not resolved it.[19] (See U.S. Supreme Court decisions in *Grutter v. Bollinger* and *Gratz v. Bollinger*.) The affirmative action debate is often described as a contest about the possibilities and prospects for a "color-blind" society.[20] It is rarely described as a debate about the legitimacy of competing regimes.

The U.S. Constitution is the overarching regime that organizes the American polity. At its adoption, the Constitution did not extend full rights of citizenship to African-origin blacks but gradually the rights of black Americans were expanded and extended. Their quest for full citizenship culminated in the civil rights laws passed during the middle 1960s.[21] By then, the regime that describes the mutual rights and responsibilities of citizens and their government had extended the Principles of Equal Opportunity and Nondiscrimination to members of race and ethnic minority groups. A sitting President, the Congress and the Supreme Court took actions that legitimized extending these key principles to groups that had been previously denied full civil, social and political rights.

Extension of the principles to black Americans did not claim unanimous consensus in the 1960s but only a small minority opposes the regime today. The Principles of Equal Opportunity and Nondiscrimination are endorsed by large majorities of black *and* white Americans and by persons who hold mainstream political views. The principles' legitimacy is enhanced by their satisfaction of the impartiality condition and by the legitimacy of the founding documents on which their claims to legitimacy rest (i.e. the Declaration of Independence and the Constitution). Finally, the social conditions that are presumed to follow from their implementation are consonant with the constitutive elements of the founding documents as the regime-legitimating formulas that linked them to the new regime claimed.

The history of affirmative action practices is often traced to the early 1940s but their roots were established much earlier. As an example, in the late 19th century, the U.S. Civil Service opened its doors to black males and others who had been denied entry. Before that time, only free white males were eligible for positions in the federal civil service (Krislov, 1967). However, it is noteworthy that the federal civil service did not abolish a provision that required photographs to accompany applications until the 1940s. That apparently simple policy revision can be viewed as a more stringent application of the Principle of Equal Opportunity.

The Principle of Equal Opportunity subsumes and implies the Principle of Nondiscrimination and the earliest affirmative action policies and procedures were designed to ensure increasingly strict adherence to both principles and to extend them to excluded classes of citizens (Glazer, 1975). New policies and policy proposals that promoted greater equality of opportunity in the workplace were common through the late 1960s and their implementation spread to other areas of social concern including housing, higher education, political participation and access to quality medical care.

Some organizations began using targeted discrimination during the final years of Lyndon Johnson's administration and its use accelerated during the Nixon years.[22] Many in the civil rights community had assumed that the reduction and eventual abolition of race discrimination would produce an equilibration of socially desirable outcomes for black and white Americans. Targeted discrimination was introduced to create more racially proportionate outcomes. The U.S. Supreme Court announced its decision in the Bakke case (*Regents of Univ. of Cal. v. Bakke*) in 1978 and the issue of race discrimination seemed to have come full circle. Affirmative action had begun as a set of policies designed to reinforce the abolition of discrimination and to ensure that members of other groups had opportunities equal to those of white males. The decision introduced *diversity* as a goal and affirmed the legality of targeted discrimination. The decision amounted to de facto authorization of the policy and led to refinements in the practice of discrimination that advantaged women and members of race and ethnic minority groups.

Proponents of targeted discrimination – the *new* affirmative action – treat diversity as an intermediate social goal. That is, diversity is envisioned as a first step in creating a desirable set of ultimate ends. Those ends include more racially proportionate distributions of: (1) college and university graduates; (2) members of selective occupations and professions; (3) incomes, and so on. The "diversity argument" implies that invidious comparisons based on race, ethnic heritage and gender are valid (i.e. legitimate) if they contribute to organizational or institutional diversity. In higher education, advocates claim that diversity is important to educational institutions because it optimizes the learning environment. (See the quotation from Lee Bollinger, the University of Michigan's former president, reproduced in Rothman et al., 2003.) The regime-legitimating formula for targeted discrimination includes these ideas in all their complexity. Figure 3 is a bare-bones representation of processes involved in the legitimation of a regime that includes targeted discrimination.

Figure 3 puts concrete elements on the skeletal description of the spread of legitimacy described by Fig. 2. As Glazer (1975) points out, the principles in the leftmost box are accepted legitimating principles incorporated in the American creed. As I suggest above, advocates of black civil rights assumed that extending full civil rights to black Americans would eventually produce the benefits

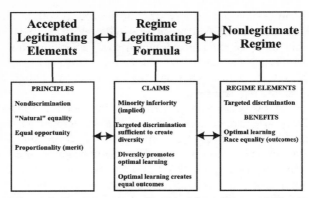

Fig. 3.   Schematic Representation of Legitimation of Targeted Discrimination.

described in the right-hand box. The regime-legitimating formula is represented by claims in the center box. The formula consists of a set of claims that link the nonlegitimate regime elements to desirable social benefits. It makes little use of the principles I describe as accepted legitimating elements.

Legitimized regimes are remarkably stable in the absence of substantial changes in an organization's environment. The stability of legitimized regimes makes it difficult for American educational institutions to legitimize targeted discrimination because the procedure violates the Principle of Nondiscrimination. (See the left hand or ALEs box in Fig. 3.) Proponents use a regime legitimating formula that claims the practice will lead to optimal learning and the equilibration of educational outcomes for members of various race and ethnic minority groups. Figure 3 includes three additional principles as accepted legitimating elements, the principles of: (1) natural equality; (2) equal opportunity; and (3) proportionality. The Principle of Natural Equality as expressed in the Declaration of Independence asserts that all men are created equal. The Principle of Equal Opportunity asserts that every person ought to have an equal opportunity to compete (e.g. for jobs, positions in educational institutions, etc.). Finally, the Principle of Proportionality is a familiar idea from theories of equity and distributive justice (Homans, 1974). Essentially, it asserts that individuals ought to receive benefits in proportion to their contributions.[23]

The regime legitimating formula claims that targeted discrimination is sufficient to establish diversity within select organizations.[24] In turn, diversity creates an optimal learning environment that benefits the institution, its majority and minority members and society in general. As a result, targeted discrimination is (or ought to be) legitimized because it leads ultimately to a host of desirable ends – ends that are assumed to flow from the application of accepted legitimating elements described in the left-hand box. Put simply, advocates of such policies imply that creating an optimal learning environment and statistical equality of races and ethnic groups on educational outcomes trumps the Principle of Nondiscrimination.

The affirmative action controversy highlights a common occurrence. A regime can claim legitimacy although it incorporates conflicting or contradictory principles (Zelditch, 2001). In some instances, regimes with seemingly contradictory principles function smoothly because the principles' domains of applicability – while within the same system – are mutually exclusive. As an example, the Principle of Natural Equality proclaims that all men are created equal while the Principle of Proportionality permits individuals to realize unequal outcomes. The Principle of Natural Equality is a general principle that applies to every member of a group or organization. The Principle of Proportionality is normally applied in specific performance domains where it implies different outcomes than the Principle of Natural Equality. In any domain in which group members are responsible for some output or action that is rewarded, the Principle of Proportionality implies that group members can expect equal outcomes if, and only if, they produce equal inputs.[25]

Regimes with conflicting principles raise special legitimation problems when the principles have overlapping domains. Chief among such problems is accommodation or resolution of conflict between the principles. As an example, consider what Fig. 3 implies about the processes through which expansion of the Principle of Nondiscrimination to race and ethnic minorities initially achieved legitimacy.

The framers of the U.S. Constitution permitted unequal treatment of blacks and Indian peoples and *required* unequal treatment in some instances. Those policies were often justified by the claim that blacks and other affected groups were not human. Civil rights activists and organizations used a two-pronged strategy to legitimize the extension of civil rights to minority groups that had been denied them. The strategy amplified and exploited basic contradictions in the nation's regime. First, proponents proclaimed the essential humanity of blacks, Indian people, and others (i.e. their "natural equality"). Second, they linked the Principle of Nondiscrimination to other tenets the country's founding documents extended to all humans (e.g. they are "endowed with unalienable rights"). The strategy was successful but only after a protracted, arduous and bloody struggle.

The example under study describes attempts to legitimize a regime that includes conflicting principles or practices (i.e. nondiscrimination and targeted discrimination). It also offers a framework for demonstrating how legitimized elements can affect situations outside an organization's boundaries. The regime-legitimating formula in Fig. 3 includes a principle or proposition that occupies the interstices between the Principles of Natural Equality and Proportionality. The regime-legitimating formula includes the claim that, with respect to race in higher education, present-day diversity can only be achieved through targeted discrimination (see Note 24). In language devoid of political and legal jargon, members of targeted groups cannot be expected to achieve results equal to those achieved by members of the majority. Label this idea, the Principle of Minority Inferiority.[26]

Any institution of higher learning that legitimizes the regime-legitimating formula described in Fig. 3 also imbues the Principle of Minority Inferiority with legitimacy. Affirmative action regimes are institution-specific but the implications of such programs spread far beyond organizational and institutional boundaries.[27] In an organization that subscribes either wittingly or unwittingly to the Principle of Minority Inferiority, all members are subjected to the principle. They may not attribute propriety to it initially but the principle is authorized. The principle is endorsed when substantial numbers express their approval of it and the principle has de facto endorsement if substantial numbers fail to express disapproval. Legitimacy theory implies that authorized and endorsed regimes generate pressures that influence individuals to attribute propriety to regime elements.

Once individuals accept the propriety of a generalized principle like the Principle of Minority Inferiority, the principle exerts influence beyond narrowly-defined organizational or institutional boundaries. Moreover, policies and procedures whose legitimacy depends on a principle's objectification reinforce its "truth." A principle that is treated as a matter of objective fact generates substantially greater influence on actors' behaviors than principles whose propriety is suspect. As a result, principles activated to achieve narrow, organization-specific legitimacy can have powerful implications for processes and behaviors outside the organization's boundaries.

The Principle of Minority Inferiority has served an important negative role in the history of race and gender relations in the United States. It was used to justify the exclusion of blacks, Hispanics, American Indians and women from a variety of occupations, organizations and institutions. Indeed, much of the early thrust of the modern civil rights movement centered on demonstrating the principle's falsity. Today, the principle is fiercely denounced but its acceptability is implied in the nuances of pronouncements of supporters of present-day affirmative action policies and procedures. Moreover, public opinion polls show that a sizable minority of white respondents continues to express beliefs consistent with the principle. For example, 11.7% of respondents to the 2002 General Social Survey (GSS) (Davis et al., 2002), expressed the belief that blacks lacked the innate ability to move up economically. The 2002 figure represents significant progress during the quarter century since the GSS first asked the question. In 1977, 25.8% of the population expressed similar views (Davis & Smith, 1977). However, the significance of the percentage reduction is tempered by other data. Many white Americans believe that black Americans simply lack the will to improve economically. More than three-fifths (61.7%) held that view in 1977 and almost half (48.1%) of respondents expressed that view in the 2002 survey.[28] With these data drawn from the adult population of the United States as a backdrop, data from a recent survey are not surprising and are consistent with predictions from legitimacy theory.

Rothman, Lipset and Nevitte (2003) report findings from a recent survey of faculty, administrators and students at 140 American and Canadian colleges. The researchers collected data from 4,083 respondents (1,643 students, 1,632 faculty and 808 administrators). A majority of faculty (56%) agreed that colleges and universities ought to practice nondiscrimination in college admissions and hiring but only 48% of college administrators agreed with that position. However, an overwhelming majority of students (85%) agreed with the Principle of Nondiscrimination. Moreover, three-quarters of students but only 57% of faculty and 55% of administrators expressed their displeasure with relaxing admission standards (i.e. a form of targeted discrimination) as a way of raising the number of minority admissions.[29]

Faculty and administrators are members of educational organizations whereas students are described more accurately as clients. An organization's affirmative action regime is authorized and members will presume that it is endorsed unless there is persistent and organized protest against it. Authorization and endorsement buttress a regime's validity and exert influence on every member's evaluation of its propriety. Legitimacy theory implies that members ought to offer greater support of an organization's regime than marginal members or nonmembers. Rothman et al.'s (2003) findings are consistent with the implications of legitimacy theory. Their data show that college and university employees are less supportive of nondiscrimination policies and more supportive of targeted discrimination than students.

Legitimacy theory also implies that individuals who accept general principles like the idea of minority inferiority will apply them outside an organization's boundaries. Few published studies report data relevant to this implication. The 1990 GSS (Davis & Smith, 1990) asked workers if their employers had affirmative action programs. Under the assumption that current affirmative action programs use some form of targeted discrimination, the model implies that the presence or absence of such programs ought to affect employee attitudes about members of ethnic minority groups and minority employment. Data from the survey are difficult to interpret. Slightly more than half of workers (51.8%) reported that their employers had affirmative action programs. Compared with those whose employers did not have such programs those who reported that their companies had affirmative action programs were no less likely to believe that black economic disadvantage was due to: (1) discrimination; (2) the innate ability of blacks; or (3) education deficits rooted in black poverty. However, those who worked for employers with affirmative action programs were *less likely* than other employees (56.9% compared with 64.8%) to attribute lagging black economic progress to the (lack of) motivation of blacks. These data clearly offer no support for this particular implication of the extended theory.[30]

DISCUSSION AND SUMMARY

Formal organizations affect every facet of modern life and the typical modern organization has an administrative structure that includes hierarchical systems of power and domination. Organizations establish hierarchical systems of command and control in order to coordinate members' actions and to achieve stability as they pursue specified goals. Power exercise is destabilizing and every organization has an interest in legitimizing its coordination, command and control operations (Weber [1918] 1968). Students of legitimacy processes have studied the role of legitimacy in order-creating processes since the dawn of human inquiry and theorists of organizational behavior have taken up the challenge in the modern era.

The multiple-source, multiple-object theory of legitimacy (Dornbusch & Scott, 1975; Walker & Zelditch, 1993; Zelditch & Walker, 2003) provides a useful framework for understanding legitimacy processes in organizations. More than three decades of experimental and nonexperimental research supports the theory's basic claims. The major correlates of legitimacy, validity, authorization, endorsement and propriety, have important effects on organizational behavior including the stability of authority structures. However, legitimacy theory has implications beyond the narrow focus on power and domination and the stability of authority structures and many of those implications have not been fully explored.

Zelditch and Walker's framework sets the stage for understanding much of the routine day-to-day activity that characterizes life in the typical organization. Moreover, the theoretical model implies that the effects of legitimacy processes *within* organizations extend beyond organizational boundaries. The processes through which organizations legitimize their regimes rest on accepted legitimating elements and use regime-legitimating formulas to link them to the elements of regimes they wish to legitimize. Legitimized elements, those that are valid, influence group members to attribute propriety to the regime in question. Attributions of propriety depend on acceptance of the principles embodied in accepted legitimating elements and the regime-legitimating formulas (RLFs) that link accepted legitimating elements to the regime. The effects of beliefs in a regime's propriety are not confined to a narrow, organizationally-defined set of issues. The theoretical model implies that organizations whose regimes are not legitimized or those whose regimes are contested can use accepted legitimating elements from legitimized regimes and regime-legitimating formulas to establish legitimacy. As such, the model implies a more general explanation of the legitimation of organizational forms and institutional isomorphism (Hannan & Freeman, 1989; Meyer & Hannan, 1979; Meyer & Rowan, 1977). The combination of institutional isomorphism and the stability of legitimized regimes also accounts for the phenomenon described as institutional inertia – the general persistence of organizational forms within organizational fields.

The theoretical model also implies that a legitimate organizational regime can legitimize structures, processes and behaviors that occur outside its boundaries. I used "old" and "new" affirmative action policies in higher education to illustrate the processes and to demonstrate the stability of legitimized regimes. Affirmative action policies and procedures were developed initially to remedy the effects of invidious discrimination based on race, ethnic heritage, gender and so on. The earliest programs gained legitimacy by connecting the new regime to a set of legitimized principles (ALEs) set out in the nation's founding documents. Over time, the label "affirmative action" was expanded to apply to practices, like targeted discrimination, that are inconsistent with some of the principles that underlay the initial legitimation of affirmative action policies. Organizations sought to legitimize the new practices in order to achieve narrow, organization-specific goals (i.e. proportionate representation of ethnic groups or women and men in educational institutions or work organizations). However, they did so without resolving the contradictions among principles on which the new regime rested its claim to legitimacy. As a result, the new affirmative action regime has failed to gain widespread acceptance.

I used the extended example to show how attempts to legitimize targeted discrimination have been largely unsuccessful because the practice conflicts with the important Principles of Nondiscrimination and Equal Opportunity. More important, I argue that legitimacy theory implies that adoption of practices like targeted discrimination generates processes that spread the legitimacy of ideas with potentially negative social consequences to arenas outside the organizations that initially proposed them. With respect to what I have labeled "affirmative action," I argued that such programs imply the legitimacy of the idea of minority inferiority. There are few data sources that permit tests of the implication and the GSS data to which I applied the arguments produce results that are ambiguous at best. However, it is important to recognize limitations of the data.

Implications of the theory suggest that compared with workers in organizations without modern affirmative action programs, those who work for employers with such programs ought to be more likely to accept the idea of "minority inferiority." Subsequently, those who subscribe to the belief ought to be more likely than nonsubscribers to attribute lack of success to minority-group inferiority. However, it is not clear how the factors measured by the GSS are related to minority inferiority.

Blacks may have a competitive disadvantage relative to whites as a consequence of all four factors. Discrimination and poor education rooted in poverty are "causes" that stand outside the individual. The idea that members of minority groups experience disadvantage as the result of factors that lie outside their control is consistent with and one element of the rationale for targeted discrimination. On the other hand, innate (in)ability and poor motivation are characteristics of individuals. Consequently, it is possible that attempts to legitimize the new affirmative action may actually reduce the likelihood that employees (or others) attribute black disadvantage to these factors. The clearest finding is that employees governed by affirmative action programs are less likely than other employees to attribute minority economic disadvantage to black motivation. Motivation is a factor over which persons are believed to exercise control.[31] Finally, the responses of males and females diverge on some issues. The findings are curious and intriguing. Women are more often beneficiaries of modern affirmative action programs than men and, for that and other reasons, women might report different reactions to affirmative action issues than their male counterparts. However, it is unclear why their attitudes about issues involving black economic progress ought to diverge. These and other concerns make clear that an adequate evaluation of the implications I have drawn from the multiple-source, multiple-object theory awaits carefully designed studies, systematic data collection and rigorous testing.

I end this discussion by pointing out that the focus has been directed to a negative example (e.g. failed legitimation and spread of the idea of minority inferiority) but clearly the theory implies similar effects of principles that might have positive social effects. I offer brief examples from American race relations that might guide future research, and point to other findings that seem consistent with the arguments.

The plausibility of the arguments is suggested by data reported by Moskos and Butler (1996). Moskos and Butler studied the U.S. Army's concerted effort to improve the integration of blacks into all areas within the organization. The writers describe affirmative action programs that conform most closely to the "old" practices and procedures. The army disavowed preferential treatment in promotion but engaged in rigorous screening to identify black candidates for promotion among both noncommissioned and commissioned officers. The organization identified deficits in education and training and provided training to upgrade skills where necessary. As a result, the army has a somewhat better record on "minority" issues than other branches of the military. Moreover, Moskos and Butler report that, while less than perfect, black-white relations in the army are equal to or better than those in American society at large. As examples, they point to race differences in attitudes and beliefs on a host of issues from the state of American race relations to ideas about the O. J. Simpson trial. Generally, race differences among military personnel are smaller and less intense than in the general population. In this isolated instance, a large organization created and legitimized a regime change that, for the most part, did not use contradictory principles to legitimize a new – and at the time – controversial regime.[32]

Another example can be drawn from racial integration of American schools. The Brown decisions (*Brown v. Topeka Board of Education*) rendered in the mid-1950s opened the door to disassembling dual education systems in American education. The decision recognized the right of black Americans to equal treatment in education and directed educational institutions to dismantle segregated systems with "all deliberate speed." The regime, although authorized by the Supreme Court, was not initially greeted by high levels of endorsement. Moreover, it is plausible to claim that it is unlikely to garner unanimous consensus in the foreseeable future. However, the regime is consistent with what I labeled earlier the Principle of Natural Equality and it has been legitimized. It is also important to point out that majority attitudes about black Americans have become substantially *more positive* since the Supreme Court declared that dual education systems are illegal and affirmed the essential humanity of black Americans (Farley & Allen, 1989; Jaynes & Williams, 1989).

Controlled investigations have shown that an experimenter's validation of controversial authority structures increases the stability of such structures and increases the likelihood that actors will attribute propriety to them. The time has come to extend such studies to focus on general patterns of everyday action. Such processes can be studied experimentally but they are also amenable to carefully constructed survey research that can track an organization's progress longitudinally. Only with such research can the ideas described above be systematically tested and either rejected or added to the storehouse of knowledge generated by legitimacy research.

NOTES

1. The terminology in this investigative arena can be daunting and confusing. Weber ([1918] 1968) distinguished power (*Macht*) and domination (*Herrschaft*). Contemporary

scholars often translate the terms as power and authority, respectively, but many writers define authority as legitimate power. The usage makes legitimate authority and legitimate domination redundant terms. I introduce below a set of definitions in an attempt to resolve sticky terminological issues.

2. That is, the definitions do not apply to statistical "groups" or aggregates (Bierstedt, 1950).

3. In the discussion that follows, I use "power" to describe the capacity to use positive or negative sanctions. I use "domination" to describe either the actions of subordinate positions in a structure of superordination and subordination or the structure itself (e.g. a system of domination).

4. The tentacles of modern organizations are not easily escaped. For example, government regulations often require licensed midwives to supervise or assist "traditional" at home-births.

5. Simple organizations can be defined by a single regime but complex organizations may include multiple subunits and several hierarchical levels. From an analytical perspective, such complexity can be described by multiple regimes. For example, work organizations have separate sets of rules for benefits-eligible and noneligible employees. In that regard, some complex organizations can be described as sets of interdependent and interlocking regimes.

6. The idea that orientation to validity is variable is also reflected in Parsons' (1951) conception of institutionalization. More important, the variability of validity has important implications for understanding its effects on the behavior of any given actor or class of actors. I address the second point in greater detail below.

7. Just how much consensus is necessary to establish legitimacy is an empirical question. However, I point out that political regimes established by noncharismatic authoritarian figures or oligarchies cannot achieve legitimacy in the absence of "consent of the governed." Political history records high levels of compliance under such regimes but the actions of those who comply are motivated by power or force threat – not legitimacy (Goldhamer & Shils, 1939; Weber [1918] 1968).

8. Legitimizing a regime establishes constraints for all parties involved in the focal social relationships. Studies that emphasize the legitimacy of power and domination focus all too often on constraints imposed on less-powerful actors or subordinates. As a result, legitimacy's effects on more-powerful superordinates are often obscured or unobserved.

9. Dornbusch and Scott defined the terms as components of their theory of authority relations. I will argue below that the terms and their theory can be applied more generally.

10. The two forms of influence are consistent with Deutsch and Gerard's (1955) classifications of *normative* and *informational* influence. Normative influence affects behavior and informational influence affects beliefs and values.

11. Barnard (1938) located administrative commands in relation to the *zone of indifference* (i.e. a manager's domain of authority). Subordinates are not *obligated* to comply with nonlegitimate commands although they may comply for other reasons (e.g. power).

12. For unambiguous statements of the writers' general application of the theory see especially the introduction in Walker et al. (2002), and Zelditch and Walker (2003).

13. The basic legitimation assumption surveys the world from the point of view of members of a focal system (i.e. the conception is system specific). Any interests to which it refers are perceived rather than "real" interests.

14. These organizational forms represent *normative* and *remunerative* organizations respectively (Etzioni, 1961). Members do not voluntarily enter *coercive* organizations (a third type). The entry status of group members has important consequences for social control processes as analyses of mixed-type organizations show. Prisons combine remunerative and coercive elements. Prison staff volunteer for their positions and their acceptance of employment implies endorsement of the local regime and its policies. Prison inmates enter involuntarily and they usually recognize the local regime's validity. They rarely attribute propriety to it. For inmates, propriety and endorsement are low and, consequently, it is more important that staff monitor their activities to ensure their cooperation.

15. As is generally true of social behavior, other factors may contribute to employee silence or encourage vociferous protest. Strong labor unions and tight labor markets are only two factors that may encourage workers to express their dissatisfaction immediately. On the other hand, organizations that interpret quiescence as endorsement do so at their peril. For generations, managers recognized this problem and often recruited spies to report the actual mood of workers who kept their grievances hidden.

16. This example describes the failure to satisfy a condition rather than a positive instance in which the condition is satisfied. As Zelditch and Walker (2003) point out, their failures to create legitimacy in experimental situations helped them identify the four conditions they describe.

17. As I pointed out above, power exists as potential. The Law of Anticipated Reactions (Nagel, 1975) describes how actors respond to the anticipation of sanctions. Consequently, much potential noncompliance is averted without overt power exercise. The "visibility" of power is further reduced when power relations are legitimized. Subordinates comply out of a sense of obligation but the validity of power exercise (and especially exercise that is authorized and endorsed), increases the likelihood of sanctions in the event of noncompliance. As a result, the frequency of overt power exercise is minimized and the mechanisms that transform power into compliance and conformity remain hidden. Similarly, the substantial effects that legitimate authority relations have on supervisors and managers are also largely invisible (see Note 8).

18. I describe legitimacy effects that are based primarily on validity. The prevalence of informal organization attests to validity's potent influence on organization and action. That is, group members often question the desirability of organizational arrangements (i.e. they question their propriety). Under close supervision, they conform with valid regimes but establish informal structures and processes that are often as effective and efficient as the formal elements they replace (Roethlisberger & Dickson, 1939).

19. Affirmative action is an umbrella term that encompasses a hodge-podge of practices and its use is not limited to higher education. Initially implemented at the federal level, affirmative action was designed to reinforce the abolition of invidious discrimination in the workplace (e.g. as in President Kennedy's Executive Order #10925 issued in 1961). Today, many affirmative action programs promote "targeted discrimination," a practice that provides advantage to members of selected groups (Glazer, 1975). The discussion that follows centers on the latter form of affirmative action as it is employed in some institutions of higher education. The focus is on policies that use invidious comparisons to make decisions about the distribution of costs and benefits.

20. In addition to race, affirmative action policies and procedures have been applied to populations that differ on ethnic heritage, national origin, age and gender. The term "color-blind" describes policies and procedures that do not take race (or ethnic heritage)

into account. Here, I use the term in a generic sense to describe the absence of invidious categorical comparisons.

21. The unamended Constitution did not refer to either persons of African-origin or to slaves although the overwhelming majority of slaves were of African origin at the country's birth. Instead, the status of black Americans was established by reference to the residual category of persons not taxed.

22. President Johnson set the stage for such policies with the now-famous analogy of the unchained man at the starting line. However, the *new affirmative action* took root during the Nixon administration.

23. The last three principles are roughly comparable to principles identified by Glazer (1975). Glazer claims that they are integral components of an American ideal or creed and he argues that negative reactions to targeted discrimination result from the inconsistency of the practice and one or more of the principles. Despite his critical commentary a generation ago, Glazer has recently reversed his opposition to the new affirmative action and embraced targeted discrimination as a viable method for creating diversity (see Glazer, 1997).

24. Proponents do not claim that targeted discrimination is the only way to create diversity. However, they do claim that many colleges and universities cannot create a "critical mass" of black, Latino and other minority students *without* it. That is, many organizations cannot establish diversity *in the current period* without it. (See also Justice O'Connor's opinion for the majority in the *Grutter* decision.)

25. The Principle of Natural Inequality applies to "natural" differences like those described by Rousseau ([1755] 1964). Rousseau labeled such differences "inequalities" but the rankings on natural qualities like race, ethnic heritage or gender are not inherent properties of the categories. Consequently, the assignment of *unequal* outcomes based solely on natural differences is purely arbitrary. On the other hand, differences on characteristics like power, physical strength or task performance are qualitatively and quantitatively unique (i.e. they constitute ranks). The Principle of Proportionality normally applies to the second category of characteristics although it can be applied to natural categories after social groups devise systems of invidious comparisons that assign quantitative rank distinctions to them.

26. The principle does not rest on the assumption that members of particular minority groups are "naturally" inferior to members of the majority or other minority groups. (But see Note 25.) It asserts that members of some minority groups rank lower than the majority on some evaluative dimensions (e.g. intellectual skills).

27. No college, university or work organization is likely to admit that it subscribes to this principle. Most university administrators would issue vehement denials if questioned about the assumption but the language of their "diversity programs," including amicus briefs filed in the *Gratz* and *Grutter* cases, suggest differently. For these reasons, the graphics in Fig. 3 describe the principle as "implied."

28. These data are generally consistent with findings reported in Schuman et al. (1997). Schuman et al. report that the proportions of blacks and whites who express the belief that blacks have failed to move up because they lack innate ability have been very similar since 1985. They were nearly identical in 1996. Schuman et al.'s data show that a majority of whites generally oppose preferential treatment for blacks in admissions to institutions of higher education and in hiring and promotion. On the other hand, a majority of black Americans support such preferences.

29. These data do not test implications of the theory and they are consistent with alternate interpretations. For example, students are more likely to bear the costs of targeted

discrimination in admissions than faculty and administrators. Consequently, self-interest may lead them to oppose the practice. Similarly, faculty and administrators may hold more "liberal" views than students (or the general population). Their greater support of targeted discrimination may reflect political and ideological differences. However, I reiterate that support of the Principles of Equal Opportunity and Nondiscrimination is widespread among people of all mainstream political views. As a result, those who understand the process of targeted discrimination must resolve the inconsistency that adherence to it would cause. As consistency/balance theorists claim (Homans, 1974), the inconsistency can be resolved either cognitively or behaviorally. Some have taken "cognitive action" and redefined targeted discrimination as a remedy for discrimination. Others have acted to abolish the practice.

30. The data are considerably more complex than described here. For example, I divided the sample by gender and find some curious differences. Compared with those who work for employers with affirmative action programs women (but not men) who work for other employers are slightly more likely to attribute black disadvantage to discrimination ($p = 0.07$). Males who work under affirmative action programs are less likely than other workers to attribute black disadvantage to lack of ability ($p = 0.008$) but similarly placed women are *more likely* to attribute black disadvantage to lack of ability ($p = 0.025$). I will return to these issues in the discussion.

31. Innate ability is a tricky attribute from a social science perspective. It is a characteristic of individuals but individuals have limited control over its realization. Some question its existence while others point out that social and other environmental factors can impede the transformation of innate ability into actual skills and abilities. In that regard, see Gould (1981) or Herrnstein and Murray's (1994) discussions of these issues. Additionally, social factors have substantial effects on motivation and some of the most important research on race and education focuses on social determinants of motivation (Ogbu, 1978). However, the lay public presumes that motivation is a factor over which individuals have control.

32. Moskos and Butler concluded that the army has done an admirable job in integrating blacks and Hispanics into its ranks. However, its record with other groups is not positive. Notably, its policy (and that of the Department of Defense) on homosexuals and its attempts to integrate homosexuals and women into the organization leave much to be desired. In fact, the military's policy with respect to the full integration of homosexuals into its ranks violates several conditions necessary for successful legitimization (e.g. it clearly violates the consensus, impartiality and consonance conditions).

REFERENCES

Bacharach, S., & Lawler, E. J. (1980). *Power and politics in organizations: The social psychology of conflict, coalitions and bargaining.* San Francisco: Jossey-Bass.

Bacharach, S., & Lawler, E. J. (1997). Preface. In: S. Bacharach & E. J. Lawler (Eds), *Research in the Sociology of Organizations* (Vol. 17, pp. ix–xiii). Stamford, CT: JAI Press.

Bales, R. F. (1950). *Interaction process analysis.* Cambridge, MA: Addison-Wesley.

Barnard, C. I. (1938). *The functions of the executive.* Cambridge, MA: Harvard University Press.

Bell, R. S., Walker, H. A., & Willer, D. (2000). Power, influence, and legitimacy in organizations: Implications of three theoretical research programs. In: S. Bacharach & E. J. Lawler (Eds), *Research in the Sociology of Organizations* (Vol. 17, pp. 131–177). Stamford, CT: JAI Press.

Bierstedt, R. L. (1950). *The social order* (2nd ed.). New York: McGraw-Hill.
CBSNEWS.com (2003). *American airlines CEO resigns*. New York: CBS Broadcasting (April 24).
Davis, J. A., & Smith, T. W. (1977). *General social survey*. Chicago: NORC.
Davis, J. A., & Smith, T. W. (1990). *General social survey*. Chicago: NORC.
Davis, J. A., Smith, T. W., & Marsden, P. V. (2002). *General social survey*. Chicago: NORC.
Deutsch, M., & Gerard, H. B. (1955). A study of normative and informational social influences upon individual judgment. *Journal of Abnormal and Social Psychology, 51*, 629–636.
Dornbusch, S. M., & Scott, W. R. (1975). *Evaluation and the exercise of authority*. San Francisco: Jossey-Bass.
Etzioni, A. (1961). *A comparative analysis of complex organizations*. New York: Free Press.
Farley, R., & Allen, W. R. (1989). *The color line and the quality of life in America*. New York: Russell Sage.
Glazer, N. (1975). *Affirmative discrimination*. New York: Basic Books.
Glazer, N. (1997). *We are all multiculturalists now*. Cambridge: Harvard University Press.
Goldhamer, H., & Shils, E. (1939). Types of power and status. *American Journal of Sociology, 45*, 171–182.
Gould, S. J. (1981). *The mismeasure of man*. New York: W. W. Norton.
Hannan, M. T., & Carroll, G. R. (1992). *Dynamics of organizational populations: Density, legitimation, and competition*. New York: Oxford University Press.
Hannan, M. T., & Freeman, J. (1977). The population ecology of organizations. *American Journal of Sociology, 82*, 929–964.
Hannan, M. T., & Freeman, J. (1989). *Organizational ecology*. Cambridge, MA: Harvard University Press.
Hernnstein, R. J., & Murray, C. A. (1994). *The bell curve: Intelligence and class structure in American life*. New York: Free Press.
Hobbes, T. ([1651] 1998). *Leviathan*. J. C. Gaskin (Ed.). Oxford: Oxford University Press.
Homans, G. C. (1974). *Social behavior* (Rev. ed.). New York: Harcourt, Brace & Jovanovich.
Iannaccone, L. R. (1994). Why strict churches are strong. *American Journal of Sociology*, 1180–1211.
Jaynes, G. D., & Williams, R. M., Jr. (1989). *A common destiny: Blacks and American society*. Washington, DC: National Academy Press.
Keohane, R. O., & Nye, J. S. (1977). *Power and interdependence*. Boston: Little, Brown & Company.
Krislov, S. (1967). *The Negro in federal employment*. Minneapolis: University of Minnesota Press.
Meyer, J. W., & Hannan, M. T. (1979). *National development and the world system: Educational, economic and political change, 1950–1970*. Chicago: University of Chicago Press.
Meyer, J. W., & Rowan, B. (1977). Institutionalized organizations: Formal structure as myth and ceremony. *American Journal of Sociology, 83*, 340–363.
Moskos, C. C., & Butler, J. S. (1996). *All that we can be: Black leadership and racial integration the army way*. New York: Basic.
Nagel, J. (1975). *The descriptive analysis of power*. New Haven: Yale University Press.
Ogbu, J. U. (1978). *Minority education and caste*. New York: Academic Press.
Parsons, T. (1951). *The social system*. New York: Free Press.
Pfeffer, J. (1981). *Power in organizations*. Marshfield, MA: Pitman Publishing.
Pfeffer, J. (1992). *Managing with power: Politics and influence in organizations*. Cambridge, MA: Harvard University Press.
Roethlisberger, F. J., & Dickson, W. J. (1939). *Management and the worker*. Cambridge, MA: Harvard University Press.
Rothman, S., Lipset, S., & Nevitte, N. (2003). Racial diversity reconsidered. *Public Interest, 151*, 25–38.

Rousseau, J. J. ([1755] 1964). *The social contract and discourse on the origin of inequality.* L. G. Crocker (Ed.). New York: Simon & Schuster.

Schuman, H., Steeh, C., Bobo, L., & Krysan, M. (1997). *Racial attitudes in America* (Rev. ed.). Cambridge, MA: Harvard University Press.

Scott, W. R. (1981). *Organizations: Rational, natural, and open systems.* Englewood Cliffs, NJ: Prentice-Hall.

Slater, P. E. (1955). Role differentiation in small groups. *American Sociological Review, 20,* 300–310.

Stryker, R. (1994). Rules, resources, and legitimacy processes: Some implications for social conflict, order, and change. *American Journal of Sociology,* 847–910.

Stryker, R. (2000). Legitimacy processes as institutional politics: Implications for theory and research in the sociology of organizations. In: S. Bacharach & E. J. Lawler (Eds), *Research in the Sociology of Organizations* (Vol. 17, pp. 179–223). Stamford, CT: JAI Press.

Thomas, G. M., Walker, H. A., & Zelditch, M. (1986). Legitimacy and collective action. *Social Forces, 65,* 378–404.

U.S. Supreme Court (1954). *Brown v. Topeka Board of Education.* Washington, DC: U.S. Government Printing Office.

U.S. Supreme Court (1978). *Regents of Univ. of Cal. v. Bakke.* Washington, DC: U.S. Government Printing Office.

U.S. Supreme Court (2003a). *Gratz et al. v. Bollinger et al.* Washington, DC: U.S. Government Printing Office.

U.S. Supreme Court (2003b). *Grutter v. Bollinger et al.* Washington, DC: U.S. Government Printing Office.

Walker, H. A., Rogers, L., Thomas, G. M., & Zelditch, M. (1991). Legitimating collective action: Theory and experimental results. *Research in Political Sociology, 5,* 1–25.

Walker, H. A., Rogers, L., & Zelditch, M. (1988). Legitimacy and collective action: A research note. *Social Forces, 67,* 216–228.

Walker, H. A., Rogers, L., & Zelditch, M. (2002). Acts, persons, positions, and institutions: Legitimating multiple objects and compliance with authority. In: S. C. Chew & J. D. Knottnerus (Eds), *Structure, Culture, and History* (Chap. 15). Lanham, MD: Rowman & Little Field.

Walker, H. A., Thomas, G. M., & Zelditch, M. (1986). Legitimation, endorsement, and stability. *Social Forces, 64,* 620–643.

Walker, H. A., & Zelditch, M. (1993). Power, legitimation, and the stability of authority: A theoretical research program. In: J. Berger & M. Zelditch (Eds), *Theoretical Research Programs: Studies in the Growth of Theory* (pp. 364–381). Stanford, CA: Stanford University Press.

Weber, M. ([1918] 1968). *Economy and society.* G. Roth & C. Wittich (Eds). Berkeley, CA: California University Press.

Wilson, R. (2003). Fall from grace. *The Chronicle of Higher Education, 49*(30), A10.

Zelditch, M. (2001). Theories of legitimacy. In: J. Jost & B. Major (Eds), *Psychology of Legitimacy* (Chap. 2). New York: Cambridge University Press.

Zelditch, M., & Walker, H. A. (1984). Legitimacy and the stability of authority. *Advances in Group Processes: Theory and Research, 1,* 1–25.

Zelditch, M., & Walker, H. A. (2003). The legitimacy of regimes. In: S. R. Thye & E. J. Lawler (Eds), *Advances in Group Processes* (Vol. 20). Greenwich, CT: JAI Press.